THE LIFE OF MAN WITH GOD

The Life of Man
with God

THOMAS VERNER MOORE, *Carthusian*

(IN RELIGION, PABLO MARIA)

*Formerly Head of the Department of Psychology and Psychiatry
and Director of the Child Guidance Center at the
Catholic University of America
Washington, D. C.*

HARCOURT, BRACE AND COMPANY · *New York*

IMPRIMI POTEST: Ferdinandus
Prior Cartusiae
die 6 Decembris, 1955.

NIHIL OBSTAT: Barry E. Fontaine
Censor Deputatus

IMPRIMATUR: ✠ EDUARDUS J. RYAN
Episcopus Burlingtonensis
6 Septembris, 1955.

LIBRARY OF CONGRESS CATALOG CARD NUMBER: 56-7919

PRINTED IN THE UNITED STATES OF AMERICA

O Mater Dei et Mater mea
Rogo te
Ut accipias et tuearis
Hoc opusculum
Et auctorem ejus
In eremo laetum cum Deo viventem.

The Life of Man with God does not follow the usual lines of development in works on the spiritual life. Every book reflects the life history of the writer. The author of this book has been a priest for over fifty-four years. Some fifty years of his life were spent in study, teaching, and research in the fields of psychology and psychiatry. For thirty years of this period he was head of a child guidance center at the Catholic University of America. There he dealt as physician and psychiatrist, with the mental problems of children and adults. At the end of this period, in 1947, he entered upon his Carthusian life in the Cartuja de Miraflores, near Burgos, in Spain.

It is evident, therefore, that the book, here presented to the public, is not a Carthusian work, but flows from the author's training in modern empirical psychology, practical experience in dealing with matters of the mind as a psychiatrist, and, more important than all, his fifty-four years in the priesthood. While this is true, the work, perhaps, could scarcely have been written except by one who has lived in the silence of the cloister.

It would be most unfortunate if the publication of *The Life of Man with God* should give rise to the impression that Carthusian life is one of learned ease. The fact that over two years passed while this little book was being written shows that it must have been done during what Carthusians term periods for relaxation.

Nor should it suggest that if one becomes a Carthusian he will have an opportunity to write books. Very few Carthusians have written books for circulation, as manuscripts or for printing, in the nine centuries of our existence. Our life is a life of prayer, silence, and penance. It is in this that our apostolate consists—not in the writing of books.

The publication of *The Life of Man with God* has been authorized in the hope that it may help many in that life with God which every human being should live.

THOMAS VERNER MOORE

INTRODUCTION

THIS BOOK is an attempt to lead the reader onward in the service of God by making him familiar with the spiritual life of man with God from its earliest beginnings to perfect union of the soul with God. To do this as vividly as possible, the forms and stages of the spiritual life are illustrated by the personal experiences of those who lead it. "Those who lead it" have been selected to a very large extent from persons giving themselves to a devout life in the home, in the various types of religious communities, and in the priesthood. They might be described as ordinary Catholics of our country and our age.*

There are two roads to perfect union with God. Each leads the soul upward to eternal life through various levels of divine charity: the love of man for God. Each requires the attainment of perfect fidelity to the commands of God. Each necessitates patient endurance of the trials of life. But there comes a point where the common road divides. One goes on through steep, rough paths with little change in scenery. The other has many beautiful vistas that urge the traveler on to rapid ascent of the heights of perfection. These vistas are termed in this book the mystic graces.

The question may be asked: Are those who go by the way

* To understand the way this book was written, the reader should consult Appendix II, pp. 383 ff.

of the mystic graces necessarily holier than the others? And the answer is: No. The measure of holiness is the height to which one ascends. There are in fact many trails up the mountain of perfection. They all lead through the same heights to one and the same summit.

We must realize at the outset that it is not possible to choose the path by which we ascend. The soul can take only the path opened to it by God. One cannot decide to go by the way of the mystic graces and then enter it at will. God gives the mystic graces, or does not give them, for reasons we cannot fathom. They may be given to one who is much occupied with the duties of the home, and not given to another whom God has called to a strictly cloistered life. It would seem that God has willed to illustrate, in the spiritual biographies of souls, all sides of the wonderful mountain of perfection.

If we are led along one road by God, it would be a great mistake and a block to spiritual progress for us to allow ourselves to desire any other way. If one had been given many mystic graces, it would put an end to his progress if he commenced to regard himself as better than those who have received none.

Should the danger of causing souls to desire what God does not intend them to have make it undesirable to illustrate, in a general book on the spiritual life, all sides of the mountain of perfection? It would seem that a full knowledge of God's dealings with souls would stimulate us to live so that God will find us such that He can lead us anywhere, when and how He pleases. It would be a mistake to deprive souls of useful knowledge for fear they might be puffed up with vanity. Would it not be better to give knowledge along with principles that tend to reduce the dangers of vanity?

Why have we drawn largely on the experience of ordinary members of the faithful rather than from the lives of the saints? The answer is suggested by the following passage from St. Augustine. The great doctor has been commenting on the passage, "unless the grain of wheat falling into the ground die, itself remaineth alone." He dwells upon the great truth that in our life with God we must make a complete renunciation of all that does not concern us. But many are afraid of the hard ways of renunciation and to them he addresses the following words:

" 'For the sake of the words of Thy lips I have kept hard ways.' [1] Why dost thou fear the hard ways of sufferings and tribulations? Christ Himself passes by. But perhaps you answer: That is *He*. The Apostles pass by. And still you answer: They are *Apostles*. I grant it. But answer thou now: Many mere men pass by. Blush now: Many women also pass by. Hast thou entered into thy passion as an old man, fear not death, precisely because you are nigh unto death. Are you still young? The young men also pass by who had their lives stretched out before them. Mere boys pass by. There pass by also, the little girls. How can that way still be rough which has been trodden down by the feet of so many?" [2]

This passage from St. Augustine breathes the spirit in which *The Life of Man with God* has been written. That life is exemplified by the daily religious experience of ordinary human beings, living in our own day, in the midst of modern activity, surrounded by temptations, harassed by distractions such as no era, perhaps, has ever before known. Sanctity and the union of the human soul with God are sublime ideals and one may with good reason point to the saints in whom the perfection of Christ has found a finite expression. But many might say: "But they were *saints*. I pray thee, hold me excused." And so it will be helpful to many to see the ideal to which Christ calls them, in process of realization in ordinary men and women of our day, young and old, in the world and in the cloister, in all walks of life in the laity, in the priesthood, in the various religious orders of the Church for men and for women.

Sanctity comes as the end product of obedience to the law

[1] Psalm XVI, 4.
[2] St. Augustine. Sermo 306; in Nat. Martyrum Massae candidae. cap. 10-11. Quoted from *Breviarium Monasticum*, Feast of St. Placid II, p. 665.

of Christ to love God as much as you possibly can love Him and to love your neighbor as yourself. The psalmist speaks of our journey to God as keeping hard ways. But St. Augustine asks: How can that way still be rough which has been worn smooth by the feet of so many? We shall learn, from those who speak to us in this book, that long before one passes to eternal life, those who follow the star, whithersoever it may lead, attain to a peace that surpasseth all understanding.

CONTENTS

Part One

THE DAILY LIFE OF THOSE
WHO LIVE WITH GOD

CHAPTER I

Soldiers in the Field

TRUTH lends itself to expression as statements of facts and principles. Sanctity manifests itself in deeds and in the life of man with God. But the life of man with God is a hidden life. It flows through the mind and the heart. Holy deeds are done in secret. Prayer is seen by God, Who seeth in secret.

There are plants that wither if exposed to the light of the sun. Sanctity perishes in those who make it known to others that they may be honored by men. And so the attempt to stimulate men to holiness by letting them see the inner life of those who live with God is likely to meet with difficulties. We have tried to overcome the righteous desire to remain hidden in some, who are living an inner life with God, by the assurance that their accounts of what goes on between God and themselves will not be made known that they may be honored; but they themselves will still remain hidden, while from their accounts will flow rivers of living waters to God's little children in the ways of the spirit.

We commence our account of the life of man with God, not with the weighing of the evidence that demonstrates its moral necessity; but with a series of pictures. These pictures sample the typical daily experiences in the various ways of living to be found in the Church: in the wide-open world; in the priesthood; and in the cloister.

3

The Catholic Worker and the Life of Man with God

The first picture that we shall study is that of a young man who lives alone in a little room. Morning and evening in this little room, and throughout the day, working as a steam fitter, he lives with God. Let us listen to his own account.

"My alarm clock goes off at six o'clock in the morning. I have to be on the job by eight and in order to get to seven o'clock Mass this is about the best time to waken. The location of my work changes from time to time and I have found it convenient to attend Mass at a church near the job, to eliminate the possibility of being late. Fortunately, in a large city, there is usually a church near at hand.

"After the morning ablutions have gotten rid of some of the sleepiness I say my Morning Offering before the wall crucifix. My mind is still sluggish from slumber however and a little stimulus is provided by reading a bit from the 'Imitation' or perhaps the *preces* from the day's feast in the Missal. These I can recall later at Mass.

"In church comes a renewal of the Morning Offering in our Lord's sacramental presence. During the Holy Sacrifice I pray for various intentions: for the Church suffering, not only in Purgatory but here on this globe, in those countries that say: 'there is no God,' and the State is master of the destiny of man; for peace, if it be God's will to lift the scourge of war and the fear of still more war; for all those in their last agony or in danger of dying impenitent, that they may recall God's love and mercy; for those who are weighted by the cares of the world; for those whose life has become dull and meaningless that they may taste the Lord and see that He is sweet and the joy of life; for the grace of final perseverance.

"After communion the time left is spent in thanksgiving. The inestimable gift of Christ, true God and true man, makes me wish I might prostrate myself in complete humility on the floor of the church. With the possible exception of night prayer, this is the most peaceful moment of the day. With your eyes closed, you feel the greatest intimacy with the Saviour. The church with all its familiar furnishings disappears for a few minutes and you are in a vast measureless void, surrounded by the infinite Immensity of the Blessed Trinity. But the minute hand moves quickly on and severs this sweet bond. The world, the flesh and the devil are waiting outside; but I have fortified myself with charity, and He is a seal upon my heart.

"At eight o'clock I've changed into my work clothes and I and my partner (we always work in pairs) either continue on our previous day's work or see the foreman for new work. The contracting shop we are working for is air-conditioning a large office building. There are over seventy pipe fitters on the job and they are occupied with various facets of the work. Some are in the basement installing the centrifugal compressors that chill the water, others are piping connections to the pumps that will send the chilled water coursing through the individual units on all the twenty-six floors.

"I'm engaged in connecting the individual units (forty on each floor) to the supply and return pipes coming up from the basement. These units are amazingly light things consisting of finned coils over which a forced draft of air blows. One is placed under each window. They are connected by copper tubing to the aforementioned supply and return pipes. A small tank of Prest-o-lite gas, a torch and soft wire solder are used to sweat the joints together.

"This part of the job is not particularly strenuous but in hot weather that torch makes the perspiration flow faster. Then occasionally you may accidentally flick a droplet of hot solder onto your hand and that's something you can offer up. A truck loaded with iron pipe will come every so often and after you have helped to unload it, you have a very keen appreciation of how our Lord's shoulder must have felt under the weight of the cross.

"In general, there are very few serious accidents, the safety-first factor having been driven home by both the contractor and the union.

"Work ends at 3:30 and while everyone has his own work pace I know I'm fairly tired by then. Of course there is a certain satisfaction in seeing the results of your work.

"During the day, one must naturally keep his mind on what he is doing, but there are little pauses and moments of transition when one can make silent aspirations to keep Christ in the picture. In a small booklet by Dom Norbert Schachinger, the author calls this the 'Little Secret'. Since we 'ought always to pray' and do all for the glory of God, these silent aspirations provide us with a nearly continuous prayer life even during our working hours when the noon-day devil is rampant.

"On the way home I stop in at a Catholic church which is near my room and make a visit. The beautiful little booklet by St. Alphonsus Liguori containing devotional matter for these visits is easily carried in the pocket and is a joy to use. Sometimes I feel too tired for even this little prayer and then I simply kneel there offering to our Lord my fatigue, discomfort or distraction. At times that same weariness seems to bring forth a simple tender prayer of humility and affection as though one were laying his head on the shoulder of Christ and remaining wordless, but trusting.

"Back at my room, a fervent 'Deo gratias' to the crucifix for a safe return to my nest. Then the grime gets washed off and I take a nap if I am tired. A few technical books on heating and ventilating are on the shelf and I'll pore over a chapter to help me get some of the theory to complement the practice I've had all day.

"In the evening I like to visit a Catholic library which has a good assortment of books. If I start meandering through the Catholic Encyclopedia, it's generally the warning bell at closing time that ends my absorption in its riches. Supper is usually at the automat nearby. Perhaps once a week I visit my sister in the suburbs and eat with her.

"I don't have too many books in my room. There are a

good many periodicals such as 'Life of the Spirit' and 'Worship' which I get at the bookrack in St. Francis of Assisi Church. I found an interesting little book there recently called 'Secular Institutes'. Beside my bible is the 'Imitation'. Next to that stand two books by St. Francis de Sales (whom I like above all): 'Introduction to a Devout Life' and 'Spirit of Love'. Next is the 'Lay Apostle after the Heart of St. Benedict' by Dom Schachinger of Kremsmuenster Abbey, Austria. Last but not least is a slim volume called 'Self-Discipline and the Interior Life' by Dom Idesbald Ryelandt of Glenstal Priory, Ireland. It gives one a wonderful spiritual buffer against the pressures of everyday life: thirty-two pages, but all gold.

"There is also a big fat 'Liber Usualis' on the shelf. I've always loved the chant but never as a participant. Of late I've been attempting to learn its deceptively simple ways. Properly done it seems to have inexhaustible beauty; and 'he who sings prays twice.'

"Bed-time is approximately 10:30 when I take into my hands a little book containing the office of Compline. By now the mental wheels are running smoothly, so after a short examination of the day's faults, I chew over something from de Sales and try it on me for size. In case I can't focus on one thing, I'll switch off the lights and say the rosary. Mary never fails to tuck me in: *Mater amabilis.*"

Those who are incorporated into the mystic body of Christ become apostles by their work and their sufferings. This pipe fitter at his morning Mass and holy communion exercises a powerful apostolate. The silent petitions he makes during the Holy Sacrifice reverberate through the Divine Immensity, and throw into vibration the heartstrings of those who know not God, and so he co-operates with Christ in the salvation of souls. And in his day's work he offers to God the "sacrifice of the shoulders" contributing his share to the apostolic work of the mystical body of Christ.

A mind at peace is not a rebellious mind. If the workers of France at the end of the eighteenth century had been living the life of the Kingdom, France would have been spared

the horrors of the revolution and their condition would have
been alleviated in an unbloody manner. If the workers of the
United States can be introduced to the life of the Kingdom,
many great social problems of our day will find a happy
solution.

Out of the Running, but Knights of the Kingdom

"Out of the running": these words recall to my mind the
image of a tiny figure on a little gocart that enabled her to
get about the apartment in which she lived. Because she was
so tiny she always seemed to me a child, and then too she
was ever as happy as a child. She wrote an interesting autobiography [1] of great psychological value as an account of the
development of the human mind in one who could not talk
or walk and so was deprived of the ordinary means of education. Education was made possible for her by her sister,
who devoted her own life to the care of this little sister who
suffered from an extreme form of spastic paralysis. Neither
she nor her relatives were Catholics; but the spirit of God
breathes where it will, and by her own reading she came to
a knowledge of the Church as the pillar and ground of truth
established by Christ for the instruction of man in the things
of eternity. She entered the Church and lived without friction
with her sister a beautiful interior spiritual life.

The true value of a man is measured by his charity: his
love of God and his fellow men for the sake of God. Consequently we shall all be surprised when in eternal life we
shall see how the first shall be last and the last shall be first.
One thinks here of the feeble-minded. I have been surprised
how children with low intelligence quotients have a surprising
insight into the truths of religion. I remember the death of
a little Mongolian low-grade moron. She had been for a year
or two under the care of nuns in a little school and then
returned to her mother. A year or so after going back to her

---

[1] Grace Gertrude Hoopes, *Out of the Running*, Springfield, Ill., Charles
C. Thomas. 1938.

mother she was taken sick and was dying. She knew perfectly well that she was dying and had not the least fear of death. She had worked out in her own simple English an adequate commentary on the words of Christ: Suffer the little children to come unto me for of such is the kingdom of heaven. She told her mother how happy she was that she was going to Jesus and how she wanted to play with Him in His garden in heaven. The pastor was asked to come to see her and if possible give her viaticum. She had never made her first communion and he doubted that a feeble-minded child could be allowed viaticum. He came. When he heard her talk of how she loved the Christ Child and wanted to be with Him in heaven, he exclaimed: "No one can hear this child talk and refuse her Holy Communion." And so he prepared her for death and gave her viaticum that Christ Himself might lead her into His garden in heaven. Shortly after, she died in peace and happiness: a true knight of the Kingdom.

When I think of the death of this child I call up by contrast a man whom I visited many years ago in a German sanatorium who was suffering from tuberculosis. He was in one of those periods of elevation of temperature, not uncommon in that disorder and not always fatal. He resented my visit, which I made with friendly intentions. His state of mind could be described as fury and horror. He was angry against God and overwhelmed with the fear of death. So great was his emotional excitement that it alone prevented the subsidence of his fever. He went down in defeat, with all his education and experience, before that which our little knight of the Kingdom conquered with ease.

I come now to a strange account and one that will seem to some an utterly impossible story but I will give the facts as I obtained them by personal investigation. It concerns a colored man with gray hair whose age is not known exactly. He told me that he would be sixty Christmas 1953 and that he was born in the time of the Spanish-American War in Florida. But if that is true he must be only fifty-five for that war took place in 1898. He is one of those southern darkies who never learned to read or write and who have only a vague concept of how old they are and one which does not keep tally with the passing years.

He told me that he never went to school at all, but as soon as his muscles were strong enough he helped out in farm work. He attended a Protestant church. About eighteen years ago, on seeing the little children going to the Catholic church, he felt that he ought to be a Catholic, but he did not see how he was ever going to manage it. His people, too, were bitterly opposed to any such strange procedure. "It kept working on my heart and mind," he said, "and while I was sitting in the Protestant church, I thought of how I would like to be in the Catholic church."

Four years ago he had a vision as he was going home after dark. Everything seemed to light up with a strange light, and as he got out of the woods into a clearing he saw a ship in which there were two men. At first it seemed to be on the ground but when he got over to it it was so high in the air that he could not get in it. Then he commenced to call: "Come and see the wonderful ship." It then seemed to him that people came running from all directions, but before they could get to him the ship went on up into heaven. And so he said to them: "Too late, too late, the ship has gone to heaven." Then there was no ship and there were no people around him, but in his mind a firm conviction: I have got to be a Catholic.

I could not at first see how that conclusion was drawn from the premises—or I should say from the vision. I asked him to explain, but he could not. It was like a symbolic dream of the night, the meaning was perfectly clear but it seemed to have no relation to the symbolism. So I attempted the novel task for a psychiatrist of interpreting, not the dream, but the symbolism of the dream; and so I said to him: "The Church of Christ is often spoken of as 'the bark of Peter' and the two men may have been St. Peter and St. Paul. You were not in the ship and could not get in. Then the ship went up to heaven. You want to go to heaven and having seen the ship that goes to heaven which is the bark of Peter, the Catholic Church, the vision left you with the firm conviction: I must get in that ship. I have got to be a Catholic."

A little later he developed an intense yearning to read. This was increased after he became ill with tuberculosis and various good Protestant clergymen gave him books to read. It was interesting to hear him recount how very gently, and with every effort to avoid hurting their feelings, he thanked them but when they asked him to receive communion in their Church he quietly made known to them that he hoped some day to be a Catholic. The good, old-time darky from Dixie Land is a definite type of the perfect gentleman and this trait is plainly evident in this neophyte. A priest visited him and he also gave him books, assuming that he could read.

One day he was thinking about how he used to take chances in a lottery and how everyone was looking forward to the day when the prizes would be distributed. This made him think that the day of the last judgment is coming, when everyone will receive his due. He told me he thought: "I can't read and I can't get ready for the judgment. Then I begged my heavenly Father from the bottom of my heart that I might read and prepare my soul for the judgment. I asked Him to open my mind and let me read and understand the Holy Bible.

"The night after, there came and sat on my bed a little child, tiny like a baby, but with wings like a bird. It leaned over and put its arms about my neck and said: 'God loves you.'" Our *caballero* from Dixie Land then tried to express to me the joy that he felt that the good God could love a poor old man like himself. One thinks of the words of the Negro spiritual "Swing Low, Sweet Chariot": Like the ship that he saw in his vision the sweet chariot that takes man to heaven will have to swing low, way, way down to reach far enough down to get the poor forsaken darkies of Dixie Land. And then he went on to tell me how the little creature with wings like a bird reached over and handed him a book and said: "You can read the Bible." "The next morning," he went on, "something said to me: 'Take the Scriptures and read' [like the *"tolle lege: tolle lege"* of St. Augustine that he heard in the garden], and I picked up my Bible and I read." He then leaned over and said to me slowly with a tone of conviction and accentuation that is impossible to any except the darky from Dixie Land: "Father, if you really 'needs' something and you 'asks' your heavenly Father in faith, you 'sho' gets it." About two months after this incident he was baptized.

Does he read? He spends the time allowed at the sanatorium in which he now is, sitting in the sun, learning by heart a couple of rather large catechisms along with the fine print with quotations from scripture. He has an extraordinary memory and one can ask him a question anywhere and he will give you the answer, word for word as a rule. But every now and then he will slip in a few synonyms for some words in the book, thus showing that he understands what he is reading. His pronunciation of unfamiliar proper names is always interesting. Thus Cilicia is shortened to "silly."

The sister who is in charge of the house where he lives at the sanatorium made a few experiments. She took his missal and he would read off any Epistle or Gospel she selected at random; but strange to relate he could not read the newspaper. This is not a question of eyesight for he memorizes passages of fine print in smaller type than is found in the newspaper. This point would be worth further investigation. But there can be no doubt that he does read. Making a rough guess I would say that he reads, on the level of the eighth- to tenth-grade, books that have a religious content.

Did he ever go to school? When he came to the sanatorium he could not write even his first name—Arthur. He learned to do this with great difficulty and later to add his last name —Johnson. Had he learned to read in school, he surely would have been taught to write much more than his name. This corroborates his own account, which has all the marks of honesty, that he never went to school and was unable to read until he saw the little creature with wings like a bird.

Asking pardon for this digression we may now consider his daily spiritual life. He gives the following account of it: "When I 'wakes' up my mind is on the Rosary and I 'says' prayers to the Virgin Mother, then the Apostles Creed, the Our Father and then I 'says' the morning offering and the prayer to my guardian angel, 'Angel of God, my guardian dear.' " He goes to Mass and Communion every day and he said: "O, Father, every hour of the day my heart and mind are on God."

I thought I would teach him the method of affective mental prayer and told him how Bernard of Quintavalle once watched and listened to St. Francis of Assisi spending the night in prayer. From time to time St. Francis murmured the words: "My God and my All." These words filled his mind with an overwhelming knowledge of God and of all God had been to him. And as he murmured them he rose to the heights of the knowledge and love of God, and then after a while, like an eagle soaring high in the heavens, as he sank gradually toward the earth he would move his wings again and on the wings of contemplation uttering 'My God and my All' he would soar to God in the region of inaccessible light. "O Father," Arthur Johnson said, "isn't that wonderful," and then went on murmuring again and again: "My God and my All! My God and my All."

Among those who are "out of the running" is the mother who has little of the goods of this world. But when such a mother brings up a large family and successfully floats her children in a stormy world, she enters the running in the true sense of the word and gains the prize at the end of the race.

The mother who wrote the following account was severely handicapped in the race of life, but she won in the end. She has done a great work for the Church of God and performed a magnificent service for society. She had very little schooling and came of poor French-Canadian parents. Her account has been re-edited. But nothing has been added, in the re-editing, to her original manuscript. Her little message at the end is given entirely in her own words.

"I married at 23 and in 18 years I had 9 children. The last child died when 9 months of age. In these years I tasted all the sorrows in life. My husband was Irish, and a good man in his way. But if ever I was sick, he was sure to come home so drunk he did not know his name. People used to say to me, 'why do you have a large family when he does what he does?' I always answered: 'When I shall stand before my Judge, I have to answer only for what I do.' The world laughs at you when your children are small, but when they are all grown up, how they want to know you. I get the surprises of my life from my children now: two doctors of medicine in my own family. My two girls are married and own their own homes. My oldest son is home with me and is my support now. All my daughters-in-law and sons-in-law love me as much as their own parents.

"When I married I prayed to St. Anthony to find us a home near a church and a school. I knew a mother would often be unable to go to morning Mass if she lived far from a church. I bought a beautiful picture of St. Anthony and had it put in a costly frame and then hid him away in a closet until he found me a home. It was only three doors from the church. I would get up early, nurse my baby and spend my first 45 minutes with our Lord at the Holy Sacrifice of the Mass. I am the only poor one in my family. I was always pushed aside by all. No one wanted a whole lot of youngsters around. But Mass every morning made all things easy, even though I had to work from early morning till late at night. We had no auto, none of the comforts of life, only a roof over our heads. But how happy I was when my boys were able to go to church with me in the morning and serve Mass.

"I never believed in young folks going out and having a good time and leaving the little ones with a 'baby sitter'. Children are little such a short time and big so long. You enjoy them most when they are little. How happy it made me to give them their bath, put clean nighties on them, gather them all around me and say our night prayers together; and then go off, put them to bed, and give each one a good-night kiss. Those happy days are gone with the wind.

"Company is nice, but my children and their playmates were ever my company from the time they were able to go out and play. Mama baked every day and everybody knew it. As the girls grew older, I let them 'fix up' as they liked. Don't ask your children to stop what you couldn't stop doing yourself. And O, how many happy Sundays we spent together: all my family at home. The girls brought their boy friends, and the boys their girl friends, with twelve to fourteen for dinner on Sunday afternoon. What fun we had! All our parties were at home. We were poor; but we proved that prayer books are more powerful than pocketbooks. It was my daily morning Mass that gave me all this happiness. Every move you make, those little ones around you watch and do likewise. If I could only call all young people together and tell them, as I told my children when they left home to get married: 'Stay close to God. The world has nothing to offer. All is vanity.'"

The Catholic Physician and the Life of the Kingdom

We would like, now by way of contrast, to present a knight of the kingdom in professional life. Our physician is a "self-made" woman leading a single life. It will be readily seen, however, that her spiritual life is not necessarily connected with the work of a physician but may well serve as a model for anyone in professional life. What others are actually doing or have done is much more useful to know than to read even a very well-written dissertation on what one ought to do.

"I am a woman physician, single and 56 years old. I have been practising my profession in this city for 28 years. Thanks be to God!

"As a child I had the great privilege of attending a Catholic school, but inasmuch as it was necessary for me to secure my high school education and at the same time support myself, I worked in the daytime and attended night school and consequently had to attend the public night school classes. The same was true with regard to my college education and that too was in a non-Catholic institution—but Our Dear Blessed Mother watched over me and my faith and trust in her help was increased with each year.

"I have done a great deal of spiritual reading the past ten years—the books I have read have been varied such as 'One with Jesus'—'Difficulties in Mental Prayer'—'The Apostolate of Suffering'—Tanquery's 'Doctrine and Devotion'—'Autobiography of St. Teresa of Avila'—'Life of the Little Flower'— St. John Eudes' 'Whom Thou Seekest'—Bishop Sheen's books (nearly all of them), as well as most of Thomas Merton's books. 'The Following of Christ' and the 'New Testament' as well as Goodier's 'Life of Christ' are frequently read, that is I pick them up and may use them for meditation for a time and then use something else only to pick them up and use them again.

"Thanks to God's Grace I have been a daily Communicant since the December before the starting of World War II— when I heard the then Msgr. Sheen's appeal to spend one hour a day in prayer, and urged Catholics to go to daily Mass and Holy Communion if possible. Previous to that time I had gone perhaps once or twice a week to Mass and Holy Communion.

"As a member of the Third Order of Discalced Carmelites, I follow our rule and make at least a half hour meditation daily, say the Little Office of Our Blessed Mother, make daily visits to the Blessed Sacrament, if possible, and practise the Presence of God. In accordance with this our Holy Rule I do all to the best of my ability. I say my morning and evening prayers and make a daily examination of conscience—The Rosary has been a daily prayer since I was a mere child.

"One way which I have found helpful is to remember the presence of the Blessed Trinity within me. It was suggested by a priest friend many years ago. On my desk I have a crucifix and a small statue of Our Lady. I change these by placing them in various spots on my desk and since they are always being moved they do not become routine fixtures and that helps me to remember. Also I have the practise of making the 'Sign of the Cross' every time I pass thru a certain door. In my home we have a cuckoo clock and for years it has been my practise every time it strikes to repeat with each stroke the words 'Jesus' and when it finishes to say 'My Jesus Mercy, Mary help me.'

"The circumstances that make my prayer life more intense are the closed retreats which I have been privileged to make. I have made at least one or two closed week-end retreats yearly for many years, as well as many five and eight-day closed retreats. Also I have had the privilege of attending many classes and lectures relating to the 'Life of Perfection' during the past ten years. Then, of course, the most important of all is having a good Spiritual Director which I think is indispensable for those desiring to perfect their lives and grow closer to God.

"I have a great personal friend in Our Blessed Mother. I talk to her as I would to my own earthly mother. It is only because of Our Dear Mother that I am what I am today and She knows that I give Her all the credit. She never refuses me anything that is for my good; even finds me parking places when it would seem impossible to most people. The *Memorare* to me is one of the most powerful prayers we have. Thanks, Dear Mother.

"I am not married therefore have no children of my own; but I do have many whom God has permitted me to bring into this world and I love them all."

The Life of the Kingdom in the Catholic Home

The Kingdom of God is a social unit whose antiquity, vastness, and complexity transcend the powers of our mind to conceive. It commenced at the very dawn of creation when

God spoke and the angels came into being. It appeared in this world with the creation of man. It has grown and extended on earth from that day to this. Of this vast social order, the Christian home is a tiny unit. Tiny though it is, it must be assimilated to that universal social order over which God rules in His Kingdom: the transcendent Intelligence in a world of intelligent beings. It is, therefore, clearly evident that the home must be, in its essence, a school of the service of God.

The main object of marriage must be the development of a family that will grow together in the knowledge and love of God. The ever-increasing percentage of childless or one-child marriages [2] in the United States shows that many do not enter upon marriage with the idea of establishing a school of the service of God, but from selfish motives. Thus the joy of life and the inestimable privilege of living for eternity in the Kingdom of God is denied to millions. For this deprivation selfish parents must answer before the throne of God. Father, forgive them for they know not what they do.

Parents should realize that it is a great privilege for them to have it in their power to bring into the world children whom they can train in the knowledge and love of God, drawing them out of nothing, giving them the boon of existence, and incorporating them into the Kingdom of God.

Let us learn how this is actually being done.

"My husband and I are both graduates of Catholic schools and colleges. I am very sorry to say that he received very little on the subjects of marriage and family life at college so my knowledge has to suffice for us both—thank the dear Lord for the good Sister who gave the *family course.*

"We were married six years ago and God has blessed us with four wonderful boys; and we are expecting the fifth

---

[2] It is clear that two children to a marriage would not suffice to maintain the human race, for some of these would die and others would not marry. Not even three children suffice. It has been found statistically that an average of four children to the marriage would suffice to maintain the race and provide for its moderate increase.

boy(?) in November. My vocation in life, I am sure, is to raise our children as real Catholics.

"Father, you have no idea of the amount of criticism we receive for having the children so close together from relatives, friends, neighbors, *doctors*, Catholics and non-Catholics, even the butcher. Not a day passes that a few remarks aren't passed. At first they bothered me some; but now I feel sorry for these people that God hasn't been as good and kind to them as He has been to us.

"I have very little time every day for formal prayers. We have a seven room home, and I do all the housework, cooking and taking care of the children myself (I'm really not killed), for at this point we can't afford any help. My husband has set high standards for us and I couldn't possibly try to attain them without his help and that of the children; we pray, work and play together. Each morning I dedicate all my work to God and in that way feel my day is just one big active prayer.

"Since Lent I have been unable to assist at daily Mass—the most wonderful way to start the day. Recently many things happened; our second boy had his worst attack of rheumatic fever and demanded my constant care for his joints were excessively painful. Finally they took him to the hospital and then the running back and forth began. At the time I had morning sickness and then my mother became ill. Things were in a turmoil and the daily Mass suffered, although, now I am able to go a few mornings. My boy, thank God, is almost completely recovered without any heart damage—our first family miracle.

"At night my husband and I say the Rosary novena together before going to bed and if we have any misunderstandings or difficulties during the day it seems to erase them from our memories, and we go on loving each other more each day.

"We also belong to a Cana group but have not been as active as we would like to be. My husband has been going to graduate school at night for the past five years and our activities have been somewhat curtailed, although I have been active in parish societies and manage to get to novena on Monday nights.

"Now to the children—they say a homemade morning prayer and grace after meals. At night they say five of our most-said prayers alone and usually a decade of the Rosary together. During the day they are ever mindful of their guardian angel *who is my best helper.*

"We are both very anxious for our children to have a good Catholic education. This past year our oldest boy went to kindergarten at the parochial school. It was a great effort to take him back and forth but the joy of his first formal Catholic learnings more than compensated for my effort.

"My summer catholic action work has been helping a neighbor who recently has decided to become a Catholic. Her husband is a rather poor Catholic so she turned to me for help. I was amazed to find that it was only three weeks before her scheduled Baptism and she didn't even know the ten Commandments. Needless to say we did three weeks of intensive study, but she still needs so much more help.

"Father, I really didn't intend this letter to be so lengthy but I hope that it may help you a little in your great work. If you only could convince these young people that children are what make happy marriages and happy family lives, it would be a great triumph."

This letter raises the question of the duty of the Catholic college to give specific training in the duties and spiritual life of the home. Another person writes thus:

"My college years taught me to know and love God. One of the Professors strove constantly to develop in us a perfect passion for the love of Christ. But during those years daily communion was the real essence of intimate and personal love of God. I am convinced that the Eucharist is the essence of love and of all Catholic life. Daily communion in this age is the most powerful force in the making of saints.

"But while my college years taught me to love God, I am not so sure that they taught me as well as they might how to serve Him, for I was still in love with self and filled with worldly desires and standards. I do not feel that they trained me sufficiently for the job of wife and mother. My College is doing a better job now, due largely to the efforts of one sister. In discussing this with her, she agreed and put it well: 'They taught us to love everything except the things we would have to do.' She did not elaborate, but she might have said that they failed to teach us to love with complete forgetfulness of self; for marriage, and sainthood too, is the love of sacrifice and death to self to live with God."

Our religious life consists not only in prayer but also in trying to meet the difficulties of everyday life in a Christlike spirit, in recourse to God in every problem and gratitude to Him for every good that comes to us. This is exemplified in the life of a mother who wrote the following account:

"I am a woman in my thirties, married at the age of twenty-six and now the happy mother of four children aged two to six. My education included twelve years of Catholic grade and High school and four years in a Catholic College. After college I had a very interesting position as a cooking instructor and assistant Home Service director.

"Last year our religious reading included various Catholic periodicals. This past summer we joined a book club and enjoyed, 'Calvary in China' very much. I think I read more for a Catholic knowledge of world affairs than for spirituality. I try to receive Holy Communion every Sunday. As our children until this year seemed to arrive quite rapidly I am very grateful to the Holy Father for permitting a dispensation for coffee and water before receiving Holy Communion. New babies and Mothers are on a night and day schedule and fasting in that case is difficult. I think I enjoy receiving Holy Communion most when I know I am carrying a little child. It is so wonderful to bring Christ so close to your own little ones.

"My husband gave me a golden rosary the evening before we were married. Since that evening we have said it together every night in bed or alone wherever we happen to be. Other prayers include Grace before meals, the children's 'Angel of God' and 'Hail Mary' and frequent aspirations as, 'Dear God help me to be patient' many times a day. The prayer I love the most, which would grant me the most happiness, if I could only follow it more and which is kept right over the kitchen sink, is 'Learning Christ.' I believe it is by Thomas a Kempis and it starts:

> 'Teach me, my Lord, to be sweet and gentle
> in all the events of life
> in disappointments
> in the thoughtlessness of others
> in the insincerity of those I trusted'
> etc. etc.

It is a prayer which touches so many things in your everyday life and seems to increase your faith as you say it.

"Sometime during the day I dedicate the day to our Lord. Mentally I try to model our family after the Holy Family and work simply and happily as Mary would. We pray to the Infant of Prague and Mary and various Saints in making big decisions—as six years ago finding the right position for my husband. We attribute the sudden raise in position he always seems to get right after a new baby to God's blessing as well as to my husband's ability.

"I want my relationship to God and the Saints to be as that of very dear friends. As a girl, St. Ann was besought to find a husband; The Holy Ghost helped out with college exams; St. Joseph helped us to find a house big enough for a family, which we could afford.

"The children have their May altar and Christmas crib. Each day they pray that God will help Daddy to make a number of good sales; and at night we thank God for everything. We try to associate God with many things as once when Daddy took us for a ride shortly after a severe operation and our car got stuck on a lonely road in a snow storm and we were so worried that Dad would hurt himself. The children and mother in the car said three Hail Marys and immediately three cars in a row stopped to help us out. It was the fact that three cars stopped after three Hail Marys were said that made them realize so vividly that God was really listening to their prayers."

Let us by way of contrast consider the life of one who grew up and established her own home without the consolations of religion such as the Eucharistic life and daily prayer, and when her husband was dead and her children married found peace in the Church.

"My father died before I was three years old. I was baptised in the Episcopal church as an infant; and when I was nearly fifteen, my Mother was married to the rector of our parish. Brought up in the Church, it would seem I should have imbibed some rudiments of Church teachings but I cannot see that I did. In Church Doctrine and Theology I had no instruction whatsoever, other than the catechism. Before I was confirmed at thirteen I do recall an emotional fervor; but it soon evaporated. I went to all the services. I liked going, it was not forced. There was no instruction such as that with which the Catholic Church arms her children for life's battles—there wasn't a notion in my mind that there would be any battles. Of sin, as an offense against Almighty God, I never heard. Sin was, rather, an offense against nice people, who I was led to believe, did not do 'such things'. Grace, too, was quite unknown.

"I married early and from then on was too far away to see my family often. Also my husband's continual illness kept me close to him. He was by baptism a Swedenborgian, but in reality a Pantheist. When our children came, they were baptised, I heard their evening prayers, but I did not give them any particular religious instruction. It is a hard thought for me today.

"Sunday was our day 'at home'. My husband looked forward to it; it was his day of relaxation. Being at home always, he liked his friends to be free to come at any time. Every moment of my time was taken: growing children, an uncertain income, a sick husband. It was not an easy life but I had the devoted love of my husband, my children and many friends: happiness and peace, in spite of constant care. In those crowded years I felt no need for God.

"But after thirty years, my children married, my husband died. Having built my life entirely around him, my world crashed. The last years had been very difficult. My husband could not walk more than a few steps. He did not sleep at night, sat up in his chair and liked me beside him; in fact I was always within call, at any time, if not with him. I had very little sleep in the last eight years of his life and was more tired than I knew.

"Now I know how good God was to me. He left me my husband's great love, my home, as long as my husband lived. This sustained me, I did not look to God for help. Material worries I could by-pass. I was used to them, but the certainty of being loved, of being necessary; these I couldn't have done without. But after his death, there came seven much harder years. I found occupation in the care of the widow of an old friend. She was a manic-depressive and I was with her for seven years. Psychiatric nurses came and went. There were periods when she was in a mental hospital. It was hard and nerve racking. When she was on the up-curve, she was entirely self-sufficient and resented me: when she was depressed she clung to me desperately. She was suicidal and often had to be watched closely. I was worn out mentally and physically.

"I had however, happened on a copy of the Imitation of Christ and had begun to read it regularly. It was the first leaven to stir my soul. Finally, I realized that I must get away. It was not easy, I had been there so long. I was longing to be near one of my children and God guided me to go near my son. About then, too, I came across Aldous Huxley's Perennial Philosophy. For a long time the Imitation and Huxley's book were my chief reading. I still was 'able to see good in all religions,' still 'really wished I could accept Catholicism'. Catholics seem so happy; but I thought, 'I cannot accept the Catholic beliefs'. This, without giving these beliefs even a passing glance. Yet it was readings from the Catholic Fathers that held my attention and kept me interested. To me one of the wonderful things in Catholicism is that it is intellectually exciting as well as able to fill our deepest religious needs. But I still looked for help from people, and there was no help. A physical ailment was keeping me in constant pain. And then God took pity on me. This was the first time in years that I had no one dependent on me directly. I did not know how to live that way and was completely lost and empty. I was of no real use to anyone and I neither would nor could accept it. My son loved me I knew; I also knew I was (necessarily in my state of mind) rather a complication in his life, than a help.

"About this time, my son and his wife—who were childless, adopted two children, brother and sister. The elder child was old enough to start school but when my son looked into the public schools he was very sure he would never send his children where the secular education was poor: the religious education entirely absent. They did not want to send them to private schools. They loved them and wanted them at home.

"I should have said before that they had left the Low Episcopal Church—not liking the teachings of the new liberal rector and were going to a High Episcopal Church. Here they used an English version of the Missal and followed to a degree the Catholic ritual. However, it seemed neither one thing nor the other, after my son had an inkling of the riches of the Catholic Church. Still looking for a school he went to see the Parochial schools—liked them—became interested in the Mass. He went to see the priest of the church nearby, became more and more interested and told him of his desire to be a Catholic and to enter the children in the parochial school. It was all so simple after the initial step had been taken. Soon he and his wife began instructions and then were baptised. The children were also baptised. Next, I too took instruction and was baptised, and was confirmed at the same time as my son and daughter-in-law.

"I did not have the struggle that many converts have, nor did my son. His wife was not so ready at first—but is now a devout Catholic. For myself, after the lonely years I had gone through, it was such a blessed comfort to have at last all I had been longing for (without knowing what it was, or how to find it) I was in no mood to quibble. I accepted with contrition and love the dogmas of the Church, grateful every moment for each grace with which God had blessed us all. Five people made safe and children of God—through my son's anxiety for his children. In this too we of course see God's hand.

"I find I have not said here, that my great sorrow now is that I did not have Catholic training early. It would have made, not only my life but that also of my family, so different."

Those who lead a devout life can even find a special blessing and consolation in the death of a much-loved father or mother. The power of religion in consoling the family in its bereavement of a good father is illustrated in the following letter.

"I am 38 years of age, I was the third oldest in a family of eight children. My parents were both Catholic and our home was a Catholic home, altho I don't think we were made to feel that God should be first in our lives. There was a constant struggle for material things, and God was looked upon as a fearful God. I am the mother of three boys, 17—16—7, my husband expired 4 years ago, and at the present I am working for a Doctor, in the capacity of receptionist.

"My religious education was only what I had acquired in High School, I went to the same school for 12 years. My husband had attended a University, and had absorbed much of the Jesuit philosophy, which was a help for me too. I had taken courses in child-parent relationship from which also I learned a great deal. In the last three years I have had a great desire to read spiritual books, and from them I have gained a deeper knowledge of my faith. Bishop Sheen's books, *Peace of Soul, Lift Up Your Heart,* Thomas Merton's *Seeds of Contemplation, We Live with Our Eyes Open* by Dom Hubert VanZeller, *Progress through Mental Prayer* by Edward Leen and *Simplicity* by Raoul Plus, S.J., are some books that I have read, and the ones I think I have enjoyed the most. The books that I seek most, are those from which I can gain a knowledge of the supernatural. I feel that I know so little of God, and if I knew Him better that I could love Him more than I do.

"Some weeks I go to the sacraments most every day, then again maybe 2 or 3 days apart and to Confession every 2 weeks. I would like to go to Communion every day. It's sheer laziness that I don't. My prayers consist of a short morning prayer, and at night I say the prayers of the devotion: The Secret of Happiness, the fifteen prayers revealed by Our Lord to St. Bridget. I attended Novena services to St. Anthony every Tuesday night. I try to say a rosary every day, but fail many times. It is easy for me to think of God during the day and many times I offer up at the present moment whatever I am doing, also to thank Him for His goodness. I have felt closer to St. Joseph and to St. Anthony since the death of my husband; to St. Joseph for his help in keeping my home intact, and to St. Anthony because he was my husband's patron saint. He was born on his feast day and died just a few days from it, he died on the first Saturday of the month and was wearing his brown scapular on which I had sewn the blessed lily of St. Anthony. He had also received Holy Communion and confession one hour before his death, and that day was also the Vigil of Pentecost. So I constantly pray to him and ask for his help too, for I am sure he must be with God, because I couldn't have received all the graces given to me without his intercession. Altho the boys have missed their father very much we often speak of him, how happy he is in Heaven. They pray, as I do, to him to help them with their problems. Heaven hasn't seemed too far away and is a reality to them. They have mentioned that they hope never to be out of the state of grace, for fear of dying and not going to heaven with him. His death has brought the realization to us of the importance of the spiritual which has helped me contrast to them, the futility of the materialistic side of life."

The following letter is valuable in showing how religion consoled the parents in the death of a child they tenderly loved.

"I am a very ordinary Catholic, trying to be a better one, but I will tell you what I do:

"My husband and I receive the sacraments as often as we can, although right now that means once a week as it is impossible at any other time. If there is one sure way of becoming a good Catholic it is that.

"The daily rosary has become a part of our lives, especially the Rosary Novena. Our Blessed Mother has been very dear to me since teen age, and never has failed me. Sometimes it's impossible to say the whole rosary at one time, especially if there are children. I often say it while giving the baby her bottle or a part of it at a time when things are slow for a while.

"Every morning I offer my whole day to our Sacred Heart, asking Him to help me make it perfect (it is a big job, asking Him that). I think that few Catholic married couples are ever asked to do anything extraordinary. If we can only do each day's work as well as we can, asking His guidance in everything, that is what God expects of us and no more.[3] There are so many irritations and trials we can offer to God in family life: for instance a word that hurts, misunderstandings, thoughtlessness. Instead of a sharp retort, I try to offer it up to God in reparation for my sins and those of the world. But many a time I forget. My Irish nature is hard to subdue.

"I try to mortify myself by not eating that extra piece of cake or by giving up something I specially like at dinner. I love to eat, Father, so this is really hard for me. Again I go

---

[3] This must not be taken as meaning that the married are not called to the heights of the spiritual life. The reader will find further on examples of several mothers who have "troubled the golden gateway of the stars."

for days without thinking of giving anything up. So you see, I have a long way to go.

"Sometimes we are tempted by the devil. The main thing is to recognize he is behind the temptation. It is easier to overcome then.

"One of the most obvious ways a person can get close to God is to ask Him to bring you close. I try to leave all my problems and decisions to Him. It saves a lot of worrying. Our Lord has given us many blessings, among them, giving us a little saint. My husband and I prayed very hard for our sick little girl. We asked that she become well, if it was God's will. He knew best though, and took her to Himself. We can see it was the best possible thing He could have done. Taking her in our Lady's month seemed to be a special sign that it was His answer to our Rosary Novenas.

"Thinking of our destination during the day helps to bring the right perspective to our duties. Depending on God for even the simplest problem is a good habit. I usually ask my favors through the Blessed Mother and have never been refused.

"A mother could have no better model than Mary. I ask God to help me be like her. If I can be even a little like her I will be happy."

Such is the life of the soul with God as it is lived in the Christian home. But in spite of the humble simplicity of the account, one sees shining through the pages of the letter the eternal brightness of the light of glory. Should anyone who thinks he has settled down to live out his life in unbelief read these pages, let him stop and acknowledge that the life of the soul with God as a matter of fact has great value, a value that nothing else can give. Some mothers protest against the daily routine of manual labor in the home. I remember one mental patient whose presenting symptom was rebellion against washing dishes and diapers. Sometimes the loss of a beloved child is followed by a sad change in a mother's life which may last for years without clearing. William James, the psychologist and the pragmatist, said [4] that whatever one may think about religion one must admit that it works where nothing else can work; and that one should have a profound respect for anything that will enable one to say with Job: "Although He should kill me, I will trust in Him." [5] The young mother, a college graduate, who wrote this letter, is perfectly happy in her household work and was able to unite her will with the will of God and even see in the death of her child God's loving answer to her prayers. She lives the "life of the Kingdom" and has attained to the peace of God which surpasseth all understanding. [6]

We may close with the example of a mother who has attained to a beautiful spiritual life.

"I am forty-seven years old, a widow of one year—with two grown sons in college. My education has been completely in public schools and extended to about a year and a half of college work.

"At present I care for an eight room home with outside help one day a week. Extra-curricular work consists of one morning a week spent at one of the old peoples' homes conducted by the Little Sisters of the Poor. During that morning I take care of whatever correspondence they have. Also I make calls for the Catholic Charities to investigate boarding homes for infants and determine whether they may be recommended for a license. I take part in the work of various Catholic organizations.

"My religious education has consisted of Catechism instruction as it is given to public school children in preparing them for First Holy Communion and Confirmation. During my teen-age years most of my girl friends were attendants of Catholic schools and this was a particular blessing to me. My two sons have always attended Catholic schools until their graduate college work; and during the years of their school-

---

[4] I read the passage some years ago but have been unable to locate it.
[5] Job XIII:15.
[6] Philippians IV:7.

ing I learned very much about God and the teaching of the Church. Family discussions with them, coupled with extensive reading, were an immeasurable help to me. I formed the habit years ago of typing their school papers for them, as a help to them surely, but primarily because I could take time to read and digest. And when questions followed the typing they were always patient and happy to help. By their interest in such discussions they have been a source of help and inspiration. In recent years they acquired a nice typing ability themselves, so now my interest has been forced to a very frank delving into all they write.

"Spiritual reading: Some years ago my regular confessor, a Jesuit, introduced me to Father Plus. Since then I have never been without one of his slim volumes for occasional reading. Father Leen's writings on mental prayer, and Bishop Alban Goodier's Public Life of Our Lord have been strong influences. Both writers draw me back again and again. Goodier's writings about Our Lord not only help me to a 'living image' of the Sacred Heart, but they draw me strongly back into the times in which He lived. I become tired when He was tired: sad and discouraged as He was saddened by men's coldness. And there is a tremendous and deep impression of His Love.

"I go to daily Mass and receive Holy Communion every day. I receive the sacrament of Penance twice a week, with the permission of my Confessor or rather with his approval. This practice was begun during Lent two years ago when I was praying for a conversion. At the end of Lent when my prayers had as yet not been answered I asked his approval of a continuance. As to my relation to Our Lord in the Blessed Sacrament, I do not know what it is. I can only give the effects; it is difficult for me to face the possibility of *not* offering my Mass each morning and receiving Him in Holy Communion. There was a period of perhaps three years when I seemed to have been given great happiness and a certain sweetness of contemplation during Mass and for a period after Mass during my Thanksgiving. For the past two years there has been a sense of silence. In using the words contemplation, happiness and silence I do not assume extraordinary gifts. I use the words in an attempt to describe things for which my words are neither precise nor truly expressive.

"I pray regularly, morning and night prayers and the Rosary daily—though not the *family* rosary. During the day I am in the habit of offering certain favorite prayers, the *Hail, Holy Queen,* and the *Memorare* being most frequent with aspirations to the Sacred Heart. The aspiration of complete trust in the Sacred Heart is of constant recurrence together with an aspiration of my own that I have used for years.

"I try to keep united to the Sacred Heart during the day, returning to Him each time I am conscious of having forgotten. During the last two months I have tried to keep united to the Blessed Virgin by regarding her as my Superior, and asking her help and guidance: her care for my carelessness, her remembrance to supply for my forgetfulness. I have prayed to her for years by asking her to do for my two sons all that I have neglected to do, all that I cannot do.

"The circumstances that make my prayer life more intense are circumstances of sorrow. I have a desire to share and offer joys as they come to me; but an infinitely closer association in prayer is given to me in sorrow, for I have known and experienced the tremendous graces He gives in times of affliction. His gifts seem to be a deluge of His Love that hinges only on our plea to Him. I have always felt that I am not close enough to His Blessed Mother. There seems an urgent need to take steps I haven't found in this regard—as though one had not yet tried the right key to a door that is closed.

"To make religion *real* to my children I have always believed that the only way this is done is through its growing reality in my own life. If I strive constantly for a growing reality of religion in my own life the reflection of it will be in theirs. Words never seem as strong as actions sincerely and earnestly performed."

CHAPTER **II**

In the Footsteps of the Apostles

THE LIFE of Christ with his twelve apostles was the prototype of every religious community in the Church that has come into being since the days of Our Lord on earth. It was a life of complete renunciation of all things in order to follow Christ. This we learn from the account given us of the calling of the apostles. After the miraculous draught of fishes "Jesus said to Simon: Fear not from henceforth thou shalt catch men. And having brought their ship to land, leaving all things they [Peter, James, and John] followed Him." [1] A little later Christ "went forth and saw a publican, named Levi, sitting at the receipt of the custom; and He said to him: Follow me. And leaving all things, he rose up and followed Him." [2]

It was a common life to which they were called. The apostles went wherever Christ went. They had no fixed abode. It seems that they often slept in the open, for Our Lord warned one who would follow him: "The foxes have holes and the birds of the air nests; but the Son of man hath not where to lay His head." [3] St. Francis of Assisi and his first companions imitated this manner of living exactly. There was a common purse from which were supplied the de-

[1] Luke V:10-11.
[2] *Ibid.*, 27-28.
[3] Matthew VIII:20.

33

mands of charity and simple needs of the apostolic college. Thus when Judas left the room on the night of the last supper "Some thought, because Judas had the purse, that Jesus had said to him: Buy those things which we have need of for the festival day: or that he should give something to the poor." [4] It was a life of absolute obedience of the apostles to Christ. And so they lived, consecrated to God and isolated from the affairs of men—except for Judas, who, going out of the cloister established by Christ for His apostles, so entangled himself in things of the earth that he needed money and betrayed Christ.

After the ascension of Christ into heaven and the descent of the Holy Ghost the apostles were confronted with the task of organizing in Jerusalem the first Christian community. They seem to have remembered the words of Christ to the young and wealthy ruler of a synagogue who came to Him seeking perfection: "If thou wilt be perfect, go sell what thou hast and give to the poor and thou shalt have treasure in heaven. And come follow Me." [5] And so the first Christian community was organized by the apostles, on the lines of the perfection of Christ, as an extension of their own corporate body, and became a religious community living under obedience to the prince of the apostles, St. Peter. "The multitude of believers had but one heart and soul. Neither did anyone say that aught of the things he possessed was his own; but all things were common to them. . . . For neither was there anyone needy among them. For as many as were owners of lands or houses sold them and brought the price of the things they sold and laid it down before the feet of the Apostles. And distribution was made to everyone, according as he had need." [6]

Soon there were Christian communities in all the greater cities of the Roman Empire. But they formed a wonderfully united body and the unfortunate in one region were helped

[4] John XIII:29.
[5] Matthew XIX:21.
[6] Acts IV:32-35. See also II:44-45.

by the charity of all. Thus St. Paul speaks of the "collections that are made for the saints," [7] that is, for Christians in need.

In the latter part of the second century Tertullian wrote of the collections made in his day. "Each man deposits a small amount on a certain day of the month or whenever he wishes, and only on condition that he is willing and able to do so. No one is forced, each makes his contribution voluntarily. These are, so to speak, the deposits of piety. The money therefrom is spent not for banquets or drinking parties or good-for-nothing eating houses, but for the support and burial of the poor, for children who are without their parents and means of subsistence, for aged men who are confined to the house; likewise for shipwrecked sailors, and for any in the mines, on islands or in prison. . . . The practice of such a special love brands us in the eyes of some. See, they say, 'how they love one another'; (for *they*—the pagans—hate one another), 'and how ready they are to die for each other.' (They themselves—the pagans—would be more ready to kill each other.)" [8]

Nor did these collections for the needy ever die out in the Church of Christ. For example, in the first half of the third century the Bishops of Numidia wrote to St. Cyprian, Bishop of Carthage, asking him to send money for the redemption of captives. He took up a collection among clergy and people amounting to 100,000 sesterces (about $5,000). "From Rome, where Pope Cornelius had fed 1500 poor persons, Pope Stephen sent relief to the Churches of Syria and Arabia." [9]

Nor was Christian charity limited to the giving of money. In the year 251, during the reign of the Emperor Gallus, there broke out in Rome a terrible plague. The pagans were afraid to do anything. The Christians took the situation in

[7] I Corinthians XVI:1.
[8] Tertullian, *Apology in the Fathers of the Church*, N. Y. Fathers of the Church, Inc., 1950, chap. 39, pp. 98-99.
[9] Rev. Fernand Mourret, S.S., *A History of the Catholic Church*, trans. by Rev. Newton Thompson, St. Louis, Mo., B. Herder Book Co., 1946, Vol. I, p. 411.

hand. They cared for the sick, comforted the dying, and buried the dead. Many of them attained to a new type of martyrdom by themselves dying from the plague.[10] The charities of St. Basil in the fourth century extended to all types of the unfortunate and a whole town grew up from the construction of the buildings he planned to house those in need.

And so one might go on and write volumes. But all works of charity in the Church are directly descended from that organization in Jerusalem of the first Christian community in which distribution was made to everyone according as he had need. The primitive fervor of early Christianity far from dying in the first century is alive and active in our own day. The growth of Christianity into a world religion made it impossible that all Christians should give all that they possessed to one common universal fund. In fact, the words of St. Peter to Ananias indicate that even in those early days it was not laid down as a necessary obligation that everyone should sell all he possessed and give the money so received to the apostles for distribution to the poor. Each one was free to do so or not, but practically all did so spontaneously.[11]

The development of institutions for the care of the sick, the poor, the aged, and the lepers demanded a personnel to staff these institutions, as well as to preach and to teach. From very early ages this was done by various organized groups leading a special devotional life and consecrating themselves to their work of charity for all their days on earth. Already in the latter half of the third century it was possible for St. Anthony to find a community of Virgins to whom he could entrust the care of his little sister, when he was called by God to give up all things and enter upon a solitary life.[12]

The charity of the first community of Christians still lives on and in our own days every year thousands of young boys

[10] *Ibid.*, p. 408, quoting Eusebius, *Church History*, Vol. VII, p. xxii.
[11] Acts V:4.
[12] St. Athanasius, "Life of St. Anthony of the Desert," Migne, *Patrologia Latina*, Vol. LXXIII, trans. by Robert T. Meyer, Westminster, Md., The Newman Press, 1950, p. 20.

and girls not only give up all that they possess but vow their lives to the service of God in religion and to a life apart in prayer, work, and penance for the salvation of souls.

The secular priest is in a very special manner a successor of the apostles in the life of the Kingdom. He is not bound by what are technically known as the vows of religion but he is bound earnestly to strive to realize in himself the ideals of the priesthood of Christ, to obey his bishop, and live in chastity. His ordination involves a blessing by which he is set apart from all that is worldly and consecrated to the service of God. Before receiving the subdeaconate the bishop says to him: "Again and again you ought to consider attentively what manner of burden you seek today of your own accord . . . that if you receive this order it will no longer be lawful to recoil from your resolution, but you must forever live with God and with His help keep an inviolate chastity." [13]

What are the ideals of the priesthood? They are beautifully expressed in the epistles of St. Jerome. He says that a cleric is one who serves the Church of Christ. He derives the word cleric from the Greek Κλῆρος which in Latin means *sors* or in English, lot or the part that falls to one by inheritance or in any other way. So a cleric is one whom Christ possesses as His special allotment or one who possesses Christ as his inheritance. "He who is the share of the Lord, or who possesses the Lord as his share, should conduct himself in such a manner that he may possess the Lord or be possessed by the Lord. He who possesses the Lord and says with the prophet: the Lord is my portion [Psalm XV, 5] can have nothing else except the Lord." [14] It is the philosophy of St. John of the Cross absorbed into the ideal of the priesthood. "Having food and clothing," says St. Jerome, "with these I am content. Naked myself, let me then follow the naked Cross." [15] It is the night of sense and the night of the spirit

[13] From the Rite of Ordination.
[14] St. Jerome, Epistola LII Migne: *Patrologia* Latina, Vol. XXII, p. 531.
[15] *Ibid.*

through which we must pass to attain perfect union with Christ.

The foundation of the priestly life according to St. Jerome is the pursuit and the possession of wisdom. A priest who pursues wisdom from youth to old age will eventually reap in full measure the fruit of his labors. "The old age of those who have taught from their youth the arts of honest living and who have meditated on the law of the Lord day and night, becomes more learned with increase of years, easier by experience, wiser with the lapse of time and finally they reap the fruit of the happy hours spent in the years that have passed." [16] It seems that St. Jerome is here giving expression to his own personal experience, for in the beginning of the letter he writes: "My hair is white, my brow is furrowed and the skin hangs from my chin in a double fold."

Let us now turn to the struggles of a young priest in the beginnings of his priestly career and let us pray that when his hair is white and his brow is furrowed and the skin of his face hangs in folds that he will have attained to the fullness of wisdom by having taught others for many years the arts of honest· living and by having meditated on the law of the Lord day and night.

Parish Work

"I have been ordained only three years. When I came to the church where I am now assigned I arrived rather late in the afternoon. The next morning I slipped out, after saying an early Mass, and took a walk in a neighboring park. I will never forget the quiet peaceful beauty of that walk and how in the sweet freshness of the morning air my mind was closely united to God. And I said to myself, 'I will commence every day, while I am here, with a meditative walk like this'. I did not realize how in a very short time my hours would be so taken up with many duties that leisure for anything like a walk would simply not exist.

[16] *Ibid.*, 529.

"I came to my appointment with a firm resolution to make sure of three things every day: a half hour of meditation every morning and every afternoon and the anticipation of Matins and Lauds, so as to be sure never to crowd the recitation of the Divine Office, and the devotion of some time daily to holy reading. After a few weeks I found it impossible to get in the time for my afternoon meditation and sometimes I miss my spiritual reading even though I never take time out for recreation except visiting my relatives on Sunday evenings. Sometimes also I fail to anticipate Matins and Lauds.

"One who takes an interest in instructing converts soon acquires a reputation as a specialist in that kind of work. The result of this for me is that an hour and a half every evening has to be devoted to this field of the apostolate, for in one way or another converts are referred to me from all over the city. It seems impossible to tell a convert that you have no time to instruct him and so since the convert can seldom come except after working hours, the evening schedule is filled to the breaking point.

"By rising every morning at five, one can make sure of the morning meditation and Little Hours before Mass. But there are days when even that is impossible. Once for instance about five in the morning I had to go out on an urgent sick call. This was followed by other sick calls, by people asking for advice in the parlor, by the poor, begging help, until the time came for the evening schedule with the converts; and only at ten o'clock was I able to commence the office of the day. Because of continually falling asleep it took much longer to say office than usual. I am well aware that a sound opinion in moral theology [17] would dispense me from at least a part of the office on such a day. But it is certainly more meritorious to say it. And why not lead a penitential life to make with Christ reparation for my own sins and those of the world?

[17] "Those are excused from the Hours who are occupied all day long in duties of religion or charity, which cannot be omitted without scandal or serious detriment to themselves or others." St. Alphonsus Maria Liguori, *Theologia Moralis*, Rome, Vatican Press, Bk. IV, Ch. ii, #156, p. 580.

Our Lord said: "If any man will come after Me, let him deny himself and take up his cross and follow Me," [18] and the word for denial in the original Greek means to deny *utterly* and *completely*. One does not rise to the heights of utter self-denial when he allows himself to avoid something that he finds very hard and difficult.

"Taking communion to the sick in the morning is always a beautiful spiritual experience. Carrying Our Lord, hidden in the pyx, through the noisy streets and communing with Him in prayer is something sublime, far more wonderful than the quiet peace and solitude of that early morning walk in the fragrant freshness of the park air after sunrise.

"And then there is the big hospital not far away with its fatal illnesses and accidents and souls to be prepared for death and relatives to console. Furthermore any priest who will listen patiently, and help when he can, and when help seems impossible say kindly words of comfort and give a ray of hope by pointing out that after our Lord's death on the Cross came the joy of His resurrection on that first Easter morn, any such priest wherever he may be, will become a channel through which Christ will pour His assistance and light and strength to many souls. But a burden will be placed on his shoulders that will ever grow and can never be laid down.

"Such a burden would be an unbearable dead weight, if it were not for the sanctification of the priests' work by the morning Mass, and living the life of Christ interiorly by reciting attentively and devoutly the Divine Office through the changing liturgical seasons of the year. Thus one lives with Christ, and does His work in the world."

On the Foreign Missions

The following letter from a missionary in China gives us an insight into the life of the Kingdom under the dramatic circumstances of the foreign missions. It was written about five years ago. Now conditions have changed, most missionary

[18] Matthew XVI:24.

priests have been martyred and the few that are still alive are under torture. But Christ will rise again and sit on the throne of His Kingdom in China.

"December 1950

"Dear Father:

"You no doubt are following the events in this part of the world and keeping the work in your good prayers and sacrifices. These past twelve years have been troubled ones for China. It may seem contradictory but they have been very happy ones for a missioner. A missioner finds his greatest opportunities in the midst of the world's deepest wounds. In these hours people really need help and even though they cannot prescribe for their own sorrows and lack of peace they can recognize it when they experience it. You and I know it's the Peace of Christ they are looking for and the Priests of Christ are schooled in this science of love.

"A real missioner after the heart of the Master never calls his Brothers in Christ foreigners and so he is at home everywhere. This is a high ideal and needs the constant reminder of Christ. In living Christ and his life of love for men two great helps are ever present—the Blessed Sacrament and our Blessed Mother—Christ and Mary. We meet Christ and Mary at every turn of the day.

"Each day begins with the preparation for the greatest event that can take place in any land—our Mass. It's usually early so that all other events of the day might have on them the imprint of this great sacrifice and prayer. It gives order and priority to each new day as God gives them to us.

"A usual day of late has had 300 or more at the dispensary. It is here with the Sisters and Fathers and Catechists we are reminded of how Christ went about healing all manner of diseases and sicknesses. Even our Sister Doctor admits Christ still has to work the miracles of cures after the proper medicine is given. Most of our patients are people whose hearts are sicker than they really know and a Christ-like kindness arouses a Christ-like note of appreciation on their faces. It is all a very wonderful spiritual exercise for Clerics and Religious.

"From the dispensary work comes the invitation to visit homes. If it were not so, we might just become mechanical in our manner of pill passing. In the homes there is the reminder of how Christ went about doing good so that many began to follow Him. These more intimate visits open the way to inviting the people to study in a catechumenate. The 'pearl of great price' becomes something others want, too.

"Visits to the country stations in Oriental countries enact the scriptures before a missioner's eyes—'Behold the harvest' —'the sower went out to sow his seed'—'and he saw a tumult, people weeping and wailing greatly'—'I am the good shepherd, and I know mine and mine know me'—'and He passed through towns and villages teaching and making his way towards Jerusalem'—'Jesus too was invited to the marriage and also his disciples.'

"There is time most always after lunch to spiritually renew the good resolutions of the morning. A brief get-together with the Catechist Sisters and men sets a pattern for the Christ-like care for the new 'followers' studying in the afternoon and evening classes. It is not enough to have the doctrine taught well. Those studying must be set on fire to share their new developing 'Faith' with all their relatives, friends and neighbors.

"One of the great blessings in these times has been what the Legion of Mary has taught us. Besides being a great help in bringing a greater love of Christ's Mother to us and our people, it has helped to make our Christians more apostolic; it has multiplied our own hands for the good of many more souls and it has uncovered leadership where academic books on the subject have never found them. Our Mother has taught us new ways and yet Christ-like ways of seeing in those about us other Christs and, therefore, people to be served in the same manner she served Christ.

"The day is long especially with evening catechumenate classes or following a long trip to the country topped by evening prayers, talk and confessions for the morning Mass. Often going over the events of the day with a fellow Priest, however, gets things in shape for Christ. Those final parts of each day with Christ in the Blessed Sacrament fill up the weak spots and the privilege of preaching the unsearchable riches is a great pillow of Peace.

"In being so close to Christ no distance can separate us or our works for Christ. May we be less unworthy of 'this and Heaven too'. Pray please for the Chinese.

"May our Blessed Mother help you and your work of being and helping others to be wholly Christ's.

"Yours in Christ through Mary."

At the Gateway to Eternity

At the gateway to eternity the roads that we have all followed together in time meet and then divide into two. We must then go either to the right or the left. There is no other choice. The path to the right has indeed a stopping place for some in purgatory. But once on the path one is certain of eternal life and the joys of heaven. Lazarus left his suffering and hunger and poverty and was carried at once by angels to Abraham's bosom, the limbo of the just. The rich man left his sumptuous banquets and, as our Lord tells us, "was buried in hell." [19] And there he was told by Abraham, "Between us and you there is a great chaos: so that they who would pass from hence to you cannot, nor from thence come hither."

The Catholic hospital is indeed a place where physical care is given to all; but it is also a place where one enters an atmosphere of prayer that is made, not only for the recovery of the patient's health, but also for the salvation of his soul. The work of the Catholic nursing sister passes on to those of our day the love of Christ for the suffering, afflicted, and the sinful. An insight is given into the life of these sisters by the following note.

[19] Luke XVI:22.

"Our day begins at 5:25 in the morning when in our building a sister rings the bell to awaken us. Then she knocks at each door and says: 'Let us bless the Lord,' and receives the answer, 'Amen'. We say a prayer while putting on our religious habit. At 5:40 the bell rings again which means that we have only five minutes before prayers begin in the chapel. Every day at due time we recite in choir the whole Little Office of the Blessed Virgin. At 5:45 we say the Angelus to our dear Lord in the Blessed Sacrament, followed by a prayer. We then hold an interior conversation with our Lord for half an hour.

"The priest comes at 6:30 and Mass begins. During Mass we receive our dear Lord in Holy Communion; and He works with us and through us all the day long.

"At seven o'clock we have our office in choir, followed by breakfast which is eaten in silence in the Sisters' refectory, except on first class feast days when we are allowed to talk at breakfast. After breakfast we make a visit to the Blessed Sacrament.

"There is a short walk from the convent to the infirmary which gives one a few minutes of contemplation, especially on a nice morning. In the infirmary one meets patients from all walks of life. Inspired by the charity of Christ we minister to those who are sick and weak of body and often also to those who are weary and sick of heart. There are various duties to perform for God's patients: making beds, giving baths, taking temperatures, pulse and respiration, making rounds with the doctor, following out his orders and giving various treatments. Sometimes one tarries with a mother who is lonesome for her children, again one listens while a patient unburdens his heart and tells of his home troubles and even of a wicked life in the past. For such patients one prays with special earnestness before our Lord in the Blessed Sacrament. The silence and solitude of illness sometimes help the patient to think and face seriously the problem of eternity and come back to God.

"One patient told me the following: Sister, I am a Protestant, but my wife is a Catholic. We were married by a justice of the peace and now never go to any Church. Will it be all right for me to go to the chapel to hear Mass? When I was a young boy, I used to go around with Catholic boys; and when we got home early on Sunday morning, they would say: Let's stay up and wait for the five o'clock Mass before going to bed. I would wait and go to Mass with them. After Mass when I arrived home to go to bed, for some reason I felt so glad I had been to Mass. I didn't know what it was all about, but there was something I can't explain. You know there is something in the Mass, I would like to learn about. Could you find time some day to talk to me about the Mass?

"Later on the patient's wife came to see him. He told her there was a chapel on the floor and that she should make a visit, which she did. The rosary is regularly said in the infirmary over the loud speaker. In this way he learned it himself. So I gave him a rosary and he felt very proud to say the beads like the rest of the boys.

"Later he received a pass for a visit home. While there he told his wife that he wanted to become a Catholic like she was. She was delighted, not only about his conversion, but also because it made it possible for her to return to the Sacraments. He took instructions from our Chaplain, was baptized, made his first communion and had his marriage blessed. And then went on to get completely well and go home—and let us say: 'to live happily ever afterwards.'

"Some time ago there was a man here in an advanced stage of tuberculosis who had been unfortunate and had led a very bad life. He told the Sister in charge some of the things he had done. She urged him to go to confession, but he would not; and so she pointed out to him how foolish he was to tell her about his sins and she could not give him absolution, and might go around and talk about them, whereas if he told them to a priest no one would ever hear about them and he would receive absolution. He had seen some of the patients die from a sudden hemorrhage and his one great fear was that he would die choked to death by his own blood. 'In those days', said the Sister, 'death by hemorrhage was very common. We never knew when our guimpe might suddenly be spattered with blood. Since the new injections, death by hemorrhage is rather rare.' But he, in spite of his danger, concluded to let things ride and would not go to confession. And so she started to pray. A little later, he asked her one morning to get some priest to hear his confession. This she did at once. She saw him a little later and grace had worked a wondrous transformation. His sins were no longer mere wild escapades of the past but crimes against the love of Christ. 'Sister,' he said, 'I am not afraid to die. I want to die and that too by hemorrhage. The least I can do is to shed my blood to atone for the past.' Only a few days later he had his hemorrhage and died in his own blood, but saved by the blood of Him Who died for all men upon the Cross."

The Life of a Teacher in the Kingdom

The following account is from a nun who is head of a college science department in a religious community and who has been in the convent for thirty years.

"The least conscious time of my day is the hour after the rising bell has rung. Out of mere habit I am usually up and dressing before I am really awake. And then the day goes something like this.

"Rising: 5:15 A.M. 'Jesus here is another day for us to live together'. On the way to Prime, I light the vigil light at the Immaculate Heart Shrine—my charge; and then I go to chapel. In choir we recite Prime in English, and pray that the whole world may do God's will this day. Then comes meditation— rarely more than a drowsy period. My real union with God in prayer comes during the day, and that too at odd moments.

"Meditation is followed by Mass: that glorious time each day when I, too, can offer Christ to His Father. At the memento I pray daily for my family, for those who have directed me in the spiritual life, for our Lady's intentions and so on. At last the moment comes when Jesus and I are truly united in the sacrament of the Eucharist and my heavenly Spouse is all mine. First I give my Beloved to my Father, that the Father's will may be done in all things. Then I offer Him in reparation for the sins of all I would pray for and for my own: to purify all we have done badly, to fill in all we have left undone, in payment of all our debts and the debts of the whole world and the debts of the souls in purgatory. After these few moments I rest in my Beloved and turning to God the Father and to God the Holy Spirit, I say: We love you. We thank you. We ask you for all that I and the world may need. And then turning to the Blessed Mother I say we, your Christchild and I, love you.

"A second Mass follows and during it I generally try to make up the morning's meditation so often lost in sleep or drowsiness. Tierce, Sext, None and sometimes Vespers are said privately.

"Then follows breakfast and after that the hours in the school room. I love teaching and I love to help my students get all they need to meet government requirements. Dinner is at 12:10 followed by the midday examination of conscience and the Rosary. Then I say Matins and Lauds, anticipated early, a privilege of our order.

"Sometimes the afternoon brings me a class or two, or gardening work, photography: developing or printing, or there are guests to be attended to and various other things. Twice a week Benediction is given. Supper follows and then recreation except for the faculty and students, for otherwise there would be no time for preparing class work.

"Compline is sung about 7:15 PM followed by the Salve Procession. At 7:45 there is a free period which I spend as a holy hour in adoration before our Lord in the Blessed Sacrament. This I end with an examination of conscience. I then make my confession to Jesus and bow in silence for His forgiveness. A Spiritual Communion follows and at 9 PM I go to my cell, where I work or pray until 10 PM.

"Finally I get to bed with my rosary in my hand and 'Hail Marys' on my lips. The day in itself has been busy, perhaps very busy; but Jesus was ever with me. In every one of its problems I turned to Him. Jesus help me to open this box— You are so strong. I have to explain a difficult problem: Jesus, my Wisdom, tell me what to say.

"And so the days come and the days go. The years pass quickly. The day of the eternal nuptials draws near: *The Spirit and the bride say: Come.* O Christ, my Spouse, I yearn for Thee! *Come, Lord Jesus!*"

CHAPTER III

On the Top of the Mountain

WHEN Moses was leading the children of Israel through the desert a powerful nation, the Amalecites, rose up and went out to fight against them. "And Moses said to Josue: Choose out men, and go out and fight against Amalec. Tomorrow I will stand on the top of the hill having the rod of God in my hand." [1] The next day Moses saw that the Amalecites were driving Josue back, so he lifted up his arms in prayer; and then Josue advanced against the Amalecites. But becoming weary he lowered his arms only to see Josue commence to yield to the Amalecites. So Aaron and Hur stood beside him and held up his arms until sunset when "Josue put Amalec and his people to flight, by the edge of the sword." [2]

"What things soever were written were written for our learning," [3] that is to say, to serve as a lesson for us. The evident lesson in the above incident is the power of prayer. Had it not been for the prayer of Moses on the mountain, Josue might have been defeated; and the people of Israel might never have entered the promised land. God allowed his ultimate design to be accomplished by the prayer of Moses. Pius XI goes so far as to say that prayer is a more powerful apostolate than

[1] Exodus XVII:9.
[2] *Ibid.*, 13.
[3] Romans XV:4.

preaching. "It is easily understood that those who perform the office of prayer and penance contribute more to the growth of the Church and the salvation of the human race than those who cultivate by labor the field of the Lord; for unless they brought down from heaven an abundance of graces to water the field the evangelical laborers would certainly receive more meagre fruits for their toil." [4]

Holy Mother Church has never lacked those who supported the toil of her missionaries by prayer and penance: in the first place, the latter days of the Blessed Mother from that first Pentecost to her Assumption into heaven; then the virgins who imitated the Virginity of Mary by a life apart in their own homes. Perhaps the earliest reference to the latter is found in the letter of St. Ignatius to the Smyrnaeans written somewhat before 110, the year of his martyrdom: "Greetings to the families of my brethren, including their wives and children, and to the virgins who are enrolled among the widows." [5]

It is hard to persuade the mute inmates of the silent cloisters to speak of any personal details of their inner life, and so instead of a note from a solitary of our own days we present instead what St. Athanasius by personal contact wormed out of the founder of monastic life in the Church of Christ, with whom he lived and whose solitude and penitential life he shared.

St. Anthony of the Desert

Sometime around the year 270 a young man about nineteen was left alone in the world, except for a little sister, by the death of his parents. One day while on his way to church, he commenced to ponder on how the apostles renounced all things and followed Christ. And then he went on to think of how the Christians who "were owners of lands or houses

---

[4] "Constititio Apostolica" of Pius XI, *Umbratilem*.

[5] *The Epistles of St. Clement of Rome and St. Ignatius of Antioch*, trans. by Jas. A. Kleist, S.J., Westminster, Md., The Newman Bookshop, 1946, #13, 1, p. 95.

sold them and brought the price of the things they sold and laid it down before the feet of the Apostles." [6] And then he pondered on our future life and the hope that is laid up for us in heaven. Turning over these things in his mind, he entered the church, just as the gospel was being read in which the Lord said to the rich young man: "If thou wilt be perfect, go sell what thou hast and give to the poor and thou shalt have treasure in heaven. And come follow Me." [7]

His parents had left him a fertile farm of about 150 acres and various other goods. The words of the gospel, however, seemed a voice from heaven directed personally to himself. He obeyed at once. He gave his farm to his neighbors. One can well imagine them saying to him, "We will keep your farm for you and you will have it back as soon as this strange mood of yours passes away." But he never came back and was later to say that when one makes the great sacrifice and leaves all things for God he must never return to his old haunts again, but live alone with God forever afterward. All his movable goods he sold for a considerable sum of money which he at once distributed to the needy. His little sister he placed under the care of a much-respected group of holy virgins. He then went forth to be known in history as St. Anthony of the Desert, dying when he was over a hundred years old.

Free from all worldly restraints, he placed himself under the direction of a holy hermit who lived in a small field not far from his home town. He gave himself to a life of prayer. But praying also while he worked, he was able to earn his living by selling the products of his toil: probably mats which everyone in Egypt needed at that time, even as we now need beds. Part of what he earned he gave to the poor.

We are told of him that he lived in *"places* only a little distant from the town." We may take this as meaning that he became a precursor by a thousand years of St. Francis of Assisi and, homeless himself, he picked first one abandoned

[6] Acts IV:34-35.
[7] Matthew XIX:21.

shelter, and then another whenever the owner claimed possession.

There must have been at that time in Egypt a number of quasi-hermits, like the old man in the little field near his home town, for when St. Anthony heard of anyone leading a solitary life with God, he sought him out and lived with him until he had learned what he could by precept and example. He then returned to some shelter around about his home town and tried to put in practice what he had learned from the solitary whom he had visited.

Seeing the good in the lives of others is the royal road, as we shall see, to intellectual humility.[8] Imitating the good we see is the foundation of virtue. St. Anthony seems to have spent about ten years in this kind of novitiate, during which time he took Elias as his model [9] and so was a precursor of the modern Carmelites. Then in quest of greater solitude he went to live in the tombs of the graveyards near his home town. This period was not long. During it he underwent the temptations that artists have delighted in depicting. In the last of these, after a severe conflict with demons he saw a light from heaven and spoke to the light that appeared to him, saying: "Where were you good Jesus? Where were you? Why were you not present from the beginning that you might heal my wounds?" And a voice came to him from heaven saying: "Anthony, I was here, but I waited to watch your conflict. But now because you did not quit fighting manfully, I shall always be your helper, and make you known all over the face of the earth." [10]

What a consoling incident! In our temptations and in trials that seem to last so long and when God seems so far away, let us remember that Jesus is looking on though we see Him not, and if we continue fighting, He will truly be our helper forevermore.

[8] Intellectual humility is described by St. Benedict in the seventh chapter of his rule in the six and seventh degrees.

[9] St. Athanasius, "Life of St. Anthony," Migne, *P.L.*, Vol. LXXIII, Chap. VII, 131.

[10] *Ibid.*, Chap. IX, 132.

At this time St. Anthony was about thirty-five years of age. Some twenty years later after long solitude and fasting his physical appearance at fifty-five is thus described: "All were astonished at the beauty of his face and the dignity of his bearing. He had neither grown gross by lack of physical exercise, nor had his features become wan by fasting and conflict with the demons. But on the contrary, time had wrought no change in him and the youthful comeliness of his body remained." [11]

Just after the vision of the light from heaven, the idea came to him of departing deep into the desert and living there, all alone with God, far from the haunts of men. He had, no doubt, been much disturbed by visitors in the various shelters where he had lived around his home town. And so he went to his "novice master," the old hermit who had been guiding him, and suggested that the two of them go off together to live alone with God in the heart of the desert. But the idea appeared to the old man as an unheard-of novelty and furthermore he held himself excused on account of his age.[12] So St. Anthony set out alone, going deep into the heart of the pathless desert, carrying with him, we are told, a six months' supply of bread and some water. Rosweyd in his *Vitae Patrum* suggests that the bread was in the form of a kind of soldiers' biscuit, akin perhaps to what we now call hardtack. The concept of enough for six months must be measured not by the principles of modern dietetics, but by the common practice of solitaries in the days of St. Anthony. After walking for some time he found an old deserted fortress in which he walled himself up and commenced his solitary life, singing the psalms, all of which he knew by heart. In his temptations he was able to pick and sing a psalm which answered the wiles of Satan and put him to flight. Here he remained for twenty years without being seen by men, and when finally he emerged his physical appearance was that of youth and freshness as we have just pictured above in the

[11] *Ibid.*, Chap. XIII, 134.
[12] *Ibid.*, Chap. X, 133.

words of St. Athanasius. Solitude had wrought in him, after twenty years, nothing that was unseemly, nor the daily conflict with demons aught that was unkind.

Sometime after he walled himself up in the fort, friends found him. They threw food over the walls. They knew he was alive, for they heard him sing the psalms; and weird noises came from within during his strange conflicts with demons. During those twenty years his unseen example alone drew men into the desert to live alone around him. He became a strange kind of abbot, one who never saw or spoke to his monks and yet led them on to the heights of sanctity. Finally he emerged and gave them conferences. Not only those who had established themselves around him, but also visitors listened to his conferences. His manner of speaking "led the hearts of many to despise earthly things and was the beginning of their entrance into the solitary life." [13]

He pointed out a fundamental principle of the spiritual life: it must be centered in the love of Christ. His words "prefer nothing to the love of Christ" were incorporated by St. Benedict into his Rule.[14] And then he stressed what might be termed the simple logic of faith that we find in St. Paul: "The sufferings of this time are not worthy to be compared with the glory to come that shall be revealed in us." [15] He had no patience with one who boasted of having given up great possessions to enter the solitary life. For the earth and all its treasures should be reckoned as nothing in exchange for God and the eternal joys of heaven. And then he pointed out that death will soon rob the richest man of all that he possesses. In the words of Ecclesiastes: "Nothing is lasting under the sun." [16] Why, therefore, in order to gain the heavenly kingdom do we not go further and renounce now what must be lost when the light of life fades into darkness? What then should we seek and hold on to? Wisdom, chastity, justice, virtue, a watchful mind, the care of the poor, a strong

[13] *Ibid.*, Chap. XIII, 134.
[14] *Ibid.*, Chap. IV, 21.
[15] Romans VIII:18.
[16] Ecclesiastes II:11.

faith in Christ. We need not go far in pursuit of virtue. The Kingdom of Heaven is in every spot on the face of the earth. Hence our Lord said in the Gospel: "The Kingdom of God is within you." [17] Hence wherever we are we may come into the Divine Presence and know God, as it is given to man on earth; and love Him and live with Him preferring nothing whatsoever to the love of Christ.

Such thoughts as these constituted the burden of the conference that he gave to those around his fort when after twenty years he first emerged from solitude. He remained to direct this first community of solitaries for only about five years and then, again seeking to be all alone with God, went still further into the desert. But here again men sought him out who wanted to leave all and live with God. He remained with them about forty-five years. St. Jerome fixed the date of his death, when he was 105 years of age, at 356-357.[18]

While St. Anthony was still living, St. Pachomius came on the scene, organized and wrote the first rule for a community of monks living together and devoting themselves to prayer and corporate manual labor. Whereas the life of St. Anthony and his monks living together in caves or huts around a church was a prelude to Carthusian life, the monks of St. Pachomius living together and doing productive manual labor became a prelude of the modern Trappists, though there is no historical descent from one to the other.

Just after the death of St. Anthony, St. Basil entered the desert (357-358) to study monastic life with the intention of eventually founding a monastery and living there with his monks. He wrote a rule for monks which still directs many cenobites in the East. To St. Basil, the foundation of the spiritual life was theology and its living expression was the liturgy. Study and the chant largely replaced the manual labor of St. Pachomius. He became not only a precursor but one who profoundly influenced Benedictinism, especially in its later developments.

[17] Luke XVII:21.
[18] Cuthbert Butler, "St. Anthony," Catholic Encyclopedia.

He was not only a monastic founder but also one who, as a bishop, led the laity to participate in the chanting of psalms and the common celebration with him of the Divine Office. He tells us how rising in the dark of the night they sang Matins and Lauds and went forth from their song to the work of the day.[19] In the Middle Ages the devout rose for the midnight office, went to the church and prayed in silence during the chanting of Matins and Lauds. There grew up around various Benedictine monasteries, groups of the laity who tried to lead a spiritual life and participate as far as they could in the life of the monks.[20] They became known as Benedictine oblates. The Franciscans, the Dominicans, the Carmelites, still have their third orders that go back to the Middle Ages. Therefore, many who for various reasons cannot enter a cloistered life attain spiritual perfection in the cloister of the home, either as a member of the Benedictine oblates or of one of the third orders.

In the Cloister of the Home

The cloister of the home often shelters the sanctity of the monastery, as we may gather from the following report of a young girl.

"MY SPIRITUAL WAY

"On awakening in the morning, I offer all the prayers, works and sufferings of the day to Our Lord. Both the day and the night and my soul belong to Him! Then I petition to be allowed to share in some special suffering of Christ and His Blessed Mother . . . Give me O Lord, through the day some of the Agony you felt when the Cross was thrown upward against the sky; when your blessed Mother met You at the Fourth Station. The most important hour of the day arrives with the celebration of 7 o'clock Mass and the reception of

[19] Opera Omnia. Edited by Benedictine monks of the congregation of St. Maurus, Paris, 1839. Epistola CCVII, Vol. III, p. 450.
[20] M. P. Deroux, *Les origines de l'oblature Bénédictine*, 1927, p. 28.

Holy Communion. This is a necessity for me to live through the day. I must know which saint or feast we are celebrating. I must be reinforced in joy and love. I must pray to God at Holy Communion for my special virtues—humility, obedience and joy. I must constantly remember two sayings of St. Paul and St. Augustine, while I look at the large white crucifix and the pictures of the Nativity, Crucifixion and Resurrection over the altar: 'Love God and do what you like.' 'I live, now, not I, but Christ liveth in me.'

"Then I start my day of work as librarian and teacher. I put on a mask of sweetness and human charity to cover irritations and vexations. This mask must eventually lead me to Divine Love and complete trust in God. Everything I say or do must be an example for everyone who is thirsting for truth. I love the most difficult because Jesus is there. I perform details while meditating on a glorious end. I try to cultivate a Divine Franciscan laughter and be not moved by praise or blame.

"At night I have discussions with my mother on the Sunday sermon, on a passage of Frater Louis, on a human failure to taste the joys of God. We talk about my sister, Mary, a Dominican contemplative, and what she is doing. We connect God with everything and think about His parables as if they were newly spoken. Mother and I recite the litany of the Saints. I go to bed early and kneel before the crucifix. I say the rosary with arms extended to St. Thomas Aquinas to help my sister to persevere. I concentrate on the physical agonies of Our Lord on the Cross. Then I explain all my problems to Jesus and Mary and the Saints and I try not to forget the last prayer: 'Father, into Thy hands, I commend my spirit.' It is perhaps a weakness not to welcome temptations to prove your love. A temptation may be easy and queer. You resist with prayer and the cross. I must not consider my cross personally but how little I am doing. I must beware of sentiment for myself and bring Christ into everything. I try not to let people distract me and to be serious about salvation only.

"I treat sickness as a cure for my own high opinion of

myself. I try to guard against love of argument and laxity of deed and work on my thoughts harder than on my actions. I pray constantly to St. John Vianney with his 18 hours in the confessional daily, that I may never lose the power of consciously loving God all throughout the day."

There is a beautiful simplicity about the spiritual life of this child of Christ in the cloister of the home. Let not the intellectuals misunderstand it. For we must never forget that Christian perfection is measured by the true intensity of our love for God and not by the heights of our intellectual illuminations in prayer or by the depth of our knowledge of theology. A deep knowledge of theology is a great aid to prayer, but it is not necessary to attain to the heights of perfection. It is an aid, a means only. The intellectuals who possess it will be held responsible by God for the use of the talent He has given them; and unless they use it well they may be far surpassed by such as my *"caballero"* from Dixie Land who could not read until the little creature, like a child, but with wings like a bird, came to him and put its arms about his neck and said: "God loves you." [21] The last shall be first, and the first shall be last.

Contemplative Life in Carmel

Let us now consider a few examples of contemplative life within the cloister, commencing with a picture of a Carmelite day in a monastery of the reform of St. Teresa, the history of which she told so interestingly in her *Book of the Foundations*.[22] Something of a distinctive character has been impressed upon the foundations of St. Teresa of Avila. She was a devout girl who commenced to lead a good spiritual life and entered an uncloistered community of nuns in 1536 when she was twenty-one years of age. After about twenty

---

[21] See above, p. 11.

[22] In *Complete Works of Saint Teresa,* trans. by E. Allison Peers, New York, Sheed and Ward, 1950, Vol. III, pp. xi-xviii and 1-206. The article "Carmelites" by Benedict Zimmerman in the Catholic Encyclopedia is an authoritative account of the whole order.

years she commenced to pass through various stages of mystical experience to a state which she termed spiritual marriage. In 1562 she was able to open her first house of enclosed Carmelite nuns. Anyone who reads her writings will see that she was not only called by God to pass through the stages of mystical experience to their very heights, but also to describe what she experienced. As a result of her experiences and her descriptions of the stages of the spiritual life,[23] a definite aspect of the religious life has tended to stand out in bolder outlines than ever before. The religious life has not ceased to be a life of prayer and penance but it tends to become more than it ever did before, a life in which the soul as the bride of Christ lives in intimate communion with her spouse. This life of communion with Our Lord was known even in the days of St. Anthony of the Desert from whom we have the phrase: *Prefer nothing to the love of Christ.*[24] It stands out clearly in the letters of St. Ignatius of Antioch and in the German mystics. But no one before St. Teresa of Avila so clearly described its stages and its culmination in spiritual marriage with Christ. She is the psychologist of mystical experience, who has no equal, and was called to be what she was, and was made what she was, by God Himself. This life of the communion of the soul with God can exist in the active life as appears from the biography of St. Francis Xavier.[25] But cloistered life is the garden where it thrives and grows most rapidly. One who enters upon this spiritual way of living with Christ attains to a certain independence and stability in which, by the Grace of God, one triumphs easily over all trials and difficulties.

A CARMELITE DAY

"A Carmelite's day begins at a different hour according to the time of year. From Easter until the Feast of the Exalta-

---

[23] See particularly her *Life* or autobiography in the above-mentioned translation and also *The Interior Castle.*
[24] See above, p. 54.
[25] By Jas. Broderick, S.J., N. Y., Wicklow Press, 1952.

tion of the Holy Cross, we rise at 4:45 AM and from then until Easter we rise at 5:45 AM. All the year round we go to bed at about 11 o'clock. Therefore to fill out the 7 hours of sleep, during the summer we take an hour's siesta in the afternoon.

"The summer schedule is as follows: There is a peculiar happiness, even when one is very sleepy in rising before the birds to consecrate oneself anew to the adorable Trinity and to Our Lady of Mt. Carmel. The Carmelite clothes herself in her holy habit and goes down to the choir to devote the first hour of the day to familiar and loving converse with God. The Carmelite Order is especially devoted to the practice of mental prayer, so it is fitting that we should devote the first hour of each day to it. We find our greatest happiness and strength in this exercise. It must not be thought that it is a selfish activity (or in-activity) because the purpose of St. Teresa's Carmelite Reform is to offer all our prayers, penances and good works for the needs of Our Holy Mother the Church, for prelates, priests and all who work for the salvation of souls as well as for all sinners and for the Souls in Purgatory. Our very efforts to sanctify ourselves are not for ourselves alone, for no one lives to himself alone, since we are all members of Christ and united more intimately than we can possibly conceive. We, who are separated from the world by very strict enclosure, are all the more aware of the strong spiritual bond which binds us all together in Christ.

"At 6 o'clock we recite the Little Hours, which is followed by Mass and Holy Communion, which the Chaplain administers to us through a little window in the grate, which separates the nuns' Choir from the public Chapel. After our thanksgiving we have our morning coffee and, having made a visit to the Blessed Sacrament, we go to our work, whatever it may be. Whenever it is possible, we work in our cells, and our work is of such a nature as not to hinder the spirit of recollection. Wherever and whatever our work is it is done in silence, so we are ever joyfully conscious of the Lord before whose face we stand.

"Before dinner we assemble in Choir for a brief examination of conscience. Our meals are eaten in the Refectory in silence, but one of the nuns, appointed for the week, reads aloud from the Holy Scriptures and other spiritual books. After dinner there is an hour of recreation in common, during which we do our ordinary work (generally sewing of some sort). Conversation is lively and merry. Recreation over, we make a brief visit to Our Lord in the Blessed Sacrament before retiring to our cells for an hour's rest (in summer only).

"At 2 o'clock the bell calls us to Vespers which is followed by spiritual reading in our cells until 3 o'clock.

"We work again from 3 till 4:45 PM when we prepare for our evening hour of mental prayer. At 5 the bell summons us to the choir. So here at the end of the day, as at the beginning, we spend an hour of 'loving converse, wherein the soul often communes alone with Him by whom it knows it is loved.' (St. Teresa) At 6 o'clock we go to the Refectory for supper, which is followed by an hour of recreation and Compline. The time between Compline and Matins is spent in our cells, working or praying or reading.

"At 9 o'clock we go to the Choir for Matins. Our Holy Mother, St. Teresa, had great devotion to Our Lord's Agony in the Garden which took place at about this time. She desired that her nuns should give Him comfort. So may it truly be that by way of the Divine Eternity, our praises of God give comfort to that Heart that has loved us so much!

"After Lauds we spend 15 minutes examining ourselves on faults committed and graces received during the day and make acts of sorrow or thanksgiving. Then we bid goodnight to Our Lord in the Blessed Sacrament and go up to bed.

"In our cells we have a little table, a stool and a picture or two. Our beds consist of boards on trestles, a straw mattress, rough woolen sheets and sufficient covering. No one need sympathize with us for they are very comfortable. How I wish that everyone knew how happy one can be with just the necessities of life! There is, I believe, a direct correlation between the spirit of detachment and the realization of the fruit of the Incarnation which is our Divine adoption. Insofar as we lose ourselves, we find Jesus in Whom we have access to the loving embrace of His Father, and we experience the bliss of intimate communion with the Holy Spirit in Whose company every desire of the soul is realized."

Cloistered Benedictine Life

The life of St. Benedict and the history of the Benedictines teaches us by the mere facts of history that when a man gives up all things for God and devotes himself wholly to a life of the soul with God, he may accomplish an apostolate that reverberates all over the world.

St. Benedict was born about the year 480 and was sent by his parents to be educated at Rome. Already in the days of St. Augustine (354-430) the life of St. Anthony of the Desert had gone through Roman society like a best seller in our modern days. It might well be that this life of St. Anthony was in part responsible for the resolution taken by this young adolescent from Nursia to retire to some hidden cave and live all alone with God. At all events, this is precisely what he did, without any intention of ever taking an active part in the conversion and civilization of the barbarian hordes that were then destroying Roman culture and civilization. For some years he lived a completely isolated hermit life in his cave. Then followers grouped themselves around him. Later he retired with his followers to the top of Monte Cassino, halfway between Rome and Naples. There he wrote his Rule for Monasteries: a rule for monks leading a common life that could be adopted by any monastery, anywhere. He died about 540.

The rule of St. Benedict was copied and sent all over Europe and soon supplanted, more or less completely, all other rules. It became a powerful factor in the conversion of the barbarians and the civilization of Europe. A group of monks would enter an out-of-the-way region deep in the lands of the barbarians, settle down in peace, chant the office, and till the fields. Their abode would become a center for the relief of the poor and sick; a center, too, from which monks eventually went out and preached to the barbarians in their own tongue. Gradually the whole region would become Catholic, and the barbarians ceased to be nomads and learned to till the soil and ply the various arts of civilization. In out-of-the-way places, some regions knew no other law for centuries than the rule of St. Benedict.

The rule lives on in our days; and there is no more beautiful expression of the spirit of the Gospel than is found in Benedictine religious life.

"Hearken, O my son to the precepts of thy Master and incline the ear of thine heart; willingly receive and faithfully fulfil the admonition of thy loving Father, that thou mayest return by the labor of obedience to Him from Whom thou didst depart by the sloth of disobedience." [26] Thus did St. Benedict exhort all coming to monastic life to listen to all that Christ has taught and see in God a Father against Whom he has sinned and to Whom he must return, with certainty of a welcome, along the hard road of obedience. To live the life of Christ in its perfection is the essence of the Benedictine vocation, and that of all religious communities. A picture of Benedictine life at the present day is given in the following account from an enclosed community of Benedictine nuns. [27]

LIFE IN A CLOISTERED BENEDICTINE CONVENT

"When I looked forward to entering an enclosed Abbey of Benedictine nuns, I resigned myself to a life in which I would be cooped up for the rest of my days in rather narrow quarters. I was much surprised when, after my arrival here, we went for a walk in the enclosure garden. It stretches out for acres. The trees here are glorious and everything is beau-

[26] Opening words of Prologue to Rule of St. Benedict.
[27] Holme Eden Abbey, Carlisle, England.

tifully green because of frequent rains. We are very near to Scotland and its Scotch mists, that are really rains that one does not like to face without some kind of protection. A river runs through our enclosure garden and cows and chickens live within it and help support the community.

"The order of our day is as follows: We rise at 5:00 AM and chant lauds at 5:30. Mental prayer from Lauds until Prime at 6:30. Tierce and Sext are said before Mass at 7:00. Thanksgiving after Mass until breakfast at 8:00. After taking care of our cells we find the 'places' for the day's office. The postulants memorize a part of the rule each day and have a conference on the rule each week by the Lady Abbess. Holy Reading or study from 9:00-10:00 and manual labor from 10 until dinner at noon. Recreation follows dinner: a happy lively period, until 1:30. Then we have manual labor until 3:15. We have 'Tea' from 3:15-3:30; and None and Vespers from 3:30 to 4:00. From 4:00 to 6:30 we devote ourselves to prayer or study. Supper at 6:30 followed by recreation until 7:30. Compline and mental prayer until 8:10 when we chant matins. Curfew is a half hour after Matins.

"Imitating Christ in his life of adoration and praise of the Eternal Father, Benedictine life is built around the Holy Sacrifice of the Mass and the Divine Office: the official prayer of the Church, which continues down throughout the centuries the worship offered the Eternal Father by the Incarnate Word.

" 'Let nothing be preferred to the *Opus Dei*,' says St. Benedict in his rule. In a monastery of cloistered contemplative Benedictine nuns, all else is subordinated to the *work of God*. As a result the daily life is permeated by the Holy Scripture and each day's interior prayer flows from the only true source of prayer: the Holy Spirit Himself. Intimate contact with Christ and through Him with the Blessed Trinity is developed through the celebration of the great mysteries of our Faith and the feasts of those members of Christ's Mystical Body who now enjoy the eternal possession of Him in the midst of the Most Blessed Trinity.

"The *Opus Dei* is a *work* in a very real sense. When performed as it should be, with reverence, attention and devotion it demands the 'first fruits' of one's energies. It in turn provides the spiritual power necessary for human beings to effect that joyful obedience which is the echo of Christ's words: 'My meat is to do the will of Him that sent Me.' [28]

"St. Benedict wrote a rule for cenobites, that is, monks or nuns living together, permanently established in the framework of a family, with an Abbot or Abbess over them. The activity of a monastery apart from the *Opus Dei*, or one might say, in support of it, is the labor connected with the maintenance of a family. Food and clothing are necessary. When possible without hindering the *Opus Dei* the nuns produce these by their own labor: farming, weaving, sewing, knitting and other such activities. Surplus production can be sold for money needed for services that must be rendered by people outside the monastery.

"A Benedictine monastery asks nothing more of an applicant than that she be 'truly' seeking God. No special talent or gift is required. However, every one is endowed by God with various special gifts: intellectual, artistic or manual, and every opportunity is provided for their development and exercise so that God may be glorified through them.

"Contemplative prayer, which according to St. Francis de Sales, is a loving attention to God, requires silence and solitude. These are well provided for by St. Benedict, in that, only absolutely necessary conversation is permitted outside of the short daily recreation periods. Each day, certain hours are set apart for Holy Reading which in Benedictine life does not differ from mental prayer. One passes from reading to petition and contemplation so that to use the words of the holy Abbot Smaragdus: 'When we read, God speaks to us, and when we pray, we speak to God.'

"Here one experiences that beautiful simplicity of a life in which poverty and purity of heart free one for the only

[28] John IV:34.

reality worth possessing: the spirit of God by Whom we are made children of God and heirs to His Kingdom. The peace, the joy and the charity that are constantly apparent in the lives of the nuns are evidence that in the words of their Holy Father St. Benedict: 'as they go forward in life and in Faith, they, with hearts enlarged and unspeakable sweetness of love, run in the way of God's commandments.' " [29]

Life in a Carthusian Hermitage

Carthusian life may be briefly described as a happy blending of the hermit life with that of monks living together in community. Day and night, the Carthusian is nearly always alone in his hermitage. Only for special reasons and with permission from the prior does anyone in the community ever visit him. He sings the midnight office with his fellow monks. With them he sings also the Conventual Mass and vespers. He lives in complete silence except for a recreation with the community on Sunday afternoons and a common walk usually on Monday. This lasts for several hours and is taken in the open, outside the enclosure. Hence the charterhouse,[30] as a Carthusian monastery is known, is located, as a rule, in some secluded region. After the common walk the Carthusian says to his companion: "Good-by until next week," and retires to the silence of his hermitage.

To many, Carthusian life will seem a strange and useless type of existence. But not to one who has arrived at an understanding of the concept of the mystic body of Christ. The mystic body co-operates on earth with Christ in the great work of the salvation and sanctification of man. This it does by prayer, penance, and works of various kinds. In the human body the many members do not all perform the same functions but each has its own specific activity. The functions of

[29] Prologue to Rule of St. Benedict.

[30] The word *charter* is here merely an English corruption of the French *chartreuse* (name of the mother house) to which was added the superfluous *house*. In Spanish a *chartreuse* is termed *cartuja;* in Italian, *certosa;* in German, *Karthause.*

the Carthusians are prayer and penance, not only for themselves but also for the whole world.

In every charterhouse, besides the choir monks, each one of whom lives alone in his hermitage, there are lay brothers. In a well-developed charterhouse the various trades are represented, and young brothers coming in learn one trade or another. So our houses, often in far out-of-the-way places, are relatively independent of the outside world. Cloth, clothing, and shoes are all made in the monastery. Cooks, plumbers, carpenters, farmers, and others take care of the various necessities of life. But the lay brother has a devout interior life. He rises at night with the monks for matins and silently prays in his choir while the monks sing in theirs. He learns to pray while he works. Each has his own room. Sundays and holy days of obligation are days of silence spent alone with God. He serves one of the fathers very often at Mass in the morning. He lives in silence separated from the world, but united to God.

From the days in which Henoch "walked with God and was seen no more," [31] various souls have been called by God to leave the world and live all alone with Him. "And I said: Who will give me wings like a dove, and I will fly and be at rest? Lo, I have gone far off, flying away; and I abode in the wilderness." [32] "Therefore I will allure her and will lead her into the wilderness and I will speak to her heart." [33] And then a hermit who in early youth had been called into the desert prepared the way for Christ and became "a voice of one crying in the desert: Prepare ye the way of the Lord, make straight His paths. And the same John had his garment of camel's hair and a leathern girdle about his loins: and his meat was locusts and wild honey." [34]

One of the Superior Generals of the Carthusian order wrote that the Carthusian spirit consists in three things:

[31] Genesis V:24.
[32] Psalm LIV:7-8.
[33] Osee II:14.
[34] Matthew III:3-4.

"*First*, that the one who adopts Carthusian life should show by his works that he has truly chosen the part of Mary; and therefore he endeavors to devote himself to the one thing necessary at the feet of the Lord, having rejected worldly and transitory things and given up all interest in them.

"*Second*, that he should sit alone and in silence according to the prophecy of Jeremias and lift himself above himself, having given up superfluous conversation with men.

"*Third*, in order that he may fulfil in the most faithful and secure way of which he is capable the conditions of discipleship with Christ, let him deny himself, take up his cross and follow our Lord." [35]

That all this may be brought about efficiently one not only leaves the world, but leaves it forever and enters a cloistered life. And why? For no other reason "than to make use of Carthusian solitude in order to attain to union with God in this life." [36] And then he continues: "It is the very substance of the soul which should be united to God, not merely its faculties. And as we see in things of which we have experienced by our senses, two things cannot be joined together until they have been stripped and cleansed of all other things, so that each being completely isolated, they touch each other and no extraneous thing lies in between them. So it is necessary that the soul should be stripped of everything and be established in complete solitude that it may be wholly united to and made one with God. For if there remain the most insignificant thing between God and the soul, to use our mode of speaking in this matter, the soul itself does not touch God but whatever it is that is held on to and placed between God and the soul. As when one touches a hand protected by a glove, one does not touch the hand but the glove." [37]

When a postulant enters a Carthusian house he is at first given a room in the guest house. In all probability he will

---

[35] Innocentius le Masson, *Disciplina Ordinis Cartusiensis*, Monstrolii, Typis Cartusiae S. Mariae de Pratis, 1894, p. 12.

[36] *Ibid.*, p. 16.

[37] *Ibid.*, Chap. IV, § 26.

remain there only a few days and then he will be taken to his hermitage. Here, though only a postulant, he will commence to lead a life in all its essentials just the same as he will lead it, should he persevere, until the day of his death.

Let us suppose that he has entered his hermitage in the late afternoon after supper, which is at about 4:30 P.M. He puts his bags away and takes a look around. He finds himself in a two-story house [38] about thirty-five feet square, built centuries ago. On the second story where he now is, there is a rather large room with an alcove for a bed and another for clothes. In one corner is a small stove for a wood fire. There is a simple table in this, his bedroom and study, with a single chair. His bed has a straw mattress, well hardened by long use, with various hollows and humps that will eventually be trained to fit into the humps and hollows of his back. The pillow is an article that commands his interest. It feels as if it were filled with chopped cornstalks and leaves. He will get completely accustomed to it in time.

Opening off his study is a chapel about fifteen by twelve feet in size, with an altar at one end and a choir stall at the other.[39] A big crucifix hangs over the altar and beneath it stands the Madonna with the Child Jesus in her arms. Here he does not say Mass, but he will recite in this chapel, every day of his life, the whole Little Office of the Blessed Virgin and compline of the day and, except on the greater feasts, also the Little Hours of the day.

He goes downstairs to take a closer look at his hermitage. He passes through a room piled with wood and notices a chopping block and an ax. This room leads into a big room, known as the *Ave Maria* because when he enters it from the cloister he always goes at once to a kneeler before a picture of the Blessed Mother and says an *Ave Maria*. He notices a little window beside a cupboard. The window passes through the stone wall of his hermitage to the cloister, forming a little

---

[38] All Carthusian houses are similar, but differ in various details. The hermitage described here is at Miraflores in Burgos, Spain.

[39] Sometimes an alcove opening off the study.

tunnel through the three feet of stone masonry. In this tunnel a lay brother will, at stated hours, deposit his meals. Letting down the door of his cupboard, he finds he has a table. Here after the liturgical grace he will take his meals alone and in silence, perhaps reading a bit now and then from an appropriate spiritual book. On Sundays, however, and the great feasts he will eat with the others in the refectory, listening to the reading. He will never get breakfast and never under any conditions, meat. His first meal from Easter to the feast of the Cross on September 14 will be at 10:15; from this feast until the following Easter, at 11:15, except in Advent, Lent, and the various fasts of the Church, when it will be at 11:45. In the period from September 14 to Easter, only one meal a day is allowed, with, however, bread and water for supper. Once a week, usually on Fridays, only bread and water are allowed. Eggs and milk products are not taken in Advent nor from Quinquagesima to Easter.

Let us now continue with our examination of the hermitage. Just off the *Ave Maria* is a gallery with an outer wall of glass windows. This hermitage faces south and the gallery on bright days is a pleasant spot nearly all through the winter. A door leads from the gallery to the garden, which is about thirty-five feet square. No eye can look into the garden except from your own hermitage. A previous occupant had obtained stones, perhaps carrying them home one by one when on a *paseo* [40] and had laid a walk around an inner space covered with grass. When I first inspected the garden, in the center of the grass plot was a beautiful bush with its branches bending down with some fifty large white peonies. Four little plots in the corners were planted with shrubs, flowers, or vegetables; and a tree heavy with big purple plums, not yet ripe, gave promise of the future. I learned that what grew in your garden, you were allowed to eat with your meals—but not at any other time. So thereafter I specialized in vitamins from tomatoes and carrots. But most of all I enjoyed the walk where one could say rosary after rosary hidden away from every human eye, all alone with God.

[40] The weekly walk.

The Angelus rings at 5:30, if the following day is a twelve-lesson feast; at 6:00 if there is a feast of three lessons or a ferial. The Carthusian then says, in his chapel, compline of the day followed by compline of the Blessed Mother. For a week after my arrival the novice master always appeared to recite with me the various offices to be said in the hermitage and to train me in the rubrics of the private recitation of the hours. For the Carthusian does not say office in private in any kind of a posture, but kneels, stands, bows, or reclines on the miserere of his choir stall, with hood on or off according to definite rubrics.

After compline, he retires for the night. Five hours after the bell for compline the bell rings for the Carthusian to rise and recite matins and lauds of the Blessed Mother alone in his oratory. Having finished, he goes to the door of his hermitage so as to be ready to open it at once and go quietly, when the big bell rings again, to the church for matins and lauds of the day.

Matins and lauds of the day may become one of the most deeply spiritual functions in Carthusian life. I was surprised to find that I was very seldom sleepy. The whole office is sung from beginning to end. Just as one can enter into a fervent pleading before the throne of God when one sings one of the beautiful plain chant Kyries at Mass, so one enters easily into such a prayerful pleading in singing the *invitatorium* or the hymns or the psalms or the responsories. In a low Mass, or private recitation of the office, this is not so easy. One cannot linger as one would. The singing helps us to plead before the throne of God.

The result of one's pleading in the interior of the soul is often what might be termed a beautiful and wonderful peace experience. Now, what I describe here is *not* proper to Carthusian life alone, but common to all who sing or even recite privately the divine office, with dignity, attention, and devotion.

The midnight rising helps. The world seems dead and the soul alive to God. The chant vivifies without destroying the silence of the night. All seems so peaceful that the soul, too, is at peace. There may be distractions, but sometimes they are almost entirely absent. In the background is a consciousness of the Divine Omnipresence and of being surrounded by the vast immensity of the Blessed Trinity. Occasionally a sudden cognitive quasi-perceptual realization of the Divine Presence may illumine the intellect and quickly fade away, as a wave of the ocean breaks on the sand of the shore and rolls back into its depths. But the dominant element in the peace experience is the warmth of the love of God. This divine charity does not burst into flames as the love of God often does; it glows, without any flickering, rather than sends out piercing flames. This glowing warmth of love is not affected by any distractions as long as the peace experience lasts. It varies in intensity only gradually. It allows one to understand the psalms one is singing, perhaps helps one, and is the source of many beautiful interpretations of their meaning. One pleads: Thy Kingdom come! Thy Will be done, on earth as it is in heaven. And one can be perfectly sure that this pleading reverberates through the immensity of God in the hearts and minds of men all over the face of the earth. One is filled with joy and happiness that one can love and praise God with the angels and saints in heaven, and by prayer co-operate with Christ in the salvation and sanctification of men on earth.

If this peace experience suddenly disappears its loss is felt at once. One may continue to make volitional acts of recollection, but they do not bring back the peace. It is a good deal like striking matches, one after another, when the electric light current is turned off. Often, however, the peace experience carries one through matins and lauds, continues through prime of our Lady and the *Missa Sicca*, which the Carthusian recites when he returns from the main church to the little chapel in his hermitage, and may even be with him when he awakes the following morning, and continue into the functions of the following day.

The *Missa Sicca*, or dry Mass, is a beautiful little exercise with which the Carthusian vigil always closes. It is the Mass of the Blessed Virgin for Saturdays, from the Introit to the last Gospel of St. John, but with the preface and canon omitted. One recites it in union with some Mass going on somewhere in the world as the Carthusian is closing his nightly vigil. During its recitation one may make a final plea: Thy Kingdom come! Thy Will be done, on earth as it is in heaven. And then one may retire. The Carthusian's dark day is over and he goes to bed to waken and greet the bright day when it dawns.

The time for the second rising is 5:15, 5:30, or 5:45 according to the dignity of the feast. On rising one says prime of the day in his chapel on ferials and lesser feasts and then devotes one's time to mental prayer until 7:00 when one goes to the church where all spend fifteen minutes in adoration of the Blessed Sacrament. The litany of the saints is then recited, after which the Conventual Mass is sung. Private Masses follow and then one returns to his hermitage. Some time every day is devoted to manual labor. But this is for cleaning house or relaxation and penance and has little or no productive value. You might, however, look on chopping wood for one's stove in winter as a means of lowering heating expenses.

During the novitiate one's day is distributed by a fixed schedule; for there is a great deal to learn about how to live Carthusian life. For one not yet a priest the novitiate is followed by some years of philosophical and theological studies. Only after one's solemn profession does one enjoy the fullness of Carthusian life. For then he can spend his day to a great extent in prayer and holy reading. One should continue the study of theology, but this can be a beautiful period of prayer and holy reading.

In general the peace experience just spoken of, as possible during the night office, carries over into the day or perhaps the recollection of the day prepares the soul for the peace experience in chanting the office. In reality there is an interaction between the two, so that Carthusian life becomes a life of union with Christ the spouse of the human soul. The practice of silence, a cloistered life within the monastic enclosure, the absorption of the mind in the things of God, all lead to that abiding, quiet stillness and peace in which the soul glows with the warmth of divine charity and the intellect bows in adoration before God the Eternal Father of all. But only when the union of the soul with God attains its perfection, is the peace of God's presence uninterrupted. Before that there are more or less long periods in which the Beloved is absent.

Out of the soil of this abiding peace there grows a plant which in due season comes to flower. The plant is the theological virtue of charity; and the flower, an ardent desire to see and be with Him Whom the soul has loved in solitude for so many years. Sometimes this growth is rapid, and the flower bursts suddenly into bloom. When this takes place, there is all at once a transformation in the spiritual life of the soul. Nothing on earth appeals to it any longer, for the yearning to see God face to face has become so intense and all absorbing that everything temporal has lost its charm. The soul, attracted now only by eternal values, stretches forward in hope to the region of inaccessible light where alone it can be united with the Eternal Word, its true and only spouse. Nevertheless it must tarry for a while in the things of time. And as it tarries the yearning burns, but it purifies and sanctifies while it burns. The pain of separation increases as charity continues to grow. But Christ loves the soul infinitely more than the soul loves Christ. Now that the soul is transformed, He will not wait long to bestow the reward of charity. Soon Christ will call His Carthusian to Himself, and, in the union of eternal love, he will behold the very essence of the Blessed Trinity, and be like God because he will see Him as He is.[41]

[41] A little more space has been given to the description of Carthusian life, for most of the books in English dealing with Carthusians were destroyed during the bombing of London. The best available article on the Carthusians at present is to be found in the Catholic Encyclopedia. A very beautiful expression of the Carthusian spirit is to be found in a well-written book, *The White Paradise*, by Peter van der Meer de Walcheren, with a preface by Jacques Maritain. The translation by F. E. Holden preserves the beauty of the original Dutch. New York, David McKay Co., Inc., 1952. See also the anonymous, *The Carthusians*, Westminster, Md., The Newman Press, 1952.

CHAPTER **IV**

The Apostolic Value of a Life of
Prayer and Self-Denial

W HAT IS it that ordinarily impels a human being to leave the world and live with God in a life of prayer and self-denial? A true vocation to contemplative life is a special call that God gives to only a small percentage of human beings. It does not arise from failure and disappointment. It is not a call to literary ease, or historical research, or to a profound study of theology. It arises from a peculiar, quiet, ever-recurring consciousness that God is calling one to lead with Him, all alone in the desert of the cloister, a life of divine charity. Like Abraham, one hears the voice of his Creator: "Go forth out of thy country, and away from thy kindred, and out of thy father's house, and come into the land which I shall shew thee." [1] Hearing the call, one obeys.

In listening to this call many have not, at first, thought of anything more than of living with God a life of charity to the end of their days and thereby save their souls. The idea of doing a work for others does not necessarily enter the mind when one first embraces a cloistered contemplative life. But the concept of the Mystic Body of Christ soon makes one realize that no one lives for himself alone, but all live for one another.

[1] Genesis XII:1.

75

One cannot love God without loving his fellow men, each one of whom God loves with infinite affection, and for each one of whom Christ suffered and died upon the Cross. And so in entering a cloistered contemplative life, one embraces a life of intimate union with God in silence and contemplation, and at the same time immolates oneself with Christ for the salvation of all mankind. "In this have we known the charity of God, because He hath laid down His life for us: and we ought to lay down our lives for the brethren." [2] In entering cloistered contemplative life, we give ourselves to God and with Christ lay down our lives for the brethren.

St. Paul pictures to us Christ, the priest forever according to the order of Melchisedech: "Who in the days of His flesh, with a strong cry and tears, offering up prayers and supplications to Him that was able to save Him from death, was heard for His reverence . . . and being consummated, He became, to all that obey Him, the cause of eternal salvation." [3] And now, "offering one sacrifice for sins, forever sitteth on the right hand of God," [4] carrying out the celestial liturgy of the eternal priesthood.

Those who lead a contemplative life are in a special manner assimilated by prayer and penance to the eternal priesthood of Christ. This assimilation finds its expression in the Holy Sacrifice of the Mass and the Divine Office. "Where there are two or three gathered together in My name, there am I in the midst of them." [5] Christ sitteth at the right hand of God, "the brightness of His glory and the figure of His substance and upholding all things by the word of His power," [6] making purgation of sins, "reacheth from end to end mightily and ordereth all things sweetly." [7] As the Eternal Word and the second person of the Blessed Trinity, He is ever present in the hearts of His faithful, as that which is known is in the

[2] I John III:16.
[3] Hebrews V: 7, 9.
[4] *Ibid.*, X:12.
[5] Matthew XVIII:20.
[6] Hebrews I:3.
[7] Wisdom VIII:1.

mind of the knower and as One Who is loved hovers before the consciousness of the lover. Therefore, when any group, small or great, has been formed in His name to give glory to His Eternal Father, and plead for the conversion of sinners and unbelievers, there He is present in a special manner in their midst. The Divine Service which is carried out by the group becomes His liturgical act, and has its value from union with Christ, being unified and inspired by Him and offered by Him to the Eternal Father as He "sitteth on the right hand of the Majesty on high." [8]

Christ is the center of all apostolic activity. All the power of the spoken word, the silent missionary appeal of a holy life, the fire of oratory, and the efficacy of prayer have their ultimate source in Him, as He carries out the liturgical functions of the eternal priesthood surrounded by the angels and saints in heaven.

The power of the apostle of Christ is not determined by the type of apostolic work that he does, but by the sanctity of his life. There is a passage in the prophecy of Jeremias that brings out this truth in a striking manner. "And the Lord said to me: If Moses and Samuel shall stand before me, My soul is not towards this people. Cast them out from My sight and let them go forth." [9] The passage implies that God would do for Moses and Samuel what he would not do for others. What was outstanding in Moses that gave him this special power of intercession? God Himself said of Moses that "he is most faithful in all my house," [10] and we read also that in spite of the great dignity to which Moses had been raised that he "was a man exceeding meek above all the men that dwelt upon earth." [11] And who was holy like Samuel in his day, when "all Israel from Dan to Bersabee, knew that Samuel was a faithful prophet of the Lord"? [12] The sentence implies also that God will do some things for those who have not attained to the ex-

[8] Hebrews I:3.
[9] Jeremias XV:1.
[10] Numbers XII:7.
[11] *Ibid.*, 3.
[12] I Kings III:20.

traordinary sanctity of Moses and Samuel. And God does these things when they *pray*. The concept was expressed by St. James: "Pray for one another that you may be saved. For the continual prayer of a just man availeth much." [13]

Is it only the cloistered contemplative who can exercise the apostolate of prayer? By no means. It is indeed the special duty of the cloistered contemplative; but the passage from St. James indicates that all the faithful should share in the apostolate of prayer: the worker on the shift, the stenographer who goes every day to the office, the mother in the home, and the little children whom she teaches to say a Hail Mary to make all men good. What would happen to the world if these prayers were silenced and the Divine Office were hushed and ceased to be an unbroken prayer offered up all over the world day and night?

The sanctity which is so necessary for apostolic work the soul attains in its life with God. This life of the soul with God in the cloister extends beyond the chanting of the Divine Office in choir. It glows also with special brilliancy in the times devoted to mental prayer. Sanctity is a perfect consecration of the soul to God in a life of charity. This is brought about for the contemplative negatively by seclusion from the world and cloister; positively by the possibility of living a life of contemplation which feeds the flames of divine charity. From the love of God there flows into the soul an abiding peace, manifested by the great joy that one experiences in a habitual realization of the Divine Presence. This union with God in thought and by an abiding love is an analogue in the soul of man of the life of the Blessed Trinity: "In the beginning was the Word: and the Word was with God: and the Word was God." [14]

The Word was with God comprehending the Divine Essence and living that eternal, unchanging infinitude of divine charity which constitutes the life of the Blessed Trinity. Christ as the Second Person of the Blessed Trinity was re-

[13] James V:16.
[14] John I:1.

splendent with the glory that He had before the world came into being by His own creative act. For, though creation is an act of the Divine Nature, and therefore of the three Persons in the one Divine Essence, the existence and structure of all created beings is attributed to the Eternal Word. "All things were made by Him and without Him was made nothing that was made." [15]

This act of creation, which proceeded from the Infinite Goodness of God diffusing His goodness throughout a world of creatures, was the primeval manifestation of the Being of God. And in the Word was life, and His life became the light of men. And so the light shone in darkness, but the darkness did not comprehend it. Then, to illumine the darkness of human minds, the Eternal Word undertook the sublime apostolate of the Incarnation.

God willed to associate human beings with Himself in the work of His apostolate. "As the Father hath sent me, I also send you." [16] But all the power of the human apostle comes to him from the Eternal Word. "I am the vine, you the branches. He that abideth in Me, and I in him, the same beareth much fruit: for without me you can do nothing." [17]

The fundamental and essential thing in the apostle of Christ is that he should abide in Christ. This he does by the life of divine charity: keeping the commandments of God and living in union with God a life that bears a distant resemblance to that of the Eternal Word, in the bosom of the Father, before time was in the infinite and unchanging present of eternity. From that life of the soul with God is derived the power and efficiency of any human apostle. Whether his apostolate will be that of prayer or preaching depends on the call of God. Its power will depend on the spotlessness of a life of sanctity which allows God's grace to flow through the apostle, more or less unimpeded, to the souls of others.

There are various examples and admonitions in Holy Writ

[15] *Ibid.*, 3.
[16] *Ibid.*, XX:21.
[17] *Ibid.*, XV:5.

that warn us to associate some kind of penance or sacrifice with our prayer if we want to insure its being heard.

When Daniel set himself about begging God earnestly for some amelioration of the lot of his people in captivity he commenced to practice severe works of penance. "I set my face to the Lord my God, to pray and make supplication with fasting and sackcloth and ashes." [18] And when the angel appeared to him to tell him that his petition had been granted, he said: "Fear not, Daniel, for from the first day that thou didst set thy heart to understand, to afflict thyself in the sight of thy God, thy words have been heard and I am come for thy words." [19]

Baruch said: "I have put off the robe of peace and have put upon me the sackcloth of supplication, and I will cry to the Most High." [20] The words "sackcloth of supplication" indicate that penitential acts of some kind should accompany our prayer.

Naturally no amount of self-imposed pain can make up for persistence in sin. To turn away from sin is the fundamental requisite in any life of self-denial. A perfect work of sorrow for sin and doing penance resulted from the preaching of Jonas. "The men of Ninive believed in God; and they proclaimed a fast and put on sackcloth from the greatest to the least. And the word came to the king of Ninive; and he rose up out of his throne and cast away his robe from him and was clothed with sackcloth and sat in ashes. . . . And God saw their works, that they were turned away from their evil way: and God had mercy with regard to the evil which he had said He would do to them, and He did not do it." [21]

But the apostle himself must do penance for his own sins, not only that he may more effectively help others, but also that he may save his own soul. And so St. Paul tells us: "I chastise my body and bring it into subjection, lest perhaps

[18] Daniel IX:3.
[19] *Ibid.*, X:12.
[20] Baruch IV:20.
[21] Jonas III:5-10.

when I have preached to others, I myself should become a castaway." [22]

The life of all those who undertake to become apostles of Christ must have in it an element of penance and personal self-denial. God in His way will make known to them in what this will consist. It is a mistake to think that everyone must imitate the severe penances of some of the saints. When God calls to such penances He gives the ability to endure them. But He does not call all to extreme acts of penance and self-denial. The words of St. Benedict are classical for their wisdom and prudence: "Every one has his proper gift from God, one after this manner another after that." [23] To find one's own measure demands honesty and courage.

The self-denial that demands in the long run the maximum of fidelity is that which is involved in forever forsaking everything that does not concern us, separating ourselves from creatures as God calls us and abiding in Christ.

We have just seen that the power and efficacy of all apostolic work derive from the intimacy of the inner life of the soul with Christ. "Without me you can do nothing." We must live with Christ even as the Eternal Word abides in the bosom of the Father. It was for this that our Lord prayed on the night before His Passion not only for His twelve apostles but also for all those "who through their word shall believe in Me" and in their turn be my apostles in whatever century they may live: "I in them and Thou in Me: that they may be made perfect in one; and the world may know that Thou hast sent Me and hast loved them as Thou hast loved Me." [24] The apostle of Christ must live with Christ, whether he does his work by prayer or preaching. From his life with Christ he derives all the power of his apostolate.

From the fundamental necessity of an abiding union with Christ arises the most important element in our life of self-denial: separation from creatures. There is a certain amount

[22] I Corinthians IX:27.
[23] Rule of St. Benedict, Chap. XL, quoting I Cor. VII, 7.
[24] John XV:5.

of separation from creatures that is incumbent on every Christian. He has been taken from the world from the time that he came, or was carried, to the baptismal font and the priest laid his stole upon him and said: "Enter into the temple of God that your lot may be with Christ in life eternal" and the wicked one was told to depart from Him "that he might be made the temple of the living God and the Holy Spirit might dwell within him." After his baptism a white linen cloth was laid upon him and he was told to "receive this white garment which mayest thou carry without stain before the judgment seat of Our Lord Jesus Christ, that thou mayest have life everlasting. Amen." Hence arose an obligation to renounce all contacts with creatures that might in any way stain his baptismal innocence. And if, as most men do, he remains in the world and develops his own home and family, he must renounce all creatures that conflict with a holy life in the cloister of the home.

But if he is called to the apostolate of preaching or of prayer he is bound to a much more extensive renunciation than those who must be in the world but not of it. Thus in the early days of the Church at Antioch when the first Christians "were ministering to the Lord and fasting, the Holy Ghost said to them: '*Separate me* Saul and Barnabas, for the work whereunto I have taken them.' " [25] And so Saul, or as he was later called, Paul, and Barnabas left all things and entered on those missionary journeys that were to turn the Greco-Roman world to Christ. All interests in other things were laid aside, however lawful or innocent they might have been, and, as St. Paul expressed his manner of life, "forgetting the things that are behind and stretching forth myself to those that are before, I press towards the mark, to the prize of the supernal vocation of God in Christ Jesus." [26] And in spite of the labors and prisons and stripes above measure, the shipwrecks and journeyings with all their perils, the watchings, the hunger, the thirst, the fastings, the cold and the naked-

[25] Acts XIII:2.
[26] Philippians III:13-14.

ness, he so lived with God as he walked with man, and he had given up so completely all that was so dear to him in his former life that he could say: "I through the law, am dead to the law, that I may live to God. With Christ I am nailed to the cross. And I live now, not I; but Christ liveth in me." [27] Thus did St. Paul abide with Christ; and this abiding was one source of the miraculous spread of Christianity all throughout the Greco-Roman world, so that our Lord's prophecy was fulfilled, even before the death of St. Paul: "Amen I say to you that there are some of them that stand here who shall not taste death till they see the Kingdom of God coming in power." [28]

One who is called to the apostolate of preaching, whether in a city or country parish in his own country or in foreign lands, must separate himself from creatures that he may live with Christ. Persons and things must never more stand between him and his prayer and work to see the Kingdom of God coming with power in the field of his apostolic labors. But this renunciation of creatures is made in order to live with Christ and by abiding in Christ he derives all the fruit of his apostolic labors. How, as a matter of fact, does a priest abide in Christ? He rises in the morning to his mental prayer in which he communes in a most intimate manner with Our Lord. He unites himself to the passion of the Savior in his morning Mass and experiences Christ's eucharistic abiding in his Holy Communion. He recites the Divine Office with Christ pleading for the salvation of all mankind. He administers the sacraments trying to realize that he is but an instrument that should be holy and spotless and clean, that Christ uses to impart grace to man. He lives in the Divine Presence all throughout the day. And when he preaches, he gives expression to what he is ever learning by prayer and holy reading.

To continue leading a life with Christ day after day as the years roll by without any interruption will imply great

[27] Galatians II:19-20.
[28] Mark VIII:39.

faith and many acts of self-denial in the renunciation of creatures. Unfortunately it is all too true of many that having given themselves to God as a block, whole and entire, they take themselves back, chip by chip. But if one remains faithful in his life of renunciation, he finally becomes conscious of the habitual presence of the Blessed Trinity in the depths of his being and the attraction of all that does not pertain to God fades into insignificance.

The renunciation of the cloistered contemplative is somewhat different. By his very entrance into the solitude of the cloister he loses almost completely and forever all contacts with persons and things in the outside world. Furthermore, throughout his hermit life he has no support from seeing the results of his apostolate, except by some accidental bit of news that may find its way into his hermitage. He lives a life of faith. Perhaps his faith will be tried by the murmurings and suggestions of natural reason acting independently of the principles and illuminations of divine grace. Reading or hearing of the brilliant results of this or that active apostolate, human nature is likely to say, "Action after all is the great if not the only apostolate." But this would be to fall into the error of Pelagius.

One who is gradually sanctified in the cloister will attain a deep insight into the words of St. Paul: "Faith is the substance of things to be hoped for, the evidence of things that appear not." [29] The apostle of the cloister prays for the thousands he has never known and whom on earth he will never see. In general he remains entirely ignorant of the results of his life of prayer and sacrifice. In entering cloistered contemplative life, like Abraham he obeyed the call of God and "went out not knowing whither he went." [30] And like the prophets of old he will die "according to the faith, not having received the promises, but beholding them afar off." [31] And yet he will send ahead of him and lead with him and

[29] Hebrews XI:1.
[30] *Ibid.*, 8.
[31] *Ibid.*, 13.

draw after him an unknown and unnumbered multitude saved by the powerful apostolate of a life of prayer and penance.

This apostolate is not confined to the cloister, but can be exercised by any Christian. It can be entered upon by those to whom all other openings are closed and whom the world rejects: the hopeless invalid, the blind, the cripple, the poor, the ignorant; for all these can love God and offer sacrifice to Him: the sacrifice of prayer, the sacrifice of justice, the sacrifice of suffering, sorrow, and disappointment, the sacrifice of the shoulders. Wherefore ye little and forgotten ones who suffer, "lift up the hands which hang down and the feeble knees." [32] "Having so great a cloud of witnesses over our head, laying aside every weight and sin which surrounds us, let us run by patience to the fight proposed to us": the apostolate of prayer, "looking on Jesus the author and finisher of faith, Who having joy set before Him, endured the Cross, despising the shame, and now sitteth on the right hand of the throne of God." [33]

[32] *Ibid.*, XII:12.
[33] *Ibid.*, 1-2.

Part Two

THE INNER LIFE OF THOSE
WHO LIVE WITH GOD

CHAPTER V

The Theology of Mystical Experience

I T IS a fundamental principle in Christian mysticism that God dwells in a region of inaccessible light and nothing whatsoever that man can do, by his own efforts, can bring him into that region.

There are outside the Church many mystics in a philosophical sense. Are there any in a theological sense? As we shall see, true mystical experience comes from God acting on the substance of the soul transformed by the action of sanctifying grace. If there is true mysticism outside the Church, sanctifying grace must have been bestowed, on those who are elected to this mysticism, by the baptism of desire.

We shall allow St. Thomas to explain for us the baptism of desire:

"The sacrament of baptism can be wanting in two ways: *First*, both actually and in intention. This happens to those who have the use of free choice and who are neither baptized, nor do they want to be baptized. And, therefore, such as lack baptism in this way cannot attain to salvation, because they are neither sacramentally nor mentally incorporated in Christ through whom alone is salvation.

"*Secondly*, the sacrament of baptism can be wanting to someone actually but not in intention, as when one desires to be baptized but death accidentally intervenes before he receives baptism. Now such a one without actual baptism

89

can attain to salvation on account of the desire of baptism which proceeds from faith working through love by which God sanctifies man interiorly whose power is not bound by the visible sacraments. Hence, Ambrose said of Valentinian (in his book *De Obitu Valentiniani*, a little beyond the middle) who died a catechumen: 'I lost him whom I was going to regenerate; but the grace that he asked for, he did not lose.' " [1]

The following passage makes quite general the conditions of the baptism of desire:

"Baptism of water has its efficacy from the passion of Christ. [It has its efficacy] furthermore from the Holy Spirit, as from the first cause. Although the effect depends upon the first cause, nevertheless the cause transcends the effect. Nor does it depend on the effect. And therefore without the baptism of water one can obtain the effect of the sacrament from the passion of Christ in so far as one is conformed to it by suffering for Christ.[2] Hence it says in the apocalypse (vii, 14): 'They have come from great tribulation and have washed their stoles and made them white in the blood of the lamb.' By a similar process of reasoning it can be shown that by the power of the Holy Spirit, one attains the effect of baptism not only without the baptism of water, but also without the baptism of blood. When, for instance, by the Holy Spirit one's heart is moved to believing and loving God and repenting of his sins. Hence this is called also the baptism of penance." [3]

No intellect can perceive a being that by its essence exists on a plane of existence other than its own, for there is nothing in its perceptual apparatus that can come in contact with the higher plane of being. Thus, no creature existing in three dimensions could in any way come in contact, by means of its perceptual apparatus, with a creature existing in the fourth

---

[1] *Summa Theologica*, 3. Q. LXVIII, ii, corpus.

[2] This phrase seems to generalize the concept of baptism of blood in martyrdom. And so some who suffer behind the Iron Curtain may have hope. Such suffering, though, implies at least an implicit baptism of desire.

[3] *Summa Theologica*, 3. Q. LXVI, xi.

or any higher dimension. It is conceivable, however, that almighty power could endow an intelligent being existing in three dimensions with some modification of its perceptual apparatus by means of which it could take cognizance of higher dimensions of space. We have used this simile drawn from the concepts of geometry of *n* dimensions merely to illustrate a difficult problem. It is evident that other beings can transcend our order of being in many other ways than those of space. They lie outside the range of our perceptual apparatus.

It is evident, too, that the Divine Essence infinitely transcends the order of every conceivable creature, by the very fact that the creature is finite and God is uncreated and infinite. But it is possible for God to give to every being, endowed with the power of intellectual knowledge of the truth, a special addition to its perceptual apparatus by means of which He can make His own very Being an object of immediate perception.

This created addition to the intellectual perceptual apparatus is termed by St. Thomas the light of glory. Furthermore, in the act of perception by which the creature sees God as He is, there is no created light that shines on the Divine Nature and is reflected on the perceptual apparatus of the creature. But the Divine Nature itself functions in the place of any such created light and God acts immediately on the mind of the creature through a modification of its being that is an addition to the perceptual apparatus that was originally bestowed on the creature.

To put the matter in the words of St. Thomas: "Everything which is elevated to something which exceeds its nature must be adapted by some disposition, which is above its nature. . . . When, moreover, any created intellect sees God by essence, the very essence of God is the intelligible form of the intellect." [4] That word "form" is likely to confuse the modern reader. The *soul* of man is a *substantial* form organizing the ultimate matter of a man to develop into and to be

[4] *Ibid.*, 1. Q. XII, v, corpus.

what he is. The *concept* is an *accidental* form organizing consciousness for the moment and determining the mind to know an object in the light of a definition that gives expression to the concept.

· When, therefore, we see God face to face, we do not obtain a mere idea of God; but the Divine Nature functions *in the place of* a finite concept (which might be expressed by a definition) and the Eternal Word reveals to our mind by His own action the very being of God Himself which cannot be expressed by any definition.

Having considered the vision of God in its perfection when we shall behold God face to face and be made like Him because we shall see Him as He is, let us look at the beginning of our spiritual life and the course of its development. This knowledge of that toward which we are going will enable us to understand some things that come to pass along the road.

Our spiritual life commences with our baptism. Baptism may also be termed the beginning of our mystical life with God. In discussing the effects of baptism St. Thomas Aquinas points out that by baptism we are incorporated into the mystical body of Christ. That means that after baptism there commences to flow from Him, as the head of the mystical body of the faithful, the fullness of grace and virtue in accordance with the words of St. John: "Of His fulness we have all received, and grace for grace." [5] He quotes also St. Paul: "He saved us by the laver of regeneration [baptism] and renovation of the Holy Ghost; whom He hath poured forth upon us abundantly, through Jesus Christ our Saviour, that being justified by His grace, we may be heirs, according to hope of life everlasting." [6]

What now is the nature of this sanctifying grace by which we are born again and made over by the Holy Spirit? It is something that is going to change the perceptual apparatus of man so that it will make possible what we have above de-

[5] John I:16.
[6] Titus III:5-7.

scribed: the vision of God face to face. In meditating on this problem St. Thomas seems to have tried to discover a way of making it possible for man to see God face to face and still remain the same species of being that he is. This must come about by some kind of qualitative change. No mere intensification of the natural powers of man could make him capable of perceiving a being that infinitely transcends the plane of human existence. There must be a new manner of knowing. St. Thomas conceived of this new capability of knowing as a new quality bestowed upon the essence of the soul. And yet he does not identify this new quality with a new mental faculty. Were this so, it would change man into a new species so that he would no longer remain the human being that he is. Thus the difference between man and any brute animal lies essentially in the possession by man of a faculty with which no brute animal is endowed: abstract intellectual thought and the power of reason. If now man were given a new faculty by which to see God so that he would not perceive Him by human intellect, man would cease to be man and become another species of being. Thus St. Thomas says that if an ox or a horse were endowed with reason they would cease to be an ox or a horse.[7]

St. Thomas solved the problem in a different way. The quality, bestowed upon the essence of the soul, was not conceived of by him as a new faculty but rather as an abiding habit.[8] God's action, in bringing on this abiding quality, flows over into the faculties of man [9] producing the whole train of infused virtues, the theological along with the moral and intellectual.[10]

---

[7] *Summa Theologica*, 1. 2. Q. LXVII, iii, corpus.
[8] *Ibid.*, 1. 2. Q. CX, iv; 3. Q. LXIII, ii, LXIX, iv.
[9] *Ibid.*, 1. 2. Q. CX, ii and iii. See also Q. XXVIII, *De Veritate*, ii, ad. 7.
[10] *Summa Theologica*, 3. Q. LXIX, iv, v, vi; 1. 2. CX, iii. See also "The Sacrament of Baptism," *Catechism of the Council of Trent*, trans. by John A. McHugh, O.P., and Charles J. Callan, O.P., Wagner, New York, 1949, pp. 188-189. The concept is given explicit expression by the Council of Trent: "Whence in justification itself, along with the remission of sins, man receives all these things: faith, hope and charity: through Jesus Christ into Whom he is incorporated [*inseritur*]. For faith, unless hope and charity are

Sanctifying grace flows over into the intellect producing divine faith. It flows over into the will producing divine hope and charity. And so also each of the infused intellectual and moral virtues is produced in its appropriate faculty. That is to say, in the intellect or the will, for that which is merely sensory, or organized matter, cannot properly be the subject of habit or of virtue.[11] In being incorporated into the mystic body of Christ, of His fullness we all receive.[12] With the theological virtues, there are necessarily infused also the gifts of the Holy Spirit with which they are connected as a plant to its roots.[13] The gifts of the Holy Spirit are different from the natural virtues in this: The natural virtues help us to follow the light of reason; the gifts of the Holy Spirit, to follow the light of grace by which man is directed by God to his supernatural and eternal end. "As therefore, the natural light of reason is something over and above the acquired virtues, which are so called [acquired] by reason of their relation to this same natural light; so also the very light of grace itself, which is a participation in the Divine Nature is something over and above the infused virtues, which are derived from that light; and by it they are regulated." [14]

A note may be entered here concerning infused moral and intellectual virtues. The concept of *infused* virtues is foreign to modern psychology, which has no idea of the existence of any habits other than those acquired by the exercise of our functions. Catholic philosophy recognizes with modern thought that man is helped in attaining his natural ends in life through the development of good habits by repeatedly striving to make his actions conform to high ideals. Enlightened, however, by revelation, Catholic theology, using philosophical concepts, conceives of God directing each and every

joined with it, neither brings about perfect union with Christ nor makes one a living member of His body." Sect. VI, Chap. VII, Denzinger-Bannwart, *Enchiridion Symbolorum*, p. 800.

[11] *Summa Theologica*, 1. 2. Q. LV, ii.
[12] *Ibid.*, 3. Q. LXIX, v.
[13] *Ibid.*, 1. 2. Q. LXVIII, iv, ad. 3*um*.
[14] *Ibid.*, 1. 2. Q. CX, iii, corpus.

man in the world to his supernatural end: the immediate and intuitive vision of the Divine Essence, face to face for all eternity. This divine direction gives a tendency to think as God thinks and act in conformity with the divine will. Such tendencies of thought and action constitute the infused virtues, bearing the same names as the intellectual and moral virtues, but differing from them because produced in a different way. These virtues are infused with faith, hope, and charity in baptism. They must be nurtured, however, by cooperation with God's grace in the course of life.

The concept of infused virtue is not without basis in revelation. In the Book of Ecclesiasticus we read that God will fill the one who fears Him "with the spirit of wisdom and understanding." [15] St. Thomas quotes these words and says: "But wisdom and understanding are certain forms of habit. Therefore some habits are infused into man by God." [16]

God's action, producing sanctifying grace as a qualitative change in the soul, flows over into the human intellect and produces a change in it, in virtue of which the mind of man can be acted upon by God immediately and directly without the intermediation of any image, phantasm, or concept. In virtue of this immediate action of God, man will know by unclouded perception the divine nature as it is in itself. Were it necessary to know God by some concept, we would be unable to see God as He is in Himself. We could only learn by the concept something about God. But from Scripture we learn that "When He shall appear, we shall be like Him: because we shall see Him as He is." [17]

The qualitative change by which we see God as He is, when we are face to face with Him, is termed by theologians the *light of glory*,[18] as if the human intellect became all resplendent when acted upon by the Eternal Light.

But since the Divine Being itself makes, by its own essen-

[15] XV:5.
[16] *Summa Theologica*, 1. 2. Q. LI, iv.
[17] John III:2.
[18] St. Thomas, *Summa Contra Gentiles*, Bk. III, Chap. LIII.

tial brightness, the human intellect all brilliant with the Eternal Light which is Himself, it is evident that God Himself is the true Light of Glory.[19] "This is the light of which it is said: 'In Thy light we shall see light',[20] that is to say of the Divine Substance. It is also said: 'The city of the blessed hath no need of the sun nor of the moon, to shine in it. For the glory of the Lord hath enlightened it'.[21] Again it is said: 'Thou shalt no more have the sun for thy light by day, neither shall the brightness of the moon enlighten thee: but the Lord shall be unto thee for an everlasting light, and thy God for thy glory'.[22] Whence, also, because the Divine Being is all one with His Intelligence, and is unto all the cause of their knowing, God is called the Light: 'That was the true light which enlighteneth every man that cometh into this world.'[23] "[24]

We must consider this last sentence with its quotation in relation to a passage in the *Summa Theologica*. St. Thomas has been discussing the distinction between *prevenient* and *subsequent* grace: grace which goes on before and grace which follows after. He has pointed out that any grace which precedes and leads on to another is prevenient and all the graces of a lifetime which lead to the soul's entrance into glory are prevenient to the light of glory which is subsequent. He then says: "From the fact that subsequent grace pertains to glory, we see that it is not numerically different from the prevenient grace by which we are now justified. For just as the charity of our present life is not done away

---

[19] In reading St. Thomas on this subject, one may have various difficulties unless one bears in mind a distinction:

1. God Himself, acting directly on the mind of man, without the intermediation of any concept, and manifesting Himself, as He is, to a human being, is the *uncreated Light of Glory*.

2. The reaction of the human mind to this direct activity of God is an act by which a human person knows God, as He is. This reaction may be termed the *created light of glory*.

[20] Psalm XXXV:10.
[21] Apocalypse XXI:23.
[22] Isaias LX:19.
[23] John I:9.
[24] St. Thomas, *Summa Contra Gentiles*, Bk. III, Chap. LIII.

with but perfected in heaven, the same is to be said of the light of grace, because neither in its very nature implies any imperfection." [25] In other words: the light of glory by which we see God face to face is essentially the same thing as the sanctifying grace bestowed in baptism. God by His action on the soul in heaven performs the function of a concept in the human mind. God thus acting through sanctifying grace, without the aid of the ordinary channels of perception, awakens the mind in this life to know Himself, not as He is unveiled in glory; but as we can know Him now with His majesty veiled so that it is possible for us to see Him and live. God said to Moses: "Thou canst not see My face: for man shall not see Me and live." [26] Elsewhere St. Thomas says that "grace is nothing else than a certain commencement in us of glory." [27]

The following words of J. de Tonquédec, S.J., bear upon this point and warn us against an extreme: The mystic experience "does not in any way involve the clear vision of divinity. It has nothing in common with that vision 'face to face' reserved for heaven. Quite the contrary, none of its characters is more strongly dwelt on by the mystics, particularly Denis and St. John of the Cross, than its obscurity. It is not even of the same order as that in which the object presents itself in full light and offers itself freely for examination." [28]

It is evident that sanctifying grace, an abiding quality of the soul that flows over into the faculties of man giving rise to the infused virtues and the gifts of the Holy Spirit, must be that by means of which man is enabled to live with God the mystic life of contemplative union.

Before going further let us consider some communications

[25] 1. 2. Q. CXI, iii, ad. 2um.
[26] Exodus XXXIII:20.
[27] Op. cit., 2. 2. Q. XXIV, iii, ad. 2um.
[28] "De la certitude dans les états mystiques," Novelle Revue Théologique, 1953, Vol. 25, p. 403. Garrigou-Lagrange has expressed the same concept. The author would replace Tonquédec's "It has nothing in common with" by "It is vastly different from."

that came to us in answer to question 20 in "The Degrees of the Spiritual Life." [29] They seem to be honest statements of facts that really occurred; and anyone familiar with St. John of the Cross will feel that they may possibly be concrete incidents of what is dealt with in general in his *Dark Night of the Soul*.[30]

1. "For years I have been in the habit of commencing a period of prayer immediately on going to bed. At first it was the Rosary, later the Stations of the Cross. No attempt was made to stay awake until either was finished. On the contrary, I hoped to fall asleep praying, the devotional duties of the day having already been accomplished. Still later I simply attempted to enter into the divine presence and make acts of love in words or to love God with all my heart and soul with no attempt to give verbal expression to my love. One night, a strange thing happened: something I had never experienced before and have never known since. After I had made my usual attempt to enter into the divine presence, I seemed to come before Him in a peculiar perceptual manner. I seemed to be gazing at Him as it were with the eyes of the soul. Gazing, I saw nothing; and perceiving I beheld no more than the divine *presence*. There was no special attribute of God that I was given to know better by this peculiar quasi-perceptual experience. I seemed to be looking at God and to know nothing; to perceive without becoming aware of any detail of what I perceived. And still I knew that I had a quasi-perceptual awareness of the divine presence.

"As I remember the experience now it was almost exclusively intellectual. The love of God was in the background of consciousness. This seems strange to me. One would think that in a perceptual awareness of the divine presence one would be all on fire with the love of God. But I was not.

[29] See below, p. 390.
[30] Bk. II, Chaps. XII and XIII.

"Then, there was something still more strange. I seemed every now and then to close the eyes of the soul and no longer behold the divine presence. Then, I would open them; and there was the presence before me, just the same as ever; even as one looks, with the eyes of the body, at an external object, closes the eyelids and no longer sees it; opens them and sees it again. It is possible that the 'closing of the eyes of the soul' was something due to the process of going to sleep. After ten minutes or so of this experience of seeing, and then again not seeing, I went to sleep."

2. "There was a time in my spiritual life when God gave me at times to actually experience what I have read about in spiritual authors as a quasi-experimental knowledge of God. Then these experiences ceased. One morning on kneeling to say my morning prayers, I actually exclaimed: 'Here Thou art again!' I had been once more vouchsafed the quasi-experimental knowledge of God."

The following collaborator illustrates for us how God, by His mystic graces, sometimes makes us realize the fullness of one of His attributes far more completely than could possibly be done by a profound study of theology. I once was told, or perhaps read, about a theologian who had some kind of a vision. After the vision he is said to have prayed to God to give him no more visions, for to him the study of theology was amply sufficient. If the story is true, I am inclined to think that this theologian made a great mistake unless he implied that God would give him in his study of theology what can ordinarily come to us only by one of God's mystic graces.

Mother Juliana of Norwich in her *Revelations of Divine Love* distinguished thus between what she knew by visions and what she knew by the ordinary teaching of the Church: "And yet in all this time, from the beginning to the end, I had *two* kinds of beholdings: the *one* was endless continuous love: with sureness of keeping, and blissful salvation, for of this was all the shewing. That *other*, was the common teaching of Holy Church, of which I was before informed and grounded, and wilfully having in use and understanding. And the beholding of this went not from me; for by the shewing I was not stirred, nor led therefrom in any manner whatsoever." [31] The purpose of the mystic graces when they concern theological doctrines is not to teach what is unknown but to make ordinary truth glow in the mind with the warmth of charity.

3. "During Matins and Lauds this morning, there came to me a series of experiences that centered in a peculiar vivid consciousness of God's love for me, that is the love of the Blessed Trinity which was usually expressed as the love of the Eternal Father. It seemed to me a manifestation of the divine humility [32] that such a *tender* affection should be made known to me. There came with it a feeling of how terrible it would be if I ever should do the least thing that would be displeasing to God, Who loves me so tenderly and so intensely. Then there came a desire to suffer with and for Christ; and a sense of obligation never to undertake anything incompatible with this life of love. May our dear Lord Jesus grant that I never may. In some way may I be given the grace of living this life of love with Him until I die. During the *Miserere* at Lauds, I felt great sorrow for all my sins; and there came to me in thought rather than in innerly spoken words: 'All your sins are now forgiven and the time will come when you will be with Me in eternal life.' And this seemed to come from the Eternal Father. Kneeling at the end of Lauds, I looked at the tabernacle and pleaded with

---

[31] *Sixteen Revelations of Divine Love Shewed to Mother Juliana of Norwich (1373)*, with a preface by George Tyrrel, S.J., London, Kegan Paul, Trench, Truebner and Co., 1920, p. 111. A few words have been modernized. The last word *whatsoever* replaces *point*, which I take as a survival of the intensified double negative of the Normans; the *any* in the original is *no*. The phrase in the original is "in no manner point."

[32] There are many dealings of God with sinful man which would be regarded as abject humility in a great ruler's relations with his subjects.

Christ to make me faithful to the love of the Eternal Father which, strange to say, I had been allowed to *experience* in the dark before the dawn."

We may now ask: How are these cognitive realizations and intellectual quasi-perceptions produced in the soul?

If we may trust the introspection of those who experience them and the verdict of the great spiritual writers they cannot be produced by the natural working of man's human faculties with which he is endowed by nature.

Nor do they belong in the category of operations like a good meditation filled with holy thoughts, or perhaps more or less barren, which it seems possible for anyone to enter upon by God's ordinary grace at will.

Spiritual writers following the lead of St. Teresa of Avila recognize an infused contemplation which is due, not to God's ordinary illuminating and inspiring graces, but to a very special divine assistance.

What is the specific character of that assistance? When we look at the Thomistic concepts of sanctifying grace and the beatific vision outlined above, and consider also his claim that sanctifying grace is one and the same thing, essentially, with the beatific vision, as the charity with which we love God in this life is one and the same thing with our charity in eternity, the following possibility presents itself.

In the beatific vision God replaces by His own Divine Essence the activity of the human concept when we see Him, face to face, as He is. Our immediate perception of the Divine Essence flows to our intellect through that special abiding qualitative change in the soul termed sanctifying grace, and not through the ordinary channels of perception. In these supernatural cognitive touches, God by the action of His own Divine Essence on the soul of man, through this same abiding qualitative change, termed sanctifying grace, allows at times enough of the brightness of His glory to shine on the human intellect to awaken a cognitive realization of His own very presence.[33] At times there may be more light and one has a "showing" of one or more of His attributes or aspects of His being, such as the vivid experiencing of God's love described in 3 above.

Sometimes these divine touches awaken an ardent love of God in the soul. This love seems directly produced in the will and arouses the whole being of the one who receives it. Love naturally derives from the perception or memory of the one who is loved. But these outpourings of love arise suddenly and spontaneously without the mediation of any perception or memory. This should not surprise anyone who has attained a true concept of the theological virtues which are directly produced in the soul by divine action and not by the natural workings of the human mind.

St. John of the Cross speaks of these touches as follows: "To the soul that God wounds and lifts to the heights of love, He is wont to give certain hidden touches of love which, after the manner of an arrow of fire, wound and pierce the soul and leave it aflame with the fire of love. . . . These influences inflame will and affection to such a degree that the soul burns with the fire and flame of love, to such an extent that it seems to be consumed in that flame, so that it is made to go out of itself and be completely renewed, and to pass to a new mode of being, like unto the phoenix which is consumed in the flame and born again." [34]

One defect in our questionnaire is that we did not enter a special query on these touches of love. However, the following is taken from the history of the spiritual life of a collaborator.

4. "For a number of years I have experienced certain sudden bursts of the love of God. They may break in on my life at any moment during any of the duties or occupations of the day. They may be flames of love that suddenly shoot high

---

[33] Garrigou-Lagrange in various places has expressed essentially the same concept.

[34] *Spiritual Canticle*, Stanza I, commentary of line "Having wounded me."

and in a moment subside. Again, and more often they are peaceful experiences and seem to be essentially a silent intense consecration of my whole being to God. It seems to me that they have always been much more than naked acts of the will. They seem in some strange way to be also intense emotional experiences, even though they are characterized usually, by little or no excitement. The usual experience is described best as a glowing, quiet, peaceful, intense outpouring of my whole being in an act of consecration of all that I am and have to God whom I love with every fibre of my being.

"They come during periods which may last from one to several days. Sometimes during one of these periods, once the first awakening has been experienced, it seems possible to turn to God with all the warmth of intense affection at almost any moment. I then think, hereafter, I shall always turn to God in this fire of love again and again in the day. But when the next day comes, I find out that these 'turnings' are no longer possible."

These experiences, which St. John of the Cross terms "touches of love," may be conceived of as being produced in the same way we have suggested that the intellectual quasi-perceptions are brought about: the inflow of divine action by way of that abiding quality which is sanctifying grace. In the intellectual quasi-perceptions the divine action flows into the intellect; in the touches of love, it awakens the will and the whole affective apparatus of man.

Is there any reason why the one to whom we owe experience 1, recorded above, should be troubled because during his perceptual awareness of the divine presence he was not all on fire with the love of God? Not according to St. John of the Cross.

"From what we have said it may here be inferred how in these spiritual blessings, which are passively infused by God into the soul, the will may very well love even though the understanding understand not; and similarly the understanding may understand and the will love not. For, since this dark night of contemplation consists of Divine light and love, just as fire contains light and heat, it is not unbefitting that, when this loving light is communicated, it should strike the will at times more effectively by enkindling it with love and leaving the understanding in darkness instead of striking it with light; and, at other times, by enlightening it with light, and giving it understanding, but leaving the will in aridity (as it is also true that the heat of fire can be received without the light being seen, and also the light of it can be seen without the reception of heat); and this is wrought by the Lord, Who infuses as He will." [35]

St. John of the Cross conceives of these illuminations to know and inspirations to love as purgations of intellect and will. In a more advanced stage both are purified simultaneously. "But before this state is reached, it is more usual for the touch of the enkindling of love to be felt in the will than for the touch of intelligence to be felt in the understanding." [36]

There is a type of mental prayer usually termed the prayer of quiet which seems to be a combination and prolongation of these more or less transitory touches of the will and understanding, with God's action on the will being more accentuated than His illumination of the intellect. St. Teresa of Avila thus describes it:

"The first kind of prayer I experienced which seems to me supernatural I should describe as one which, despite all our efforts, cannot be acquired by industry or diligence, though we can certainly prepare for it, and it must be a great help if we do. This prayer is an interior recollection felt in the soul, which seems to have acquired new senses, corresponding to its exterior senses, and appears desirous of withdrawing from outward tumult. Consequently it sometimes carries the exterior senses away with it, being anxious to close its eyes so that it

[35] *Dark Night of the Soul*, Bk. II, Chap. XII, p. 7, trans. by E. Allison Peers, *Complete Works of St. John of the Cross*, Westminster, Md., The Newman Bookshop, 1946, Vol. I, p. 439.

[36] *Ibid.*, Chap. XIII, p. 2, Peers's translation, Vol. I, p. 440. The reader would do well to study these two chapters, XII and XIII, of the second book of *Dark Night of the Soul*.

may neither hear nor see nor understand anything but what is then occupying it—namely the possibility of converse with God alone. In this state there is no loss of any of the senses or faculties, which are all fully active: but their activity is concentrated upon God. . . . From this recollection there sometimes springs an interior peace and quietude which is full of happiness, for the soul is in such a state that it thinks there is nothing that it lacks. Even speaking—by which I mean vocal prayer and meditation—wearies it: it would like to do nothing but love. This condition lasts for some time, and may even last for long periods." [37]

Further on we shall deal more fully with the prayer of quiet; but to bring it into relation with the theology of mystical experience we shall give here an account by a priest collaborator. His account is probably a good description of what often occurs in the prayer of quiet.

5. "Very often, in the period of my mental prayer, I enter promptly into a state of mind the dominant characteristic of which may be termed *peace*. This peace, however, lives with the love of God. In general, however, no special acts of the love of God are made. I love God silently but intensely, without uttering a word. The intensity may however rise and fall gradually like the long low swell of the ocean after a storm. At the same time there is a dim consciousness of being face to face with God. It is a twilight consciousness and never brightens to the brilliancy of direct sunshine. Perhaps as a result of

[37] Relation V, Peers's translation of *Complete Works of St. Teresa*, Vol. I, pp. 327-328.

Is the prayer spoken of here as "supernatural" what St. Teresa terms the prayer of quiet or what she calls the prayer of recollection?

The prayer of recollection is a meditation that starts with the concept: God is everywhere, therefore within me in the depths of my being. It is possible to anyone with the ordinary grace of God. It is *undertaken* by the one who makes it, not *bestowed* by God. "It is called recollection because the soul collects together all the faculties and enters within itself to be with its God." (*Way of Perfection*, Chap. XXVIII, Peers's translation, Vol. II, p. 115.)

The prayer described here is not the prayer of recollection, for "despite all our efforts" it "cannot be acquired by industry or diligence."

this consciousness, a hush comes over my whole being, that flows over into the muscles. I remain quiet and motionless. When this stillness is very profound I do not tire and change from a kneeling to a sitting position; but simply remain motionless, knowing that God is looking at me, and that I dimly behold Him. When the time of prayer is over and I must turn to some duty of the day, the hush abides for some time in the midst of activity. It never utterly leaves me, except for periods when I have to discuss some matter with others and not always then. When the hush is not deep, the mind may wander to various distracting thoughts even in the time allotted to mental prayer. But, in a strange way, a quiet continuous love of God persists in spite of the distractions.

"This peace experience goes way back in the history of my spiritual life to the thanksgivings I made after communion. Even the carry-over into the activities of the day was felt in my seventeenth year. But only in recent years has the 'peace experience' dominated habitually the periods devoted to mental prayer. The longest the carry-over has ever lasted was on one occasion when the 'peace experience' abided during all activities for several days."

As we have seen above, sanctifying grace according to St. Thomas "is nothing else than a certain commencement in us of glory." In the beatific vision the very essence of God replaces the *species intelligibilis*, the intelligible form of the intellect, termed the concept in modern psychology. The light of grace and the light of glory are one and the same identical thing: just as the charity with which we love God now is the same virtue of charity by which we shall love, when face to face with Him, in eternal life. When does the light of grace first awaken the soul to the living consciousness of the divine presence? In mystical experience, the first glimmer of which comes to us with the prayer of quiet.

CHAPTER VI

The Heights and Depths of the Way of Life

S

T. JOHN, in the Apocalypse, gives us a glimpse of one phase of that great event toward which all creation moves—"when the Son of man shall come in His majesty, and all the angels with Him" [1]—"And I, John, saw the holy city, the new Jerusalem, coming down out of heaven from God, as a bride adorned for her husband." [2]

This new Jerusalem is the Church in glory after the resurrection of the dead. This vast cloud of witnesses is a body of individuals and has no existence except in the human beings that comprise it. The new Jerusalem is said to be adorned as a bride for her husband because each soul in that vast throng has been espoused to Christ for all eternity. Though their number is vast, still they constitute one body, the mystic body of Christ, whose soul is the Holy Spirit. "The marriage of the Lamb is come; and His wife hath prepared herself. And it is granted her that she should clothe herself with fine linen, glittering and white. For the fine linen are the justifications of the saints. And he said to me: Write: Blessed are they that are called to the marriage supper of the Lamb. And he saith to me: these words of God are true." [3]

[1] Matthew XXV:31.
[2] Apocalypse XXI:2.
[3] Apocalypse XIX:7-9.

And so we learn that all those who will be saved on the last day and will enter with Christ into His glory will be espoused to Christ and reign with Him for all eternity. The spiritual marriage of the soul with Christ is, therefore, the final and normal terminus of our growth in sanctity to be attained by all the blessed in heaven. We must hope for it and pray for it and do all in our power not to block the designs of Christ for the sanctification of our soul.

If true matrimony is a pact of perfect friendship, no one should shrink from the term spiritual marriage with Christ as the normal terminus of the development of our spiritual life. Let us look at the matter further. On the night before He died our Lord said: "Greater love than this no man hath, that a man lay down his life for his friends." [4] For whom did Christ die? "Christ died for all." [5] If that is so then Christ offers His friendship to all and seeks the love of human beings in return. All men are *potential* friends of the Eternal Word; but actually "you are my friends, if you do the things that I command you." [6]

If then you are to be truly the friend of Christ, the Eternal Word made flesh, you must offer Him no mere casual acquaintanceship but the highest perfection of friendship. This is implied in Christ's formulation of the greatest and the first of all commandments: "Thou shalt love the Lord thy God with thy whole heart, and with thy whole soul, and with all thy strength, and with all thy mind." [7] Your friendship, therefore, with Christ must be all-sacrificing, indissoluble, and eternal.

St. Ignatius Loyola in his contemplation on spiritual love describes how this love consists in God, the lover, giving to the soul, the beloved, all that He has and that the soul can contain. For God is infinite, and the finite cannot hold the infinite. Therefore God gives the soul all that the soul can receive and that will enhance the beauty of its being; and the

[4] John XV:13.
[5] II Corinthians V:15.
[6] John XV:14.
[7] Luke X:27.

soul gives to the Infinite Lover all its tiny being without reserve along with its power to be, to do, and to suffer. And this intercommunication of goods should go on without ceasing and forever.

How does this pact of friendship and intercommunication of goods differ from marriage? St. Thomas Aquinas raises the question whether or not the marriage between the Blessed Virgin Mary and St. Joseph was a true marriage. And he answers: Yes; because in it was verified the fundamental and essential character [*forma*] of matrimony, namely an inviolable and indissoluble union of minds by which each spouse is bound to maintain an unbroken fidelity to the other.[8] As the soul passes through the various stages of the spiritual life it advances step by step to the marriage feast of the Lamb. In a broad sense we are betrothed to Christ our spouse in baptism. We renounce the devil and his pomps and the priest says to us: "Receive this burning light, and keep thy Baptism so as to be without blame: observe the commandments of God, that when our Lord shall come to His nuptials, thou mayest meet Him together with all the saints in the heavenly court, and live for ever and ever. Amen." But we shall have a long way to go between that plighting of troth on the day of our baptism and that state in the life of the soul with God known as the spiritual betrothal; and far, far beyond that, the state of spiritual espousal or the marriage of the soul of man with the Eternal Word. But no matter what our walk in life, we must remember that we are all destined to a higher spiritual matrimony which blesses all human marriage and is its ideal and prototype: "Husbands love your wives as Christ also has loved the Church and delivered Himself up for it." [9]

Let us approach now the problem of describing the ascent of man to God, from the lowest depths of human iniquity to the spiritual marriage of the transformed soul to Christ, the Eternal Word made man. This study will be based on an

[8] *Summa Theologica*, 3. Q. XXIX, ii, corpus. For a fuller discussion see Chapter XIV.
[9] Ephesians V:25.

analysis of reports obtained from a number of persons in various stages of the spiritual life rather than on a study of the classic authors.[10]

We may ask in the first place, what is the theoretical starting point in the spiritual life of every baptized Christian in the present order of grace? It is a state of perfect innocence and freedom from every stain of sin whatsoever. Nevertheless it is not like the state of innocence of our first parents. For while baptism takes away original sin it does not entirely do away with concupiscence, that is to say, a sensory urge to commit sin.

This being the case, can we hope to find individuals who have preserved themselves entirely free from every shadow of venial sin, both voluntary and semivoluntary, throughout a long lifetime? The Council of Trent condemns the statement that it is possible "throughout an entire lifetime to avoid even all venial sins, except by a special privilege of God as the Church holds of the Blessed Virgin Mary." [11] We would not expect, therefore, to find that anyone could say that he or she had always been in stage seven of our questionnaire throughout an entire lifetime.[12]

Theologians point out that the wording of the Council of Trent says simply *all venial sins*, making no distinction between voluntary and semivoluntary venial sins. Therefore it might be possible, without a special privilege such as granted to the Blessed Virgin, for one to have lived his life without having fallen below stage six, which admits of semivoluntary venial sins. A semivoluntary venial sin is one that one slips into without a cool deliberate choice. One is bound to control his temper, but occasionally manifests impatience without really choosing to do so, but because of a weakness of emotional control which he should have acquired. Such acts of impatience are termed semivoluntary venial sins. They are not imperfec-

[10] See Appendix II, pp. 383 ff.
[11] Council of Trent, Session V, #5, Denzinger-Bannwart, 792; Session VI, Canon on Justification, Denzinger-Bannwart, p. 833.
[12] See p. 289.

tions in the strict sense of the word. A sin is an offense against the law of God. An imperfection is an offense against a regulation we have imposed upon ourselves, as something over and above what God demands. It was imposed in order to strive by the grace of God for a more perfect life; hence the term imperfection. Thus if one resolves to deny himself something not demanded by the law of God or by the specification of a divine law by the Church, during the season of Lent or at any other time, and without any laudable excuse breaks the resolution, one does not commit a sin but an imperfection, because one has not broken any law of God, but only a resolution that God left one free to make or not to make as he would.

This concept of imperfection is not admitted by all. Et. Hugueny in the article on "Imperfection" in the *Dictionnaire de Théologie Catholique* (ed. by A. Vacant *et alii*) denies the existence of any imperfections that are not venial sins.

According to Hugueny the law of charity is expressed by *affirmative precepts*, telling him who loves God what he ought to do, and by *negative precepts*, telling him what he should not do. It is easier to formulate precisely the prohibitions than the precepts. What each individual should do in detail comes to him by the inspirations of the Holy Spirit. But all are not called to the same life. What the priest should do is different from what a layman should do. What this priest should do is not the same as what every other priest should do. Not all are called by the Holy Spirit to the same minutiae of a penitential life. What the Holy Spirit calls you to do is the law of God for you. If you refuse to do some *little* thing He asks you to do, it is an offense against the law of God and therefore a venial sin.

This concept splits the affirmative precepts of the law of charity into two subdivisions: those that derive from the general law for all, and those that derive from the way in which the Holy Spirit specifies the general law for the concrete individual. The general expressions do not determine what is sinful for the individual in all the little details of life. This is done by specific inspirations given to the individual. Disobedience to these specific inspirations in the minutiae of life are venial sins and matter for absolution in confession.

The fact that most theologians say, with St. Alphonsus, that imperfections do not constitute matter for absolution in confession would indicate that, implicitly at least, Hugueny's concept is contrary to the principles of the majority of theologians. Furthermore it would seem that the Eternal Wisdom cannot only command but also advise. When He commands we are bound to obey under pain of sin. A kind and loving father can say to a son: My son, I do not command you in this matter as something I lay upon you by my authority as a father, I am merely telling you that I know by experience that you will get what you are aiming at more certainly and with less trouble if you do as I advise you. In like manner our heavenly Father may well say in regard to many things: I would advise you thus; but I don't command you this under pain of sin. If you listen to my advice you will attain to true sanctity much more easily and with less suffering than if you do not. I am pointing out to you the easier way; but if you take the harder way, you will not sin, but you will suffer. When we do not do as God advises, we will have our follies to repent of as well as our sins. Follies are not indifferent acts. They amount to neglecting good advice, but do not involve disobedience to the law of God. The psalmist draws this distinction: "O God, Thou knowest my foolishness; and my offences are not hidden from Thy eyes." [13]

It is to be doubted that it is psychologically possible for anyone to say with certainty that Chautard's stage seven [14] was the lowest he was ever in during his whole lifetime. A slight involuntary venial sin makes so little impression on the mind that it is easily forgotten. Then our own judgment of ourselves is not always God's judgment. For this reason it would seem that six is the highest degree one can hope for as the starting point of one's spiritual life and below which one

[13] Psalm LXVIII:6.
[14] See below, p. 289.

would never fall,[15] assuming that one is not given special help such as that given to the Blessed Virgin. It is otherwise with mortal sin. No normal person who ever commits a mortal sin completely forgets that he has done so.

Let us now raise the question: How does it happen that one descends from baptismal innocence or the negative sinlessness of the unbaptized infant to various depths of sinfulness? The answer, so far as it is given by our material, is the lack of proper instruction in childhood and an inadequate home and either no living parents to care for the child or parents who had no appreciation of a spiritual life or were themselves in various ways morally inadequate.

The following pathetic little autobiography gives the picture of a calamity that is all too common and also shows the way in which God often sanctifies inadequate parents by the instruction given to their children in a Catholic school.[16]

"I feel that I have come a long way since I commenced to know and understand my religion. I always attended a public school since no Catholic schools were available. So I did not get the Catholic foundation that the kind sisters give in their schools. Thus it came about that I committed sin. When I married I took care to put my children under the training of the sisters. As they grew up I learned from them to know and love my religion. And now I feel that I am nearing perfection. I would love to know how to get the habit of mental prayer and what is mental prayer."

What happens to baptized Catholics in unfortunate circumstances very often takes place in various ways outside the Church.

But God, whose Intelligence is without limit and whose Mercy is infinite, can make due allowance for innocence lost by children through no fault of their own because they grew up in moral and spiritual ignorance and were exposed to temptations that they had no proper training and equipment to resist.

[15] Only one of our collaborators picked seven as the lowest degree.
[16] See also pp. 30 ff.

In discussing the power of penance St. Thomas points out that by sin man loses a twofold dignity: first, that of sanctifying grace and, second, that of innocence. It was this second dignity of innocence in which the elder brother of the prodigal son gloried when he said: " 'Behold for so many years do I serve thee, and I have never transgressed thy commandments.' " [17] This dignity the penitent cannot recover. Nevertheless, the penitent gains at times something of greater value. For as St. Gregory says (*Hom. de centum oves* 34 in *Evang.*, a little from the beginning): " 'Those who know that they have forsaken God make good their former loss by later gains. There is greater joy over them in heaven, even as a general is more pleased with a soldier who, after turning his back to the enemy, returns to the thick of the fight, than over the one who never turned his back, but never entered into the thick of the fight.' " [18]

But in our day there are many outside the Church who gather not with Christ and therefore scatter. They are, as it were, soldiers who ignorantly, through no fault of their own, joined the forces fighting against the great King. They sin, or rather, sometimes in an amoral manner, commit sinful acts not knowing what they do. They are not really immoral. They fight against the great King not realizing that He is indeed the King of Kings and the Lord of Lords. When the truth dawns upon them, they leave the forces of rebellion and fight for Christ the true King. Sometimes they enter the thick of the fight and God gives them what St. Thomas terms something greater than innocence. This is exemplified in the case that follows.

"When I was a child I suffered greatly. My home was broken and I became a ward of the juvenile court. I felt alone in the world as indeed I was. I had no contact with my parents nor any kind, sympathetic relative to whom I could confide my troubles. With or without cause I suffered from what seemed to me to be the taunts and ridicule of other children.

[17] Luke XV:29.
[18] *Summa Theologica*, 3. Q. LXXXIX, iii, corpus.

Nor did I know anyone to whom I could go for consolation. I was placed in one home after another by the court, for the reason that the families with which I was placed were not stable residents of the city. One after another they moved away and turned me back to the court for replacement.

"A certain man, learning that I was fond of a large shepherd dog belonging to a priest in the city, gave me a novel which recounted various shameful things against the Catholic Church. I took it to the priest and asked if what was said there was true. He said: No. Therefore I referred the matter to the juvenile court. I was called in and was asked to show that I was sorry for having referred the book to the priest by consenting to be boarded at the house of the man who gave me the book. I lied and consented. Then followed years of scolding and humiliations. Naturally I did not take kindly to the religion of my foster-father. And when I went to college I cut all ties with the Christian religion, though some principles hung on in my mind from my childhood training.

"I went against the natural light of reason and committed serious sin and before long I was at the bottom of Chautard's scale in Stage 1, *Hardness of Heart*. I knew my acts were wrong, though I had no well formed concept of sin, such as a well instructed Catholic would have. Nor did I know the difference between mortal and venial sins. There was a stifling of remorse. I did not pray. But I cannot say that I denied the existence of God. In the midst of my wretchedness, I was constantly seeking for some explanation to the problem of unhappiness and suffering, which I saw all around me; and which medicine, psychiatry and allied sciences seemed powerless to solve.

"How did I rise and commence my ascent to God? I remember telling a girl who was working with me that I would never become a Catholic for the Church demanded too much. Not long after that I was dining with a very close friend of mine, a good Catholic. She said to me half in joke and half seriously: 'You love the unfortunates so much that it is a pity you do not give some of that love to God.' My instinctive reaction was one of anger. My friend had touched a very sensitive spot. I could not deny the justice of her remark, but I loved her so much that an angry retort was out of the question. I quickly changed the subject, but her words had set me thinking.

"A little later I was invited to a Holy Hour at a Catholic Church. The priest chose for his text the beautiful verse from the First Epistle of St. Peter (II, 9), 'But you are a chosen generation, a kingly priesthood, a holy nation, a purchased people: that you may declare His virtues, Who hath called you out of darkness into His marvelous light.' As he proceeded to explain the meaning of these words and to extol the superiority of the Catholic faith, I felt the hot anger surge within me. As I sat there, touched to the quick, I said with great conviction: 'If they can prove that, I will become a Catholic'. As I left the Church, I kept turning over in my mind the remark of my friend and the words of the priest.

"The next afternoon there was a lull in my schedule, and as I sat in my office, I reviewed my fragmentary knowledge of the history of religion. One thing was clear, the Catholic Church is the original Church founded by Christ on St. Peter. I knew from my reading that this was so. The Catholic Church, I realized, has a better claim than any other. At least it was worth investigating. I rose immediately and went to see a friend. I asked her to refer me to some priest for instruction.

"As I ran up the steps of the rectory, the thought flashed through my mind: 'If you ring that bell you will go through with it. You could turn back now.' I brushed the thought aside and rang the bell. Strange to say during the interview the priest said to me: 'No man putting his hand to the plough and looking back is fit for the kingdom of God.' [19] 'The kingdom of heaven suffereth violence and the violent bear it away.' [20] These words had a profound effect and though I did not formulate any resolution, the will to go ahead from that

[19] Luke IX:62.
[20] Matthew XI:12.

point on, no matter what the consequences and where they might lead, was very strong. Since then, though there have been minor fluctuations, there has been an increasingly conscious endeavor to be faithful to that first grace and live with God.

"I have striven for true compunction of heart and have tried, by careful reception of the Sacraments of Penance and the Eucharist, to blot out venial sins and grow in purity of heart ever since my baptism. Being more or less a coward in the matter of self-denial, I have frequently said the following prayer, asking myself, even as I said it, whether I really seriously meant it in all its implications. And since I experienced resistance to it, I asked our Lord to overlook my resistance and grant my request anyhow: 'O Lord, grant me to know the obstacles which I more or less place in the way of Thy grace working in me, and grant me grace to overcome them. And if I do not do so, do Thou remove them for me, though I should suffer greatly.'

"Desire for self-sacrifice has been growing and I often ask the grace of generosity in self-denial from our Lord during the Holy Sacrifice of the Mass. There is a real hunger for the Holy Eucharist; and at times, especially during Communion, the desire for perfect spiritual union with Christ is intense and profound. There have been various graces of infused contemplative prayer; and this almost from the time of my entrance into the Church. I believe that God often gives these graces to converts to detach them from their past life and to fortify them in meeting rebuffs from old friends who have little tolerance for the Catholic Church. These graces have been more frequent during the past several years. But only a little while ago I was in a state of aridity, probably through my own fault. I feel that the spirit of sacrifice in me is less well developed than the spirit of prayer. But God knows what I am. Yet in spite of my weakness and propensity to evil He again and again lifts me up towards the regions of His inaccessible light. With Pentecost, my aridity vanished and I have been flooded with light and strength."

In the following case we are not told how a soul passed from baptismal innocence to what it considered the lowest of our stages: hardness of heart. But it illustrates how divine grace can lift a soul that was sunk in the depths for twenty-three years and elevate it to the heights in the time that it takes to kneel before the Blessed Sacrament and make an act of contrition. Having made the act of contrition the soul regained once more the baptismal robe of sinlessness. For many years, co-operating with the grace of God, that soul has lived in the higher regions of a holy life.

"The writer was for some 23 years living in a state, objectively considered anyhow, of grievous sin and under excommunication. Faith seemed to be extinguished or at least, so obscured as to be inoperative. In addition there were personal, social and other reasons that made a return to Catholic practice appear morally impossible. Then, for no easily discernible reason, the person in question stopped his car one day outside a church where the Blessed Sacrament was exposed (forty hours, perhaps). He went in, knelt down and made an act of contrition for the first time in all those years. He left the church conscious that he could go to confession and return to Catholic practise.

"Since that time, the practice of religion, including the state of chastity, has been relatively easy and full of consolation. The significant feature of this experience, for which the writer lays claim to nothing miraculous, is the overwhelming conviction it gave and continues to give of the power of divine grace. The habits of nearly a quarter-century of scepticism, as well as sinning against the sixth commandment were destroyed and rendered as though they had never existed within the few minutes the person used to make his act of contrition before the Blessed Sacrament. A general confession and a return to the practice of frequent Communion seem to have re-created a spiritual personality which had, apparently, been totally destroyed."

He rates himself now as being in stage six of our schema; but would probably place himself in seven if he could say that he truly thirsts for self-denial and humiliations. At times he hungers for our Lord in heaven so much that it is painful to remain on earth. He devotes to prayer all the time he can possibly spare. He can truly say that, "I have found Him Whom my soul loveth. I held Him, and I will not let Him go." His union with Christ rises at times to such heights that, were moments to broaden into eternity, he would seem to possess the joy of eternal life. He entered upon this life and forsook twenty-three years of sinfulness and loss of faith, immediately and without relapse, following a single act of contrition before the Blessed Sacrament. There is no adequate explanation of such a conversion unless one admits that God by a direct interior action on the soul illumines the mind and inspires the will and works a change and transformation in the soul, by which one who was the slave of his passions, suddenly accomplishes what would otherwise be impossible.

CHAPTER VII

Temptation

WE CAN learn something about the psychology of temptation from conditions termed double and multiple personality. A number of cases of double personality are characterized by alternating periods of consciousness with profound changes of memory and of mood.

The patient may pass from what may be regarded as his normal and primary phase of consciousness suddenly into a secondary phase; or the passage from the normal phase may be mediated by a clouded or twilight stage of consciousness. This latter condition happens to some epileptic patients; and in their phase of consciousness initiated by an epileptic seizure and mediated by a twilight period, they may perform criminal acts of which they have no memory when they more or less suddenly return to the normal phase of their mental life.

An important characteristic of the double personality is the change of mood that follows the break in the memory chain. The sequence: break in the memory chain and the appearance of different emotions, desires, and interests, probably points to a causal nexus between the two events. Your old interests can no longer appeal to you if you have lost all memory of the events of life that awakened that interest. The joys and sorrows of your previous life disappear with the break in the memory chain that obliterates all conscious trace of the experiences on which those joys and sorrows depended. Perhaps this explains why electric shock therapy is so helpful in pathological depression. It gives a period of complete relief. Repeating these periods allows the patient to master his emotions.

Sometimes in the secondary phase the patient may even lose a considerable portion of his educational acquisitions. The elimination of moral principles from the mind of the epileptic in his so-called twilight phase would account for the criminal acts that are at times committed during that phase.

We have introduced these considerations to throw light on what happens in the time of temptation to sin. In the period of temptation, one passes from the normal state of one's mental life to a secondary phase. There is not the sharp, rough difference between the two phases that exists in cases of multiple personality; but there is a similar difference in mood, interests, desires along with a similar retreat of one's educational acquisitions into the background of consciousness. This concerns particularly one's moral principles.

The presence of an appealing opportunity to indulge a human sensory craving tends to banish from the mind for the moment all considerations of right and wrong. The further one enters into the temptation, the more profound is the change in mood from perhaps a normal cultured reserve to a reckless disregard of consequences; or perhaps an intense longing dominates the whole field of consciousness to the exclusion of everything else.

If the mental endowment of man did not contain anything more than sensory cravings, and impulses to enjoy them, man would be a slave to his drives just as the brute creation. But the history of man is replete with instances where the ideals of religion or patriotism have led countless numbers to undergo death itself rather than follow the drives of sensory nature. Such a phenomenon is unknown in brute animals because intellect and will in the true sense of the words are found only in man.

How is this possible? The existence of intellectual ideals in the mind is not the whole story, because in the hour of temptation man enters a world of sensory cravings in which the intellectual ideals sink below the level of consciousness. And they remain there unless another factor comes into play. This factor is peculiar to man among all the creatures of the earth. It is the power of volitional control. This power exerts its most effective influence by bringing from the subconscious the vanishing intellectual ideals and former acquisitions of education and experience. Volitional control is able indeed to do something by brute resistance, like the center rush in a game of football. But unless it calls to its assistance the intellectual ideals, tender memories of past experience and former resolutions of fidelity, there is great danger that the battle will be lost.

Most cultured readers will recognize in this analysis a true expression of what occurs in periods of temptation. But, though essentially true, it does not tell the whole story. Many see in temptation a mere natural conflict between the pleasure-pain principle and reality. A large school of psychiatrists dealing with the moral problems of adolescence can see nothing more. When one adds to this a loss of respect for the moral law, one can easily see that such psychiatry cannot deal with man as he is and direct the troubled mind to its true end.

Anyone who recognizes God as the Infinite and Absolute Good, the source and origin of all that is, will see that this involves a society and fellowship of all intellectual beings. In this society the transcendently Supreme Intelligence lives with every person and directs that person to attain the supreme end of his power to know and to will in the unending knowledge and love of Himself: the Eternal Truth and the Infinite Good. This means that God takes an active part whenever man is tempted. This fact is made known to us by revelation: "It is God Who worketh in you, both to will and to accomplish, according to His good will." [1] But He does not move us about or discard us like a tool in the hands of an artist. We must work with Him, and so St. Paul wrote, "With fear and trembling work out your salvation." [2]

[1] Philippians II:13.
[2] *Ibid.,* 12.

While we are assured of God's assistance in the hour of need and told that we must accept it and by means of it work out our salvation, we are also warned that the assistance of God is so profoundly necessary that we can never attain to the unending knowledge and love of Eternal Truth and Infinite Good without His illumination of our minds and inspiration of our wills.

Christ compares all human society to a vine which is Himself and the Eternal Father is the husbandman and we are the branches destined to bear fruit in due season. "Abide in Me, and I in you. As the branch cannot bear fruit of itself, unless it abide in the vine, so neither can you, unless you abide in Me. I am the vine: you the branches. He that abideth in Me, and I in him, the same beareth much fruit: for without Me you can do nothing." [3] If anyone forsakes Christ and loses himself in a life of grievous sin he will wither and die; "and they shall gather him up, and cast him into the fire, and he burneth." [4]

As long as man remains on earth, no matter who he is or where, he lives in some manner with God; not merely because God is everywhere but because He never ceases to call from sin to the observance of His commandments. "I have spread forth My hands all day to an unbelieving people, who walk in a way that is not good after their own thoughts." [5] God is ever entering into the moral struggles of man, helping, advising, persuading, but not forcing and destroying freedom.

Many will agree with me fully up to the present point. They have no difficulty in recognizing a natural element in temptation: "Every man is tempted by his own concupiscence." [6] They will agree also that God "will make also with temptation issue, that you may be able to bear it." [7] But they will not go further and admit a satanic element in any temptations. It is a widely prevalent error of the present day that

[3] John XV:4-5.
[4] *Ibid.*, 6.
[5] Isaias LXV:2.
[6] James I:14.
[7] I Corinthians X: 13.

Satan plays no role in the affairs of governments or in the lives of individual men. But no one can admit that the scriptures are the word of God and hold any such concept. All temptations are not from Satan but many are. St. Paul warns us: "Our wrestling is not against flesh and blood; but against principalities and powers, against the rulers of the world of this darkness, against the spirits of wickedness in the high places." [8]

Two vast societies are in conflict on earth. One is the society in which God rules supreme in the spiritual world of His angels and saints in heaven in union with His Church on earth. The other is the world of Satan, who for pride was expelled from heaven, but allowed to infest the earth and tempt men, that having been proved by temptation they may "receive the crown of life which God hath promised to them that love Him." [9] And therefore the psalmist prayed, "Prove me, O God, and know my heart. Examine me and know my paths. And see if there be in me the way of iniquity and lead me into the eternal way." [10]

There can be no doubt as to what the ultimate result of this conflict will be. Why does God allow temptation and trial and all manner of suffering? To develop in man heights of sanctity that could never be attained in a paradise of pleasure. Satan and those who follow his standard on earth will persecute the just and fight against Christ. And "for a time and times and half a time" the children of the kingdom will seem to be banished from the face of the earth. Satan, his evil spirits, and those whom he has seduced on earth, "shall fight with the Lamb, and the Lamb shall overcome them, because He is the Lord of lords, and King of kings." [11] No other outcome is possible when finite creatures rise up against the Almighty. But in the very midst of the trials from which we suffer at the present day, the Almighty from Whom

[8] Ephesians VI:12.
[9] James I:12.
[10] Psalm CXXXVIII:23-24.
[11] Apocalypse XVII:14.

all came forth and to Whom all return, renews to us the promise He made of old: "I am Alpha and Omega, the beginning and the end. To him that thirsteth I will give of the fountain of life, freely. He that shall overcome shall possess these things, and I will be his God; and he shall be My son." [12]

One cannot understand the vital currents of history nor the conflict of the present without taking cognizance of the fact that in the history of nations, as well as in the lives of individuals, purely human forces, economical and psychological, are not the only factors in all that transpires.

The providence of God directs the life of men as individuals and enters into the counsels of nations. "By Me kings reign, and lawgivers decree just things. By Me princes rule, and the mighty decree justice." [13] At times individual rulers have been chosen, all unknown to themselves, to carry out the will of God. "Thus saith the Lord to my anointed, Cyrus, whose right hand I have taken hold of, to subdue nations before his face . . . I am the Lord Who call thee by thy name, the God of Israel. . . . I girded thee and thou hast not known Me." [14]

But Satan is allowed to rise up with all his cunning against nations. "And Satan rose up against Israel: and moved David to number the people." [15] Christ became incarnate to destroy the works of the devil: "He that committeth sin is of the devil: for the devil sinneth from the beginning. For this purpose the Son of man appeared, that He might destroy the works of the devil." [16] After Christ the sphere of Satan's activity was restricted for a long time, expressed in scripture by the mystic phrase: a thousand years. But there will come a time, and perhaps it has now come, when "Satan shall be loosed out of his prison and shall go forth and seduce the

[12] *Ibid.*, XXI:6-7.
[13] Proverbs VIII:15, 16.
[14] Isaias XLV:1, 3, 5. See also Jeremias XXVII:6: "Nabuchodonosor king of Babylon my servant."
[15] I Paralipomenon XXI:1.
[16] I John III:8.

nations." [17] But when that day comes we must all remember the warning, "Behold I come quickly: hold fast that which thou hast, that no man take thy crown." [18]

In the meantime the war goes on. It is a hand-to-hand, or shall we say a mind-to-mind, conflict of a soul with an evil spirit. Our Lord has taught us much concerning that personal conflict so that we may understand and be prepared. He has told us that Satan instills false principles into the minds of men, and makes them propagate his principles, like the crypto-Communists who are told to keep their connection with the party unknown, but to propagate everywhere its principles and policies. But for the most part men do not realize that they have become emissaries of Satan.

"He that soweth the good seed is the Son of man. And the field is the world. And the good seed are the children of the kingdom. And the cockle are the children of the wicked one. And the enemy that sowed them is the devil. But the harvest is the end of the world, and the reapers are the angels." [19]

Let us take a closer look at the wheat and the cockle. Who constitute the wheat? Everyone who, leading a holy life, becomes by word or example a channel of truth and virtue for others is a child of the kingdom. And who constitute the cockle? Everyone who by word or example leads others away from the ideals of Christ or causes others to slacken in the pursuit of Christian perfection belongs to the cockle sowed by Satan in the field that Christ bought for the Eternal Father by the sacrifice of His life on the Cross.

Christ has also taught us that Satan takes the good principles of the Gospel out of our minds. We may pause here to consider the development of principles in the human mind, from barren concepts to determinants of action. There is a first period in which a certain principle has never found entrance into the mind in any way at all. At a definite moment, in reading, conversation, or listening to a lecture, the truth

[17] Apocalypse XX:7.
[18] *Ibid.*, III:11.
[19] Matthew XIII:37-39.

of this principle dawns on the mind. The mind may then harbor the principle for some time without availing itself of it, even on occasions which call for its use.[20] Its first employment may come suddenly and unexpectedly, with a resultant glow of success. There then follows a stage in which, by effort, one puts the principle in practice whenever an opportunity arises. Finally the principle, as it were reflexly, dominates conduct. Such acts, however, remain free and meritorious because of their ultimate cause in the period of trial. A cashier in a bank never stops to consider whether or not he will put some of the money before him into his pockets. "Don't take what does not belong to you" has become for him a principle that, as it were, reflexly dominates conduct. There was a time in childhood when in some way he was first taught the principle, and the original childish tendency "to lay hold at once of anything you want" commenced to be restricted and subjected to reason. It is in this period of transition that Satan is active. "The seed is the word of God and they by the wayside are they that hear. Then the devil cometh and taketh the word out of their heart, lest believing they should be saved." [21]

It is well for us to remember that we may be tempted by Satan at any time and everywhere. "Be sober and watch because your adversary the devil, as a roaring lion, goeth about seeking whom he may devour." [22] However, as St. Augustine points out, since the days of Christ, he has been chained like a dog and can only bite those who come within the reach of his chain. So long as we remain within what we might term the cloister of our state of life, we are never within the reach of his chain. When duty calls us into perilous regions and we go with the blessing of authority, the dog is muzzled. Anyone, however, who remains physically within the cloister and breaks his rule goes within reach of the chain.

[20] For an example of this interesting phase, which was noticed in the process of bibliotherapy, see T. V. Moore, *The Nature and Treatment of Mental Disorders,* New York, Grune & Stratton, 2nd edition, 1951, p. 226.

[21] Luke VIII:11-12.

[22] I Peter V:8.

Let us now consider the data from our material; the positive answers to question 22 in our schema. "Have you ever experienced any molestations that seemed to come from Satan, other than ordinary temptations?"

1. "At times when I am trying to sleep, I seem to be horribly tempted by impure thoughts that do not even appeal to me by day."

2. "Once Satan appeared as Christ in an extremely subtle temptation. For a few moments I was puzzled and knew something was wrong; but my heart went out in love to our Lord as He really is, and Satan vanished."

3. "I had repeated trials of something akin to despair. It seemed to me to come from Satan. There came a consciousness of the presence of our Mother Mary. My trials ceased. They were followed by deep peace and a closer conformity with the adorable will of our loving Father and a feeling of gratitude and increased love for my brethren in religion."

4. "False consolations, but they were after a short time easily recognized as false. They seemed in some way to come from the exterior."

5. "Once in our dormitory cell at night, during a period when God was granting me a very great favor, Satan or some other evil spirit seemed to enter the cell in a small human form. Close to my ear where I lay he angrily hissed threats and arguments to make me *fear*, and lose my trust that God was taking care of me. I paid no attention and he went out still fuming. The incident may have been a dream, though I seemed to be awake."

6. "Perhaps, here is the answer to my temptations of thought which I fight against continually."

7. "For seven months I was enveloped by this evil, suffocating, black fog during which time I felt that if a spiritual substance was capable of annihilation, my very soul would vanish into nothingness, as a moth in a furnace. Then one night after sleepless hours spent in mortal combat with the Spirit of Darkness (nothing was present to my bodily senses but he was there!) who suggested with appalling vividness

that I commit suicide, I heard the words in my mind: 'There's a razor blade in the drawer'. Suddenly all was quiet interiorly and a modicum of peace returned. It was as if Christ had calmed the storm with His familiar words, 'Peace be still'. Other great trials continued, but those frightful temptations never returned."

8. "I have had horrible temptations far worse than ordinary. One was against hope and the love of God. It lasted over a period of months. Some very strong temptations against purity, but I doubt if they were worse than what others have."

9. "Shortly after I went to sleep one night I woke (for me a rare event) and heard the words (interiorly spoken): 'Call upon Satan'. So far as I know, I had not been dreaming. The words seemed to have no connection with my thoughts on going to bed. I had, of course, not the least intention of doing any such thing. But suddenly there was a void in my conscious life as if I had lost the presence of God and was no longer bound to Him. It distressed me greatly, I immediately commenced to make acts of adoration and love for Christ. I seemed wide awake as if I could not go to sleep again. But in a short time I was sound asleep. When I rose, the void was gone. I thought nothing could make me more miserable than to have that sense of loss abide indefinitely. It gives me some appreciation of what the pain of loss must be to a lost soul. Then, too, it teaches me that I live in a constant state of peace, resting in the love of Christ, but do not realize it. When it is suddenly taken away, I become conscious of an aching void."

10. "While saying office one night, I was surprised at the recurrence of an imaginal-intellectual grace that was given me many years ago during a long period of temptations. In that time of stress and storm, I perceived often, if not abidingly, a beautiful white Easter lily that seemed to rest in or on my chest without any known method of support. It was a peculiar tactual-visual sensory experience, but dominantly an intellectual insight into the symbolism. At the same time

there seemed to be close in front of me, and a little to the left, a cruel fiend who wanted to tear the lily from my bosom with his clawed talons. But he never could. On this night there came the consciousness: 'You still possess your lily'. And I seemed to ask our Lord: 'Shall I present it to You now?' And the answer came: 'Keep it and present it to me when you come before Me to be judged'. O Christ, my Spouse, do not Thou forsake me: 'Unless the Lord keep the city, he watcheth in vain that keepeth it'." [23]

The above are instances which seemed to the persons concerned as possibly temptations that came from Satan or an evil spirit. Can we be sure that the surmise is correct? Unless a temptation is associated with preternatural phenomena incapable of explanation by natural causes, and certainly not produced by God, there is no absolutely certain way of determining their diabolic origin. On the other hand there is no way of demonstrating conclusively that any temptation is purely natural and has no immediate connection with Satanic activity.

One should insist on the concept that it is not necessary for us to know whether our temptation is a purely natural reaction to present circumstances or comes to us through the unconscious from a complex of past experience or is due to the direct action of Satan on the mind. The one thing necessary is to know that what one is impelled to do in any temptation is against the will of God. And the all-important thing to do is to turn immediately from the consideration of the immoral act and go about one's ordinary duties when this is possible, as in the daytime; or when this is not possible, as in the night, to enter into communion with God by prayer and loving adoration. "Be subject, therefore, to God. But resist the devil; and he will fly from you. Draw nigh to God; and He will draw nigh to you." [24]

By what signs can we know that there is some likelihood that a temptation is diabolic? Tanquerey gives this answer:

[23] Psalm CXXVI:1.
[24] James IV:7-8.

"When a temptation is sudden, violent, and protracted beyond measure, the devil is largely responsible for it. One can especially suspect his influence if the temptation casts the soul into deep and prolonged turmoil; if it excites a desire for the spectacular, for strange and conspicuous mortifications, and particularly if it induces a strong inclination to be silent about the whole affair with our spiritual director and to distrust our superiors." [25] Not all these signs will be found in every temptation. Examples of some will be found in the cases just cited: the violence in 1, 7, and 8; the protracted character in 7, 8, and 10; just what Tanquerey means by deep and prolonged turmoil is vividly pictured in case 7. The last also illustrates a character of diabolic temptation which is not mentioned by Tanquerey: a persistent drive in a *mentally normal* individual to an act that is abhorrent and lacks all lure from a sensory craving. The sudden and complete clearing of such a condition without analysis would distinguish it from a compulsion neurosis.

How does Satan tempt us? There is a phrase in St. John which is suggestive: "the devil having now put it into the heart of Judas Iscariot, the son of Simon, to betray Him." [26] In some way Satan puts evil thoughts and intentions into the minds of men. St. Thomas teaches that he cannot directly put thoughts into the human intellect or directly move the will itself. For God only can illumine the mind directly, without making use of the channels of sense, the human mind or directly move the will to action. [27] It is certainly difficult for us to conceive how any finite being could awaken ideas in the human mind except through the channels of sense. And in his *Summa Contra Gentiles*, [28] St. Thomas points out that it would be contrary to the all-caring-for providence of God to allow the human will to be directly moved and not by some

[25] Adolphe Tanquerey, *The Spiritual Life*, Westminster, Md., The Newman Press, 2nd edition, 1930, p. 116.
[26] John XIII:2.
[27] *Summa Theologica*, 1. Q. CVI, ii; 1. 2. Q. IX, iv.
[28] Bk. III, Chap. LXXXVIII.

form of persuasion which man is equipped to resist or to accept by a free and responsible act.

The problem of the power of Satan to read directly what is in our minds and put thoughts into our minds immediately and not through the channels of sense is approached by St. Thomas from a metaphysical investigation of how one angel speaks to another. It is an attempt to penetrate a little further than the data of revelation by the gift of reason.

Essentially, conversation is a mutual manifestation of thoughts carried on by two or more individuals. It does not by its very nature demand the use of the spoken word or other sensory signs. The angels being pure spirits make no sounds and utilize no sensory symbols. St. Thomas solves the problem of conversation between good angels enjoying the beatific vision by reminding us that in the beatific vision we behold all things that concern us. The angels, therefore, "always behold one another in the Word." [29] In that vision they see all that concerns them. What one angel wants to make known to another concerns each. And so, as the Holy Spirit abides in the soul of man along with the Father and the Son, so the Blessed Trinity abides in the angelic hosts and one converses with another by a wonderful interior locution mediated by the light of glory. But what one angel does not intend to communicate to another does not concern that other and remains, therefore, hidden within himself.

But as for Satan and his evil spirits any such means of locution is excluded. It seems, however, necessary to suppose that one evil spirit is capable of communicating with another. "But because even in the state of nature, in which they [the angels] were created, they were able to talk to one another, and even now, the wicked angels speak with one another, it is to be said that just as the sensory apparatus is thrown into activity by a sensory object, so the intellect is moved by an intelligible object. As, therefore, the sensory apparatus is stimulated by a sensory sign, so by *some* intellectual power [*per aliquam virtutem intelligibilem*] the mind of an angel

[29] *Summa Theologica*, 1. Q. CVII, i, ad. 3um.

may be awakened to attention." [30] In other words St. Thomas, recognizing the necessity of intercommunication between spiritual beings, merely postulates an unknown power of carrying on this intercommunication.

St. Thomas appeals to revelation to prove that as a matter of fact no being other than one's own self (and God) can know what goes on in our own mind. The passage he cites is thus translated by Ronald Knox: "Who else can know a man's thoughts, except the man's own spirit that is within him? *So* no one else can know God's thoughts, but the spirit of God." [31]

By considerations such as these the tradition has been developed in Catholic theology that Satan cannot read any thought in our mind unless we ourselves in some manner manifest it. Satan cannot instill directly any thought into our intellect unless we allow it to enter through the channels of sense. St. Thomas, as we have pointed out above, holds that it would be against the all-caring-for providence of God to allow Satan to move our wills to action directly and not merely by persuasion. The same argument may be invoked to maintain that the intellect of man can never be the playground of evil spirits unless man himself admits them through the channels of sense. It is generally admitted on the basis of scripture that Satan can tempt by audible or innerly spoken words. Cases 5 and 9, cited above, seem to be illustrations of such activity. And woe betide him who in such a moment does not turn at once to God, in prayer!

Theologians hold that Satan is capable of acting on our exterior senses in general. In case 2 he seems to have appeared in the likeness of Christ. Satan and evil spirits are also capable of awakening mental images and intensifying in some way sensory desires and emotional states. And so when your attention is called to something done by a person to whom you have a feeling of antipathy, you may, perhaps, say to yourself: Could anything be more stupid? And with that there

[30] *Ibid.*
[31] I Corinthians II:11.

may surge a rising tide of contempt for him and what he has done. Perhaps others do not think and feel as you do. Perhaps later you will see that had the same thing been done by a special friend of yours, you would have thought it most opportune. But what was the cause of your prompt, rash, and unkind judgment? It may be that the whole affair was not a purely natural event with no more than various psychological roots in your own past history. It is possible that it should be, but in reality it may not be. All our wrestling is not against flesh and blood. The Holy Scriptures point to the possibility that some evil spirit was whispering to you and blowing the bellows that fan the fire of emotional drives. If we could realize that Satan and his emissaries are sowing the seeds of hatred and rebellion on all occasions and everywhere we would check our tendency to pass harsh judgments, to nourish hatred against a fellow creature, and to exclude others from the circle of our friendship. Perhaps after all the clenched fist of our modern days is the clawed talon of Satan.

The cases we have cited afford various examples which might well be due to Satanic activity. No one who accepts revelation as the word of God can deny the possibility that many temptations of various kinds may be the activity of evil spirits. Theologians hold that the statement that evil spirits often tempt men to sin is a matter of divine faith known to us by scripture and the universal teaching of the Church down through the centuries.

Many diabolic temptations, however, seem to be mere natural occurrences. In two hundred responses to this question, thirty-seven (18.5 per cent) thought that they might at times have been tempted by Satan. Those who at the time of filling out our questionnaire were in stages three and four of Chautard (the lowest found in our material) recognized no Satanic activity in their temptations. St. Paul's phrase "Our wrestling is not against flesh and blood" would indicate that at some time all men enter into direct conflict with Satan or his evil spirits even though each one may be often tempted naturally by his own concupiscence. Satan has a natural intelligence of a high order. He will use all possible natural means to lead us into sin. He will arrange meetings in a casual way, get books into our hands, lead us into opportunities to sin, and all the time seek to remain unknown. The great point in his strategy in modern times is to lead men to the conviction of his own nonexistence.

Those whose life is made difficult by many persistent temptations must not think that they are, therefore, sinners beyond the rest of mankind. They must pause to realize that no temptation is ever by its very nature a sin; but all temptations are destined by God to be means of strengthening virtue and to become sources of great rewards in eternal life. And so St. James wrote the consoling words: "Blessed is the man that endureth temptations; for when he has been proved, he shall receive the crown of life, which God hath promised to them that love Him." [32]

Our strategy must be to avoid as far as possible all conflict. We must never go within the range of the chain by which the dog is tied. We must never go outside the cloister of our state of life. When duty calls us into dangerous paths, our heavenly Father will muzzle the dog till we pass by. We must live with God and pray for that state of the spiritual life in which the consciousness of God's presence abides with us from our morning communion until we lie down to sleep in the protecting arms of our eternal Father. And so we must live, until God grants us a quiet night and a perfect end and eternity dawns and the shadows retire.

[32] James I:12.

CHAPTER VIII

Lukewarmness and Desolation

THE LOWEST stages of Chautard's analysis of the spiritual life that we encountered as the *present* level of the individuals who constitute the material of our study were the third and fourth degrees. Those in these stages constitute also a relatively small group of all souls attempting to lead a devout life. Those in the first and second degree are neither leading nor attempting to lead a devout life.

There are several individuals who placed themselves in stages three or four who are so much alike that we may regard them as constituting a special syndrome, which we may term lukewarmness. The symptoms of this syndrome are: 1) neglect of mental prayer, 2) neglect of self-denial, 3) general tepidity or lukewarmness, 4) irritability, 5) antagonism to others, 6) self-isolation and a consequent interior desolation. Individuals presenting these symptoms have fallen from a higher stage of the spiritual life to their present condition, or their spiritual life has become stagnant for some years in their present unhappy state. Sometimes, though the present degree in which they are is also termed the highest they have ever reached, they nevertheless in accompanying notes or explanations say "there was a time when this or that was true." There are, therefore, various secondary levels in each of Chautard's stages.

Lukewarmness cannot properly be described as a stage of the spiritual life, any more than an adolescent schizophrenic condition can be regarded as a stage in the course of mental development. Neither should uncomplicated lukewarmness be regarded as either a mental or a physical disorder. I say "uncomplicated" because lukewarmness may at times be associated with a mental or physical disorder. An incipient schizophrenia or a severe anemia and various other things can take the zest out of life and give rise to the symptoms we have enumerated above as characteristic of the syndrome lukewarmness. Tepidity in the spiritual life which does not yield to honest effort and co-operation with a good superior and the spiritual director should be investigated both from the psychiatric and the medical point of view. Genuine uncomplicated cases should yield to good spiritual direction if the subject co-operates with honest endeavor.

Let us present a case.

"I learned my prayers at my mother's knees. Family prayer was always a part of my life. During the summer months, when hours were irregular and farm work hard, we did not have the family rosary, when we were small; but as we grew older it was a year round practise. My mother read us the Lives of the Saints. At the age of fourteen or fifteen, when ploughing in the field, I would enjoy talking quietly but aloud to God. In the religious life we have had many wonderful helps and conferences, but I continually find myself 'busy about many things', rather than 'the one thing necessary'. The desire to be otherwise, is very strong and even painful, but this last year has been one of silence-breaking, irritability, complaining and even judging others."

The prayer life of this individual is not bad. But it is not what it formerly was. She tells us that she has not forsaken all that is not God, "because my prayer life is not what it should be." *Now*, there is a definite lack of intimacy between the soul and God. *Once*, she seemed to be running rapidly toward God in her spiritual life, but now this is all a thing of the past. There was a time a few years ago, when in prayer she was sometimes so absorbed in God that she was oblivious to her surroundings and, when she, as it were, came to, it seemed that God had been in her soul and she in God. But this is, now, no more.

If a person gives himself up for some time to the fervent practice of prayer, there comes a time when the period allotted to mental prayer seems all too short, and if the regime of community life makes it possible, the period of mental prayer is willingly prolonged. Later, as the love of Christ grows in the soul, the time of mental prayer, as well as Mass and Communion, is looked upon as a precious opportunity to be with Christ, Him Whom the soul loveth. As a result, in every spare moment of the day the soul, as it were, runs to Christ to enjoy His presence and commune with Him and life flows on in a sweet joy and wonderful union with Christ in divine charity. There was a time when this soul was approaching this habitual union with Christ in a life of prayer. But this time is now passed. The joy of Christ's presence is not felt and the soul does not turn to Christ during the free interstices of the day.

When one lives with Christ and things happen to go wrong, each such incident is a spiritual opportunity to demonstrate by loving patience the strength of divine charity. Those who allow themselves to get upset are weak in the love of God, or perhaps are overburdened by physical ills. That this latter may be the case with our "patient" is suggested by the remark: "When too many things go wrong I even allow it to make me sick and get a headache or an upset stomach." It is possible that lack of emotional control can cause a headache or an upset stomach when there is no purely physical cause for any such disturbance.[1] However, a kindly intelligent su-

---

[1] For an interesting case of the successful psychiatric treatment of such symptoms in a nun with an unsympathetic superior, see T. V. Moore, *The Driving Forces of Human Nature and Their Adjustment*, New York, Grune & Stratton, 1948, pp. 184-188. See also T. V. Moore, *Personal Mental Hygiene*, New York, Grune & Stratton, 1945, Chap. XIV, Hysterical Manifestations in Children. For organic treatment of minor mental symptoms see Moore, *The Nature and Treatment of Mental Disorders*, Chap. VII, Mental Conditions Secondary to Organic Conditions.

perior would ask a good physician to look for any possible physical factors in the condition. When such factors are absent an intelligent spiritual director with good common sense will be able to handle borderline cases of pure *uncomplicated* lukewarmness, without recourse to a psychiatrist.

Our patient did not answer the question: What works of self-denial and bodily penance do you usually practice? The reason may be that she had none to recount. But in others suffering from this syndrome we have such answers as the following: "Almost none. Sometimes I try to offer up what I can't avoid. I used to do some small act of mortification daily; but gradually I got away from it." Another says: "Those only, prescribed by our Rule. Certain penances of custom I omit for slight reasons." Another writes: "Nothing planned: merely put up with discomforts when they are forced on me. I am at present at a standstill or sliding down."

Generally, tepidity and lukewarmness are indicated by negative answers to questions 1, 2, 3, 6, 8, 10, 11, 14b,[2] as well as by those that indicate an inadequate life of prayer and self-denial. In our patient these are all negative. To question 6 she answers: "I really want to please Him, but my self and my activities get so involved in everything."

Another who qualifies for the syndrome of lukewarmness answers these questions thus:

1. "I entered the religious life to find God, but unfortunately I cannot say that I *Now* forsake *all* that is not God."

2. "I seek God's will in a general sort of way, but in the duties of each day, I seek my own interests principally."

3. "The answer is *no* because small things bother me too much, proving I am full of myself."

6. "I must answer no, not because I don't want to please God, but the pleasing of myself is quite a motivating force in my life."

8. "The greatest obstacle is the practice of charity towards those with whom I must live; at times it seems next to impossible and I get very discouraged and careless."

[2] See Appendix, pp. 388 ff.

The answer to 10 and 11 was in each case a simple *no*. To number 7 she answered: "I am afraid to die in my present state, although so far as I know and by God's grace, I do not think I am in the state of mortal sin, but tepidity I guess."

As one turns from God one is likely to center everything in oneself. It is the love of God that makes easy a life of self-sacrifice for other human beings. Self-centering is likely to lead to one encasing oneself in a regime that fits into the circumstances of one's life. One becomes interested in doing certain things at certain times. One manages to select from the activities open to one certain things that attract one. In this way one becomes blind to the needs of those about one. Woe betide the one who breaks into that regime especially during the period of an afternoon siesta. The false sacredness of that regime makes the one whom it encases deaf to the call of charity and blind to the needs of those one might so easily help. Their occasional just pleas only arouse anger and antagonism in the hardened cadre of a rigid regime.

When, however, we look more closely into the life of the patient, whom we have taken to give a general picture of the syndrome of lukewarmness, there are various little things that betoken a beautiful humble sorrow, for all her faults and for her own guilt in having slipped from what may well be termed a high state of the spiritual life down to habitual tepidity. She is evidently desolate because of her condition, the isolation it has imposed upon her, and also because of a deep salutary sorrow for having turned away from God and the beautiful spiritual life of her childhood and earlier years as a religious.

Her condition is perhaps not nearly so bad as it seems. She is certainly not like the Pharisee who "standing prayed thus with himself: 'O God, I give Thee thanks that I am not as the rest of men,'" but rather like the publican who "standing afar off, would not so much as lift up his eyes towards heaven, but struck his breast saying 'O God be merciful to me a sinner.'"[3]

[3] Luke XVIII:11, 13.

There is a mental darkness that purifies and sanctifies. Perhaps her grief, her isolation, and her desolation are truly a dark night that precedes the dawn.

How does it happen that a soul falls from a good stage of the spiritual life and settles down to lukewarmness?

We may say that it is at least a general rule that the syndrome of lukewarmness belongs on the third to fourth level of Chautard's stages. Chautard's stages depend on three conditions: mortal sin, venial sin, habitual state of the life of prayer. Chautard's third and fourth stages both imply the presence of mortal and venial sins. We may say, therefore, that no one falls into lukewarmness who keeps himself habitually free from deliberate venial sins. The development of habitual deliberate venial sins must therefore be reckoned as a necessary factor in the descent of the soul from a good degree of the spiritual life to lukewarmness.

Looking at the symptoms of the syndrome we see that neglect of prayer and self-denial belong to its very essence. They may be regarded as fundamental and preparing the way for venial or mortal sin.

Turning now to general experience, I would say that an important factor in lukewarmness is the contagion of example. Whenever a body of human beings are united together in some great enterprise some push ahead in the vanguard, others lag behind in the rear. The religious life is a great enterprise to which one devotes all the days of his life. The goal is personal sanctity and union with Christ in a life of perfect charity, no matter what the special work of the community. Full success is impossible without complete renunciation of everything that conflicts with the great enterprise in which all are engaged. "Every one of you that doth not renounce all that he possesseth cannot be my disciple." [4] The tendency is to get interested in the special work of the community and forget that it cannot be carried out successfully except by those who attain to personal sanctity and union with Christ in a life of perfect charity. There grows up a nucleus of shortsighted

[4] Luke XIV:33.

members who look upon themselves as having common sense and being eminently reasonable and practical. There is a tendency among them to seek various relaxations on account of the heavy burden they have assumed. They want everyone to live as they live, and, should some carry out the ideal of the rule and the constitutions and lead a life of prayer and penance, such observance they regard as a criticism of themselves, even though nothing is ever said. They sometimes urge a younger member to be sensible and not to trouble the golden gateway of the stars; and so by word and example they infect others with the syndrome of lukewarmness from which they suffer themselves. Should a zealous soul yield for various reasons to the temptation to neglect prayer and take things easy in regard to self-denial, it is like the exposure to cold and dampness that makes it possible to succumb to an infection and pneumonia.

We all belong to the one mystical body of Christ. The sins and imperfections of any member of the mystical body lead others in various ways to sins and imperfections. The various virtues and fidelities of any member of the mystical body lead others to be virtuous and faithful. What we are is not a matter that concerns ourselves alone, but our concepts and actions circulate in the mystical body. Let us make it our supreme care, therefore, to strive vigorously and continuously for personal sanctity and to live in union with Christ a life of perfect charity. "Seek ye therefore first the kingdom of God and His justice, and all these things shall be added unto you." [5]

Let us suppose that we should one day notice in ourselves an antagonism to one or another among the brethren. Suppose that this should lead us to make a careful examination of our whole manner of life. And finally let us suppose that this examination should reveal to us some of the symptoms of the syndrome of lukewarmness. Memories of the past would rise up of a time when our constant prayer was that Christ would purify our souls and sanctify us and lead us on to the life of

[5] Matthew VI:33.

perfect union with Himself. We would go back in memory to a time when we looked forward with joyful anticipation to the periods and moments we could spend with Christ in mental prayer, to those years when we felt a real sorrow for having been unfaithful to Him and grieved because the world knows Him not, and tried to prove our sorrow and make reparation by a penitential life. It is a great grace that God caused us to stop and think. It is a still greater grace if He enables us to realize that our present life saddens His Sacred Heart, that our eternal salvation is in danger, and that we are a source of contamination to others. Perhaps it will now dawn upon us that in minimizing the importance of the inner life of the soul with God and priding ourselves on being practical men of vigorous action, we became like the Pharisee who said within himself: "O God, I give Thee thanks that I am not as the rest of men." It is high time for us to fall on our knees and cry out, "O God, be merciful to me a sinner." [6]

To fall on our knees and ask God's forgiveness from the bottom of our heart and beg His help to do better is the first step in any attempt to bring about a change in our manner of life. And then: *Felix qui potest rerum cognoscere causas* (Happy is he who can know the causes of things). The study of our material makes it abundantly clear that the cause of the syndrome of lukewarmness is to be sought in falling away from a life of prayer and self-denial. Therefore, after first begging the grace of God and the help of His Blessed Mother, we must return to Christ in our interior life and launch forth again into the sound practices of a penitential life.

"From the days of John the Baptist until now, the kingdom of heaven suffereth violence, and the violent bear it away." [7] There are some among the spiritually lukewarm, but vigorous men of action, who shudder at such passages and murmur, "Alas one more unfortunate soul who is tainted with Jansenism." But the error of Jansenism was not to call out with Christ and St. John the Baptist, "Do penance for the kingdom

[6] Luke XVIII: 11, 13.
[7] Matthew XI: 12.

of God is at hand," but to take charity from its supreme place in Christian life and subordinate it to the rigors of penance. There is no danger of Jansenism in the soul whose main endeavor in life is to live with Christ our inner life of divine charity, and, saddened by its own sins and the ingratitude of the world, tries to make reparation by a life of penance within the confines of an approved rule and the sanction of a superior or the approval of a spiritual director. The great danger in the America of our day is not Jansenism, but the error of Quietism. The Church has condemned the proposition that "the voluntary cross of mortifications is a heavy and useless burden and therefore to be laid aside." [8]

The time comes when in one way or another our Lord speaks to the lukewarm soul and says: "Thou hast left thy first charity. Be mindful therefore from whence thou art fallen: and do penance, and do the first works. Or else I come to thee, and will move thy candlestick out of its place, except thou do penance." [9] One must then pick up at once the observances of the rule under which one lives or ask special instructions from one's director and do penance. But penance must be vivified by charity that extends its supreme dominion over the soul in its inner life with Christ. But soon one shall be filled with a spiritual peace that will overflow and diffuse itself around one as a delicious aroma. It will envelop all the many works of the day. And one will see that what one once thought and said was impossible one will know as a living reality by daily experience. No work is ever neglected, but every external activity is sanctified and made efficient by Him Who abides within one, while one abides in Him.

Not all in stages three and four suffer from the syndrome of lukewarmness. Some have really not commenced to lead a spiritual life at all. By a spiritual life we mean an earnest attempt to lead an inner life of prayer with Christ and to deny ourselves and take up our cross daily and follow Him. Some

[8] Innocent XI, 1682, Denzinger-Bannwart, 1258.
[9] Apocalypse II:4-5.

go to Mass on Sunday and forget about God till Sunday comes again.

Some, however, are on the way to higher things and have not fallen from a higher state but are merely passing through stages three or four in the ascent to God. What a different picture these present to those who are lukewarm. Let us take an example.

"I rise a bit early in order to go to church and serve Mass. I return home and say the rosary with the arms extended in the cruciform position. Then follows a day of manual labor. But sometimes the peace of the morning Mass stays with me while I work.

"My mental prayer is made at night just before going to bed. First comes a short prayer to the Holy Spirit to ask His help. Then I try to recollect that I am in a very personal and intimate sense, coming into God's presence.

"As the full realization of this act (a sinful creature presuming to address his all-holy Creator) deepens, there comes with it a feeling of great humility and self-reproach for the faults of the day. Sometimes this sense of compunction increases and crowds out all further thoughts and words. I can merely keep on re-echoing St. Peter's words: 'Depart from me, for I am a sinful man, O Lord.' [10]

"If this sense of contrition passes shortly, I usually will try to think of God as He is at that particular season (in post Pentecostal time as Holy Spirit and Teacher, in June I think of His compassionate Sacred Humanity and so on).

"After a varying amount of meditation on these points, I may petition Him to help me overcome my common weaknesses: those of which I am aware, and those which have their roots so deep that they are like tough weeds. I have been pulling up the top part without getting at the roots.

"Then a fervent act of love to Christ and the 'Memorare' and I am ready for 'a quiet night and a perfect end.' "

The following words of our Lord in the Sermon on the Mount should be often before the mind of every soul who

[10] Luke V:8.

tries to lead a devout interior life: "Be you therefore perfect, as also your heavenly Father is perfect." [11] No matter how far we may advance in a holy life there will ever remain an infinite distance between any shadow of holiness to which we may attain and the infinite divine perfection of the Eternal Father. Therefore, as long as we are on earth we never enter any stage of the spiritual life to take up our dwelling there and stay. In each stage there are various levels. We must ever be in transit, passing on to higher things. "We have not here a lasting city, but we seek one that is to come." [12]

[11] Matthew V:48.
[12] Hebrews XIII:14.

CHAPTER IX

Our Life of Prayer

T HE FIRST lesson that should be taught when giving instruction on prayer is that prayer, in its broad sense, must dominate our whole conscious existence. It is not an exercise merely to which one devotes a set time, usually early in the morning, after which one has nothing more to do with prayer until the following day. One young man wrote a very good description of his method of prayer, and, having described the way he concludes it, added: "and then I depart from the presence of God." As we shall see, when prayer reaches its higher levels, one does not depart from the presence of God when the period devoted to prayer is finished. In such levels God Himself takes over the direction of our mental activity in the time allotted to prayer, and after we must leave our place of prayer He often continues to dominate the mind and the heart while we go about the ordinary occupations of the day. In this way, without any effort on our part, it is possible to continue to live on throughout the day in peace and to glow with divine charity and still do efficiently all that duty demands.

But before this time, which may indeed be long in coming, one does not say good-by to Christ when the time allotted to mental prayer comes to an end. By no means! On the contrary, again and again in the course of the day one elevates the mind to God, becoming for a moment conscious of how God is omnipresent; and, therefore, one is at this very moment face to face with Him. Realizing this, one bows interiorly before Him in a moment of adoration; and sends forth a swift act of love which like an arrow pierces the cloud of unknowing and falls at the foot of the throne of God on high.

It is thus seen that the broad sense in which the word prayer is used here may be defined as the *elevation of the mind to God*. An examination of the data to be presented will show that in some persons prayer (as an elevation of the mind to God manifested by a peace that glows with the love of God and sporadic illuminations, at varying intervals, in which the mind is conscious of the divine presence) may last for hours after the morning's mental prayer, and even dominate the entire day. There is no continuous intellectual activity by which God is known in a quasi-perceptual manner. But there is a continuous peace experience due to God's action on the soul rather than any natural human activity.

One would hesitate, in a general book on the spiritual life, to point out this continuity of abiding in charity as the natural end to which the practice of prayer should lead us were it not that a number of souls in our own day and time actually are elevated to this life of union with God. Furthermore, our Lord seems to hold it before our minds in various passages of the Gospel.

"If anyone love Me, he will keep My word, and My Father will love him, and we will come to him, and will make our abode with him." [1] Does this abiding of the Blessed Trinity, here referred to, mean only that God will be in the souls of the just as He is everywhere in nature? It certainly means more than this. The sanctification of the soul means the bestowal of sanctifying grace which is not only granted but is preserved in the soul as long as the soul does not deliberately turn away from God. If, therefore, one keeps the word of Christ in all things, as one should, God will dwell within one and act upon the soul continuously by sanctifying grace. He

[1] John XIV:23.

will give the soul a tendency to Himself, even as all things on
the earth have a tendency to its center by the force of gravity.
But of this divine action on the soul, the mind has no direct
and immediate perceptual awareness.

But does it mean more than this so that we can look forward to a state in our spiritual life in which we may live
habitually in conscious communion with the Blessed Trinity?
Some of the saints, certainly, have attained to such a conscious
communion with God. It seems to be the terminus of the development of charity. "God is charity and he that abideth in
charity, abideth in God; and God in him." [2]

Christ Himself has given us a commentary on this passage.
"As the Father hath loved Me, I also have loved you. Abide
in My love. If you keep My commandments you shall abide
in My love; as I also have kept My Father's commandments,
and do abide in His love." [3] We are, therefore, to abide in the
love of Christ even as Christ Himself, the God-man, abides in
the love of the eternal Father. Now according to St. Thomas
and most theologians, Christ always enjoyed the beatific vision, and, therefore, always abode in the love of His Father
consciously and without interruption. We may conclude that
if we keep the word of Christ in all its fullness, and without
any self-seeking in sin or voluntary imperfection, we may
hope that we shall one day attain to an habitual conscious
abiding in the love of Christ. Very few souls ever attain to
this state, but some do.

St. Teresa of Avila writes: "I seem always to be having this
intellectual vision of the three Persons and of Christ's humanity. . . . My interior peace and the little which joys or
troubles can do to deprive me permanently of this presence
make it so impossible for me to doubt the presence of the three
Persons that I seem clearly to be experiencing the truth of
those words of Saint John that He will make His abode with
the soul. And this not only through grace, but because He is
pleased to make the soul conscious of that presence which

[2] I John IV:16.
[3] John XV:10.

brings so many blessings that they cannot all be described." [4]

There are many stages of approximation to this continual intellectual vision of the Blessed Trinity, some of which we shall describe in discussing the material at our disposal. We may look upon them all as the fulfillment of our Lord's promise: "He that hath My commandments and keepeth them, he it is that loveth Me. And he that loveth Me, shall be loved of my Father: and I will love him and manifest Myself to him." [5]

Much of that manifestation is the perfection of faith and peace without vision. "Peace I leave with you. My peace I give unto you: not as the world giveth do I give unto you." [6] One lives a life of prayer, and prayer helps one to keep the commandments of Christ. And the innocence that grows through obedience leads to perfect prayer: "Blessed are the clean of heart for they shall see God." [7] From the data to be given and analyzed below [8] it is an empirical truth that what is known as the prayer of quiet appears sporadically and imperfectly in our spiritual life long before it becomes habitual. It commences also sporadically to hang on after the period devoted to prayer has elapsed and to invade the day.

But is there not danger of many lapsing into vanity and false mysticism if they are encouraged to aspire to this peace in the presence of God? As a matter of fact, the prayer of quiet makes its appearance so unobtrusively, quietly, and naturally, from time to time, that the soul does not advert to its presence. This stage is often preceded by an attempt to recall the divine presence in the course of the day and make acts of love and adoration. Few would have any objection to the *life* of prayer led by the physician who gives us the following account.

"Since my time for meditation is limited due to my employment, I usually make it early in the morning during one of the Holy Masses which we are privileged to have in our parish. During my meditation period I do not follow the missal but

[4] Relation VI, Peers's translation, Vol. I, pp. 335-337.
[5] John XIV:21.
[6] *Ibid.*, 27.
[7] Matthew V:8.
[8] See below, pp. 193 ff.

make my offering at the offertory and consecration. Therefore, I usually take with me a small book like, 'The Following
of Christ', 'My Way of Life', 'The Cenacle', etc., and read
from it until the Holy Ghost inspires me to stop and talk to
God. When I am physically tired or mentally upset I may do
what I have heard called 'meditative reading', otherwise my
mind will wander too much.

"When on week-end retreats or my annual five or eight
day retreat I spend a great deal of time in mental prayer and
find it easy to meditate then. During the working days, however, I try to make little darts of loving prayer or acts of love
during the entire day. I have made it a habit of placing my
right hand over my heart and, in doing so, lift my mind to
God, as an act of love. I can do this during my work and
still not neglect my duty."

I I

Having determined to lead a *life* of prayer, it is important to
set apart a special time in the day for mental prayer. This
should be, if in any way possible, early in the morning before
one goes out to Mass and Holy Communion. If there is not
time for both Mass and the morning meditation, one goes to
Mass. During Mass interior recollection centers in the Holy
Sacrifice and the offering of oneself as a victim soul. One also
converses at times interiorly with Christ or abides in silent love
and adoration. All this may well be a period of mental prayer
that cannot be surpassed.

But granted that there is also time for a period of mental
prayer, how does one set about it? The starting point in mental
prayer is usually what is known as meditation. For this there
are a number of methods. Pre-eminent among them is the
method of Saint Ignatius. The following is an abstract of his
method.[9]

One commences with a preparatory prayer that all one's

[9] See R. P. Joanne Roothan, *Exercitia Spiritualia S.P. Ignatii de Loyola*,
Augustae Vindelicorum (Augsburg), Huttler, 1887.

thoughts and desires, deeds and activities may be directed solely to the service and praise of His Divine Majesty. This prayer might well include the attempt to come consciously into the Divine Presence recommended specifically by most authors. St. Ignatius advises that in our meditation we should take certain preliminary steps which he terms: preludes.

The first prelude in a meditation on a scene in our Lord's life is to read over an account of that scene. This is naturally omitted when we are not meditating on a visible scene, but on such a subject as sin.

The second prelude is an attempt to form a visual image of the scene that one intends to consider, such as the death of Christ upon the Cross.

The third prelude is to formulate the particular good you hope to derive from the meditation, such as the quickening of your love of God, a deeper sorrow for sin; and then ask God to grant that you may obtain what you seek.

St. Ignatius gives then a general method of dividing the matter to be considered: Who is present; what do they say; what do they do.

After meditating on these three points one concludes with a colloquy with our Lord or His Blessed Mother. It has been pointed out that the purpose of the preludes and the points is to serve as a scaffolding to rise to the plane of an intimate conversation with our Lord. If one can at once enter into communion with Christ making many fervent acts of love or kneel in His presence in silent love and adoration the scaffolding of preludes and points is laid aside as superfluous.

There is also what is termed the method of St. Suplice. Its essential elements are the following:

1. *Adoration.* We adore God in some one of His various attributes, such as love (God is love) or sanctity or mercy, or Christ as the model of obedience or sacrifice.

2. *Communion.* We pray that in some manner we may participate in that which we have adored.

3. *Co-operation.* We determine to practice what we have adored in God or Christ. We then think of a definite way in

which we may actually imitate what we have adored in God or Christ and resolve to do so on that very day.[10]

In many communities there is a custom of reading points for meditation to the community assembled for mental prayer in common. One of our co-operators in this book, a nun, found herein difficulty on account of distractions.

"Mental prayer is made twice a day according to rule. The points for meditation are read first. We are free to follow them or use any subjects or method desired. I try to meditate on the points read, but am greatly troubled by distractions."

Those who practice meditation as a habitual method of mental prayer will be very likely to have serious difficulties unless they make a *preliminary meditation the night before* in which they prepare the matter for the next morning's meditation. Then, when the time for morning mental prayer opens, they must launch vigorously into the meditation outlined the night before and pass, and perhaps repass more than once, to the colloquy in which they commune with Christ in silent love and adoration.

In our entire group relatively few practiced habitually some form of meditation at their mental prayer; and these have simplified the usual schemata given by writers on the spiritual life. The following may be taken as an example of meditation.

First I place myself in the presence of God and ask Him to help me make a good meditation. Then I proceed to make acts of faith, hope, love, humility, et cetera. After this I try to picture in my mind the mystery or event in the life of Our Lord that this particular meditation proposes. Then I think about the moral or the lesson I can derive from it and make my resolution. Then I end my meditation much the same way that I started, and I ask our Lord to help me keep the resolu-

---

[10] For a fuller presentation see Adolphe Tanquerey, *The Spiritual Life*, pp. 335-339. A very simple and beautiful method of mental prayer is given in the early chapters of the *Introduction to a Devout Life* by St. Francis de Sales. Of great value for beginners is *A Primer of Prayer* by Joseph McSorley, C.S.P., New York, Longmans, Green & Co., 1939. A select bibliography on prayer is found in *The Home and Its Inner Spiritual Life* by a Carthusian of Miraflores, Westminster, Md., The Newman Press, 1952, pp. 251-253.

tion, and conclude with some more acts of love, hope, et cetera.

A novel method of family meditation is presented by the Baroness Maria Augusta von Trapp in her *Yesterday, Today and Forever.*[11] A scene or a topic is selected for family meditation. Each member of the family is assigned a portion of the New Testament to read through and pick out passages that will be pertinent in the family discussion of the scene or problem. The family meets at the appointed time and all take part in the discussion, even, at times, the little ones.[12] It is remarkable how illuminating such a family meditation may be.

An ingenious and apparently very effective modification of the Ignatian method of mental prayer is the following:

"THE USUAL WAY I MAKE MY MENTAL PRAYER

"I have compiled the actual words of Our Lord as recorded in the New Testament, and have arranged them chronologically from a Gospel harmony. My mental prayer is based on contemplation of Our Lord's words: I am present at the time and place, and follow Him through His public life as if I were an ever-present disciple.

"No actual, formal composition of time and place is needed —as the scenes are immediately present to me. Our Lord teaches, exhorts, and loves; it is easy to realize His love and to love in return.

"My weaknesses stand out with remarkable clarity—yet do not discourage me as Christ's unfailing love usually surrounds me.

"My prayer at the end is usually a brief sense of confusion at my failures and a petition for grace to love Our Lord more. Throughout the day I carry with me a rather vivid realization of His love—and of my love for Him."

Such personal modifications of the usual methods are very helpful to the individual who makes them. They stimulate the

[11] Philadelphia, J. B. Lippincott Co., 1952, p. 220.
[12] Such participation of children with adults is a powerful stimulation to mental development and should be sympathetically encouraged by the whole family.

throwing of oneself heart and soul into one's morning prayer. Such wholehearted efforts draw down on the soul the grace of God, and so one attains to a close union with our Lord during morning prayer and the peace of love which abides through the day. If one is always inattentive and drowsy during mental prayer, one should seek the cause in oneself.

As Pourrat points out, mental prayer practiced according to a fixed systematic plan appeared rather late in the history of asceticism.[13] St. Benedict set apart some two hours every day to reading.[14] This reading we may well assume was in general from the holy scriptures and devout works of the Fathers. This is suggested by a passage in Smaragdus: "When we pray we ourselves speak with God. When we read God speaks with us . . . for prayer does not differ from reading, nor is reading different from prayer."[15] We may, therefore, conceive of these two hours of the day as being devoted to meditative reading which one must regard as one of the various methods of mental prayer. One reads until one finds an illuminating passage. It expresses a truth that seems important to the reader in his own spiritual life. He pauses and thinks how he can make that principle dominate his conduct, and begs God's help. Such meditative reading was probably the earliest form of mental prayer in the spiritual life of Christians.

Meditative reading forms an important part in the life of prayer of the nun from whom we have the following:

"I sometimes sleep during the time of meditation. But in the time I spend alone before the Blessed Sacrament, I am wide awake and feel greatly drawn to Our Lord in the Eucharist and through Him to the three Divine Persons. It is during meditative reading of Scripture that I find most relish in prayer.

"I also prepare myself for days or weeks ahead for some special mystery or feast. Thus during Advent I try to saturate

---

[13] *La Spiritualité Chrétienne*, Paris, Lecoffre, 1943, Vol. III, pp. 19 ff.
[14] Rule of St. Benedict, Chap. XLVIII.
[15] Comment in Reg. S. Benedicti, IV, 57, Migne, *P. L.*, Vol. CII, p. 784.

myself with the Advent liturgy and repeat throughout the day some fragments from the Breviary (antiphons at Lauds, for example) as a means of keeping in close contact with the mystery; and try to orient spiritual reading around the mystery.

"I try to devote my free time to prayer and holy reading."

Closely akin to meditative reading is to read a passage from the scriptures or the liturgy of the day, think about it, and make it the starting point in a series of aspirations of love, petition and adoration.

Thus a priest writes:

"I usually take some bible text or a phrase in the Mass of the day and develop it. I no longer labor over points. I try to listen to what Christ has to say to me. Besides this, my prayer is largely of aspirations and acts of faith, sorrow, love, loyalty and so on. To a very large extent, my prayer is, 'taste and see that the Lord is sweet.' "

Another collaborator writes as follows:

"My morning meditation and mental prayer is usually made this way: I read either the epistle or the gospel of the day's Mass very slowly. When I come to a thought that strikes me as significant, I stop and think about it and talk to our Lord or our Lady about it. Then I try to make some practical applications for the day and end with some kind of prayer for a special grace. I think that meditation is best which accompanies the theme and life of the daily liturgy in either its temporal or sanctoral cycle.

"I seem more inclined to spend our required period of adoration in quiet recollection and adoration of God, listening to His voice whenever He gives that grace. However, I have been taught by the Benedictines that next to the Holy Sacrifice of the Mass, the Divine Office is the most perfect prayer and so I often force myself to read the Office of Our Lady of the Short Breviary during the periods of adoration and preparation for Holy Communion."

The following shows what a powerful factor the liturgy is in the spiritual life of the nun who wrote it.

"My prayer is exceedingly simple. Some thought from the text of the day's Mass or Office has perhaps already absorbed me, and when the time for mental prayer comes, I dwell on it.

"For example, this year at the Easter Vigil service, these two exclamations from the 'Exultet' stirred me more profoundly and seemed more luminous with meaning than ever before: 'O wondrous condescension of thy mercy towards us!' 'O incomprehensible goodness of love: to redeem a slave Thou didst deliver up a Son!'

"During Paschaltide these have been uppermost in my consciousness and given the keynote to the season. At the time of mental prayer, I savor their meaning. I say little, if anything to Our Lord but I hold myself in His presence with sentiments of admiration, contrition, thanksgiving and love. The days have abounded in thanksgiving more meaningful than ever before.

"At other times, it may be a fragment from an antiphon that holds me for days, like this one from the Office of the Exaltation of the Holy Cross: 'O great work of Love'. Or, it may be a text from St. John or St. Paul referring to the 'excess of love' wherewith God has loved us (John XIII-XVIII; I Epis. John; Eph. II, 4). My desire is to be a witness to His love and to let it have its way with me to the full (I John IV, 17). I would be rooted and founded in love and so to measure 'in all its breadth and length and height and depth, the love of Christ which passes knowledge' and so to be filled with all the completion God has to give (Eph. III).

"However, my prayer is often distracted and sometimes at the period of mental prayer made after the midnight office, I am slothful and yield to drowsiness. But I beg the grace that God will strengthen my weakness with a power that will reach my inmost being and I have the firm hope that He Whose power is at work in us is powerful enough, and more than powerful enough, to carry out His purpose beyond all my hopes and dreams."

A young priest writes of his liturgical prayer as follows:

"My mental prayer is usually begun by placing myself in

the presence of God. It is an active recall of the Indwelling of the Trinity; a very brief act of contrition, faith, hope, love, in a rather formal way. Then I may simply speak to God, adoring Him, thanking Him for His great glory, asking for a further understanding of this great bond of union which I have with the Trinity. This may just be ideas, acts of the will without use of words. It may be a sort of 'basking' in His presence. But, perhaps because of a lack of sufficient direction in this, I feel that I often allow this to degenerate into a sort of 'Quietism' in mild form—that there are no longer acts of the will being made, that I'm actually loafing, wasting time.[16] At times I begin to get drowsy here, so I 'push on'.

"Any formal meditation as such is difficult, even distasteful. But this may not be because I can no longer meditate; it may simply be my laziness or lack of sufficient preparation. Often I take the Mass text and use that as a taking off point for reflections and acts of the will. The only other printed helps I normally use are some reflections on the Indwelling, or, for example, a few paragraphs from a book like *Reminiscences of Sister Elizabeth of the Trinity*. I use no formal conclusion in this period. Usually it ends abruptly when I realize that 'my time is up' and I have to prepare for Mass.

"I feel that I am on the edge of a deep interior union with God—but I never quite 'make it'. It seems that He desires and wills great things of me if only I cooperate with His graces, but perhaps through lack of a competent interested and available spiritual director there has been little progress in this. Reading St. Teresa, St. John of the Cross, even Sister Elizabeth of the Trinity are helps, but remain 'theoretical' for the most part.

"The thirst for God has been there for some time, but because there seems to be so little cooperation on my part in comparison with the great graces He seems to be presenting me, the will to keep desiring God seems at times to begin to fail. The idea, momentarily at least, becomes distasteful (es-

---

[16] In all probability, this is not the case. But it is a thought that often comes to those on the threshold of contemplative prayer.

pecially with the 'pull' exerted by the world). But our hearts
are restless until they rest in Him. And true union will not
be fully enjoyed until the Beatific Vision. So perhaps it is
God's will that I remain on the edge of this deep life of union
for some time."

One should note that mental prayer which commences with
pondering on a text of scripture, or an introit or antiphon
from the liturgy, and leads on to aspirations and various acts
of faith and charity, does not by any means confine itself to
pondering and making acts of various kinds. It may well pass
very quickly into what is termed the prayer of quiet. The
frequent acts based on the chosen text may be reduced to occasional one-word aspirations, indicative of what Poulain
terms the prayer of simplicity. The whole period of mental
prayer may be a mixture of this prayer of simplicity, periods
in which aspirations are multiplied and time in which they
cease altogether in the prayer of quiet.

III

What is this prayer of quiet? [17] It may be described as dominantly a peace experience which seems *produced* in the soul
rather than the resultant of its own activity. It is a period in
which repeated acts of mental activity come to an end. But
it is far from inactivity. It is possible for the soul to analyze
this peace experience while it is going on, but it does not like
to do so. Such an analysis shows that it is dominantly an intense
abiding love of God. In the period of acts, ardent flames of
love burst out, shoot up toward heaven. But in the peace experience flaming ceases; and the fire of charity settles down
to a constant glowing, which now is white hot, again more
or less red, but never ceases to glow. By this figure I do not
intend to ascribe anything like color to the warmth of charity,
but merely to point out that it varies in intensity during the
period in which the soul enjoys the prayer of quiet. But love
is not the only mental activity in the prayer of quiet, though

[17] See also pp. 104, 200 ff.

it has a tendency to dominate the focal region of consciousness. There is also a subconscious intellectual realization of the presence of God. He is very near, certainly He does not seem far away. And then from time to time there are likely to take place more or less dim flashes of a quasi-perceptual seeing of the Divine Immensity, but through a glass, as it were, and in a dark manner. All muscular activity ceases of its own accord and the body may remain motionless in whatever position it may have been when the mind was inducted into the prayer of quiet. I say inducted because the soul cannot by any effort of its own exercise the prayer of quiet at will.

The prayer of quiet has a tendency to remain as a beautiful peace experience long after one has finished the period allotted to prayer. In fact it may abide with the soul the whole day long. That it may abide all day long should be recognized, by those who lead a life of prayer, as the normal terminus toward which that life is developing, even though few attain it. Several of our collaborators have actually attained a habitual all-day life of prayer that goes on day after day without cessation.

Thus a lay woman writes as follows:

"For many years mental prayer has consisted in placing myself in God's presence in silent adoration and love. All external duties in the day are done as acts of perfect love which do not interfere with His presence within me."

The following is a young man's description of his ordinary period of mental prayer.

"Sometimes if praying in a place where there may be external distractions I begin my prayer by saying to God, 'I love you', a few times. After this I remain in a very peaceful and loving contact with God. I strive to remove all thoughts from my mind and simply rest in this state of peaceful love.

"Usually I do not need to say, 'I love You' at the beginning of prayer but simply enter into the aforesaid prayer. Also, often, during this prayer I find any movement, even the moving of the lips in vocal prayer, undesirable and requiring an effort."

One is not always capable of entering into the prayer of
quiet even after God has made it relatively habitual. Mental
sorrow or physical pain may make it necessary to return to
acts and aspirations. Thus a nun writes of her difficulties in
attaining to perfect recollection in prayer:

"In times of peace my usual form of prayer is simply allow-
ing myself to be penetrated by the Divine Presence—a simple
reflection sufficing to recollect me, for example, 'quoniam tu
solus sanctus' or 'tomorrow eternity' or a psalm verse or
thought from current liturgy or office. Most often I experience the perfect silence of receptivity.

"In times of trial my prayer often consists of: acts of resignation; thanking Our Lord for the suffering and begging
help; lifting up my soul with all its misery to be purified. In
times of illness or fatigue there may be nothing more than
simple endurance of the time allotted for mental prayer."

A priest has made his prayer the center of an organized
plan.

"MY MENTAL PRAYER

"1. Remote Preparation—constant search for *truth*—be my
true self—never tell Jesus anything I do not mean,—avoid all
falsity, acting on human respect, etc. Desire for the *reality* of
God—and His will—not words or images or feelings.

"2. *Presence* Try to divest myself of all that is not my true
self, so that I can face the presence of God at
the summit of my soul as I am and as He is, not
with delusions or useless activity born of pride.

Activity The simple activity of love trying to call God to
myself in the darkness and depth—realizing all
the while that He is there. Using the Holy Name
of Jesus, as a kind of communion.

Rest Quite often pray without many distractions with
a sense of deep *awareness*, of being *more alive*
than at other times of the day, of being *more
real*, a new person, 'in Christ' or 'in God'—sense

of freedom as if I had the sky opening up inside me.

"However, I often fall asleep at thanksgiving, although before and after drowsing there are moments of valid prayer, and the effect of Mass and Communion always seems to be very deep and lasting. Prolong thanksgiving—½ or ¾ hours. No capacity to do anything at that time. Can't read."

Not all methods of prayer are easily classified and graded. Thus, a dear, simple lay brother once told me that in the time prescribed by rule for mental prayer he went to his room and sang quietly one hymn after another during the whole period. A priest once told me that he composed little poems of his own and sang them during the time for meditation.

St. Teresa of Avila tells us of a nun who came to her in great discouragement because she could not practice mental prayer. St. Teresa asked her how she tried to pray. The nun told her that she merely said over and over again the "Our Father" and "Hail Mary" thinking of our Lord in some scene of His passion. On further questioning she found that in her Paters and Aves she enjoyed pure contemplation and occasionally God lifted her to perfect union with Himself.[18] Let no one, therefore, say that the rosary cannot become pure contemplative prayer; and let us all try to say it so perfectly that God may lift us to perfect union with Himself.

Perhaps our minstrels of Christ ascend in their songs to the heights of contemplative prayer. At all events the singing of the Divine Office cannot be regarded as mere vocal prayer. During the singing or private recitation of the Divine Office, God can and does lift souls to perfect union with Himself.

Mental prayer, after all, is nothing more nor less than the actual living of the life of man with God. One lives this life, not only during one's morning and evening devotions, but also throughout all one's waking hours. It is evident, therefore, that anything that clouds the relationship between the human mind and the Divine Lover interferes with mental prayer.

[18] *The Way of Perfection*, XXX, Peers's translation, Vol. II, p. 126.

There are many things that cloud the relationship of the soul with the Divine Lover in those who are in stages three or four of Chautard. None of those in our group who placed themselves in either of these stages enjoyed habitually the prayer of quiet.

Furthermore, anything that helps toward the union of the mind and heart with God will develop the life of man with God. Self-denial which promotes the turning away from creatures to God should be a factor in the development of the life of prayer and its neglect might stunt spiritual growth. As a matter of fact we find that those in stages three or four either practice no self-denial at all or reduce it to a minimum.

This group has not yet conquered grievous sin. They bear witness to the truth: Blessed are the clean of heart for they shall see God. It is in mental prayer that we see God, as well as He can be seen in this life: as through a glass and in a dark manner. All men are called to this vision of God. He who would heed the call of God to live with Him in union of mind and heart, "let him refrain his tongue from evil and his lips that they speak no guile. Let him decline from evil and do good: let him seek after peace and pursue it." [19] "Let him deny himself and take up his cross daily and follow" Christ.[20]

[19] I Peter III:10-11, quoting Old Testament.
[20] Luke IX:23.

CHAPTER X

Penance and the Cross and the Joy of Life

Our Life of Penance in the Mystical Body of Christ

AND AFTER that John was delivered up, Jesus came into Galilee, preaching the Gospel of the kingdom of God and saying: The time is accomplished, and the kingdom of God is at hand: Repent, and believe the Gospel." [1]

What is the fullness of meaning in these words with which Christ opened His public ministry?

In the first place, *believe* must mean the acceptance of the entire body of the teaching of Christ, in accordance with His last instructions to His apostles: "Teaching them to observe all things whatsoever I have commanded you." [2]

Secondly, it means the conformity of our daily life with the sublime truths of our Lord's teaching: "Blessed are the poor in spirit, for theirs is the kingdom of Heaven." [3] One believes the gospel as one should when the Kingdom of Heaven in eternity becomes in one's mind the great reality. Then, all his life long, he will be waiting "till the day break and the shadows retire." [4] Life in eternity is the day: the pleasures of time

[1] Mark I: 14-15.
[2] Matthew XXVIII: 20.
[3] *Ibid.*, V: 3.
[4] Canticle of Canticles II: 17.

164

are the shadows. That which is eternal is the reality we can lay hold of: that which is carnal escapes our grasp like a shadow.

Life has its sufferings, its mourning, its trials, and its failures. "Blessed are they that mourn, for they shall be comforted." [5] But no comfort is in sight. Youth is gone and the days are upon me that please me not. The silver cord is broken. The golden fillet has shrunk back. The pitcher is crushed at the fountain. The wheel is broken upon the cistern. And the dust is ready to return into the earth whence it came.[6] It makes no difference. *Repent and believe the gospel.* In spite of all, they that mourn shall be comforted, for the *spirit* returns to God Who gave it. "The sufferings of this life are not worthy to be compared with the glory to come that shall be revealed in us." [7] *Repent and believe the gospel.* "In my Father's house there are many mansions. If not, I would have told you: because I go to prepare a place for you. And if I shall go and prepare a place for you, I will come again and will take you to myself: that where I am, you also may be." [8] *Repent and believe the gospel.* And when you are beset with trials and difficulties on all sides, no matter how human they may seem, believe the gospel: "Blessed are they that suffer persecution for justice' sake: for theirs is the kingdom of heaven. Blessed are ye when they shall revile you and persecute you and speak all that is evil against you, untruly, for My sake: be glad and rejoice for your reward is very great in heaven." [9]

When Christ speaks to your soul, repent and believe the gospel. He is calling you to a Eucharistic life with Himself in time and in eternity, in union with the saints in heaven and the faithful on earth in the mystical body which is His Church. Repent, therefore, and believe the gospel with a living faith. Know and live the sublime truths of faith and "continue in those things which thou hast learned and which have been

[5] Matthew V:5.
[6] Cf. Ecclesiastes XII.
[7] Romans VIII:18.
[8] John XIV:2-3.
[9] Matthew V:10-12.

committed to thee" [10] that thou mayest know Christ and live with God.

Our penitential life is lived in the mystical body of Christ. It would be a false concept of the penitential life to consider it apart from this mystical body of Christ. And it would be a false concept of humility that led one to say: "Who am I that I should do penance for others?" All penitential works must be offered up with the sacrifice of Christ upon the Cross and therefore not for oneself alone but for all. We should not only say prayers, but lead a life of prayer for everybody: not only make penitential sacrifices, but lead a life of sacrifice for all the world: not only hear Mass at the altar before which we kneel, but, in bowing down before God where we are, to adore Him and offer ourselves as a victim soul with all the faithful on earth on the altars of the world and also with the angels and saints in heaven where Christ, "offering one sacrifice for sins, forever sitteth on the right hand of God." [11] By prayer, praise, and penance we live, with all the faithful, the life of the mystical body of Christ. "For in one spirit were we all baptized into one body, whether Jews or Gentiles, whether bond or free; and in one Spirit we have all been made to drink. For the body also is not one member, but many. . . . But now there are many members indeed yet one body. . . . And if one member suffer anything, all the members suffer with it; or if one member is glorified, all the members rejoice with it. Now you are Christ's body, organs of it depending on each other." [12]

We realize the great truths of man's fall and his redemption by Christ. "All we like sheep have gone astray, everyone has turned aside into his own way; and the Lord hath laid upon Him, the iniquity of us all . . . for the wickedness of my people have I struck Him." [13]

But now we belong to the mystical body of Christ, which

[10] II Timothy III:14.
[11] Hebrews X:12.
[12] I Corinthians XII:13-27. The last verse is the translation of Msgr. Ronald Knox.
[13] Isaias LIII:6, 8.

is the Church, with "one Lord, one faith, one baptism, one God and Father of all, Who is above all, and through all and in us all." [14] To this body of the faithful, whose head is Christ, represented on earth by the successor of St. Peter in the see of Rome, there is a soul, just as in the body of man there is a soul: its principle of life, organization, and action. The soul of the mystical body of Christ is the third person of the Blessed Trinity, the Holy Spirit. And so when, as individuals, we say with the psalmist: "I know my iniquity and my sin is always before me," [15] the Holy Spirit makes the prayer of many one prayer for all and includes therein the potential members of the Church who do not pray, because they know not God.

And so the members of the body of Christ co-operate with and are subject to the Head, Jesus Christ who is "God, begotten of the substance of the Father before all ages, born of the substance of His Mother in time." [16] All the sufferings of the faithful of Christ are united with the passion of Christ. Christ suffered on Calvary for the sins of the world. Christ suffers in the body of the faithful down throughout the centuries to the end of time. "Saul, Saul, why persecutest thou Me?" [17] The Eternal Father has laid upon Christ and His mystical body the iniquities of all, both faithful and unbelievers. The faithful suffer with Christ for an unbelieving world: "Amen I say to you, as long as you did it to one of these my least brethren, you did it to Me." [18] As St. Thomas says: "The Head and the members constitute, as it were, one mystical person, and, therefore, the satisfaction of Christ pertains to all the faithful as to His members." [19] These words refer specifically to Christ, the Head, meriting for us the members.

We must note, however, that this does not mean that we contribute to the essential work of redemption as co-redeem-

[14] Ephesians IV:5-6.
[15] Psalm L:5.
[16] Athanasian Creed.
[17] Acts XXII:7.
[18] Matthew XXV:40.
[19] *Summa Theologica*, 3. Q. XLVIII, ii, ad. *1um.*

ers with Christ, meriting with Him *de condigno* salvation for man.[20] Christ alone can merit *de condigno* salvation for man. But Christ, having merited redemption for us, and assimilated us to His mystical body, we, the faithful, constitute with Him one mystical person. Co-operating with Him by a holy life, denying ourselves and taking up the cross He offers us and bearing it with patience, and moved by the Holy Spirit we can merit *de condigno* eternal life for ourselves. We can also help others to merit eternal life by meriting *de congruo*[21] many graces for them. "Pray for one another, that you may be saved. For the continual prayer of a just man availeth much."[22]

With Christ as our Head and His vicar on earth, our holy father the Pope, the mystical body of the Savior continues His passion down throughout the centuries. The sufferings of the faithful are in some manner the sufferings of Christ, their mystical Head. With Him and through Him each member of

[20] It is necessary here to explain two theological phrases: *de condigno* and *de congruo*. If you agree with a man to do a piece of work for a certain sum of money and you do it, you merit from him *de condigno*, the payment of that sum. God promises us eternal life if we keep His commandments. He urges us on to keep them and gives us all manner of helps. Though we do not merit in such strictness as the laborer does his hire, we do nevertheless merit truly, eternal life, if we die in the state of grace. The strict merit by which the laborer merits his hire is said to be with the *rigor of justice*. The less strict merit *de condigno*, with which we merit eternal life, is said to be merited *de condigno* but not with the true rigor of justice, because God gives us all the means of carrying out this law. Thus, if a man bought all the laborer's tools and fed him, but only contracted to pay him for the work alone, the expense of tools and upkeep might be well above the price of his labor, and the man would, in *rigor of justice*, not be entitled to all his pay.

If a man had a good and faithful servant, when Christmas came it would be fitting for his master to give him a Christmas present, but he would not merit the Christmas present, in the sense that he could sue for it if he did not get it. It would, however, be unbecoming in the master to forget his good servant on Christmas. The Christmas gift could be said to be merited *de congruo*. Thus we merit *de congruo* many things from God. St. Monica is said to have merited *de congruo*, by her tears, the conversion of her son, St. Augustine. We can merit for others only *de congruo*.

It is of faith that we can truly merit for ourselves eternal life. (Council of Trent, Denzinger-Bannwart, 842.)

[21] *Summa Theologica*, 1. 2. Q. CXIV, vi.
[22] James V:16.

the mystical body merits *de condigno*, eternal life for himself. But our prayers, penances, and sufferings are offered up, not for ourselves alone, but for all. For them we merit, *de congruo*, many graces, helpful or necessary for their salvation. Supreme among the faithful is Mary, the blessed Mother of God. Theologians speak of her as truly the co-redemptress of the human race, not that she merits for anyone a single grace *de condigno*, but because at the foot of the Cross she merited for man *de congruo* all that Christ merited *de condigno*.[23]

We can see, therefore, that assimilation to the passion of Christ by suffering is to be numbered among the greatest privileges granted to man by God. By union with Christ in His passion we can merit eternal life for ourselves. By suffering with Christ we may also merit, *de congruo*, for others, graces which may be all that is needed to help them rise above their temptations and attain the vision of God in eternal life.

From all this it is evident that a good Christian, in life and in death, is a victim soul, offered to the Eternal Father with the Divine Victim Who died for man upon the Cross. I remember how at one time I was afraid to offer myself as a victim soul lest God might take me at my word and I would find myself overwhelmed with some terrible calamity. But being a victim soul means no more than to enter wholeheartedly into the life of a Christian in which everybody prays and suffers and rejoices and triumphs with everybody else.

To understand Christian life we must realize that every created person was in the mind of God from all eternity. And so God thought in eternity of what He wanted you to do in time, when the aeons would sweep on to the short span of your human life. He had an ideal of your character: one of the infinite ways in which the personality of Christ could find expression in a human being. He destined for you certain trials, temptations, and sufferings by which the inherited block of your being would be chiseled into the form He wished your character to take. He apportioned to you a special way of

---

[23] See Dictionnaire de Théologie Catholique, Vol. IX, 2. Art., Marie col., p. 2389 ff.

bearing the Cross of Christ that you might co-operate with Him in the salvation of souls. It is true of you and of every created person that you were "set apart from eternity and of old before the earth was made." [24]

The realization of a divine ideal is bound to be something of sublime beauty and inestimable value. Why should we seek to substitute our human concepts for the outward expression in time of the divine mind, the Eternal Word of God? Why should we fear to accept the way marked out for us from all eternity to bear the cross and co-operate with Christ in the salvation of souls? God always makes easily possible everything He asks us to do. No one need have any fear of being a victim soul in the way God designed for him when the Creator "had not yet made the earth, nor the rivers, nor the poles of the world." [25]

Our holy father, Pius XII, points out to us that every Catholic, whenever he hears Mass and also in his daily life, should offer himself up as a victim soul: "In order that the oblation by which the faithful offer the divine Victim in this Sacrifice to the Heavenly Father may have its full effect, it is necessary that the people add something else, namely the offering of themselves as a victim.

"This offering in fact is not confined merely to the liturgical Sacrifice. For the Prince of the Apostles wishes us, as living stones built upon Christ the cornerstone, to be able as a 'holy priesthood to offer up spiritual sacrifices, acceptable to God by Jesus Christ.' [26] St. Paul the Apostle addresses the following words of exhortation to Christians, without distinction of time: 'I beseech you therefore . . . that you present your bodies a living sacrifice, holy, pleasing unto God, your reasonable service.' [27] But at that time, especially when the faithful take part in the liturgical service with such piety and recollection that it can truly be said of them, 'whose faith and devo-

---

[24] Proverbs VIII:23.
[25] *Ibid.*, 26.
[26] I Peter II:5.
[27] Romans XII:1.

tion are known to Thee',[28] it is then, with the High Priest and through Him they offer themselves as a spiritual sacrifice, that each one's faith ought to become more ready to work through charity, his piety more real and fervent, and each should consecrate himself to the furthering of the divine glory, desiring to become as like as possible to Christ in His most grievous sufferings." [29]

How can one really desire grievous sufferings? At first sight it will seem to some an impossibility. But we must distinguish in the complex termed here desire, an essential volitional element. This is a free act of will choosing an object presented by the intellect with full responsibility for the choice. In a narrower sense, desire is a sensible craving for sensory pleasures that one does not at the moment enjoy. The intellectual volitional choice may be utterly in conflict with the whole system of sensory desires.

The "desire" for suffering, to be like Christ, may be perfectly cold, but firm and determined. On the other hand it may be associated with a certain intellectual enthusiasm that betokens the yearning of one's whole being to be like Christ and suffer with Him. This enthusiasm is not sensory desire, for suffering is repellent to all sensory cravings. The desire to be like Christ in His most grievous sufferings is on the higher, intellectual-volitional plane.

Various considerations will help us to an intellectual-volitional election of suffering. Thus, one who truly loves Christ wants to be like Him: the Man of sorrows. But no one can be like the Man of sorrows without suffering. By suffering I can atone for my own sins and offer something in reparation for the sins of men who reject the love of Christ. If I love Christ, I feel a drive to make this reparation. Suffering is the coin of the heavenly kingdom. As a member of the mystical body my own sufferings, borne with patience for the love of Christ, will

---

[28] Roman Missal, Canon of the Mass.

[29] Encyclical, *Mediator Dei*, on the sacred liturgy, #98, 99, pp. 36-37, ed. National Cath. Welfare Conference, 1312 Massachusetts Ave., N.W., Washington, D. C., Vat. Library trans.

help others in the mystical body to conquer their temptations and attain the vision of God. Because I love Christ, I want to do all I can to bring this about. The offering of myself as a victim soul on the altar of suffering does bring it about. Therefore, choose suffering rather than joy. Elect to wear throughout life Christ's crown of thorns rather than a golden crown studded with precious gems, symbolic of success, pleasure, and the applause of men.

But all this comes about in proportion as God increases in the soul the virtue of charity: the love of God and man. Few, who are in deep earnest in the spiritual life, fail to feel a certain glow of enthusiasm when faced with the trials and suffering and contradictions of life. The presence of a real hunger and thirst for sufferings and humiliations and a yearning to be, like Christ, reputed with the wicked is one of the best signs of a strong genuine love of God. Not all will experience such an intensity of desire. But we should not lose courage. There is great merit in the intellectual-volitional acceptance of trial and suffering, especially when this is persevered in day after day for years until we die. But when, in the midst of trial and bitter sorrow, the will accepts in the light of reason, but the heart cries out for relief, realize that you are united with Christ upon the Cross when He cried to heaven: "My God, my God, why hast Thou forsaken me?" In the light of your own sins and the sins of all the world, as a member of the mystical body, repent and believe the Gospel: "Blessed are they that mourn for they shall be comforted. . . . Blessed are ye when they shall revile you, and persecute you, and speak all that is evil against you, untruly, for My sake: Be glad and rejoice, for your reward is very great in heaven." [30]

Denying Ourselves in Little Things and Bearing the Cross of Christ

When a person has been living a life of prayer for some time, he experiences a growing warmth in his love of Christ. He

[30] Matthew V:5, 11-12.

commences not only to know with great certainty but also to realize in his inner experience how wondrous is the love of Christ for the soul of man. He understands, as he never understood before, the great truth that Christ is the Eternal Word, the Second Person of the Blessed Trinity by Whom all things were made and without Whom was made nothing that was made. This deepening of spiritual knowledge leads him to feel the crime of the rejection of Christ by His people, and by so many in all the centuries down to our modern days. He commences also to realize, as never before, that he himself rejected the Eternal Word by his past sins. All this creates a deep sorrow: sorrow for his own sins, sorrow for the crimes of the modern world; but no anxiety. There then arises a desire to make good for what was done by himself and also in some way for what has been done by the world. He wants to make good by love and to give a pledge of his love by penitential works. Such desires, at all events, are often if not always the result of a life of prayer. They constitute the true reason and higher motive for a life of penance vivified by charity. And blessed indeed will be he who, from the moment he has received this insight from God, determines to make his whole life a life of prayer and penance even though he is called by God to live and work in the world and not in the cloister.

He feels that it would be shirking his full duty if he tried to make reparation *solely* by the sweet and gentle way of the love of Christ. Love by all means must dominate and permeate reparation; but love calls for something more than to enjoy the sweetness of the presence of the Beloved. Reparation is penance for our own sins, and, with Christ in the mystic body of the Church, for the sins of all the world.

And, as he ponders on these things in his heart, there echoes in his mind the words of St. John the Baptist: "Bring forth therefore fruits worthy of penance." [31] The Greek word for penance used here by St. Luke means, by its component roots, a change of mind. But it would be easy to show that in the

[31] Luke III:8.

New Testament the word takes on a much deeper meaning and refers to a complete change in one's whole manner of being, which results in a personal consecration of the soul to God in reparation for past sins. In this passage St. John demands of his hearers not only that they give up their past sinful life, but also that they prove it by their deeds. The people felt that an interior change of mind would not suffice, and so they "asked Him saying: What shall we do? And he answering said to them: He that hath two coats, let him give to him that hath none; and he that hath meat, let him do in like manner." [32] Here we have making reparation and doing penance by almsgiving. To the publicans or taxgatherers, he said: "Do nothing more than that which is appointed you," [33] that is to say: Don't take any more money than that to which you are entitled. All penance involves sacrifice. St. John laid upon the publicans what the psalmist speaks of as the sacrifice of justice: "The things you say in your hearts, be sorry for them upon your beds. Offer up the sacrifice of justice, and trust in the Lord." [34] It was the same sacrifice of justice he imposed upon the soldiers: "Do violence to no man, neither calumniate any man; and be content with your pay." [35]

The advice of St. John the Baptist on making reparation and doing penance is eminently practical and filled with discretion. Perhaps the first thing we should think of in making reparation to Christ is the sacrifice of justice. "Cast away from you all your transgression, by which you have transgressed, and make to yourselves a new heart and a new spirit." [36] This must be the first step in reparation for the past.

Some are moved to a penitential life by a desire to be like the saints. This is in itself a good desire, but it must be purified from any self-seeking or hidden desire for a reputation for sanctity, and it must be followed with discretion. It is said that a man once went to the Curé of Ars telling him he

[32] Luke III: 10-11.
[33] *Ibid.*, 13.
[34] Psalm IV: 5-6.
[35] Luke III: 14.
[36] Ezechiel XVIII: 31.

wanted to live the penitential life that the Curé lived. The Curé slept only two to three hours in the twenty-four, and often passed several days without eating anything, to say nothing of other penances by which he rivaled the ancient Fathers of the Desert. He told the man (to use words quoted in the Rule of St. Benedict) that each one has his own proper gift from God: one this, another, that. If God calls a man to a life of severe penance, He gives him the strength to do his work and support his heavy burden of penance. If he attempts such a heavy burden without the call of God, he collapses under what it is humanly impossible for him to carry.

However, that does not mean that all forms of corporal austerity must be eliminated from Christian life except by a very few to whom God has given a special call. Corporal austerity practiced with discretion and with the approval of a superior or confessor aids greatly our progress in the spiritual life. It also enhances the value of prayer. Did not our Lord Himself say: "If in Tyre and Sidon had been wrought the mighty works that have been wrought in you, they would have done penance long ago, sitting in sackcloth and ashes." [37] And did not the angel say to Daniel: "From the first day that thou didst set thy heart to understand, to afflict thyself in the sight of thy God, thy words have been heard"? [38]

There is a wholesome type of corporal austerity which, when practiced reasonably and with due discretion, does not at all injure the health of a normal vigorous man or woman. In fact, it may be conductive to physical well-being. I refer to fasting. Many more healthy individuals are injured by overeating than by fasting. And our Lord is authority for the statement that certain demons are only cast out by prayer and fasting.[39] Most healthy men and women could keep a strict Lenten fast with improvement of both soul and body, and the lowering of high blood pressure, should it be present.

[37] Luke X:13.
[38] Daniel X:12.
[39] Matthew XVII:20.

Hours of meals and a light or heavy breakfast are largely matters of custom. One can easily adjust oneself to a great variety of regimes without physical detriment. In doing so for the love of God, one puts up with wholesome but harmless bodily discomfort. However, in all matters of penance obedience is better than sacrifice.

When we are thinking of corporal penance that might be practiced without danger to health, we should seriously consider the renunciation of alcoholic beverages and tobacco. A sound principle for anyone in search of earnest self-denial, as a pledge of love for Christ and His Cross, would be this: I will give up everything the renunciation of which will not harm me or the carrying out of my duties, but which might prevent grave dangers in life or be seriously injurious to bodily health. Those who give up alcohol and tobacco do themselves no harm. But the indulgence in alcoholic beverages has sometimes been responsible for unfortunate developments that have ruined the prospects of many a promising man and woman; and smoking is at times a major factor in diseases of the arteries leading to such things as high blood pressure, coronary thrombosis, and cerebral hemorrhage.[40] Many would have attained to great success and would have prolonged their time of productive activity by decades had they been sufficiently courageous to sacrifice alcohol and tobacco for the love of Christ. A valuable apostolate on earth and a great reward in heaven will be the lot of those who take St. John the Baptist for their patron and "drink no wine nor strong drink" [41] and renounce all that is not God, to be cloistered by Him in the wide-open spaces of the modern world.

There is a simple type of penitential life that means real suffering, but which cannot be held responsible for any damage to our physical well-being. I refer to the "little way" of St. Thérèse of Lisieux. There is something entrancingly beautiful about this "little way" and its spirit. St. Thérèse intro-

[40] This statement is based on a number of scientific researches in experimental medicine.
[41] Luke I:15.

duces us to it with one of her beautiful similes. "How can one fear One Who lets Himself be held by one hair of our neck? [42] So we must learn to hold Him prisoner, this God Who makes Himself a mendicant for our love. In telling us that a hair can work so great a marvel, He is showing us that the *smallest actions* done for love are the actions which win His heart. Ah! if we had to do great things how much to be pitied we should be. . . . But how fortunate we are, since Jesus lets Himself be held by the smallest. . . . It is so sweet a thing to *aid Jesus* by our slight sacrifices, to aid Him to save souls He has redeemed at the price of His blood, souls which await only our help not to fall into the abyss." [43]

"Souls which await only our help not to fall into the abyss." How strange that this child, who remained a child at twenty-three when she wrote these words, should be able to envisage and express this profound truth of the mystical body of Christ. Souls who might have been lost are saved by our virtues and sacrifices. Souls follow their own willfulness and fall into the abyss who might have been held back were it not for our sins and selfishness. The thought of this child saint finds expression in the encyclical of Pius XII on the "Mystical Body of Christ": "Deep mystery this, subject of inexhaustible meditation: that the salvation of many depends on the prayers and voluntary penances which the members of the Mystical Body of Jesus Christ offer for this intention." [44] How this great truth stimulates us to a life of prayer and penance for the salvation of souls! And who can refuse the tiny acts of self-denial of the "little way"?

Many sacrifices of the "little way" are truly tiny but when given with the love of a child they have eternal value: for example, to give up little dainties we particularly like; to restrain the curiosity of the eyes, or ears; to put up with things we find hard without even interior rebellion, and, perhaps even

[42] Canticle of Canticles IV:9.
[43] *Collected Letters of St. Thérèse of Lisieux*, New York, Sheed and Ward, 1949, p. 276.
[44] #46, p. 15, edition of Paulist Press, New York.

with joy; trying our best in these ways to give Christ a pledge of our love and to offer a little mite for the welfare of all the actual and potential members of the mystical body. Cathedrals are built by the pennies of the poor. Some sacrifices, however, are not so tiny as they seem. When Thérèse was still a little child her father sent for her and Céline, her sister. Asking Céline a few questions he arranged for her to learn painting. Then, turning to Thérèse, he said, "And you, my little Queen, would you like to learn painting along with Céline?" She was just about to burst into joyful exclamations of delight when an older sister answered for her and said, "Oh, no. Thérèse is not interested in painting." At once our child saint (the incident proves she was already a saint of the Christian home) thought to herself, here is an opportunity to offer our Lord a big sacrifice, and though her heart was breaking, she kept quiet and said nothing.[45] Nor did she take back the sacrifice by very soon nestling close to her good father and telling him how much she really wanted to go with her favorite sister, Céline, and learn painting.

The little way not only demands little sacrifices but also that we ever remain little children and tiny insignificant creatures in our own estimation, throwing ourselves completely into the arms of the loving Father of mercies.

"O Jesus, how happy Your *little bird* is to be *feeble* and *little!* . . . When it wants to gaze upon the divine Sun and the clouds keep it from seeing a single ray, its little eyes close in spite of itself, its little head is hid under its little wing, and the poor little thing sleeps, still fancying it is gazing upon its dearest star.[46] When it awakes, it is not at all desolate, its little heart stays at peace; it resumes its task of *love*. . . . O

[45] *St. Thérèse of Lisieux*, trans. from her autobiography by Rev. Thomas N. Taylor, New York, P. J. Kenedy, 1926, p. 143 note.

[46] Bishop Curtis of Baltimore had a cognate concept of falling to sleep when at prayer. He once was giving a retreat at a convent. A friend called to see him. The Sister Portress looked for him everywhere and finally found him in the sanctuary of the chapel sound asleep in a big chair. She shook him and said: "Bishop Curtis! Sleeping in the presence of the Blessed Sacrament!" He promptly replied: "Can't a dog lie down and go to sleep before his master?"

divine Word . . . I love You, and You *draw* me to You. It is You, descending into this earth of exile, Who have chosen to suffer and to die to *draw* souls to the heart of the Eternal fire of the Blessed Trinity." [47]

We can say with little fear of contradiction that all the saints have been little souls in their own estimation. St. Bernard must have perceived that he was a powerful influence for good in the world of his day. And he practiced heroic penance and lived a life of union with God so close and intimate that he did not observe what was going on around him. But he could not fail to know that all the good he did was done by God through him as an instrument and that, of himself, he was altogether nothing and nothing else but nothing. St. Francis of Assisi is outstanding among even the greatest saints, and yet, considering all that God had done for him, he truly regarded himself as spiritually inferior to a bandit who was about to die on the scaffold. If God, he said, had done for that poor bandit all that He has done for the poor Francis, the bandit would surely have surpassed in virtue the poor little Francis.

Those who think such an attitude of mind is a kind of silly dishonesty should ask themselves: Has God ever given me the grace to see myself as I really am and the even more important grace to see the divine in the souls of others? No one can correctly place himself or anyone else on the scale of the true value of a human soul. The "little soul" never attempts this impossibility and places itself among the tiny beings whom God has created, and there abides in great peace and security.

But does God let all men pass through life without ever asking them to make a big and heroic sacrifice? I think that most people are given the great opportunity of making, at some time in the course of their lives, a truly great sacrifice. Think for instance of the last illness of the child saint of the "little way." Those who rise to the occasion prepared themselves for it by many little sacrifices.

Sometimes such a heroic sacrifice is asked early in life. Mary

[47] *Collected Letters*, p. 285.

Walsh, a young woman born in Ireland, was working as a laundress for a wealthy family in New York. On her way to work one hot summer morning in 1876, she noticed a tiny girl, about seven, sobbing in a doorway as only a child can sob when something terrible has happened and there is nothing else for a child to do but shed the bitterest of bitter tears. The young Irish woman stopped and asked in tender sympathy: "My child, what's the matter?" "Mother is so sick and I don't know what to do! Oh! Miss, I'm so scared." "Take me to your mother." They went into the stifling air of the tenement. A woman near to death, with a newborn infant dead by her side, was lying on a bed. Three children, huddled with fright in a corner, looked up at the lady and their sister Ruthie. The room was "a foul kennel of crushed humanity." There was nothing to eat in the house, and of course no money. But that did not cause Mary Walsh the least difficulty. She started to clean up the room, wrapped the dead baby in a torn blanket and put it out of sight for the moment, gave the mother a sponge bath, and then asked, "Where is the father?" She found out that he was in jail for drunkenness and disorderly conduct. She said to the mother: "Don't worry, God will not forsake you, and I will take care of you and the children. I will be back in a little while." On the way she prayed, "Dear Lord, aid me. Tell me how to help."

She went home, picked up what savings she possessed, begged a little money from her friends, returned and gave the poor family the first decent meal they had had for some time. She begged from policemen, firemen, neighbors. She bought fresh bedding and clean clothes for all. She paid the gas bill, buried the dead infant, and managed to make the husband promise to quit drinking and then got him released from jail, got his employer to give him another trial, with the final result that the whole family was rehabilitated and a happy home created out of squalor and misery.

Early in these activities, she visited the lady for whom she worked. The lady tried to persuade her that she was wasting her time, but gave her to understand that unless she returned to work she would be discharged. Mary said, "I cannot forsake the poor in their need." And she lost a job and was penniless herself except for being given the wages still owed to her and a donation for the poor family.

From that time on, while earning her own living, she went about among the sick poor as a friend and benefactress. She worked and begged to help those in need. Associates gathered about her, and finally she became the foundress of the Dominican Sisters of the Sick Poor, who now have several houses in the United States.[48]

The obedience of Mary Walsh to the call of charity on that hot summer morning of 1876 was one of those sublime acts of self-sacrifice which prove heroic love of God and which lift the soul at once to a higher level of the spiritual life. Sometimes, when God calls *us* to step in and make a great sacrifice we lose the great opportunity of our lives by shrinking back or suggesting that the matter be cleared and taken care of by an appropriate agency.

Sometimes the call to heroic sacrifice is our last illness; but if we accept and endure in true charity it is the great opportunity to make reparation for all our own sins and with Christ in the mystic body to offer up His eternal sacrifice for the sanctification of all mankind.

The endurance with perfect patience of a long and very painful illness terminating in death is perhaps to be reckoned among the things that are hardest for man to endure. Multiple bone cancer was the big sacrifice by which a young married woman was allowed to associate herself with the passion of Christ and die with Him in the mystic body of the Church for her own salvation and sanctification and for that of all mankind. She accepted her lot without rebellion. She was in agony and on the point of death for over a year. She sent me a little history of her life and illness.

[48] See Anne Cawley Boardman, *Such Love Is Seldom*, New York, Harper & Brothers, 1950. The author is proud to say that he knew Mary Walsh as the saintly Sister Mary, the friend of the poor, in her dark days before she put on her beautiful Dominican habit.

She was a promising student in college and after graduation held with success a number of good positions. Not very long before the onset of her illness she married. Its first marked symptom was sudden pain in an ankle on getting out of a bus. It was considered a sprain. But she commenced to lose weight. One day, after her weight had fallen to ninety pounds, in walking across the floor of her room, the right femur broke under her weight. She fell and in the fall broke the left femur and the right arm near the shoulder, but "God Almighty to Whom I screamed in agony gave me a swift and wonderful calm." In this and in various incidents throughout her whole illness we can see how, in a most extraordinary manner, religion bestowed on her a wonderful peace and even happiness in spite of intense physical pain, while she lived on without hope of recovery, face to face for over a year with impending death. "Without hope of recovery" was true objectively; and subjectively she knew that there was no hope. Still from time to time hope for a cure glimmered in consciousness. Thus she wrote: "If I can hold on till they take off this itchy iron garment." The last months of her life were spent in a body cast.

Nor were mental trials absent during the months of physical agony. "My husband," she wrote, "has taken it the hard way. . . . More than all the suffering, it hurts to hear 'I hate' and 'I'll kill myself.'"

Souls at the summit of spiritual perfection have a yearning for the Eucharist. But this poor sufferer was unnecessarily deprived of Holy Communion. "Looking to the Eucharist for consolation in my helplessness I was painfully disappointed to find that the nursing home to which I went, was visited by a priest only once a month, and 'on the run'. Oh, what a longing I had to see again the tabernacle in the shadows of the evening and the faithful red light and the empty pews, in a stolen visit to the Blessed Sacrament."

Her one consolation was the inner spiritual life that she lived with Christ. This was so much easier as long as she was all alone with Him in a private room. Financial reasons made it necessary for her to be moved to a ward; and so she lost her beautiful solitude with Christ. But she saw in the change an opportunity for the apostolate of example: unbroken cheerful submission to the way the Eternal Father had chosen for her to share in the passion of Christ and co-operation with Him through His mystic body in the salvation of mankind. "My scapulars and badges, pains, heartbreaks and small successes keep me united to the Head and members of the Mystical Body. The union was closer during the months I lay alone, yet with roommates, there is an apostolic function when cheerfulness is maintained. The Lord God has made it awfully plain that He will do with me as He wants. My visitors, family, friends, the Sisters especially always say the right thing: and have seemed actually envious of the spiritual favor of suffering sent me. I can agree with my reason, but cry out for relief with my heart."

So her account ended. A friend sent me the following message: "Tell him I would like to write more, but can no longer use my arms and am losing my sight."

Renunciation of All Things for Christ

The renunciation of all things for Christ seems at first a hard and unreasonable saying and one asks oneself: Who can or should bear it? But a calm view of things as they are shows us that it is in the long run absolutely necessary. The only problem to be settled is when and how.

There is no exception to the law of death. Death brings about a complete separation from all persons, pleasures, and interests in life. But death is not the end of all. The body dies and disintegrates, but the soul lives on. A spirit does not find delight in eating and drinking. It has new joys awaiting it: God and the vision of His Infinite Being, and the society of the angels and saints in heaven. Life is not a time merely to enjoy the pleasures of earth, but to prepare ourselves to enter upon the joys of eternal life. Into this life there shall not enter "anything defiled, or that worketh abomination or maketh a lie, but they that are written in the book of life of the Lamb." [49]

St. Paul points out to us that by baptism we go through a preliminary death to all that is of the earth earthy and rise to live on earth the spiritual life of the Kingdom of Heaven. "Know you not that all we, who are baptized in Christ Jesus, are baptized into his death? For we are buried together with Him by baptism into death; that as Christ is risen from the dead by the glory of the Father, so we also may walk in newness of life." [50] When all goes as it should be a child is born into a house where the parents have died to the world and live with Christ. The child learns gradually by the example of others in the home, by teaching and experience, to walk with Christ in newness of life. It enters adolescence having already learned to live with God. It makes its renunciations as it grows in years and grace with God and man. It plans its future, leaving aside all that does not concern it, as it forges ahead in its career. But the life of the soul with God becomes ever more perfectly a communion with a wise Guide and Powerful Protector. And so the man lives on until the evening.

It is seldom, however, that this idealistic picture is realized. Many have to learn by experience, and experience is a severe disciplinarian. And so, instead of a lifetime of little sacrifices, there are sudden blows, many sorrows, and one rises from the depths only by a heroic holocaust of all that seems dear.

The necessity of a complete renunciation in life, such as that which we all go through at death, was taught us by our Lord Himself. "So likewise every one of you that doth not renounce all that he possesseth cannot be my disciple." [51] Our Lord spoke these words just after recounting the parable of the king who was preparing to meet another king who was coming against him with superior forces. Victory demanded the emptying of his treasury and the sacrifice of all that he possessed to meet the impending danger. Our adversary, the devil, comes against us with superior forces with which un-

---

[49] Apocalypse XXI:27.
[50] Romans VI:3-4.
[51] Luke XIV:33.

aided human nature cannot cope. If we sacrifice all to be disciples of Christ, He fights for us, and Satan can do nothing.

It is an illusion to regard this total renunciation as something terrible to undertake and endure to the end. It seems to be when we look forward to it, but experience dissipates the deception. Total renunciation is the road to happiness. Unfulfilled desires are the source of torment to man. That torment vanishes when we no longer want to satisfy these desires. We become independent. We ascend higher and higher to a holy type of life on the spiritual plane. St. Anthony of the Desert was provoked with those who spoke of having renounced vast possessions to live with God in solitude. Who could say that one made a great sacrifice if he gave up a penny to gain a million?

But then how vastly superior is the peace of Christ in the midst of thorns, to the lot of those who have gone after the "wages of iniquity," "who, as irrational beasts, naturally tending to the snare and to destruction, blaspheming those things which they know not, shall perish in their corruption." [52]

Everyone must make his choice. He that gathereth not with Me scattereth. You cannot serve God and mammon. Your lot on earth and in eternity must be the wages of iniquity or the peace of God which surpasseth all understanding. St. Anthony was right, there is no great sacrifice in giving up all that the world can offer for the life of the soul with God.

In the renunciation by which the soul attains to God, half-measures do not suffice. When someone suffers some great loss, we sometimes hear it said: God wants everything; as if He took some kind of pleasure in leaving a soul empty and miserable. The phrase indicates a wrong point of view. God wants you to live with Him now and to be with Him for all eternity, because He loves you. The mystery is that God should bestow infinite love on such a tiny creature. He does not want you merely to suffer, but that you should attain the Infinite Good, which He is Himself.

St. John of the Cross expresses the necessity of total renun-

[52] II Peter II: 12.

ciation by an apt simile. If a bird is held by a slender thread, it cannot fly to the heavens until the thread is broken. It is likewise impossible for you to set your heart on retaining anything created that *does not concern* you and your work for God in the world, and attain the union of perfect friendship with God.

This comes out even more clearly in the simile quoted above, used by Innocent le Masson, a great superior-general of the Carthusians. "It is the very substance [53] of the soul which should be united to God, not merely its faculties. And as we see in things of which we have experience by our senses, two things cannot be joined together until they have been stripped and cleaned of all other things, so that each, being completely isolated, one touches the other, and no extraneous thing lies in between them, so it is necessary that the soul should be stripped of everything and be established in complete solitude [54] that it may be wholly united and made one with God. For if there remain the most insignificant thing between God and the soul, to use our mode of speaking in this matter, the soul itself does not touch God, but whatever it is that is held on to and placed between God and the soul. Thus when one touches a hand protected by a glove, he does not touch the hand but the glove." [55]

Now in all this, there is not involved anything unreasonable, nor any injustice, nor any cruelty to anyone. All your duties, without exception, are involved in that which God asks of you in your daily life. Therefore, while never failing in any duty, you renounce everything that is incompatible with duty. All this being understood, the principle holds: If you wish to attain to God, you can set your heart on nothing except God alone.

[53] It might be well to recall here that according to St. Thomas Aquinas sanctifying grace is a new quality of the soul added to its substance by God, not a habit bestowed on one of its faculties. (*Summa Theologica*, 1. 2. Q. CX, arts. ii, iii and iv.)

[54] For the laity, this means isolation from all that does not concern them.

[55] *Disciplina Ordinis Cartusiensis*, Monstrolii, Typis Cartusiae, S. Mariae de Pratis, 1894, Liber I, cap. IV, sec. 26, p. 19.

The triumph of the infant Church in the conversion of St. Paul turns the mind away from the total renunciation that it meant for St. Paul himself. In one moment he lost every relative and friend that he possessed and entered a group, some of whom at first distrusted him. "When he was come into Jerusalem, he essayed to join himself to the disciples; and they all were afraid of him, not believing that he was a disciple." [56] The inner sufferings of St. Paul in the total renunciation God asked of him are not recorded, but the totality of it and its bitterness are reflected in his words: "With Christ I am nailed to the cross. And I live now, not I, but Christ liveth in me." [57] At some time or other God leads us into our total renunciation. If we make it in the spirit of St. Paul we shall be surprised to find therein our freedom and our joy when we cease to live for ourselves and find Christ living within us.

God calls us all to a close union with Himself. If we attain our ideal we shall enter a habitual state of mind in which we shall be able to say: "I live now, not I, but Christ liveth in me." One does not at first realize that such a union with Christ is his own personal destiny. This great truth dawns on the mind gradually. We first think of avoiding all mortal sin, so that we may be united to God in heaven. Then we commence to think that when we come before Christ in judgment we want to hear the words: "Well done, good and faithful servant: because thou hast been faithful over a few things, I will place thee over many things: enter thou into the joy of thy Lord." [58] The love of Christ commences to make us brook no delay in our union with Christ, no painful waiting in purgatory, and so we begin to think of avoiding every little venial sin and imperfection. In the meantime, perhaps we have commenced to think about devoting our life and energies to something in life that would be truly a service to God: the establishment of a home that would be a school of the service of God, or the work of some religious community, or the

[56] Acts IX:26.
[57] Galatians II:19-20.
[58] Matthew XXV:21.

priesthood. Finally it dawns on the soul that Christ wants it to live in *close union of mind and heart with Him*. At the same time the soul sees the work that God wants it to do in the world. And so it becomes clear: God does want me to renounce all that does not concern me, so that I can do my duty and still live in close union of mind and heart with Him Who called me out of darkness into His marvelous light that I might know His love and enjoy the vision of His Being for all eternity.

The strict cloister of Carthusian life is a great aid in enabling the soul to live in close union of mind and heart with God. But there are analogies between the monastic cloister and the cloister of the home. Monastic cloister brings about a permanent isolation of the soul from all that is not God. The cloister of the home absorbs the interest and activities of the parents to such an extent that they no longer have any desire to indulge in anything that interferes with the life of the home: the love of one for another and those happy evenings together and the picnics in the country and the many joint activities of a happy home. But how about the solitude of the monastic cloister? It, too, has its analogue in the cloister of the home where one is alone and away from persons that might interfere with the happy life of the home: alone and away from things that do not concern one, alone in mind and heart and unconcerned with all that is not God while all in the family love one another, even as Christ loves each. Home life, in its perfection, provides an opportunity for the silence of the soul in the solitude of its union with God in the Holy Sacrifice of the Mass and in family prayer and holy reading, and becomes a living experience of the profound truth, that "God is charity: and he that abideth in charity, abideth in God, and God in him." [59] What a noble work it is for parents to contrive to establish such a home life. And who would not go forth from himself by a renunciation of all things that he might establish such a life on earth and abide in God that God may abide in him?

[59] I John IV:16.

CHAPTER **XI**

The Beginnings of the
Interior Life

WHAT is meant by an interior life? Let us briefly describe it first when it is well developed, and then proceed to study its beginnings. The interior life is a habitual life of union with God, which, when well developed, seems independent of personal efforts to remain in the Divine Presence or to come before God by frequent acts of recollection in the course of the day. This consciousness of union with God becomes continuous only at the very height of spiritual development. At a moderate degree of its development there are periods in which a beautiful peace dominates daily life, especially during one's morning mental prayer, Mass, and Holy Communion. Very often this peace hangs on after one leaves the church and lasts for one to several hours into the work of the day. There is a strange duality of a peace consciousness that is uninterrupted and an intellectual awareness of the Divine Presence, which talking about business matters or various activities cause to disappear. But the intellectual awareness spontaneously returns until the whole peace experience fades out.

There is great variety in the duration and frequency of these "visits of the Beloved," as some spiritual writers term them, and, of course, of the interims between visits. But sometimes in these interims there is an unbroken, quiet happiness deep in the background of consciousness, as if Christ had retired to a hidden room in the interior castle of the soul; but the soul knows perfectly well that He truly is in the castle and never leaves it. It is probable that this hidden happiness derives from a consciousness of freedom from sin. Should the soul slip into mortal sin, peace would at once be destroyed and there would be left the agony of an aching void.

One should note well, however, that the peace experience of which we now write is not something into which one is able to enter at will. One must await in patience the visit of the Beloved. One is powerless to shorten the interim in which He is absent. In general He enters without knocking. His presence in the soul is sometimes so hidden that its effects are perceived before the intellectual consciousness of His abiding is awakened. The psalms of the divine office, for instance, are found to scintillate with meanings that did not flash on the mind yesterday and the day before. There is an ease, not always experienced, to lift the mind to God in a quiet glowing aspiration of wordless love. Such a "visit" may or may not be accompanied by a peculiar quasi-perceptual awareness of the Divine Presence. But neither the glow of divine charity nor the intellectual awareness can be entered upon voluntarily whenever the soul chooses. There is required something that may be figuratively termed the "visit of the Beloved."

An apparent exception to this last statement is found when one discovers that for a whole day, or for several days, as some of our respondents have noted, one can at any moment pause in the activities of the day and enter into a quasi-perceptual awareness of the Divine Presence and feel the warm glow of divine charity. But this is possible because the visit of the Beloved is prolonged more than usual. A more marked exception would be found, according to St. John of the Cross, toward the close of the period of spiritual betrothal and in the state of spiritual matrimony. "There is now no door closed to the soul. . . . It is in her power to enjoy this sweet sleep of love every time and whensoever she desires." [1] That is possible because the Beloved has entered and will never again depart. This statement may seem extreme. It does not mean that there is no possibility of losing God by sin, but that it is, as we say, practically impossible. St. John of the Cross goes so far as to say of spiritual matrimony: "I think that this estate is never attained without the soul being confirmed in grace therein." [2]

In a broad sense the interior life commences when one commences to go to Mass and Holy Communion habitually every day or to make a daily meditation or both. Such a practice commences to bring about a character change for the better.

Thus one of our respondents writes of the commencement of his interior life: "When I was about 16 or 17, my teacher, a Jesuit Scholastic, taught me how to make a meditation according to the method of St. Ignatius. About the same time I commenced to read daily from the *Bible* or the *Imitation of Christ*. My mother gave me a beautiful copy of the *Bible* and someone else presented me with a copy of the *New Testament* and the *Imitation of Christ* in Latin. This latter book (in small print of pocket size) became my constant companion. Soon I was snatching every spare moment for silent prayer. I would steal short moments where I worked to hide behind the file cases and be alone with God in prayer. My ugly temper, and graver faults, faded away suddenly. I avoided successfully even slight venial sins. 'If then any be in Christ a new creature, the old things are passed away. Behold all things are made new.' " [3]

When one commences the practice of daily mental prayer, he is likely to be led on to recalling the presence of God frequently in the course of the day and speaking of his love to the Creator of his soul. He may read in one book or another

---

[1] *Spiritual Canticle*, Stanzas XX and XXI, §19, Peers's translation, Vol. II, p. 305.
[2] *Ibid.*, Stanza XXII, §3, p. 308.
[3] II Corinthians V:17.

of the ideal of continuous recollection. Here we must at once speak a word of caution. No one by personal effort, through the exertion of will power, can force himself to anything like *continuous* recollection. The effort is likely to lead to neurotic headaches, a nervous strain, anxiety states, and various mental symptoms. Continuous recollection is a wonderful spiritual gift that God seldom grants, and we should remember that it is wrong to try to produce by our own efforts what can only be caused in the soul by a special divine action.

We can, however, approach the ideal of continuous recollection in a perfect interior life with God by an indirect and circuitous route. We should recall to mind the beatitude: "Blessed are the clean of heart for they shall see God." We use our effort in co-operating with divine grace, which we humbly, earnestly, and often beg, to avoid every manner of sin or imperfection displeasing to God. We live a Eucharistic life with daily communion, and frequent visits to the Blessed Sacrament. We are faithful to daily Mass and mental prayer. From time to time in the day we relax the strain of work and come into the Divine Presence and pour forth our soul in love to God. As we do this, God commences to lay in the soul the foundations of continuous recollection by bestowing the peace experience we have been speaking about. At first it may last only a few moments but it has a tendency to flow over from our morning devotions into the activity of the day. We cannot make it last, but God from time to time will give us hours of this peculiar specific peace experience, which, when it passes, we are unable to bring back. This peace experience by its very nature excludes all tension, anxiety, excitement, and everything of a neurotic character. God's divine action perfects man in many ways; it never produces anything with the slightest semblance of a mental disorder.

II

How early in the course of the spiritual life does this peace experience make its first sporadic appearances?

For purposes of classification we distributed our data into five classes:

I. Those in stages three and four of Chautard.
II. Those in stage five of Chautard.
III. Those in stages six or seven but who do *not* find it painful to remain on earth because they want to be united with Christ in heaven.
IV. Those in stages six or seven but who do find remaining on earth painful for this reason.
V. Those in stages six or seven but who report a betrothal experience with Christ.

The following table gives the story of the appearance of the peace experience in the spiritual life, based on the first 150 reports in our material.

	Those who have had the peace experience		*Those in whom the peace experience is habitual*	
	Fraction	Percentage	Fraction	Percentage
I	12/26	46	0	0
II	47/55	85	3/55	5.4
III	35/37	94	13/37	35
IV	24/24	100	17/24	71
V	8/8	100	6/8	75

We give here the question on which this table is based: "In mental prayer do you ever enter into a period of profound peace with your whole being infused with the love of God, a peace which remains in spite of the mind wandering at times away from God?——Is your prayer habitually of this character?——Does the peace continue after your prayer is over, and accompany you into the work of the day?"

The table suggests to the statistician that the peace experience in prayer may occur sporadically in anyone who turns to God in prayer even though he may be leading a life from which mortal sin has not been entirely excluded. It was known by all our respondents in Chautard's stages six and seven. It does not, however, become habitual until one has entered into Chautard's fifth stage and mortal sin has been completely, or almost completely, overcome. *Habitual* enjoyment of the peace experience becomes more common than not in those who have conquered habitual venial sin. It would probably be a truer way of expressing this fact if one would in some way bring out the concept that it is the union with God in the prayer, characterized by the peace experience, that banishes sin from the life of man. If this is so, we should expect that God would from time to time awaken souls leading a life of sin and call them by the peace experience. And as the soul turns to God more frequently in prayer, it enjoys the peace experience ever more and more often, and all fully deliberate sin is quickly banished from daily life.

The peace experience of which we have been speaking has been long known and discussed by spiritual writers. We have described it as we have encountered it in the data obtained from our questionnaire. It is now time to give an account of it from the descriptions of St. Teresa of Ávila and St. John of the Cross.

III

St. Teresa's description of what she termed the "prayer of quiet" [4] may be summarized as follows:

1. It is something that cannot be brought about by our own efforts or entered into at will. Any psychological experience which is produced by some activity other than our own personal effort must be an awareness that is, qualitatively, quite different from one which we ourselves produce and carry on. Meditation is produced and carried on by our own activity, stimulated and guided though it may be by divine grace. The prayer of quiet may appear as an incident during a meditation, but in itself it is different *qualitatively* from meditation as such, because God produces it without any personal effort on our part. Some have maintained that between meditation and the prayer of quiet there is no qualitative but

[4] What St. Teresa terms the prayer of quiet is often referred to now as infused contemplation.

only a quantitative difference. This theory is ruled out by the considerations just put forward. There are, however, wide differences of degree in our experiences of the prayer of quiet: as to duration, continuity, and intimacy of the union of mind, will, and heart with God.

St. Teresa thus speaks of the prayer of quiet: "This is a supernatural state, and, however hard we try, we cannot reach it for ourselves; for it is a state into which the soul enters into peace, or rather in which the Lord gives it peace through His presence." [5] Again in her *Life* she writes: "This state [the prayer of quiet] in which the soul begins to recollect itself, borders on the supernatural, to which it could in no way attain by its own exertions." [6]

2. It is maintained without effort. "Everything that now takes place brings the greatest consolation, and so little labor is involved that, even if prayer continues for a long time, it never becomes wearisome." [7] This is in marked distinction to a meditation or to meditative spiritual reading in which intellectual activity is maintained by volitional effort. It is quite possible, however, that in a meditation, especially in the colloquy, one should be given a touch of the prayer of quiet and enter into a long silent pause in which the soul is absorbed in the love of God. At times in such a pause the soul may feel the nearness of God in a quasi-perceptual realization of the Divine Presence.

3. The central element in the whole experience that the soul enjoys in the prayer of quiet is the glow of the love of God. This St. Teresa expresses by saying that the "will is bound." This expression is theologically correct and exact, for the love of God is an act of the will by which a man consecrates himself to God and experiences this consecration. In the prayer of quiet this act gives rise to an abiding experience which may be likened to the glow of red-hot iron.

The prayer of quiet differs from states of more intimate

---

[5] *Way of Perfection*, Chap. XXXI, Peers's translation, Vol. II, p. 127.
[6] *Life*, Chap. XIV, Peers's translation, Vol. I, p. 83.
[7] *Ibid.*, p. 84.

union of the soul with God, in that, while the glow of the love of the soul for God does not fade completely during this prayer, nevertheless the flow of thought may wander to many things not concerned with God. By "flow of thought" we wish to express here what St. Teresa terms the activity of imagination and memory. The same concept could be expressed by a more homely terminology: Even though the soul experiences an abiding continuous love of God, the period of prayer admits of an endless number of distractions, but these distractions are superficial and do not interrupt the abiding love of God nor the peculiar sense of being established in perfect peace.[8] This is quite different from an ordinary meditation. Distractions interrupt the meditation, breaking in upon the train of thought.

There are, however, many degrees of the intensity of love, recollection, and peace in the prayer of quiet. In the deeper stages of this prayer, the train of thought does not wander but all mental activity is centered on God.

4. The term "quiet" was no doubt used by St. Teresa because quiet and peace dominate the whole experience. Love does not flash and flame. It glows like the red-hot iron. There is a tendency to avoid the slightest movement. One's prayer is often wordless or one makes use of a monosyllable as recommended in *The Cloud of Unknowing*. St. Teresa writes: "Persons in this state prefer the body to remain motionless, for otherwise their peace would be destroyed: for this reason they dare not stir. Speaking is a distress to them: they will spend a whole hour on a single repetition of the *Pater Noster*. . . . They seem not to be in the world, and have no wish to see or hear anything but their God; nothing distresses them, nor does it seem that anything can possibly do so." [9]

5. A final characteristic of the prayer of quiet is its tendency to carry over beyond the time allotted to prayer or attending the Holy Sacrifice of the Mass, into the work of the

[8] See *Life*, Chap. XV, Peers's translation, Vol. I, p. 88 ff.; *Way of Perfection*, Chap. XXXI, Vol. II, p. 128.
[9] *Way of Perfection*, Chap. XXXI, Peers's translation, Vol. II, p. 128.

day. St. Teresa says that this occurs when "the quiet is felt in a high degree." She speaks of it lasting for one or two days. "It is a great favor which the Lord grants to these souls, for it unites the active life with the contemplative. At such times they serve the Lord in both these ways at once; the will, while in contemplation, is working without knowing how it does so; the other two faculties [10] are serving Him as Martha did. Thus Martha and Mary work together. I know someone to whom the Lord often granted this favor; she could not understand it and asked a great contemplative about it; he told her that what she described was quite possible and had happened to himself. I think, therefore, that as the soul experiences such satisfaction in this prayer of quiet the will must be almost continuously united with Him, Who alone can give it happiness." [11]

As we shall see, continuous enjoyment of a *consciousness of the Divine Presence* with the heart overflowing with the love of God in the midst of all activities, lasting for years without interruption, is a psychological characteristic of the state of spiritual matrimony with Christ. Perhaps in the prolongation of the prayer of quiet this consciousness of the Divine Presence is more in the background and the foreground is the flow of divine charity.

St. Teresa dwells in various places on the great value of the prayer of quiet for our spiritual life. "This water of great blessings and favors which the Lord gives in this state makes the virtues grow much more, beyond all comparison, than in the previous one; for the soul is already rising from its miserable condition and gaining some slight foreknowledge of the joys of glory. . . . As soon as it arrives at this state, it begins to lose its covetousness for the things of earth." [12]

"A person who used to be afraid of doing penance lest he

---

[10] St. Teresa names these as *imagination* and *memory*, but it is clear that she means the whole train of thought whether running along as in a reverie and so constituting a series of distractions in the time of prayer, or as directing the work of the day and managing practical affairs.

[11] *Way of Perfection*, Chap. XXXI, Peers's translation, Vol. II, p. 129.

[12] *Life*, Chap. XIV, Peers's translation, Vol. I, p. 84.

should ruin his health now believes that in God he can do everything,[13] and has more desire to do such things than he had previously. The fear of trials that he was wont to have is now largely assuaged, because he has a more lively faith, and realizes that, if he endures these trials for God's sake, His Majesty will give him grace to bear them patiently, and sometimes even to desire them, because he also cherishes a desire to do something for God. . . . Having now tasted the consolations of God, he sees that earthly things are mere refuse; so, little by little, he withdraws from them and in this way becomes more and more his own master." [14]

Should we desire to attain to the prayer of quiet? St. Teresa speaking to the nuns of the Carmelite reform wrote thus: "You will desire, then, my daughters, to strive to attain this way of prayer, and you will be right to do so." [15]

Can we extend this pronouncement to all those who have entered upon an interior life with God and go to Mass and receive Holy Communion daily when possible and practice mental prayer and devote some time to holy reading? I would answer with a strong affirmative, but would admit that a certain few neurotic individuals would constitute exceptions to the general rule. This is far from saying that all who desire the prayer of quiet should commence at once to attempt to practice it. We shall cite later the rules of St. John of the Cross for determining when one should abandon meditation for "the prayer of loving attentiveness to God."

But how are we going to strive to attain that which is unattainable by our own efforts? Basing what I say here largely upon the second chapter of the Fourth Mansions of St. Teresa's *Interior Castle*, I would say that:

1. We must never strive to attain the unattainable by direct vigorous personal striving. We must own to the truth: our own unworthiness, weakness, and incapability.

[13] One should not take this passage as a sanction to undertake severe penances without the permission of a spiritual director or one's superior.
[14] *Interior Castle*, IV, iii, Peers's translation, Vol. II, p. 244.
[15] *Ibid.*, p. ii, Vol. II, p. 238.

2. St. Teresa points out that the way to the prayer of quiet lies through humility. But how do we attain to humility? The way to humility is a sinless life. The way to a sinless life is to live in the presence of God. This we can attempt and in some measure attain by peacefully recalling from time to time in the day the great fact that God is everywhere and we are never out of His Presence. The table on page 192 shows that the percentage of those whose mental prayer is habitually that of quiet increases from zero, in Chautard's third and fourth stages where mortal sin is by no means banished, to his sixth and seventh stages, in which fully deliberate venial sin no longer occurs. As we have pointed out, there is an interaction between prayer and freedom from sin. Be faithful every day to your morning or evening meditation and fully voluntary sin will disappear from your life. Live free from sin and God will lead you into that prayer of loving attention to God which St. Teresa termed the prayer of quiet. "Blessed are the clean of heart, for they shall see God." [16]

And then it would be well to be mindful in our daily mental prayer of the following suggestion of St. Teresa: "I only want you to be warned if you would make progress a long way on this road and ascend to the Mansions of your desire, the important thing is not to think much, but to love much." [17]

To grow in the love of Christ we must try to learn something of the sublime strength and incomprehensible tenderness of His love for us by trying during mental prayer to penetrate into the mysteries of His passion and commune with Him in loving adoration.

Thus by being truly humble and honestly recognizing our unworthiness of the close union with Christ that comes to us in the prayer of loving attentiveness to God, and by flying from sin and begging our Lord to allow us to be truly associated with Him in His passion and asking for the power to imitate Him in all things, we shall commence to

[16] Matthew V:8.
[17] *Interior Castle*, IV, i, **Peers's** translation, Vol. II, p. 233.

share in the life of the mystical body of Christ and attain to the peace of God which surpasseth all understanding.

I V

The prayer of quiet as found in the writings of St. John of the Cross is to be sought in his description of a spiritual experience that commences to make its appearance when ordinary meditation becomes difficult or impossible. "The soul waits with loving attentiveness upon God, without making any particular meditation, in inward peace and quietness and rest and without acts and exercises of the faculties. . . . The soul is alone, with an attentiveness and a knowledge, general and loving, as we said, but without any particular understanding, and averting not to what it is contemplating." [18] St. John points out to us that the beginning of this type of prayer may be scarcely perceptible. "It is true, however, that, when this condition first begins, this loving knowledge is hardly realized." [19]

St. John gives three signs which indicate that one should cease meditation and give oneself to this "loving attentiveness upon God." 1) A certain inability to employ reasonings and images in mental prayer. 2) The loss of all desire "to fix his meditation or his sense upon other objects besides God." 3) "The soul takes pleasure in being alone, and waits with loving attention on God." [20] To pass completely to this prayer of "loving attention to God" and give up all meditation, the soul must notice in itself not one or two of these signs but all three.

According to St. John of the Cross the passage from meditation to the "prayer of loving attentiveness to God" is ordinarily accomplished by going through a period of aridity which may be exceedingly bitter.[21] Besides the inability to

[18] *Ascent of Mount Carmel*, Bk. II, Chap. XIII, Peers's translation, Vol. I, p. 116.
[19] *Ibid.*, p. 117.
[20] *Ibid.*, pp. 115-116.
[21] *Dark Night of the Soul*, Book I, Chap. VIII.

meditate just spoken of: 1) the soul finds not only no consolation in the things of God, but also none in anything created; and 2) "Ordinarily the memory is centered upon God, with painful care and solicitude, thinking that it is not serving God but is back-sliding." [22]

The passage from meditation to the prayer of quiet involves, according to St. John of the Cross, the first purgation or night: the passive purgation of sense. Though he says that "the first purgation or night is bitter and terrible to sense," [23] he nevertheless points out that there are wide variations in the intensity and duration of this purgation.[24] So wide are these variations that one who would pay attention to things said about the terrors of this night might pass through it all unconsciously, and say to himself: I have entered the ways of contemplation without experiencing the passive purgation of sense.

We must remember that besides the specific difficulty that arises from the waning of the sweetness experienced in one's daily meditation and the delayed appearance of consolation derived from union with our Creator in the "prayer of loving attentiveness upon God," there are many trials, temptations, and sufferings, such as one experiences in all stages of the spiritual life. These seem to have no specific dependence on any degree of prayer or on passing from a lower to a higher degree. Many a virile soul, humbly relying on God's help, will take in stride some aridities, sufferings, and desolations and they will appear as nothing more than what is ordinarily to be expected. On the other hand, what is known as the manic-depressive temperament is subject to much more violent fluctuations of mood than are ever to be found in other types of temperament. St. John of the Cross himself points out that "these aridities might frequently proceed, not from the night and purgation of sensual desires aforementioned, but from sins and imperfections, or from weakness and luke-

[22] *Ibid.*, Chap. IX, p. 374.
[23] *Ibid.*, Chap. VIII, p. 371.
[24] *Ibid.*, Chap. XIV, p. 396.

warmness, or from some bad humor or disposition of the body." [25]

A remark of Poulain should be mentioned here: "I think that I have met with souls who have arrived at the mystic state without having passed through the night of the senses but only through other great trials which resulted in detachment. In the period previous to the prayer of quiet they felt a loving attention to God, which, however, had nothing bitter or painful about it." [26] One who derived his knowledge of the prayer of quiet from St. Teresa without having studied St. John of the Cross would be inclined to think that Poulain's findings would be the normal average experience.

V

Let us now turn to some examples of souls leading the interior life derived from the data of our questionnaire. The first is from a day laborer who truly leads an interior life. It seems that he experiences, at least sporadically, the prayer of quiet; and its peace sometimes accompanies him into his daily work.

When we look into the way in which a soul commences to lead an interior life, we find, as we would naturally expect, that God in some way makes the things and persons with which we come into contact in daily life act upon our mind and make us turn within ourselves where we find Him.

Take for instance the following report of this day laborer: "I commenced to lead a higher degree of the spiritual life about 5 years ago. It all came about because of my job. The place where I worked was around the corner from a small old church. Once a number of Catholic families lived in the neighborhood. But the district is now a business section; and the parish is dependent on small contributions that are made

[25] *Dark Night of the Soul*, Book I, Chap. IX, Peers's translation, Vol. I, p. 373.

[26] A. Poulain, S.J., *The Graces of Interior Prayer*, translated from the sixth edition, Kegan Paul, Trench, Truebner & Co., London, 1910, Chap. XV, p. 213.

by down-town workers. Because of the proximity of the church to my place of work, I commenced to go to Mass there every morning. Then I became a daily communicant.

"At the rear of the church was a well-stacked pamphlet rack, which I made use of frequently. These pamphlets were a convenient and ever-ready source of information concerning Jesus, our Lady, the saints and all manner of problems in religion and the spiritual life.

"So with faithful attendance at daily Mass and with daily communion and spiritual reading, my heart and mind have turned from worldly things to those of spirit and truth."

In this way he passed from Chautard's third to his sixth stage of the spiritual life and seems to be solidly established in an interior life of the soul with God. He makes no mention of any persons having played a role in the change that came over him. His conversion to a holy life was like the silent unseen working of the leaven "which a woman took and hid in three measures of meal, till the whole was leavened." [27] His elevation to higher things points out the apostolic value of a church in a downtown region, where the Masses are said at convenient hours, and the pastor places at the disposal of all a rack filled with well-chosen pamphlets.

His daily life is now well-leavened. "My mental prayer," he writes, "has not followed any systematic plan. It has been chiefly a monologue in which I have thanked God for His favors and blessings and asked Him for further favors." Sometimes at prayer his whole being is infused with the love of God and the peace of prayer follows him into the work of the day.

His self-denial, considering that his work is entirely rather heavy manual labor, might be termed vigorous. "No eating between meals. Usually no breakfast. No movies nor radio programs. Rather seldom look at TV. Place 50¢ in a mite box daily and when the coins have accumulated give them to the Society for the Propagation of the Faith. Rise at 4.30 A.M. Sundays to serve masses in a distant parish church." His life

[27] Luke XIII:21.

is not without mystic graces, such as: "It seems as if Christ were standing on my right side as I knelt in prayer and He was placing His left hand on my head." This consciousness of Christ's presence inflamed his love for God and urged him to closer conformity with His will.

His life has now been free for some time, not only from mortal sin, but also from all deliberate venial sin. It would seem that our Lord made that pamphlet rack play the role of a very efficient master of novices.

Physical illness can at times be associated with divine grace and turn one suddenly to an interior life.

"Some twenty years ago while I was visiting a nun crippled with arthritis, I heard an interior voice telling me that would be my condition in later years. I paid no attention to it as I thought my imagination was working. For many of those twenty years I led a life of tepidity.

"It was a few years ago, after a fall that injured my back, that I saw in some degree the condition of my soul. The Retreat Master advised me to read books on the Interior Life and have a director.

"As my back got worse and I was not able to do my work, I knelt before my crucifix and begged God to let me do my work even if I had to suffer. That interior voice again came, saying: 'Do you remember what you were told when you visited the invalid nun? Now is the time for its accomplishment.'

"I made an act of resignation. Some time after, when during one of the many periods of overwhelming joy, I asked our Lord why I, who was so sinful, should be receiving such favors. I heard within me this answer: 'It is because you are so sinful and miserable that I can manifest and glorify My mercy in you. You will suffer.' It seemed to me that I was shown a deep, dark abyss through which I would have to go. After raising my eyes from this terrible place, I saw at the other end of the abyss a brilliant white light which seemed to shine from behind a cloud. This filled me with unutterable joy. I suffer much, but experience a profound joy and peace. At times it seems that a spiritual loving embrace holds me."

Would one who is suspicious of all mystical experiences say that this nun has been in any way injured by her voices and visions? From her answer to question 11, we learn that her life flows on in sweet joy and a wonderful love of Christ, which is not interrupted by intense physical pain. And from question 14 we learn that the sufferings she experiences fill her with joy. Would anyone who looks upon all mystical experiences as nothing more than the natural activity of the imagination attribute this abiding joy and peace in the midst of intense physical pain to the natural resonance of mental imagery and not the result of God acting on the soul by divine grace? It is possible to *say* anything, but it is not possible to adequately *explain* the transformation of this soul and her joy in suffering without attributing it to God. Is there not a latent Pelagianism in the unreasonable antagonism of some to acknowledge the part played by divine grace in many mystical experiences?

The following account tells us how a soul left the house of the Father and was led back again. It exemplifies also the inadequacy of a Catholic home in which God and religion are secondary to worldly interests, and in which the importance of Catholic education is not understood. The world needs saints, but an adequate harvest is not to be expected until it is a general rule that the home is a school of the service of God.

"I was brought up a fairly conscientious, but not especially devout Catholic. At 18 years my attendance at Mass became only occasional for several years; and at 22 I left the Church completely and announced I did not believe in God. In addition to my personal culpability in this decision there were the influences of (1) professional education in a situation which made church attendance very difficult. This school was chosen for me by my parents; (2) my mother's death, my father's alcoholism and my brother's defection from the Church; and (3) a university education into pragmatism. All this sounds like 'making excuses'. The real cause of my leaving the Church was sloth and the neglect of grace. I really thought I did not believe in free will.

"After 13 years, I realized that I was all wrong. God granted me the grace to crawl back into the Church. It took some crawling, because I had married outside the Church, and I now had a time explaining to a suspicious and reluctant male why I was in the clutches of Rome after all these years. Through the prayers of the Blessed Mother of God, my marriage was rectified. I had never had much devotion to Mary as a child. No Catholic schools were available when I was little; but now I love her beyond expression.

"Before I returned to the Church, I went through several years of praying; at first to a God who might be; then with more confidence; then asking to know the truth, but with no idea that it would lead me home! I made up a religion of my own which had a proud lonely searching as its center. I never, however, attended a Protestant service. Prayer and reading the lives of the saints brought about my 'downfall'. One day I walked up and down in front of a Catholic church. Finally I went in and prayed at St. Mary's altar for her to tell me what to do. Then I went and knocked at the door of the rectory. Three months later my husband and I were married.

"After my return to the Church, for a considerable time, I had a logical and wholesome feeling of guilt and gratitude that kept me close to God. But, with the pressure of work, this wore off and I became quite self-satisfied, and glad to be only an 'average Catholic'.

"Then, by the grace of God, the most significant thing in my life happened: I mean, of course, aside from the sacraments. I became the close friend of a woman who had been an atheist all her adult life and who had sought happiness in kinds of relationships which could only bring bitterness. Although her work was such that she knew much about the intricacies of the human mind, normal and abnormal, she had been exceedingly unhappy. Then God called her, like Samuel, in the night; and like him, at first she did not know who was calling.

"I thank God every day of my life that I have had the experience of watching this soul grow, and for having been an instrument in God's hands to help her. We talked and read together till she was ready to take formal instructions. But her baptism and confirmation have not ended her growth nor mine. She helped me to grow because, like a teacher teaching a new subject, I had to keep one chapter ahead of the pupil.

"We want to be saints and are willing to suffer whatever is necessary. For myself, I am as inconstant as the moon at Mary's feet. A small trial comes and I forget my ardent prayers and firm resolutions. If trials could come with a large label, 'This is a Suffering,' I might do better. But to me it just looks like a blasted nuisance and I rebel. But I am, nevertheless, closer to God than ever before, and *seem to have an awareness of His presence even when I am deep in work.* I find a formal meditation difficult; but during the time allotted to mental prayer I *seem* to be praying wordlessly much of the time."

This history gives us an example of a definite separation between a conversion leading to return to the Church and entering on an interior life with God. It also shows the incomparable spiritual advantage of entering upon an inner spiritual life with God over a cheerful fulfillment of the minimum that the Church asks of every Catholic. Our respondent rose from Chautard's first degree to the sixth. Now mortal sin never occurs and venial sin is never deliberate. This is fundamental and essential in a holy life. Besides what is probably the prayer of quiet, which she seems to experience without recognizing it when "deep in work," there have been no mystic graces; but these are not necessary to perfection. She is determined to be a saint and is well along the way.

One respondent thus describes her preconversion period in the spiritual life: "For over twenty years I struggled along in religious life shackled by imperfections and indeliberate or, at most, semi-deliberate venial faults, mainly a tendency to criticism and censure: sometimes of my superior. I experienced difficulty in submitting my judgment in obedience. I was distracted and slothful in my spiritual exercises. Week after week in confession I accused myself of not putting sufficient effort into my spiritual exercises."

Then by a sudden grace, or series of graces, she entered immediately deep into the interior life of the soul with God.

"Not many years ago, during the annual retreat, the conference on the love of God started a series of movements in my soul. I was led to make a complete oblation of myself to God. In some way I cannot explain, this oblation gave me a power to carry out resolutions that I had never before known in all my life. I experienced many spiritual consolations in this retreat. The chief of these was a peculiar sense of *possessing* God in prayer. In return I made known to Him that I would give Him absolutely all.

"The faults I have mentioned above, as well as the habit of breaking silence three or four times a week, seemed to fall away from my soul with hardly an effort on my part. I stood in awe of what God did for me in so short a time. I gave myself completely to a life of silence and recollection. My whole being was filled with the love of God and an intense desire to love Him more and more. Loving Him became truly an 'obsession'. The love and longing for God now interrupted my work, as an active religious, as much as formerly my work had interrupted my prayer.

"As my love of God increased, so did my longing for prayer, solitude and penance. Nothing seemed too difficult to give to God and, one after the other, in quick succession, He asked for every creature comfort and satisfaction that a soul has to offer. I gave Him all that is in my power to give and begged Him to take by violence those things which the soul cannot give of itself. I began to realize what it is to live by *Love*.

"From the time of that retreat my prayer was filled with sweetness and consolations. I became immediately absorbed in God as soon as I took my place in chapel. Time meant nothing. An hour seemed like five minutes. I needed no book, no points or ideas. Love absorbed all my being. This was truly heaven on earth. I feared it could not last after the retreat was over. But it did, and for at least six months all was sweetness and consolations. This must be how God woos the soul until it is given to Him utterly. Then gradually there was less and less consolation until all became dry and desolate as it is now. All that remains is the conviction that I love God and would rather die than displease Him. Prayer-time seems to be filled with this idea and a constant reaching out for God. I can neither think nor imagine. Love is all. Is this the Dark Night of Faith? I can truthfully say that I seek no pleasure save in God; and I have no desire but to love Him perfectly. I long to go to the chapel to pray; but when I arrive there, I find myself dry and cold—in an agony of desolation. Still, I cannot make myself leave unless obedience or charity calls me.

"I was led to commit myself to a life of complete self-renunciation by a vow of Greater Perfection. My confessor finally consented. I now have it for a year. I have no choice left but to deny myself at every turn. But love makes this continual crucifixion sweet and easy. I am *all given to God* and have no desire but to love Him to folly. I obtained permission from the major superior and my confessor for various rather severe penances and extra periods of prayer.

"But God had different designs for me and made it known through my local superior. She insisted on my keeping the rule perfectly, and I did. She insisted that I add nothing to what the rule laid down; and I submitted. She happened to find out about some of my penitential practices. Then followed several months in which she criticized me for practically everything I was doing. I was subjected to the most humiliating scoldings I ever had in my life. But I can answer an unqualified 'Yes' to question 25 of the questionnaire, even though I was stripped of every penance and practice that was dear to me, even extra time for prayer. I now know what it means to be denied the satisfaction of every desire, even those that are spiritual. I felt it all so much that it seemed to me (you may not believe me) that I would die. But my confessor told me that God was closer to me then than He had ever been before; and all this was necessary for my perfect purification. I finally arrived at a state in which I could really thank God for all these difficulties and felt not the least bit of resentment toward my superior. She was but God's instrument. *Magnificat anima mea Dominum.*"

CHAPTER XII

The Development of the Interior Life

Whenever God leads the soul habitually to the practice of the prayer of quiet, it enters into a definitely higher state of the spiritual life. Previously the time set apart for mental prayer was not entirely occupied with God. One found oneself, perhaps, watching the clock to see how many minutes before one can "get to work and do something." But with the habitual appearance of the prayer of quiet, one wants ever to prolong the period allotted to mental prayer if this is in any way possible. In the *horarium* of many religious communities such prolongation is not possible. One must pass to the duties of the day. But one then finds, perhaps, that when one passes to the duties of the day, the "loving attentiveness to God" abides in the midst of work without in any way interfering with what one has to do.

In this period of one's spiritual life, various unnecessary interests are still indulged in. In our day, much time is spent in reading the newspapers, radio, television, theatergoing, novel reading, and, by the cultured, in more worthwhile pursuits, such as studying another language or the history of some period, the reading of good historical biographies, and various other wholesome pursuits. For one living in the world a few wholesome interests are important and perhaps even necessary. But it is sometimes a pity to see a religious finding much time for the "latest books that everybody reads," and, perhaps, not giving full time to spiritual duties of obligation.

After one has entered into closer contact with God by the prayer of quiet and maintained it for some time, one may be given one or more of the mystic graces. These inflame greatly one's love of God and strengthen consecration to all that pertains to God. The same result is at times brought about merely by the development of the prayer of quiet to the higher stages of its perfection.

Among the mystic graces is one that St. Teresa termed the *prayer of union*. She attempts to describe thus its essential character. "For as long as such a soul is in this state, it can neither see nor hear nor understand. The period is always short and seems to the soul even shorter than it really is. God implants Himself in the interior of that soul in such a way, that, when it returns to itself, it cannot possibly doubt that God has been in it and it has been in God." [1]

Many holy souls never experience at all this prayer of union. With St. Teresa of Avila it was a frequent occurrence. It is readily seen that even one or a few such experiences would be a powerful influence in strengthening the union of mind, will, and heart with God. At all events when the union of the soul with God becomes very intimate, it rises to another level of prayer and a higher stage of the interior life.[2] This stage is characterized by experiencing an inner call to lay aside *all unnecessary* activities, such as those mentioned above, and devoting *all free time* to communing with God in prayer.

One must, however, realize that there is occasion here for self-deception. I remember a lay sister who told her superiors that God had called her to a life of prayer, and she was now

[1] *Interior Castle*, Vol. V, p. i, Peers's translation, Vol. II, p. 251.
[2] The "prayer of union" may be desired and even asked of God. But mystic graces such as visions, locutions, and ecstasies should neither be desired nor asked of God. See below, pp. 297 ff.

unable to do any manual work at all. She felt she should spend the day alone in her room or in the chapel. And I remember, too, a choir nun in an active community who felt herself called to a solitary life in her cell and refused to take her place in choir or engage in any kind of work. God does not call anyone to lay aside the rule one has vowed to practice and to disobey one's superiors. The call we speak of here is merely to lay aside *unnecessary* activities that are not worth while and give the time to God that was formerly frittered away in trifles. What is of obedience or important in one's work must not be neglected. The problem is akin to that of the injudicious choice of electives in college or university work. Many a career has been marred by running after the interest of the moment without keeping in mind the goal of life.

The "little way" of St. Thérèse of Lisieux keeps one from indulging in will-o'-the-wisps. But after some progress in the prayer of quiet, the union of the soul with God becomes so intimate that a sense of fidelity to Christ, the spouse of the human soul, seems to demand the sacrifice of all that can be sacrificed in order to be alone with God.

Question 16 in our list was designed to discover whether or not a respondent might have attained to anything like the prayer of union as defined above. It reads: "Have you ever entered into a state of prayer in which, though you can neither see, hear, nor understand, God seems to have so entered into your soul, that when you return to yourself, you cannot possibly doubt that you have been in God and God has been in the depths of your being?"

Question 12c asks: "Do you devote to mental prayer all the time you can possibly spare?"

Is there any tendency for questions 16 and 12c to be associated? What is known as Yule's coefficient of association is a simple method of finding this out. When this coefficient is $+1$, there is a necessary connection between two items; when it is -1, the two items are mutually exclusive. When it is o, there is no relation between the two.[3] We found a coefficient of +0.52 in 192 cases. This means that, for some reason, devoting all the time you possibly can to mental prayer is more likely than not to be associated with the prayer of union. But we know aliunde that one cannot bring about the prayer of union by devoting all one's free time to mental prayer. Therefore, the prayer of union has a tendency to invite one to turn to God whenever one can possibly do so.

II

After St. Teresa has described the prayer of union in the first chapter of the Fifth Mansion, she tells in the second chapter how it works a sudden transformation in the soul. "It finds itself longing to suffer great trials and unable to do otherwise. It has the most vehement desires for penance, for solitude, and for all to know God." [4] "It neither knows nor desires anything save that God shall do with it what He wills." [5]

In the next chapter she takes up an important problem.

---

[3] Yule's coefficient is obtained by the following simple procedure. The data are arranged in a four-place table thus:

	12c present	12c absent
16 present	a = 37	b = 37
16 absent	c = 28	d = 90

Number of cases with:
  a = first and second trait both present
  b = first trait absent, second trait present
  c = first trait present, second trait absent
  d = both traits absent

$$\text{The coefficient} = \frac{ad - bc}{ad + bc} = \frac{3330 - 1046}{3330 + 1046} = 0.52$$

One can easily see that the maximum of the function is +1; the minimum −1; and that when the two traits are found together only by chance, the function fades to zero.

[4] *Interior Castle*, Vol. V, p. ii, Peers's translation, Vol. II, p. 255.
[5] *Ibid.*, p. 257.

Are the graces granted through the prayer of union necessary in order to attain to a perfect love of God, that is, to an identity in all that we will with what God wills for us? And the answer is: No. "Despite all I have said, this Mansion seems to me a little obscure. There is a great deal to be gained by entering it, and those from whom the Lord withholds such supernatural gifts will do well to feel that they are not without hope; for true union can quite well be achieved, with the favor of our Lord, if we endeavor to attain it by not following our own will but submitting it to whatever is the will of God." [6] In other words, by co-operation with the ordinary grace of God we can rise to a level of sanctity equivalent to that of those who are elevated to the prayer of union.[7] Does God, then, arbitrarily make things easy for some of us and hard for others? No, whatever God does is done with infinite wisdom, justice, and love. Some, perhaps, are given the mystic graces because they are weaklings; and some are left without them because they are more vigorous. But there are many other reasons known to Him Whose ways are inscrutable and which we can never fathom.

St. Teresa points out a certain advantage in being deprived of the mystic graces. "But note very carefully, daughters, that the silkworm has of necessity to die; and it is this which will cost you most; for death comes more easily when one can see oneself living a new life, whereas our duty now is to continue living this present life, and yet to die of our own free will. I confess to you that we shall find this much harder, but it is of the greatest value and the reward will be greater too if you [8] gain the victory. But you must not doubt the possibility of this true union with the will of God. This is the union which I have desired all my life; it is for this I continually beseech Our Lord; it is this which is the most genuine and the safest." [9]

[6] *Ibid.*, Chap. III, p. 259.
[7] For a description of this prayer see above, p. 212.
[8] "You," that is, who do not experience the prayer of union and other mystic graces.
[9] *Op. cit.*, p. 260.

The mystery of the wide divergencies in the number and types of the graces that God bestows on souls that try to lead, one and all, an interior life cannot be cleared unless we bear in mind the true nature of divine charity. Let us recall to mind the words of St. Thomas Aquinas on this point.[10]

We attain our union with God by charity. And charity alone is the measure of our perfection. "Anything is perfect in so far as it attains its proper end, which means the final perfection of a thing. But it is charity which unites us to God, Who is the final end of the human mind. For he that abideth in charity abideth in God, and God in him. And, therefore, the perfection of Christian life is above all measured by charity."[11] And again: "The perfection of Christian life consists fundamentally (per se) and essentially in charity, manifesting itself mainly in the love of God and secondarily in the love of our neighbor."[12]

Now what is charity? In solving this point St. Thomas points out that there are two groups of things that human beings desire. One group can be perceived by the senses and give rise to sensory cravings. The other group can be known only by the intellect and man chooses them by a free and responsible art of the will. God cannot be perceived by the senses and so cannot be the object of mere sensory craving. He can only be known by the intellect and therefore sought by volitional consecration. Charity therefore is an act and a virtue of the will.[13]

One consecrates oneself to God by accepting the will of God. The more perfectly, and completely, and without reservation of any kind we accept the divine will, the more perfect is our charity. In various places St. Teresa points out to us that the mystic graces, one and all, are powerful aids and lead to almost overwhelming impulses to accept without any reservation absolutely all that God wills. Then, as we have

---

[10] See also pp. 8, 282.
[11] *Summa Theologia*, 2. 2. Q. CLXXXIV, i.
[12] *Ibid.*, Art. iii.
[13] See *ibid.*, Q. XXIV, i.

just seen, she points out that they are not necessary to perfect union with the divine will in which is to be found perfect charity.

Bearing that in mind, we can understand that God wants the general picture of the spiritual life to present an endless variety of variations. If he gives no mystic graces he will give ordinary graces which will lead the soul to the same end: perfect charity.

Who can say that God cannot lead a soul to perfect union of its human will with the divine will, unless he bestows contemplative prayer (the prayer of quiet) and perhaps other mystic graces? In our investigation we found a number of beautiful simple souls who carefully prepare at night the morning's meditation. Some of them report that they are leading a life free from any fully deliberate sin of any kind. Who can say that their charity is inferior to that of others who have been granted mystic graces and have ascended to the heights of contemplative prayer? Who can say that the hospital sister, faithful to her rule and busy all day or all night long with the care of the sick, cannot attain to perfect charity by the love of God and the sick?

We have but to pose the question in its true light to see that God certainly can lead souls to the heights of perfection, without any of the mystic graces, not even the prayer of quiet.

While this is true it would seem from our investigation that most souls experience at some time, at least, a taste of the prayer of quiet. It is also clear, from the cases we shall cite,[14] that a day of hard work in the home may be accompanied by the unbroken glow of the love of God and an almost continuous consciousness of the Divine Presence.

III

Let us present here a respondent who now leads a life free from any fully deliberate sin and therefore has attained to a

14 See below, p. 218.

high degree of the love of God, but who enjoys very little of the joy and sweetness of the contemplative life.

"The lowest degree in my spiritual life was somewhere between 4 and 5 on Chautard's scale. I never committed a fully deliberate sin in my life. Though I am sure I did things at times which by their nature were mortal sins. But at the time I did them, I felt that they were not mortal. I have since wondered about this, because when I committed them, I knew that they were supposed to be grave. I never gave much thought to venial sin, but never felt I was choosing sin in preference to God. Even at times of sin I could always talk to God, which I have done freely all my life. I think now it all sums up to the fact that I thought it impossible for this wonderful person to commit a mortal sin. I never did any penance, expressly for my sins, other than that given in the confessional.

"In my present life venial sin is truly never deliberate. It is slipped into at times through half advertence. I deeply regret it, but wonder if it is *fervently* atoned for. I guard against imperfections and resist them heartily.

"As to my prayer, I make an hour of mental prayer every day, following methods suggested by St. Teresa of Avila, whose writings appeal to me more than those of any other. I put myself in the presence of God, then try to be present at some scene of the Passion of Christ; then realize that my mind has been for some time wandering all over everywhere. Sometimes I make little acts to bring it back, but it goes right off again. Sometimes I am not conscious that my mind or imagination is working thus, but sometimes I am; but I never deliberately stop prayer to think about other things. My mind is generally in a peacefully blank state. I find that a reasoned out meditation is difficult and have done so for some time. But I cannot control my imagination, that is, the flow of my thoughts. This is especially true when household chores have piled up and are waiting for me to attend to them.

"The only good thing I can say about my prayer is that

I keep at it faithfully. But it is becoming more and more of a chore, and the time drags. But every day I go to Church and make my attempt at prayer for an hour before the Blessed Sacrament. I could scarcely prolong it and get through my work.

"Throughout the day I try to keep recollected all the time I can. I keep close to God and my favorite saints all day long; but formal prayer is usually a chore. Once at prayer, about 6 years ago, I had what may have been some kind of special spiritual experience. I had been thinking on the passage in St. John of the Cross treating of all things having been created in Him and of His giving them beauty by a glance: a favorite thought of mine. Suddenly I felt seized, held in space in some way I cannot explain. I felt a bit frightened and thought: What is happening to me? I felt that in some way God was certainly present. Then it passed: all in a matter of seconds. I told my director. He made no comments. This director is no longer in the place where I live. My great trouble is to find anyone who will direct my soul. I must get along as well as I can by myself. None of the priests to whom I can now go is interested in my interior life or will give me help in my life of prayer.

"After completing my education, I became something of a 'career woman' and lived a rather worldly life. But after some years God seemed to call me, and I began more and more to turn to Him. At that time I commenced to go to Mass every day. Some years ago, I resigned my position to lead a quiet contemplative life in the world. And for some months lived as it were on retreat. My mother became very ill and I returned home. Since she died I have been keeping house and caring for my aged father.

"My works of self-denial consist in denying myself in all things as much as my nature can bear: little things that come up every minute. Needless to say I fail oftener than I succeed. I follow St. John of the Cross in *striving* to choose the least desirable; and in other things he suggests. I don't practise any afflictive penances. Once each night, when I awaken,

I get up and kneel for five minutes of prayer. Once a week, on Thursdays, when I awaken during the night, I get up and pray for an hour. I now often fail in this, but am gradually getting back to it again. It is very painful; and it has gotten so that it is definitely grace that pushes me out of bed—not my own effort at all. My self-denial goes on all day long: refraining from asking curious questions; eyes pretty well mortified most of the time; no worldly amusements, except when family life demands TV to keep an aging father company, or a movie once or twice a year when charity demands it; no flavoring on foods at table, and so on. The Sacrament of the moment calls in the home for much self-denial.

"The several years I spent in retirement away from home, but still in the world, served to teach me principles. But now I am again in the home, I find I am the same old person, with the same old faults and weaknesses. They were dormant during my learning period away from old situations. So now I am faced with a great desire for perfection, but no virtue. I commit the same old faults, even now in the light of the knowledge of perfection that God has given me. This is my great cross."

Such souls should remember that perfection is essentially the love of God, the consecration of ourselves to Him Who made us and redeemed us, Jesus Christ the Saviour of man. The strength of this consecration, that is, the degree of charity we possess, is not measured by the fervor of love, but by what love endures and puts up with for the sake of Christ. Charity "beareth all things, believeth all things, hopeth all things, endureth all things." [15] Such a soul should recall the words of the Apocalypse: "Behold, I come quickly: hold fast that which thou hast, that no man take thy crown. He that shall overcome, I will make him a pillar in the temple of my God; and he shall go out no more." [16]

One should not be too much disturbed about the persist-

[15] I Corinthians XIII:7.
[16] Apocalypse III:11-12.

ence of habitual faults. Some faults are likely to cling to the soul until it attains the state of spiritual matrimony or its equivalent. Thus St. John of the Cross writes: "Until the soul attains to this state of perfection [spiritual matrimony] whereof we are speaking, however spiritual it may be, there ever remains to it a little flock, as it were, consisting of some of its desires and petty tastes and other of its imperfections— sometimes natural, sometimes spiritual—after which it goes, endeavoring to pasture them while following them and satisfying them." [17] Sometimes one leading a deeply spiritual life is humbled by involuntary manifestations of impatience. Few indeed ever attain to the state of spiritual matrimony, but all the mystic graces tend to eliminate imperfections.

The one who wrote the above account has been given few mystic graces. It is for her to kill the worm of selfishness herself with the aid of God's ordinary grace. With perseverance this will be accomplished, and as St. Teresa says, such a victory is more meritorious than one attained easily and quickly by the mystic graces.

Quite a different picture is the following; but God alone can say which soul is superior to the other. We can only say: The one who loves God more. But to determine which one does so is beyond our power. The account is valuable as a rather detailed history of the development of the interior life.

A nun tells us how her mother was wont to pray that all her children would be priests or religious. And as they came along she begged God earnestly and persistently that none of them would ever commit a mortal sin. The nun's childhood was spent playing with her brothers and so she became something of an athlete. Her mother urged her to pray for a "vocation" and she did so, saying: "Teach me Thy will in my regard: just so it is not to be a sister."

However, during grade school she went to Mass every day. In high school she had plenty of dances, dates, and parties over and above her studies. "The thought of a voca-

[17] *Spiritual Canticle*, Stanza XXVI, Peers's translation, Vol. II, p. 336.

tion became distasteful to me. But towards the end of high school, dances and dates had lost their thrill. God commenced to speak to my soul. I thought of the Judgment and that then our Lord would say: 'Why weren't you in the convent?' I thought I would say: 'Because I didn't like it.' But I knew I couldn't justify that unless I had tried it. The next step was to think out how I could try out convent life, find out I didn't like it, come back and continue where I had left off."

Some of her girl friends told her about their intention of entering the convent. She decided to enter with them. "I assured everyone I would be back by Thanksgiving, or at least by Christmas. I entered, but found out I loved the convent. Years have passed: the happiest of my life. I am now a professed Sister and have never regretted a day in the convent.

"From the time of my Novitiate, I have always desired to be a saint. However, I was far from recollected and most of my efforts remained mere prayers in the chapel. This went on until I made my pre-profession year at the Motherhouse previous to the making of my final profession. It was during that time that I determined to strive for real sanctity. The next year, I got the marvelous grace of loving the Little Flower and really understanding the value of her 'Little Way'. (I am ashamed to say that when her autobiography was read in the refectory when I was a postulant, I had a great aversion for her which was not dispelled until I read this book myself some years later.)

"From then on, I gave into her charge my family to make into saints as she would make her own family, and I adopted her for my 'Novice Mistress'. Since then, she has obtained for me so many graces that I have speedily gained many things which I earnestly tried to obtain myself before but could never acquire, especially a little more recollection and a greater awareness of the indwelling of the Blessed Trinity. She also taught me to say the Stations with greater devotion and to love the Passion and to desire to make reparation. One day she gave me the inspiration, while in retreat, to be Our

Lord's little towel and his Simeon. When I wondered how to do this, I thought of her little way of doing little things for this intention. I determined to do everything for others and to be cheerful as a means of wiping Our Lord's face and comforting Him in His Passion.

"Sin began to grieve me much more; especially when I would hear of crimes, I would feel very sorry for Our Lord and make acts of reparation and love to Him.

"In 1953 I read the life of the Curé of Ars which inspired me with a deep appreciation of the value of penance and prayer in trying to lead others to holiness. This was especially applicable in the classroom. From his example I realized the value of crosses so I asked Jesus to give me a deep love for the cross and a sincere desire to be despised with Him if it were for His greater glory. Seemingly, that prayer was answered in the fact that I was sent to a mission to teach where the priest had recently had a nervous breakdown and was suffering mentally from it.

"Recently I made a retreat under a very boring retreat master. After three days I felt I was wasting time because he dwelt on ridding oneself of sin. Although I know I could easily fall into sin if God wouldn't help me, I am confident he will keep me from it because about three years ago, during retreat, I begged Him to let me die rather than again offend Him in the slightest way. Since then, He has kept me from— at least knowingly—offending Him. Although I have committed many faults, I think he lets me have this humiliation for my own good and doesn't take any offense. (Like a little baby who slaps his mother and pulls her hair when she stoops to kiss him in his cradle.) However, God made use of this retreat to lead me to read the revelations of St. Gertrude from which I gained many graces. I offered to exchange hearts with Jesus. I know he gets the least of the bargain but in a way He gets more since He can change my heart into a furnace of Love while, at the same time, I can be loving Him with His. I also learned from this book that one can save so many souls through desires (which fits in with the little way of

St. Thérèse and also by St. Gertrude's way of saying the litany of the Saints for the Poor Souls).

"One last thing is the lesson of littleness which St. Thérèse taught me. She makes me see in babies and children so many ideas of God's ways with us. I have been able to see that there is no need to fear death, which so many do, but rather to welcome it as a wonderful eternal 'home visit'.

"It seems that I forgot to mention the most important of all: the Blessed Mother's help which began when I was consecrated to her by my mother shortly after I was born. Later, in 1947 or '48, I made my own consecration (of Bl. De Montfort). I'm sure this is what started my devotion to the Little Flower since our Blessed Lady surely knew that was best for me.

"I don't have any special way of praying except just talking to Our Lord and telling Him that I want to be a great saint. This is necessary now because so many terrible things are happening that need a great saint to make reparation. Then I follow St. Gertrude and St. Mechtilde's method of offering to Jesus all the love of all hearts, from the beginning of the world to the end, in union with His Divine Love in reparation for sinners. I offer His Heart—which I feel He gave me—to have for the conversion of sinners.

From this description of her mental prayer there would seem to be little therein of the prayer of quiet. But from her answers to question 15 we learn that it appears usually, and often the peace follows her into the work of the day.

When she asked Jesus to trade hearts with her so that she could love Him and His Mother perfectly, she felt that He "took me up" on her request, and experienced something akin to the prayer of union. The "heart" is the symbol of the inner life of man. The granting of this request does not signify a physical exchange of hearts but the enabling of the creature to love Christ in some measure as Christ loves us. Thus she writes: "After I offered to exchange hearts, I felt very much in love with our Lord and determined never to displease Him in the slightest way."

I V

There are souls who attain to a high degree of divine charity with no mystic graces other than the prayer of quiet. They live a life of complete freedom from anything like coldly deliberate venial sins or imperfections. It may seem to them that they are entirely free from even semivoluntary sins and imperfections; but as explained below [18] this is a matter that God alone can decide. A mortal sin or a deliberate venial sin stands out very clearly in consciousness. But a momentary loss of emotional control, not manifested exteriorly, could pass without one being aware of it.

Souls in this class have an abiding consciousness of the Divine Presence. Their whole life flows on *for years* in what seems to them an unbroken consciousness of the Divine Presence while their whole being glows with the warmth of divine charity. In their daily routine they are living examples of Martha and Mary working together. Let us consider the following description of a married woman's daily routine.

"At six o'clock, the Angelus in a nearby church rings. I awake to offer up a new day to God. I say to Him: Thanks be to Thee, O God, for another day to do your Holy Will. I say my Angelus and assist spiritually at the Holy Mass I know is going on. I arise and attend Holy Mass at 7:00, receive Holy Communion, return home and get breakfast for my husband, my daughter and myself. Then I return to hear the 8:00 and 8:30 Masses. Sometimes I am privileged to have another Holy Mass at the side altar.

"During the day I am always thinking of God. Since He told me 'my delight is to dwell with the children of men,' it is easy for me to live with Him and dismiss the cares of the world. Free from these cares, every act of my day becomes a prayer.

"After my Masses, I go to the store and get my groceries.

[18] P. 289.

My shopping becomes spiritual. I say Hello! to everyone with a smile. Once the clerk at a store said to me: 'Why are you always smiling?' I said: 'To gain more merit for heaven.' I am not disturbed by sharp remarks from anyone. They produce a genuine feeling of joy. I want to be like Christ and I am happy if some thoughtless person makes a cutting remark or if I hear of something mean so-and-so said of me. I want all such things that I may be more like Christ.

"Having finished my shopping, I come back home, put away my groceries, wash my breakfast dishes, make the beds, clean house or wash and iron the clothes. At 12:00 I get lunch. Then I say my daily Rosaries. The Rosary brings me closer to the Blessed Virgin and her divine Son. I love to contemplate the sufferings of Christ and my own wretchedness. The Lives of the Saints, the pleas of Bishop Sheen, the mortifications of Father Louis astonish me with their humility. At various times I read the Bible, Bishop Sheen, Thomas Merton and G. M. Hopkins.

"I get supper at 6:00. After supper we chat until my daughter resumes her studies. Then I meditate on the love of God. I never want to lose it."

In filling out the questionnaire she placed seven as the lowest degree she was ever in during her whole life. Having her address, I wrote to her. She replied: "In answer to your question, Father, I do think that No. 7 is the lowest state I was ever in,[19] with the help of God. I have never thought of offending God and have bent my will to His as far back as I can remember. I never had any problem of not believing, because God was always my true and constant friend."

Another presents a similar picture:

"On awakening in the morning I offer up to Christ the prayers, works and sufferings of the day. I ask Christ to help me to share one small part of His agony in the Garden or some of the sufferings of the Blessed Virgin. Then I get ready to go to Mass. On Sundays the whole family goes together. On weekdays I go with my mother. Christ comes

---

[19] See below, p. 289.

to me every morning in Holy Communion to solve my problems and to share His strength; and I beg Him never to be
deprived of His love. I adore Him, and recite the 'prayer
before a crucifix' and 'Soul of Christ sanctify me', and thank
Him for all His many gifts.

"Then we go home for breakfast. On Sundays I do my
studies for the graduate courses I am taking or talk to my
mother about God. In the evening we all listen to the Ave
Maria hour. Before going to bed I say my fifteen decades
of the Rosary for my sister. I ask St. Maria Goretti to take
care of my mother.

"On week-days I take the bus after my breakfast for the
place where I am working. During the day I pray God to
keep me calm and full of love. I fall too many times into
annoyances and melancholy. I seem to forget to be gentle
like my mother and that Christ loves all creatures. But I
speak to Christ and the Blessed Virgin during the day to help
me to be good and remember my purpose on earth and ask
for patience and perseverance.

"My mental prayer extends over my entire day. It commences with my joy in the new morning: another day to
praise God. It continues during the day with fervent prayers
that I may show forth His image. I cannot let Christ be for
a single second. No, that is not literally true. He gives me a
peace in the morning which is brilliant the whole day long
with the glow of God. This peace gleams from time to time
with my prayers. I marvel at the patience of Christ. He seems
to await so humbly my spare moments. His light makes me
childlike and joyous. He never lets you go. Nothing inter-
rupts my peace. Pain disappears without a mental blow.
Something makes me thirst for humiliations but I hesitate
at the thought of great sufferings; but yearn to take them
all with consuming love.

"At 5:00 I leave for home and the saintly atmosphere of
my mother. Then there is joy and my childlike soul soars
again. In the evening I study or talk about my silly problems
with my mother. At nine we have night prayers together. I

then get ready to go to bed. I say my rosary, kneeling with arms outstretched at the sorrowful mysteries. I ask God to bear with me. My sister speaks of God with delight on her lips and love in her eyes. I have not even touched the lowest rung of a meditative life." [20]

V

We have been giving pictures of the daily experience of the soul that leads an interior life with God. It is the author's opinion that this should be the typical life of the Christian, no matter whether he lives and works among the laity in the world or is a priest or a member of an active or contemplative order. All work for God should proceed from God Who abides in our souls and has deigned to accomplish many things in and through and by the co-operation of men. Hence all Christians should be given instruction in mental prayer and the life of the soul with God. It is true that many adults are no longer capable of assimilating this instruction. But any normal mother who has received and assimilated such instruction can impart it to any normal child. If every home were a school of the service of God, all the world would soon be spiritually transformed. The present work is one little contribution to bring this about.

Let us take now an example of one who has not penetrated far into the interior life. The respondent is, by self-estimation, at present in Chautard's fifth degree.

We will repeat parts of our schema, giving our respondent's answers to the questions.

1. Can you say that you have forsaken all that is sinful and all that is not God in order to attain God? *Yes.*

2. Can you say that you seek God without ceasing? *Try to but not always successful!*

3. Does your love of God give enthusiasm to all you do for Him? *Mostly. Sometimes the line of routine makes things a trial.*

[20] This respondent rates six as the lowest degree of her spiritual life.

4. Do you feel that you cannot say with certainty that you are spiritually superior to anyone? *Yes.*

5. Do you believe in your inmost heart that you are lower and viler than all? *No. I can't say I honestly do.*

6. Do you seek yourself in nothing, not even asking God for spiritual consolations; but, forgetting self, are you ever interested in finding something to do that will please God? *No. Just occasionally!*

7. Do you really suffer and is it painful to you to remain on earth because you want to be united at once with Christ in heaven? *There's no doubt but that I'd love to be in heaven with Christ, but I do not suffer because I am not.*

8. Have you a consciousness of running, in your spiritual life, with great rapidity towards God and a perfect life, as the hart to the living waters? *I strive to move forward but I certainly am not conscious of any great rapidity—it is slow plodding!*

9. Have you a sense of such freedom from sin and all that is not God that you approach God in prayer with great intimacy and boldness and yet God seems to invite and not rebuke you? *Yes.*

10. Can you say, "I have found Him Whom my soul loveth. I held Him and I will not let Him go." And does your union with Christ rise at times to such heights that, were moments to broaden into eternity, you would seem to possess the joy of eternal life? *Yes to the first part, but I have never reached any "heights."*

11. Does your life flow on in a sweet joy and a wonderful love of Christ which is not interrupted even by intense physical pain or great mental trials and sufferings? *No.*

12. (a) Describe on a special sheet of paper the usual way in which you make your mental prayers. *I still use a book but try to talk it over with God and apply it to myself.*

(b) Do you often prolong the period set apart for mental prayer? *No, we have to keep moving along!*

(c) Do you devote to mental prayer all the time you can possibly spare? *No.*

13. What works of self-denial and bodily penance do you usually practice? *Self-denial of speech—not expressing unfavorable opinions—the unkind word—minding my own business. Penance—bearing the physical ills I have cheerfully—in reparation.*

14. (a) Can you say that you really thirst for sufferings? *No.* For humiliations? *No.* And desire like Christ to be reputed with the wicked? *No.*

(b) Can you say that you would at least suffer such things patiently recognizing in them God's will for you? *Yes. I would certainly try to, if and when they come my way.*

15. In mental prayer do you ever enter into a period of profound peace with your whole being infused with the love of God, a peace which remains in spite of the mind wandering at times away from God? *Yes.* Is your prayer habitually of this character? *No.* Does the peace continue after your period of prayer is over, and accompany you into the work of the day? *Sometimes—often I might say!*

16. Have you ever entered into a state of prayer in which, though you can neither see, hear, nor understand, God seems to have so entered into your soul, that when you return to yourself, you cannot possibly doubt that you have been in God and God has been in the depths of your being? *No.*

17. In prayer has your love of God so absorbed you that the body lost sensation of itself for some seconds? *I don't think so.*

18. Have you ever entered into a state in which you lost all awareness of your surroundings and sensation of all kinds and were completely absorbed in God? *No.*

19. Have you ever heard any interiorly spoken words (or experienced them intellectually) that seemed to come in some manner direct from God? *Yes.*

20. Have you experienced any imaginal or other consciousness of the presence of Christ or our Lady of the Saints, or have you seen them as it were right before you as sensory objects? *No—just imagined.*

21. And did such experiences inflame greatly your love of God and urge you to a closer conformity with His will? *Yes, of course, every time I imagined myself in the actual presence of Christ or Our Lady.*

"*My answers to all following questions is: No. Thank you, it makes me think.*"

Our respondent is evidently a good and holy soul, but seems by no means to have risen to the heights of the spiritual life that might have been attained with kindly stimulation by superiors and the guidance of a good spiritual director. I must speak here with considerable reserve and point out that I can only point to superficial appearances. There is a simplicity and humility in her account of herself that is very beautiful; and God alone knows what more may lie behind appearances. Without this simplicity and humility there can be no genuine life of the soul with God. But our Lord, as we shall see, wants to lead us on to something that brings us much closer to Him: a conscious realization of his abiding presence in the depths of our being: "I in them, and Thou in Me: that they may be made perfect in one: and the world may know that Thou hast sent Me and hast loved them as Thou hast also loved Me." [21]

Our respondent makes no shadow of a complaint about the lack of spiritual direction, but many do. If a subject allows himself to feel rebellious about this lack, it is a spiritual imperfection; or, perhaps, semivoluntary venial sin. God will never allow a soul to suffer because guidance and spiritual direction are lacking if that soul does all it can, with the grace God gives it, to conform its will absolutely with the divine will.

Let us, by way of contrast, present one more picture of the inner life of the soul with God.

Our respondent came of a good Catholic family. The family Rosary as a child was her first introduction to the spiritual life, and still remains a source of strength and consolation. She has not outlined the stages through which she

[21] John XVII:23.

came to her present spiritual state. But, at present, she is in Chautard's seventh degree of the spiritual life. She experiences the hunger for the Holy Eucharist there mentioned, and yearns for heaven. She speaks of dreading to leave the chapel in the morning where "the intimacy with Christ was so wonderful and return to the workaday world," even though she knows that Christ will accompany her every step she makes. When school is out "I almost run home to get to Him in the Blessed Sacrament even though He has been with me all day long. It is a case of carrying Him to Himself to adore and praise Him on the way and in the tabernacle.

"I talk to Him in my soul's depths almost constantly. I pray much for others. There are hundreds of people I tell Him about. Though teaching, I lead a life of prayer. My mind and heart are ever alert to think of Christ and speak with Him all day long. I have never changed in my love for Him: through my high school days, novitiate on through many years of community life. I've weakened at times, fallen, picked myself up, but always struggled onward; never at a standstill."

She makes use of various ruses to be spiritually alone and commune with Christ. Thus, when the teachers attended in a body a moving picture in the school theater, she closed her eyes during the whole performance and entered into a period of intimate communion with Christ.

There is a high degree of true union of her will with that of God. "I desire to advance much further in the spiritual life. But, perhaps, God does not will to give me more. In that case, I will exactly *what He* wills: nothing else, nothing more. I am gradually getting closer, but I am so weak."

Sometimes those in an active order live a life such as that just depicted, and feel that they are out of place and should leave their work and enter a strictly cloistered community. But the fact that one in an active order is lifted to a high degree of contemplative union with God does not by any means prove that God has called such a one to a strictly cloistered community. It is most pleasing to God when those in an active order do everything possible to do all their work and lead an interior life with Him. The fight to find and use all possible spare moments for communion with God is a most meritorious struggle.

VI

We have already seen that a profound peace, with one's whole being infused with the love of God which continues during prayer in spite of distractions and sometimes passes over into the work of the day, is by no means rare in the experience of those who lead a spiritual life. This experience, often to be identified with what St. Teresa called the prayer of quiet, is the flowering of sanctifying grace,[22] the spiritual life of the mystical body of Christ. Children commence to experience it in its beginnings when they receive Holy Communion. Thousands know it in their morning Mass and their Holy Communion and their living in the Divine Presence when they go forth to their daily duties. Christ intended that it would develop normally from the sacrament of the Eucharist. "My flesh is meat indeed and My blood is drink indeed. He that eateth My flesh and drinketh My blood abideth in Me and I in him. As the living Father hath sent Me and I live by the Father: so he that eateth Me, the same also shall live by Me." [23]

In discussing the concept of "life" as applied to God, St. Thomas starts by establishing its meaning in the language of everyday life. He points out that we distinguish two classes of objects in everyday experience. The first class never moves except when set in motion by some exterior force. As an example we might mention the dust on a dry road, lifted up in clouds by the wind. As objects in the other class we might point to plants that expand in height and width by some kind of force from within; and animals that move about by the action of their own muscles.

St. Thomas then broadens the concept to include the men-

[22] See Chapter V above, specifically p. 97.
[23] John VI:56-58.

tal life of man, who by intellect can conceive of an ideal and organize all his activities to its attainment. This intellectual life of man vastly exceeds in its dignity the growth of plants and the sensory pursuits of the animal world.

But the intellectual life of God infinitely exceeds that of man. God's knowledge has no limits either in time or in content. Furthermore, God not only has intellect but is by nature Infinite Understanding, and as St. Thomas says: "He has the most perfect and eternal life because His intellect is the most perfect and is always in action." [24]

And so, through the sacrament of the Eucharist, we are destined, when we attain the fullness of our spiritual development, even here on earth to live by Christ and in some manner share that life which He lives by the Father. This is a Christ-like life of conscious union of intellect and will with God Whom we know as Infinite Truth, and love as the Supreme and Eternal Good. This Eucharistic life is not a life of individuals, living independently as individuals, but as Christians incorporated into one spiritual, organic whole: the mystical body of Christ. "Abide in Me: and I in you. As the branch cannot bear fruit of itself, unless it abide in the vine, so neither can you, unless you abide in Me. I am the vine: you the branches. He that abideth in Me, and I in him, the same beareth much fruit: for without Me you can do nothing." [25]

Not every branch bursts into bloom and bears fruit; and not every baptized Christian attains early to conscious abiding union of mind and heart and will with the Blessed Trinity, even as Christ, Who lives by the Father. But there are very few earnest souls to whom this life is utterly unknown,[26] for it is the life of the Church, the mystical body of Christ.

But do not think you can enter into it by your own efforts

---

[24] *Summa Theologica,* I. Q. XVIII, iii, corpus.

[25] John XV:5-6.

[26] Should the study on which this book is based be repeated, this fact should stand out just as clearly in the repetition as in the original: see above, p. 193, and Chapter XV: *The Two Ways,* pp. 277 ff.

to live a life of recollection. The way to the life of conscious union with Christ is the keeping of the commandments. "Judas saith to Him, not the Iscariot: Lord, how is it that Thou wilt manifest Thyself to us, and not to the world? Jesus answered and said to him: If any one love Me, he will keep My word. And my Father will love him and we will come to him and will make our abode with him." [27] Behold this is the "gate" and the "strait way" "that leadeth to life: and few there are that find it." [28]

But our Lord has promised us the assistance of His Holy Spirit: "and I will ask the Father: and He shall give you another Paraclete, that He may abide with you forever: the Spirit of Truth, Whom the world cannot receive, because it seeth Him not, nor knoweth Him. But you shall know Him: because he shall abide with you and be in you." [29] And through the action of the Holy Spirit, Whom we shall know because He is in us, there will commence in our human minds a certain shadowy representation of the life of God Who is Infinite Understanding, ever in action by knowing the Eternal Good which is His own very Being.

Furthermore our Lord promised us that He would not leave us, even though he would go to the Father; for He would remain with us in the Eucharist. "I will not leave you orphans: I will come to you. Yet a little while and the world seeth Me no more. But you see Me: because I live, and you shall live. In that day you shall know that I am in My Father: and you in Me, and I in you." [30] The thought was dear to Him because this very knowing is the essence of eternal life, commenced in time and enjoyed for all eternity. "Now this is eternal life that they may know Thee, the only true God, and Jesus Christ whom Thou hast sent." [31] The commencement of this knowledge in time is given us in the prayer of quiet which, as the fruit of the Holy Eucharist, constitutes the spiritual life of the mystical body of Christ. And so our

[27] John XIV:22-23.
[28] Matthew VII:14.
[29] John XIV:16-17.

[30] *Ibid.*, 18-20.
[31] *Ibid.*, XVII:3.

Lord prayed that all the members of his mystical body would know Him thus in the Eucharist: "And not for them only do I pray, but for them also who through their word shall believe in Me. That they all may be one, as thou, Father in Me, and I in Thee: that they also may be one in Us: that the world may believe that Thou hast sent Me." [32]

[32] John XIV:20-21.

CHAPTER **XIII**

The Shadows of Charity

W HEN St. Augustine saw the truth and was finally given the grace to embrace it, he paused to consider the past and turned to the vision of eternity that was opening up before him. There came over him a feeling like that expressed by Francis Thompson.

> In the rash lustihead of my young powers,
>   I shook the pillaring hours
> And pulled my life upon me; grimed with smears,
> I stand amid the dust o' the mounded years—
> My mangled youth lies dead beneath the heap.
> My days have crackled and gone up in smoke.

But far more clearly than Thompson he saw the brightness of eternity through the dust of the mounded years; and so he exclaimed:

"Too late have I loved Thee, O Thou beauty of ancient days, yet ever new! too late have I loved Thee! And behold, Thou wert within, and I abroad, and there I searched for Thee; deformed I, plunging amid those fair forms which Thou hast made. Thou wert with me, but I was not with Thee. Things held me far from Thee, which unless they were in Thee, wert not at all. Thou calledst, and shoutedst, and burstest my deafness. Thou flashedst, shonest, and scatteredst my blindness. Thou breathedest odors, and I drew in breath and pant for Thee. I tasted, and hunger and thirst. Thou touchedst me, and I burned for Thy peace." [1]

Francis Thompson shrank back in the presence of the sacrifice that confronted him:

> For, though I knew His love Who followed,
>   Yet was I sore adread
> Lest, having Him, I must have naught beside.[2]

St. Augustine was given the vision of peace that comes by giving up all things for God. "When I shall with my whole self cleave to Thee, I shall no more have sorrow or labor; and my life shall wholly live, as wholly full of Thee." [3] And then he sensed the demands of true love and cried out to God, "Too little doth he love Thee, who loves anything with Thee, which he loveth not for Thee. O love, Who ever burnest and consumest! O Charity my God! kindle me. Thou enjoinest continency: Give what Thou enjoinest and enjoin what Thou wilt." [4] And then St. Augustine goes on to consider in detail one after another the pleasures of sense, and how he can renounce them one and all that he might cling to nothing whatsoever that would cloud or weaken or in any way prevent the perfect union of mind and heart with that Ancient Beauty of the eternal years Whom he now loved and adored with all his heart and soul.

Every generous soul that has tasted the true love of God feels rising within him the demands of love and commences to do all he can to lay aside everything which it is morally possible for him to renounce that he may open his mind to the knowledge of God and free his heart that he may cleave to the Eternal Good. It is in this way that one lays deep and solid the foundations of the spiritual life.

St. Augustine's renunciation was complete. He gave up not

---

[1] *Confessions*, Bk. X, trans. by E. B. Pusey, Mount Vernon, New York, Peter Pauper Press, 1949, p. 211. There is also an edition with a preface by Bishop Fulton J. Sheen. Modern Library.

[2] The quotations from Francis Thompson are from his *Hound of Heaven*.

[3] *Confessions*, p. 211.

[4] *Ibid.*, p. 212.

only all sinful pleasures but every trivial curiosity that might turn his thoughts from God. He had attained, when he wrote his *Confessions* at about the age of forty-three, to that stage of the interior life where one gives up absolutely every interest that is not concerned with God.[5] With him this involved not only major interests but minor wanderings of the mind to little events that engage the attention during the day. The importance he lays on these minor acts of self-denial makes him a precursor of the "little way" of St. Thérèse of Lisieux.

"True," he writes, "the theatres do not now carry me away, nor do I care to know the courses of the stars. . . . Notwithstanding, in how many most petty and contemptible things is our curiosity daily tempted, and how often we give way, who can recount? How often do we begin as if we were tolerating people telling vain stories, lest we offend the weak; then by degrees we take interest therein! I go not now to the circus to see a dog coursing a hare; but in the fields, if passing, that coursing peradventure will distract me even from some weighty thought, and draw me after it: not that I turn the body of my beast, yet still incline my mind thither. And unless Thou, having made me see my infirmity, didst speedily admonish me either through the sight itself, by some contemplation to rise towards Thee, or altogether despise and pass it by, I dully stand fixed therein. What, when sitting at home, a lizard catching flies, or a spider entangling them rushing into her nets, oft-times takes my attention? Is the thing different, because they are but small creatures? I go on from them to praise Thee the wonderful Creator and Orderer of all, but this does not first draw my attention. It is one thing to rise quickly, another not to fall. And of such things is my life full; and my one hope is Thy wonderful great mercy." [6]

There is no essential difference between St. Augustine and St. John of the Cross. St. Augustine's attempt to withdraw his mind wholly from all pleasures and interests in order to give himself entirely to God is what St. John of the Cross terms

[5] See below, pp. 242 ff.
[6] *Confessions*, Bk. X, pp. 221-223.

the *active night of sense*.[7] The following instructions for doing so are redolent of St. Augustine.

> When thou thinkest upon anything,
> Thou ceasest to cast thyself upon the All.
> For, in order to pass from the all to the All,
> Thou hast to deny thyself wholly in all.
> And when thou comest to possess it wholly,
> Thou must possess it without desiring anything.
> For, if thou wilt have anything in all,
> Thou hast not thy treasure purely in God.[8]

St. Augustine presents this sacrifice as something he is impelled to make by a burning love for God that seems to drive him to forsake everything whatsoever that he may find God and be wholly occupied with Him. But the fundamental principle is the same with each great Doctor of the Church. Thus St. John of the Cross writes: "It is the same thing if a bird be held by a slender cord or by a stout one; since, even if it be slender, the bird will be as well held as though it were stout, for so long as it breaks it not and flies away. It is true that the slender one is easier to break; still, easy though it be, the bird will not fly away if it be not broken. And thus the soul that has attachment to anything, however much virtue it possess, will not attain to the liberty of Divine union." [9]

St. John is very helpful to one who would enter into this active night of sense, in that he points out to what we must direct our efforts: 1) everything in the nature of a truly voluntary sin, however venial; 2) *attachment* to certain imperfections which one is unwilling to sacrifice to attain perfection and true union with God. "These habitual imperfections are, for example, a common custom of much speaking, or some attachment which we never wish entirely to conquer—such as that to a person, a garment, a book, a cell, a particular kind of food, tittle tattle, fancies for tasting, knowing or hearing certain things, and suchlike." [10]

---

[7] *Ascent of Mount Carmel*, Bk. I, Chap. XIII.
[8] *Ibid.*, Peers's translation, Vol. I, p. 63.
[9] *Ibid.*, Chap. XI, Vol. I, p. 53.
[10] *Ibid.*

Yielding to transitory desires that are not sinful, and which do not constitute something on which the heart is set, does not impede the habitual union of the soul with God. In general, one should not attempt that absolute fixation of the mind on God, which seems to have been St. Augustine's ideal, until it becomes the insistent demand of love. Lest one should be led by such an attempt into neurotic anxiety, one should follow the advice of a prudent director.

For the general necessity of this night, St. John of the Cross appeals to a striking passage from St. Paul. "This therefore I say, brethren: The time is short. It remaineth, that they also who have wives be as if they had none: and they that weep, as though they wept not: and they that rejoice, as if they rejoiced not: and they that buy, as though they possessed not: and they that use this world, as if they used it not. For the fashion of this world passeth away." [11]

II

St. John of the Cross speaks of a passive night of sense which the soul enters upon when it passes from ordinary mental prayer to infused contemplation [12] or loving attentiveness to God or to use the term of St. Teresa of Avila the prayer of quiet. We discuss this elsewhere in this book.[13]

After the night of sense comes the night of the spirit. It, too, has both an active and a passive phase. The active phase of the night of the spirit is discussed by St. John of the Cross in the second and third books of the *Ascent of Mount Carmel*. He was writing for the friars and nuns of the discalced Carmelites of his day, many of whom experienced frequently various types of visions and locutions. It would seem that some became very much attached to these extraordinary experiences and there was real danger that the primacy of the

[11] I Corinthians VII:29-31.
[12] *Dark Night of the Soul*, Bk. I, Chap. IX, Peers's translation, Vol. I, pp. 373 ff.
[13] Pp. 194 ff.

pure love of God would be lost sight of in the minds of many. Hence he pointed out the necessity of rejecting many of these experiences and of conducting oneself in all things so as not to stand in the way of our true union with God. This check placed upon spiritual gluttony for mystic experiences and the interest of the mind in things that do not lead to God, results in the active night of the spirit. Writing, as we do, for a more general public we have merely touched on some of the problems of the active night of the spirit.[14]

III

We may consider the passive night of the spirit as a *period* in the life of the soul which lasts from the time one enters into the habitual enjoyment of the prayer of quiet, or, as it is also termed, infused contemplation, until the soul attains to spiritual marriage or finishes its career on earth to pass to perfect union with God in eternity.

During this period, there is to be discerned a type of suffering specific to one who has developed a strong love of God due to the mystic grace of truly contemplative prayer. This suffering varies in character and is subject to remissions of longer or shorter duration.

Besides this specific type of suffering there are other trials that do not seem to flow as the natural sequence of contemplative prayer. Some of these are due to our native temperament and our mismanagement of our emotional life, and some to apparent accidents of life: bereavements, losses of various kinds, unhappy personal contacts, and many other trials.

Before considering these trials let us study that which constitutes specifically the passive night of the spirit, which is continuous in this period though it manifests various forms and is subject to marked fluctuations of intensity.

Let us first raise the question: Who enter into the passive night of the spirit? The concept that the passive night of the spirit commences when one passes from ordinary mental

14 See pp. 250 ff.

prayer—meditation and affective mental prayer—to infused contemplation seems to carry with it the idea that those who habitually practice meditation do not enter into the night of the spirit.

The solution of this problem cannot be purely theoretical. It is a question of fact. A first step may be made by trying to find out whether or not one may habitually make a daily meditation and still habitually enjoy infused contemplation. We do not ask whether or not all should give up entirely the prayer of meditation when God gives them infused contemplation. We merely ask whether or not one may enjoy infused contemplation in the course of a formal meditation and perhaps also at other times of the day.

In 152 answers to our questionnaire there were only seventeen who practiced formal meditation. Of these seventeen, three answered that a) in mental prayer they entered into a profound peace with the whole being suffused with the love of God: a peace which remained in spite of the mind wandering at times away from God; b) that their mental prayer was habitually of this character; and c) that the peace continued after the period of prayer was over and accompanied them into the work of the day.

It would seem, therefore, that it is possible for one to practice formal meditation habitually and in this meditation be lifted by God to something which at least resembles the prayer of quiet or infused contemplation.

The matter is important and is illustrated in the spiritual biography of one of our respondents.

She says that the lowest and the highest degree of the spiritual life she was ever in was Chautard's stage six in our questionnaire. This means that she is not conscious of ever having committed a deliberate venial sin.

She thus describes her mental prayers:

"When I commence mental prayer I first make the preparatory prayer. Then I read the preludes and first point of the meditation. Next, I think about what I have to read and try to see in what way it applies to my life. I ask God to help me in my daily work and in all my needs.

"Often, after reading, I make acts of faith, hope, love or contrition, depending on how the subject moves me. Sometimes, when I feel too sleepy or tired to pray, I spend the time apologising to our Lord for my failure to make the meditation.

"At other times, I fix my mind on some mystery such as the Annunciation and think about everything connected with it.

"Our life is so regulated by the rule, that there is little or no time to prolong the morning meditation. The day is so filled with work that I barely ever get to our afternoon devotions. There is little time for meditation during the day. If I am wakeful at night, I sometimes say a rosary, meditating on the mysteries.

"When there is a movie or some entertainment given for the nuns, I go. I could stay at home and make extra meditation, but I enjoy the relaxation, so I go."

At the same time, all three questions in our No. 15 are answered in the affirmative. She attains to the loving peace of the prayer of quiet habitually and it carries over from her morning meditation into the work of the day.

She has enjoyed a number of mystic experiences which inflamed her love of God and seemed to free her from various imperfections.

"When I was a young sister I heard these interiorly spoken words: 'I am a jealous God.' I was on the verge of falling into a particular friendship. These words stopped me.

"On the day of my Reception, just after I had returned to my pew after receiving Holy Communion, I saw Our Lord standing near the tabernacle. He was radiant with light, and so beautiful that no words can describe His beauty. I don't know just how long the vision lasted. When the novices rose for the last gospel, the vision faded and I stood up. Whenever I entered the chapel for years after, and even now, the beauty of that scene flashes again into my mind.

"During my novitiate days, I saw Our Lady on two occasions. Once she was carrying the Infant and presenting Him to Holy Simeon. Saint Joseph and Anna, the prophetess, were there too. For the moment, I was so wrapped up in the sight, that I was not conscious that the Assistant Novice Mistress was looking at me. She asked me what was the matter, but I said: 'Oh, it was just a light.' The conversation ended there. A group of novices were standing together in the study hall when I saw this scene.

"Another time when a group of novices were standing in the Novitiate with our novice mistress, I saw our Lady riding on a donkey. She was holding the Divine Child in her arms. He was very beautiful. His light hair was a mass of ringlets. He looked to be about a year old. At the time, it seemed that Mary was fleeing with Jesus into Egypt.

"The three experiences just described seemed to be right before me as sensory objects.

"About ten years after I entered, I began to practice a special devotion to Christ the King. Many times He seemed to be walking beside me, wearing His kingly robes and Crown. This scene was different in that I did not see Him with my bodily eyes, but was conscious that He was present.

"Once, while I was a novice, I saw two immense figures in the sanctuary. They were standing on either side of the priest, who stood at the foot of the altar to begin Mass. It seemed as though they were struggling for the soul of the priest. I thought that one was the devil, and the other, St. Michael the Archangel. This priest had a stroke that evening, and died shortly after.

"I prayed that I would see our Lord again on Profession Day. I was kneeling near the back of the chapel. All at once the Sacred Heart stood near me. He said, 'What do you want?' I was so overcome with joy and happiness, that I could only say: 'Grant me only Thy love and Thy grace. These are enough for me. I desire nothing more.' He was gone, and then I began to ask for graces for my parents and brothers and sisters, feeling sorry that I did not think of it while He was there.

"While making the annual retreat one year, I had this experience. During benediction, I offered my heart to Christ and asked Him to place it within His breast. He seemed to answer me by giving me His Heart in place of mine. I do not know whether this was a betrothal scene. It was not like any I have read about. It was repeated."

She has given us the following account of her spiritual life.

HOW I FIRST COMMENCED TO LEAD
A SPIRITUAL LIFE

"From my earliest childhood, I lived in a very holy environment. My parents attended Mass and said the family rosary daily, and received Holy Communion frequently. The family was consecrated to the Sacred Heart. My eldest brother began to serve Mass when he was six, and I frequently accompanied my parents to weekday Mass, when only four or five. My parents were generous contributors to the Church.

"I was one of a large family. All who lived were given a Catholic education in grade, high school and college.

"From the time of my first Communion, I tried always to keep my soul free from the slightest sin. At this age I made a private vow of chastity. As daily Communion was not practiced at this time, I was always looking for some excuse to receive on weekdays. I'd make a novena to St. Anthony so that I could go on Tuesdays, and to the Sacred Heart so that I could receive on Fridays. If there was a Holy day or a special feast day, that provided an excuse for me to receive. I really longed for the Holy Eucharist.

"Shortly after my First Communion, I had a very vivid dream. I seemed to be in a forest of evergreens. Looking up into the star-studded sky, I beheld Our Lady sitting on the clouds. She seemed so beautiful that I prayed that I could stay with her always. Many years after, when I entered the convent, I seemed to be standing in the same forest. Our Lady had answered my prayer. I was to be with her always.

"My years before I entered were very sheltered. The daily routine of Mass, Holy Communion, and school was followed.

My time after school was spent helping mother with the household duties, and caring for the younger children. The desire for the religious life grew as I grew, so that I felt I could not live if my desire could not be satisfied.

"When I entered the convent, I found Him Whom my soul loveth. After many years of religious life, I pray that I may never lose Him Whom I have found.

"Do not think I am satisfied with my life. I feel that under the circumstances that I have just stated, and because of the environment in which I lived as a child, that I should be more advanced in the spiritual life. The question often arises in my mind: 'Why have I not advanced? What have I done or omitted that has prevented me from rising to spiritual heights?' "

This respondent clearly illustrates how infused contemplation may enter into a formal meditation, and how such mental prayer may lead one far into the beauties of mystic experience.

It is, therefore, possible for infused contemplation to enter into the life of prayer of one who habitually practices a formal meditation. It is also possible for one to attain to infused contemplation who does not devote the time of prayer to anything but vocal prayers.

Thus a respondent was puzzled how to answer our question 12 asking for a description of the usual way of making mental prayer and whether or not it is ever prolonged and if all free time is given to mental prayer. "I hardly know how to answer this question. I say morning and evening prayers, grace at meals, two rosaries (5 decades each), my office of the Third Order of St. Francis, and some other prayers. I often make the sign of the Cross, glance with a prayer at a statue of Christ or our Lady, pray to St. Joseph, St. Anthony, the Little Flower, St. Francis. It seems to me I pray most of the time but not always holding a rosary or a prayer book." Many years ago she wrote in a letter: "All this week I have been able to pray incessantly, except when I slept, and I have wished that I could be awake to Christ through the night instead of sleeping." She seems to enjoy at times the prayer of quiet and God has granted her various precious mystic graces.

Let us try to reconstruct a fragment of her biography and her life of prayer from the various answers she made to our questionnaire.

"From childhood on I guarded against imperfections. I constantly tried to please God. I have done this all my life except once. When I was a young married woman with several children, I let the sun go down on my anger, spoke angrily to the woman the next day, and almost immediately apologized. I was deeply sorry." This seems to have been the greatest sin of her life. She terms the lowest stage of her spiritual life this outbreak of anger. Thus a sin rather than a period of sinfulness constituted for her the lowest stage of her spiritual life. We should say, not *stage*, but the lowest *point* of her spiritual life. She rates herself now in Chautard's stage six. As to stage seven she writes: "I pray even while I work. I often hunger for the Holy Eucharist and for heaven. I have received some graces of contemplative prayer. Once I asked for suffering; and when it came, I was not as patient as I should have been. So I did not do that any more. I told God I would try to bear the suffering He saw fit to send me." She had many and hard trials to endure.

It seems that she had a vocation to the married life. "When I was sixteen years old and still in high school, I experienced a real calling, I think. In prayer I said that I wished to marry and have six children, and bring them up in the fear and love of God." She did raise a large family, in the love and fear of God, though one or two children gave her some trouble.

Now as to her prayer: Is it truly what St. Teresa of Avila would term the prayer of quiet?

In the first place she has striven since childhood to lead a sinless life and seems to have succeeded without any fall greater than the one she mentioned. Sinlessness is the soil in which God plants His infused contemplation. Then, she can succeed in praying incessantly for as long as a week except during the time of sleep. "I try to live in the presence of God all the time, as any Christian should do, praying to Him and trying not to offend Him. But I can't say that my heart is lifted up in prayer, to the love of God and boundless peace, even every day, much less a big proportion of the day." These heights of divine charity seem, however, to come frequently. At times her union with Christ rises to such heights that, were moments to broaden into eternity, she would seem to possess the joy of eternal life. She speaks of enjoying boundless peace as a result of various mystic experiences.

One of these is a condition akin to ecstasy that seizes hold of her suddenly at times and with no personal effort when she glances at an image of Christ or our Lady. She has occasionally experienced words, intellectually, giving her important advice in difficult situations. At times she has experienced the presence of Christ or our Lady. Such experiences have a wholesome effect on her spiritual life, inflaming charity and urging her to closer conformity with the will of God.

On one occasion "I just knew without a doubt and without any effort on my part that Christ was giving His Heart to me; and I was giving my heart to Him." This seemed to her to symbolize a betrothal scene. "Since then I have experienced deep and boundless peace."

And withal, in answer to the question: Do you believe in your inmost heart that you are lower and viler than all? she replies, "Yes, but at the same time I know I am not in mortal sin."

The number of positive answers to this question in those who are leading a sinless life is a strange fact. Perhaps the Thomistic explanation is the only one possible. A holy life leads the soul to see the divine in others, but the human in himself. All unconsciously he compares the human in himself with the divine he sees in others. In general, those leading a very imperfect or sinful life do not see things that way. But as souls grow toward perfection they see more and more of the divine in others.

Can we say that without the prayer of quiet one does not enter into what is technically known as the passive night of the spirit? With St. John of the Cross the answer to this question is a matter of definition. "This dark night is an in-flowing of God into the soul, which purges it from its igno-rances and imperfections, habitual, natural and spiritual, and which is called by contemplatives infused contemplation, or mystical theology," [15] or we may say in the language of St. Teresa: the prayer of quiet. We must, however, recognize that God can lead some souls to perfection without making them pass through this dark night of the spirit. It is probably true that most souls who attain to the perfection of the love of God go through a period in which they habitually experi-ence the prayer of quiet with the specific suffering to which it leads along with 1) severe trials that do not arise from con-templation itself, and 2) many sufferings due to natural dis-turbances of emotional life

IV

In the prayer of quiet the soul abides in silence and in peace in a glowing love of God. This peaceful love is of the very nature of the prayer of quiet. However, in the beginning, it is what St. John of the Cross terms *dark love* (*amor oscuro*). With the commencement of the prayer of quiet "the soul im-mediately perceives in itself a true determination and an ef-fective desire to do naught which it understands to be an offence to God, and to omit to do naught that seems to be of His service. For that dark love cleaves to the soul, causing it a most watchful care and an inward solicitude concerning that which it must do, or must not do, for His sake, in order to please Him." [16]

In the beginning these questionings are not associated with a realization that they arise from the love of God which is commencing to develop in the soul. Hence, love in this period may be termed *dark love*. One who stops to think, however, will at once see that, if one did not love God, one would not

[15] *Dark Night of the Soul*, Bk. II, Chap. V, Peers's translation, Vol. I, p. 405. Note that the subtitle of Book II is "Of the Dark Night of the Spirit."

[16] *Ibid.*, Chap. XVI, Peers's translation, Vol. I, p. 455.

be at all disturbed about little things that might displease Him. The suffering due to all this carefulness will vary much according to the native temperament of the individual.

The prayer of quiet is a state which presents many degrees of development. These stages are steps in the growth of the love of God. All mental prayer tends to increase our love for God. Meditation certainly does so, and on that account one who practices it faithfully begins to give up sin whether little or great. Meditation is a type of prayer that we can practice by God's ordinary grace. It leads to the love of God; but it does not consist essentially in the love of God. The prayer of quiet is possible only by a very special grace of God. It consists essentially in the infusion by God of an experience of divine charity in the soul, and the dim or intensely brilliant glow of loving peace.

The experience of the love of God that takes place in the prayer of quiet is far greater than what occurs in meditation, unless meditation passes over into the prayer of quiet. Hence the prayer of quiet even in its first stage of *dark love* makes one very much concerned with doing all he possibly can do to please God.

At some stage the soul commences to really suffer because it has offended God in the past. This suffering is something very different from the freely floating anxiety of the neurotic patient. God gives "His suffering" at first in touches that come and are gone in a moment, but are very keen while they last. These moments of agony may follow upon such things as a special illumination by which the soul really experiences the indescribable tenderness and intensity of the love of the Eternal Father or an insight into how Christ has always loved the soul and the soul has responded so coldly to the divine love of the Savior.

St. Teresa of Avila tells us that her sorrow for her sins became so intense that it was painful for her even to live. And St. Thomas Aquinas teaches that sorrow for sin never ceases till we see God face to face in eternal life.[17] It is true that the

---

[17] *Summa Theologica*, 3. Q. LXXXIV, viii.

essence of true sorrow for sin is a free and responsible act by which man turns away from all sin and resolves never to offend God again. It can be emotionally cold. But as the love of God increases in contemplative prayer this determination becomes all the more firm; and a keen sorrow causes genuine suffering.

As love continues to grow, the soul yearns to be united with God in eternal life. This yearning eventually becomes so intense that it is painful for the soul to remain on earth. And hence St. Teresa's poem *Vivo sin vivir en mi:*

> I live yet no true life I know
> And, living thus expectantly,
> I die because I do not die.[18]

It is readily seen that love, such as we have been describing, purifies the soul from all sins and imperfections. It breaks all bonds that prevent the union of the soul with God. It is a yearning of the whole being of man for His Creator. It is a free and responsible act of the human will at its highest level of perfection, for it is made with an intellect purified and illumined by a special grace of God and a will untrammeled by blind emotional drives. And all this is the very root of our meriting eternal life.[19]

But this peaceful glowing love of God is the formal and essential principle of the passive night of the spirit. It produces suffering in various ways; but it is the love and not the suffering in itself by which the soul is purified. Crushing sorrows that are not essentially connected with the night of the spirit often add to the sufferings of this night. This peaceful glowing love meets them and consumes them. The soul sees, in virtue of this love, how wonderful is the privilege of being associated with Christ in His Passion and co-operating with Him in the salvation of souls. And every sorrow loses its sting. But it is love that purifies the soul in every trial and not the pain or sorrow. As St. John of the Cross says: "This

[18] *Complete Works*, Peers's translation, Vol. III, p. 277.
[19] *Summa Theologica*, 1. 2. Q. CXIV, iv.

dark night of loving fire, as it purges in the darkness, so also in the darkness enkindles the soul. . . . Even as spirits are purged in the next life with dark material fire, so in this life they are purged and cleansed with the dark spiritual fire of love. The difference is that in the next life they are cleansed with fire, while here below they are cleansed and illumined by love only." [20]

Intimately associated with the love of God that constitutes this dark night of the spirit is an illumination that makes the soul conscious of its defects. This illumination comes very early in this night, even before the soul is conscious of the dark love that has taken hold of it. It sees various things in the past as stupid follies. It realizes also that some things that it did not look upon as sins when they were done were in reality materially sinful.[21] It has previously exonerated itself of serious guilt by various palliating considerations. One respondent writes: "A special light dawned on me while reading the prophecy of Jeremias. I came to the words: 'Thou hast said: I am without sin and am innocent: and, therefore, let Thy anger be turned away from me. Behold, I will contend with thee in judgment, because thou hast said: I have not sinned. How exceeding base art thou become, going the same ways over again!'[22] As I read, I recalled how for years I had thrown a cloak of excuse over many things in my heart. But now, as I have entered deeper into this prayer of peaceful love of God, I can no longer do so. The reading of this passage seemed to remove all scales from my eyes and there welled up an act of sorrow for my sins in the light of this knowledge. It seems to me now that never before had I made such an honest act of contrition. I was given also to see how all the time Jesus was grieved with my self-encour-

---

[20] *Dark Night of the Soul*, Bk. II, Chap. XII, Peers's translation, Vol. I, p. 436.

[21] There is a difference between what is *materially* and *formally* sinful. An act is only materially sinful when it is sinful by its very nature but the one who commits it does not appreciate its essential wickedness. If he knows it is wrong at the time he commits it, the act is also formally sinful.

[22] Jeremias II:35-36.

aged blindness. This resulted in keen sorrow. Since then I have experienced this keen sorrow repeatedly. It comes over the mind like a flash of lightning. Did it continue, it would be hard to endure."

Every confessor will remember a certain small group of penitents who evade responsibility for their sins, and say they really could not help them. Usually such penitents continue to relapse. True contrition lifts the sinner from the mire of sin. Cases where an emotional storm renders a man unresponsible for his acts are rare. In general, violent emotions lessen guilt but do not remove it entirely.[23] Honesty with ourselves does not involve in any way a blind scrupulosity that sees sin in almost anything.

One must not think that the dark night of the spirit is one long continuous period of suffering. It is rather a long stretch of time in which day follows night and night day, but the length of day and night is not constant but subject to wide fluctuations. St. John of the Cross speaks thus of these periods of remission: "The purgative process allows intervals of relief, wherein, by the dispensation of God, this dark contemplation ceases to assail the soul in the form and manner of purgation, and assails it after an illuminative and loving manner, wherein the soul, like one that has gone forth from this dungeon and imprisonment . . . experiences great sweetness of peace and loving friendship with God." [24]

The nights in this period are sometimes due to the direct action of God. The Beloved hides His presence from the soul, that sharing in His Passion it may be purified and made ready for the closer union that is to come. While still a child St. Thérèse of Lisieux entered into one of these nights which she thus describes:

"Before sending a ray of hope to shine on my soul, God allowed me to pass through a three days 'martyrdom of an-

---

[23] See on this point the condemned propositions of Molinos, 41-53. Denzinger-Bannwart, 1261-1273.
[24] *Dark Night of the Soul*, Bk. II, Chap. VII, Peers's translation, Vol. I, p. 415.

other and most grievous kind. Never before had I so well understood the bitter sorrow of Our Lady and St. Joseph as they walked through the streets of Jerusalem in search of the Divine Child. It was as if I were lost in some fearful desert; or rather my soul seemed like a frail skiff, without a pilot, left to the mercy of the stormy waters. I knew that Jesus was there, asleep in my boat, but how could I see Him through a night of such darkness? Had the storm really broken, a flash of lightning might have pierced the clouds that hung over me, enabling me to catch a momentary glimpse of the Beloved of my heart, but even that was denied me. All around was night, dark night, utter desolation, death! Like my Divine Master in Gethsemani, I felt that I was alone, and that I could find no comfort neither on earth nor in heaven." [25] It is readily seen that the love of Christ was the psychological cause of all this suffering.

A priest describes how his spells of depression clear, and again how, though the sadness and a sense of futility remain, there comes a spiritual consolation that produces a beautiful peace.

"During the periods of depression there is a profound sadness and sense of futility in my life. But this clears and the depression lifts completely and for some time. I enter then into a period in which there is a sense of happiness and physical well-being. I am glad to have something to suffer and difficulties to overcome. If I am blocked in one way I feel that I have many other things to do which are eminently worth while. And so I go along happily in what may be looked upon as the normal phase of my mental life.

"At other times there is a different kind of relief; but the sadness does not disappear and the sense of futility remains. The peace of God enters my soul and my whole being is dominated by a silent, quiet, but wondrously intense love of God. I prefer this peace of charity in the depths of sorrow to the joy and sense of physical well-being. When Christ

[25] *Saint Thérèse of Lisieux*, Taylor's translation, p. 96.

whispers His love to the soul, nothing can cloud its interior happiness."

In the period of darkness one must never give way to despair. Remember that Jeremias in his temptations to despair cried out: "The Lord is good to them that hope in Him, to the soul that seeketh Him. It is good to wait with silence for the salvation of God." [26] It will help us to remember that God does not want us to suffer. It becomes necessary, however, to lead us through trial and sorrow, away from our self-seeking, to union with Himself.

If God is to lead us to Himself, the only true end of man, He must free us from all that separates us from Himself, and therefore, in the first place, from sin. Various persons and activities help us for a while. But there comes a time when they are no longer useful. They may even become harmful. It becomes necessary that in the course of life we must be separated from various persons and give up certain activities. This stripping is often very painful.

Some sufferings are merely opportunities to share the Passion of Christ and co-operate thereby with Him in the salvation of souls. The great Architect of the universe has designed also the life of every human being. The wise man will allow the Architect to execute His plan.

V

Many and widely different are the stories of the dark nights of individual souls. By way of illustration we present the following little biography of a soul with its description of the summer and the winter of the spiritual life.

"I am a Sister and entered the religious life as a young girl. Throughout I have been in earnest about striving toward the highest ideals of the religious life. I regret that I have not always been entirely faithful to these ideals, but I have never surrendered them, and God's goodness to me has truly been wonderful.

[26] Lamentations III:25-26.

"The first seven or eight years need little comment. They were spent as any young religious sincerely desiring holiness would spend them. I loved the religious life, and it held more of sweetness and light than serious spiritual difficulties. Then, after some happy years teaching, I was transferred. I then underwent the first great spiritual upheaval of my life. Everything in the natural order was lacking—an understanding superior, trusted friends, congenial work, and the ordinary pleasant relationships of community life. The year was dark and painful and long, broken only by a three-day retreat, a respite which gave little consolation but sufficient strength to finish the year. Throughout the year it was *not* felt absence of God and His grace which caused me great suffering; on the contrary, I clung close to Him as my one Friend. Somehow I felt that He was on my side, and I honestly believed that I was putting my best into every day's activities, both spiritual and otherwise. I had great difficulties in the school that year; and there was no comfort or consolation to be found anywhere. Although God gave me the grace not to complain, I suppose my superiors saw I was unhappy. Anyway, after summer school that year I was moved back to the same city where I had been before, though to a different school. The superior was the same I had had for some years at the other school, and we were and still are intimate friends. As I look back now at these supremely happy years, indeed it seems that this was the summer of my spiritual life. The last few years have been totally different. But first, some facts concerning the great graces of my 'spiritual summertime.' Shortly before I left the large city after the first years, I attended a series of conferences on the spiritual life. Oh! That was a glorious holiday for my soul! All was conducive to recollection and concentration, and never have I enjoyed or profited more greatly from a summer's activities. Among the many great lights of that summer, I remember distinctly my first true insight into the incomprehensible Mystery of the Trinity. I remember looking at Father with awe and thinking, 'And you knew that all the time!'

"I think I must have imbibed a great devotion to the Sacred Heart with my mother's milk, for she surely loved and trusted Him. This devotion has been and is the focal point of my entire spiritual life. About this time I wrote out an Act of Oblation to the Sacred Heart, in which I did not ask for suffering, but offered myself for *anything He saw fit to send me,* as a proof of love and as an act of reparation. Then followed the difficult year spoken of above. Apparently He 'took me up on it.' *Cum permissu,* I also adopted at this time a monthly Holy Hour of reparation from 10 to 11 of the night preceding each First Friday.

"Then, following the one year in another city, I returned here. Although there were many trying experiences during these years and I felt the happy necessity of offering earnest and extended prayers and mortifications for much needed graces to 'come out on top,' yet through the grace of God I did come out on top, and that period of my life was filled with unbounded spiritual joy and exaltation. I remember telling my spiritual director (whose advice and encouragement I am still blessed with) at this time that God would either have to take away such excessive joy or enlarge my heart to contain it! Now I know that God chose to enlarge my heart, but this knowledge is in retrospect. At this time my soul was evidently prepared for the tremendous graces which God gave me through another priest, a saintly man indeed. He gave us conferences on the spiritual life, with special emphasis on the development of the mystical life apart from the extraordinary phenomena which sometimes accompany it, though he gave consideration to these, too. His conferences were an hour long, and I was so spellbound and engrossed both by his radiant sanctity and his subject matter that I wished the hour would never end! His death has taken him away from us, but his fruits, in my soul at least, are indestructible and eternal. Before that, although intensely attracted to the mystical life, I held it to be something entirely out of the scope of an ordinary mortal. The expansion of the life of grace in me during those years can not be overstated.

I really began to *live* spiritually. During the last four years at that school, I enjoyed the close friendship of another unusually holy priest. A sincere esteem was almost spontaneous from our first meeting, and to see saintliness in daily life, all I had to do was look at him. The tremendous influence he exerted upon me spiritually (and I was conscious of it and opened my soul wide to it) was another of the greatest graces of my life. Then he went to work elsewhere. I was careful to enjoy this friendship only with the full knowledge and approval of my director.

"And then, like a bolt from the blue, came the order to be on the train the next noon (about 15 hours later). I will not try to deny that that move cost more than any other act of obedience I had ever made. That was the beginning of a vital and permanent change in my life. Summer was over; winter set in with sudden fierceness. Everything happened at once, leaving me utterly overwhelmed. To a most disagreeable teaching assignment was added the companionship of a Sister whose character and personality is the very antithesis of mine. These, together with an annoying physical infirmity and various other crosses, were but the accompaniment of the blackest spiritual destitution and abandonment. Previously I was incapable of imagining such pure agony could exist. I was swept off my feet completely. I will not attempt to describe it. I can refer you to the 'Dark Night of the Soul' of St. John of the Cross. There I found an exact reflection of my condition. One thing alone was missing: among the horrible and prolonged temptations to blasphemy, despair, and SUICIDE (I shudder to write it!), the temptation to impurity was conspicuously absent. I can thank God for that. For seven months I was enveloped by this evil, suffocating black fog during which time I felt that if a spiritual substance was capable of annihilation my very soul would vanish into nothingness as a moth in a furnace. Then, one night after sleepless hours spent in mortal combat with the Spirit of Darkness (nothing was present to my bodily senses, but he was there!) who suggested with appalling vividness that I commit suicide,

I heard the words in my mind, 'There's a razor blade in the drawer!'. Suddenly all was quiet interiorly and a modicum of peace returned. It was as if Christ had calmed the storm with His familiar words: 'Peace! Be still!' Other great trials continued, but those frightful temptations never returned. During this trial, in desperate need, I sought the help of a local priest, and through him God gave me strength if not many consolations. Then I received permission to write to my director who was in the city miles away. His kindness and understanding were wonderful, and gradually God restored to me some semblance of balance and calm. The above trial was accompanied by an almost overpowering temptation to abandon my vocation. Some power outside myself kept me from it.

"The intensity of this trial is gone, but my very soul, I believe, is essentially affected by it. Nothing is quite the same as before. My present state is hard to describe. Although I possess peace deep in my soul, yet the surface is not consistently smooth. This past year took away from me every natural liking and satisfaction in teaching, which I have previously loved so much, and in which God openly blessed my efforts. I have always been very active in doing many things for Him. At least, I thought that I wanted only to do them for Him and His honor. Now I see how much of self was in my 'holiest' actions. Now my whole being feels empty, spent, useless, weak, prone only to sin. I used to have so much enthusiasm and zest for teaching and for life in general; now all that is gone, and I am left inert and lifeless. I know God has given me great graces, but against the background of His Infinite Purity my sinfulness does not dare let me think I am superior to anyone, spiritually or any other way. During the past year my big fight has been against sadness. But my good director is still taking care of me, and he doesn't seem to be worried at all! In spite of all, I am still bold enough to hope and to pray for the highest union I can possibly attain here on earth according to God's Will for me. . . . This is very brief. One more incident I must include. When I was deciding my vocation when a young girl, among other equally 'weighty' obstacles was my sincere admiration and attachment to a young man richly gifted by nature and grace. After revolving all these issues in my mind for the nth time, one day while I was making my brother's bed I clearly and indelibly heard these words in my mind: 'There is no person in the world worth loving like I want to Love!' I've never forgotten that, and it is so TRUE. Yes, the very breath of my life is LOVE, for God, but it is still too, too weak and frail. O! That God may increase it until the vast conflagration consumes all of self!"

CHAPTER **XIV**

The Rebellion of Nature

THE SUFFERINGS that we undergo during the winter of the spiritual life are not all imposed by wintry blasts that are sent upon us directly by divine action. Some are due to the fact that we ourselves are responsible for not making the provisions we should make for the onset of rough weather, and some to the nature of the body itself, the habitation in which we live. "These aridities might frequently proceed, not from the night and purgation of sensual desires aforementioned, but from sins and imperfections, or from weakness and lukewarmness, or from some bad humor or indisposition of the body." [1] Thus, those who have what is termed by psychiatrists a manic-depressive temperament will have a tendency to far deeper and more prolonged spells of sadness than others. Those with a schizophrenic trend will be more likely to feel discouragement and want to say what's the use, and sink into a state of hopeless self-isolation.

It is possible for us to do a great deal, with the ever-present and powerful grace of God, to overcome these faults of native disposition and thus prepare ourselves for the winter of the spiritual life. The main factor in this conquest is the ever-present and powerful grace of God; but *we* must utilize

[1] *Dark Night of the Soul*, Bk. I, Chap. IX. Peers's translation, Vol. I, p. 373.

what God makes available to us. This utilization is not an easy task, like turning on the steam in a well-heated city apartment. It is more like chopping wood or mining coal.

St. Paul speaks of this transformation which Christ is going to work in our souls. "Our conversation is in heaven: [2] from whence also we look for the Savior, our Lord Jesus Christ, Who will reform the body of our lowliness, made like to the body of His glory, according to the operation whereby also He is able to subdue all things to Himself." [3]

The word "reform" of the Douay version means in the original to thoroughly renovate, to make over without destroying. If we can expect that Christ is going to renovate our whole being, we can hope for the disappearance of sins and imperfections in such a manner that we cannot attribute their disappearance to our own efforts alone. A number of our respondents have noted this. Thus one in Chautard's seventh stage writes: "Many imperfections have faded from my spiritual life in a most wonderful way; but many still remain." I might say that it is the general experience of those who report mystic graces that these graces are followed by a marked increase in a conscious love of God and the disappearance of many imperfections. One said "of practically all."

These sudden changes in the moral and spiritual life of man may come as a "conversion experience" in which one suddenly puts an end to a life of grave sin which had endured for years, with no preliminary warning or mystic grace of any kind.[4] Or they may come as the apparent result of a mystic grace that suddenly appears in consciousness. These sudden changes, according to our data, take place more frequently in those already leading a very good and holy life. When they come, some or nearly all the clouds of imperfection suddenly and permanently disappear. These facts should hold

[2] That is, our manner of life is to be like that of the citizens of heaven, the angels and the saints.

[3] Philippians III:20-21.

[4] For an example, see p. 118.

out hope to one who is struggling against sins and imperfections without apparent success. Keep up the good fight and one day Christ will enter the field of battle and at once the enemy will be put to flight.

These breaches of continuity in spiritual development demand for their explanation a factor that even in adult individuals may never have been brought into action before, or one that acts sporadically and seems to belong to something that is not found in the mental powers of man. They may well be attributed to the action of God Himself on the soul. Grace is not nature, but above nature.

Another important word in the passage from St. Paul is "body." In the original its early meaning was only the dead body, but it came to signify later the living body, and still later, the whole personality of a man. We may assume that it bears this meaning in the passage quoted. In the normal course of the development of the spiritual life of one who on his side does what lies within him, the whole personality is going to be made over by Christ by that divine supernatural action "by means of which He is able to subdue all things to Himself."

What is He going to make over? Our human nature, restored indeed to sanctifying grace by baptism and the sacraments, but still, as theologians say, suffering to some extent from the loss of that first integrity bestowed upon Adam but lost by original sin. This "integrity" involved such a dominion over emotional life that no unreasonable emotion or sensory desire could maintain its place in consciousness against the free and responsible power of the human will. As St. Thomas says: "In the state of innocence the inferior affective apparatus [*appetitus*] was entirely subject to reason. Hence the emotions of the soul were found in it only in so far as they flowed from the judgment of reason." [5]

One element in the Redemption of Christ was to restore to the soul the integrity lost by original sin. But this integrity was not to be given completely at once like sanctifying grace

---

[5] *Summa Theologica*, 1. Q. XCV, ii. corpus.

in baptism. It will not be given back in its fullness until we enter eternal life. The subjection of emotions and sensory cravings to the dominion of reason is accomplished to a very great extent by the practices of an ascetical life and the bestowal of the mystic graces. It is very helpful to hold before us as a high moral and spiritual goal: the complete subjection of emotions and sensory cravings to the demands of reason. To aid in that conquest we shall consider various human emotional drives somewhat in detail.

II

One very common unreasonable emotional drive is a fretful anxiety about how things are going to turn out, or a tendency to keep going over in the mind various unlikely and even impossible things that might happen.

Then there are a number of people, adults as well as children, who are abnormally anxious about various specific objects or situations. Thus a young woman's whole future development is blocked because she enters into a state of painful anxiety whenever she must speak to any stranger even about ordinary unimportant matters in the normal contacts of daily life.

Fear of having committed a mortal sin torments the life of many a devout and innocent soul.

Some have an acute attack of anxiety just before the time to pronounce their vows or take the subdiaconate, which involves committing oneself to a life of celibacy.

Many of these states of anxiety can be handled by good psychiatric treatment. But some of these same anxiety states would never have arisen had the spiritual life progressed to its normal level of attainment. We might say that the most powerful prophylactic measure against states of anxiety is the development of the life of the soul with God. Unfortunately the lack of this development makes the services of a psychiatrist at times indispensable.

Without underrating the value of natural prophylactic and

curative procedures,[6] let us try to point out how religion is an important factor in the prevention and sometimes in the cure of anxiety states.

Let us first dwell on the fact that anxiety by its very nature implies a defect. Therefore, it could never have found a place in the mind of Christ. The goal of our spiritual development is likeness with Christ. In the degree to which one attains to this goal, anxiety is made impossible and is eliminated from the mind.

Anxiety about how things are going to turn out arises from a weakness of faith, from an inadequate knowledge of God and weakness in the realization of His presence, almighty power, and loving providence. Because of this truth our Lord said to His apostles in the storm at sea: "Why are you fearful, O ye of little faith?" [7] Did the Blessed Virgin ever suffer from an attack of anxiety? Such was her sanctity and likeness to Christ that we must conclude that our Lord could never say to her at any moment of her life: Why art thou fearful, O thou of little faith. Sorrow, she suffered indeed, but anxiety never.

And so you also, if your spiritual life develops as it should, will attain, eventually, to a state of mind which excludes all anxiety. Perfect sanctity carries with it an abiding peace and consciousness of the Divine Presence and the glow of charity, which makes all anxiety impossible.

But we must hasten to remark that this imperturbable peace is attained only at the summit of the spiritual life. It would seem that a state of complete freedom from anxiety is reached only toward the close of the period of spiritual betrothal and more fully in the state of spiritual matrimony, or in those equivalent states of charity to which some may be raised without the mystic graces of betrothal and espousal. One grows, however, toward imperturbable peace by living with God in mental prayer. During this period God often sud-

---

[6] See on this, T. V. Moore, *Personal Mental Hygiene*, Chap. IV, Anxiety and Scrupulosity, pp. 32-49.

[7] Matthew VIII:26.

denly bestows, by His mystic graces, a peace that is alive with charity.

Scrupulosity in general needs wise guidance from a good spiritual director and at times the help of a psychiatrist. But if the life of prayer can be developed, scrupulosity may fade out as one lives closer to God in an interior life. An attack of acute anxiety or scruples just before the time for ordination, or taking one's vows, is a sign of a hidden conflict about leaving the world for the service of God. It indicates a serious lack in the true love of God. It has been found more than once that if the conflict is resolved by returning to the world the anxiety and scruples immediately vanish.

But after one has considered all the natural causes of anxiety states, there remains a group that has no natural cause. God purifies and sanctifies the soul by an intensity of emotional suffering which he bestows as a special grace. Such experiences are the shadows of charity and the darkness that leads to the dawn. One must recognize in them the hand of God in order to pass through a quiet night and attain to a perfect end.

I I I

Among the emotional states which we may unreasonably intensify is what is termed a mental depression. By this word we mean a feeling of sadness which lays hold of us, and, while it lasts, takes all the zest out of life. If one will study the onset of his depressions one will find that they are sometimes due to some trivial incident that results in a lowering of the habitual sense of personal value. A student fails to answer a question put to him in class, and for a while everything is hopeless and gloomy. On the other hand, if a young student, or an old man, should have an opportunity to display his information, there is a sudden bull movement in the inner stock market of self-appreciation. Thus many trivial incidents of everyday life give rise to elation or depression.

The serious calamities of life generally cause deep and prolonged depressions. If we live our spiritual life as we should, we can prepare for these severe trials of life that are out of our power to prevent. As suggested in the last chapter we can see in them opportunities given us by the Eternal Father to share the Passion of Christ and co-operate with Him in the salvation of others. And fortunate will that soul be who, like the Little Flower of Lisieux, learns this lesson early in life. She writes that shortly after her first communion there came to her "an ardent desire for suffering, as well as a conviction that I should have many a cross to bear. Then a wave of consolation swept over my soul—of such consolation as in all my life I have never known. Suffering became my treasure. I found in it charms that held me spellbound, though as yet I did not appreciate it to the full." [8] We must not think that this state of mind robs suffering of all its pain. The peace and joy of love bloom in the midst of thorns.

Whether our spells of depression arise from the trivialities of life or its serious calamities, there is a tendency, strange to say, to stay in a depression and try not to come out of it. I remember seeing a depressed patient in a mental hospital a number of times. At first the depression was so deep he could not carry on conversation. Finally one day I came in and he chatted like a normal person. I said: "I am glad to see you so much better." "Oh, no!" he replied, "I am much worse than I ever was." He then went on to moan about his troubles.

Sometimes there is an extraneous factor in the tendency to hold on to a depression and moan about it to others. One craves for and enjoys the sympathy thus obtained. Again the clinging to a depression is mere indulgence in a much greater vanity: the delight that some experience in pitying themselves. When no extraneous factors lurk behind the focal point of awareness many depressions may clear rapidly. But there are also physical factors: fatigue, anemia, and an obscure hereditary factor that makes some individuals fall into a depression more easily and is responsible for their de-

---

[8] *Saint Thérèse of Lisieux*, Taylor's translation, p. 76.

pressions hanging on beyond the point where any sufficient cause for sadness remains.

Many depressions, especially those that are unreasonably prolonged, exemplify the rebellion of human nature against the dictates of reason. A perfect man would be able to dominate emotions by reason, and not allow sadness to interfere with the duties of the day. Our weakness in this respect is one manifestation of that loss of "integrity" on account of which our emotions and desires are not completely subject to reason. Baptism does not restore to us fully in this life all that was lost by the fall. But, having been raised to a supernatural state by sanctifying grace, it is our problem in life to win, by the practice of all virtues, perfect emotional control. Thus will our mind approach that absolute dominion of reason over all desires and emotions that was characteristic of the mind of Christ.[9]

There is one thing true of *natural* depressions that is valuable to know about and always to take into consideration. They are rhythmic. For any one person the rhythm manifests a cycle of fairly uniform duration. The usual limits of the period of recurrence varies in different individuals from three to nine weeks.[10] I knew one case in which the subject had a weekly depression. It would come on in the afternoon. Life seemed without any hope when he went to bed, but he would awaken in the morning with all his usual zest for action. The usual cycle of one's depressions is very much disturbed when one enters into a period of stress and storm. In such a time of difficulty the periodicity is lost owing to violent reactions to the many difficulties with which one is beset.

The cycle of our ups and downs here referred to is that of normal emotional life. If we go into the manic-depressive cycle of insanity one must think in terms of months and years rather than of weeks.

The value of special mental hygiene in this whole matter is that one should try to remember in the depth of sadness:

9 St. Thomas, *Summa Theologica*, 3. Q. XV, iv.
10 See T. V. Moore, *Personal Mental Hygiene*, pp. 22 ff.

After a period of days, I shall be myself again with my former outlook on life. And so one settles down to jog along, going about his usual tasks, waiting for his sadness to clear, as if he were in bed waiting for a fever to go down. The usual duties of the day constitute the best occupational therapy.

The life of the soul with God is of great value in all depressions, even those that dip over into the pathological. This life is dominated by the ideal of praying, working, and suffering with Christ for the triumph of the Kingdom of God. Sadness, and all other suffering, is grist for our mill. The deeper our life with God, the more easily we can always bob up serenely at our post and carry on. In this interior life a mystic grace may suddenly banish a depression as if by miracle.

"One evening 'when so sad I could not sadder be' I noticed the *Autobiography of the Little Flower* on a friend's table. I had read it more than once, but not at all for several years. I borrowed it and read from it that night, opening it at random. I cannot describe what happened as I read. It was as if a person who had been confined in a dark, noisome prison were suddenly brought into the light and sweetness of home, or a person in delirium suddenly restored to clearness." [11]

This is only one example of a common experience. The grace of God acts on the mind suddenly and overwhelmingly and more powerfully than a drug which exerts a specific influence preventing or curing a definite disease.

Sadness is an emotion which in itself implies no imperfection. That a son should experience no sorrow at the death of a good mother who had always loved and cared for him would show an abnormal state of mind. But should he allow his sorrow to crush all activity, and nurse it for years, it would be a defect. Sadness is only a defect when it is deeper than what is called for by the situation, or is absent when it should be present, or is prolonged for an unreasonable length of time.

[11] See T. V. Moore, *Personal Mental Hygiene*, p. 246.

We find sadness recorded of Christ, and by that very fact we know that in itself it is normal and wholesome. We read that when our Lord was about to enter the garden of olives that "He began to grow sorrowful and to be sad" and He said to His apostles: "My soul is sorrowful even unto death." [12] And when dying upon the cross He cried out: "My God, my God, why hast thou forsaken me?" [13] No human sorrow has ever approached the agony of that moment. "Surely He hath borne our infirmities and carried our sorrows." [14] "Let us go forth, therefore, to Him without the camp, bearing his reproach." [15]

I V

One of the most dangerous of our emotional drives may be described as a tendency to isolation from friendly contacts with others. It finds expression, after some incident of emotional tension, in such a phrase as: "I am done with him. From now on we are going to part company." These phrases though they seem to be innerly spoken words proceeding from our own selves may be at times whispered to us by Satan, the father of discord. St. Thérèse of Lisieux gives the following example in her autobiography. " 'You did well to be severe yesterday,' a novice said to me. 'At first I was indignant, but after I had thought it over I saw you were right. I left your cell thinking all was at an end between us and determined to have nothing more to do with you. I knew, however, that the suggestion came from Satan, and I felt you were praying for me. Then, as I grew calm, the light began to shine, and now I have come back to hear all you have to say.' " [16]

A large percentage of mankind can be classified as having a

[12] Matthew XXVI: 37-38.
[13] *Ibid.*, XXVII: 46.
[14] Isaias LIII: 4.
[15] Hebrews XIII: 13.
[16] *St. Thérèse of Lisieux*, Taylor's translation, p. 178.

manic-depressive or a schizophrenic [17] temperament. Abnormally intense or prolonged spells of sadness are found in those with a manic-depressive temperament; the tendency to break off social relations with others and retire into life with oneself is typical of the early stages of *schizophrenia* or *dementia praecox*. Let us take another example. Francis Thompson in his essay on Shelley "describes most exactly what psychiatrists will at once recognize as a typical schizophrenic reaction. 'So beset, the child fled into the tower of his own soul, and raised the drawbridge. He threw out a reserve, encysted in which he grew to maturity unaffected by the intercourses that modify the maturity of others into the thing we call a man.' [18] But in describing Shelley, he was but telling what he had experienced himself." [19]

No one should be surprised if he hears within his mind the words: "I won't have anything more to do with him." But he should look upon it as a dangerous step if he finds himself carrying those words into effect. The reason is that this schizophrenic reaction has a tendency to keep on extending itself to other individuals with whom one comes in contact. One is then inclined to say: "I am alone with God." But the solitary life does not arise from excluding others from the sphere of our affection and kindliness, but from seeking union with God while extending love and affection to all.

The schizophrenic reaction of withdrawal could never have found lodgment in the mind of Christ, and is utterly opposed to His teaching. "Love your enemies: do good to them that hate you: and pray for them that persecute and calumniate you." [20] How can we do good to those with whom we determine never more to have anything to do? And when we determine to live within ourselves and have nothing to do with anybody? How can we be the children of our Father

[17] *Schizophrenia* was formerly termed *dementia praecox*. Hence the adjective *precox* is synonymous with *schizophrenic*. To characterize a trend toward schizophrenia we often hear *precoxy* used.

[18] *Essay on Shelley*, London, Burns and Oates, 1903, pp. 33-34.

[19] T. V. Moore, *Personal Mental Hygiene*, p. 289.

[20] Matthew V:44.

Who is in heaven, "Who maketh His sun to rise upon the good and bad and raineth upon the just and the unjust?" [21] The Church is one large happy family in which all live together, quickly forgetting injuries, and happy in the exchange of mutual love and help.

The schizophrenic withdrawal reaction originates often in trivialities, but it leads to something that may be very serious: hatred. We must, however, distinguish between emotional dislike and hatred. Some people get scrupulous about the problem of hatred because they do not know this difference. Emotional dislike toward a person is an antipathy we feel in spite of ourselves. It is involuntary and therefore cannot be a sin. But if we deliberately and responsibly resolve to do evil to or truly wish evil to fall upon the person we dislike it becomes a sin: venial if the evil done or wished is trivial; mortal, if it is serious.

Conscious volitional hatred involving serious evil is rare or nonexistent in religious communities. But one must be on guard against subconscious hatred which is masked as an act done for the true welfare of the person we dislike. Superiors should be on the lookout for a tendency to send away or treat with special rigor persons for whom they feel a strong antipathy; and subjects should be careful about the opinions they entertain about the superior whom they cannot like, and avoid anything like vigorous opposition to his policies. We must beware of what psychiatrists term ideas of reference, and say, "He means me," when as a matter of fact he is not thinking of "me" at all. We must be careful to banish from our mind the thought: "He is doing that just to be mean," when as a matter of fact he must do it because it is his duty.

Your antipathy is likely to pass into volitional hatred if you avoid all friendly contacts with the one you dislike and toward whom you have developed what might be termed a little delusion of persecution. If you do not give yourself generously to the religious exercises of the day and cease to live

[21] *Ibid.*, 45.

with God in a life of prayer, your charity for God grows cold and your mind becomes a fertile soil in which antipathies will grow luxuriously and blossom into hatred.

In antipathy and hatred, especially, is illustrated the title of this chapter: *The Rebellion of Nature*. Hatred is caused by an emotional rebellion against the sound dictates of reason. Satan stirs up the rebellion; and man nourishes his hatred.

Hatred is never to be found in any well-balanced personality, for such a one ever works to maintain cheerful, friendly contacts with all. It is mainly our love for God that establishes emotional balance. Genuine love of God, of necessity, includes a true love for all mankind. "God is charity: and he that abideth in charity abideth in God, and God in him. . . . If any man say: I love God, and hateth his brother: he is a liar. For he that loveth not his brother whom he seeth, how can he love God whom he seeth not?" [22]

V

Besides the rebellion of emotions against reason, we have to deal with the even more powerful rebellion of our desires. "A desire is a craving we experience to seek or produce a situation in which impulsive tendencies may be satisfied or natural wants may be supplied." [23] The human desires that cause the most serious difficulty are the cravings for unlawful sex pleasure and alcoholic beverages. They become exceedingly difficult to manage only after they have been excessively indulged in over a more or less extended period of time. The difficulty that arises in this way is a human responsibility, and is never directly imposed by God.

The most hopeful way out of the impossible situation in which many find themselves as a result of these cravings is to beg the help of God with all one's heart and soul, and enter upon the life of the soul with God: Morning Mass and Holy Communion, mental prayer and holy reading. Anyone who

[22] I John IV:16, 20.
[23] T. V. Moore, *The Driving Forces of Human Nature*, p. 244.

faithfully persists in these exercises will, by the graces obtained, rise out of any moral slump whatsoever. The great difficulty in the application of this remedy is that the addict seldom has any interest in making the attempt.

Prevention is far easier than cure. A good mother can introduce a child early to the love of God, and then to the value of self-denial as reparation to Christ for His rejection by the world, and as a prayer for gaining Him souls. And then she can easily encourage a resolution to habitually give up completely, for Christ's sake, all pleasures that might well lead to serious harm, but to no injury whatsoever, if they are never enjoyed. Many human wrecks would have sailed through the storms of life triumphantly had they been faithful to such a resolution.

Not all our desires are sinful by any means. Some are good, noble, and worthy of attainment. It sometimes, perhaps we could say often, happens that a man sets his heart on the attainment of one of these worthy objects of human desire. As the years roll on this object ever eludes his grasp. Yearning increases with nonfulfillment and a void deepens in mental life. There is a burning in the depths of this void that is ever purifying his soul. He is not conscious of the sanctity that is growing within him, all on account of this unfulfilled desire.

A very simple insight is capable of filling the void in his soul with peace and joy. The story is told of Agassiz that he kept a student weeks on end dissecting fish. The student had to report daily his findings. Agassiz kept saying: "There is something important that you have not found yet." Finally one day it dawned on the pupil to say: "One side is just like the other." "That," said Agassiz, "is the important fact." In due season God will give an important but very simple insight to one who has suffered for years the disappointments of life. "My child," the Divine Wisdom will say to the soul, as he said to Abraham, " 'I am thy reward exceeding great.' It makes no difference what you lose if you find Me, and live in the peace of the attainment of My love." Up to that moment the soul was being sanctified by the bitterness and darkness of the night of the spirit. But now there breaks upon it the brightness of the dawn. All that it can desire is possessed. All the attractions of the created universe fade quickly into nothingness "as the dream of them that awake. . . . Thou hast held me by my right hand: and by Thy will Thou hast conducted me, and with Thy glory Thou hast received me. For what have I in heaven? And besides Thee what do I desire upon earth? For Thee my flesh and my heart hath fainted away. Thou art the God of my heart, and the God that is my portion forever." [24]

[24] Psalm LXXII: 20-26.

CHAPTER **XV**

The Two Ways

PREPARATORY to a study of the mystic graces we would like to point to a difference in the general development of the spiritual life of those who live interiorly in the Divine Presence. From our data it stands out as a fact of experience that one group experiences no mystic graces, or only the prayer of quiet; and some good souls do not perhaps even receive that. The other group experiences various mystic graces with greater or less frequency.

What precisely do we mean by the mystic graces? The mystic graces are spiritual experiences that unite the soul with God in an intellectual awareness, at times quasi-perceptual, of his presence, or inflame the will and the whole affective apparatus of man with an ardent love of God, or both things simultaneously. This knowledge and love is often mediated by a vision or some kind of locution. A mystic grace may at times be reduced to little more than a few words, which, however, solve at once a problem by which one has long been perplexed. It is characteristic of mystic graces that they establish the soul in peace. It belongs to their essence that they are not produced by any personal efforts, however intense or prolonged. The recipient realizes that they come to him or are given to him independently of his own activity.[1]

[1] For examples see the following chapter. The term "mystic graces" is by no means original. It is found repeatedly in A. Poulain, S.J., *The Graces*

One may attain to complete freedom from anything like fully deliberate venial sin and live for years, habitually, almost without interruption, in the Divine Presence and never be directed or instructed by innerly spoken words or see any kind of a vision or experience anything akin to an ecstasy. On the other hand a person in a similar walk of life may attain to the same freedom from sin and continuity of recollection, but he will be frequently illumined by various mystic graces.[2] There are transitional pictures in which a soul receives one or a few mystic graces, over and above the prayer of quiet, in the course of a lifetime. The extremes constitute two very different ways in the spiritual life.

The question now arises: Can one attain spiritual perfection with its freedom from fully conscious and deliberate venial sin and to a large extent from even semi-deliberate venial sin without ever experiencing the prayer of quiet and even without consolations of any kind in the period of mental prayer? If there be any such, they would be at the opposite extreme of the way that encounters many mystic graces.

The following account of a soul in desolation poses the problem.

"After many years in Religious Life, I am still struggling to lead a *definitely interior* life. Except for a few years in the beginning, I have had little or no satisfaction in my spiritual life. For the most part, God has never been a Personal God, in the sense of my having satisfaction in feeling His Personal Presence. I do believe, although there have been times when I even doubted that for everything seemed so bleak. I have had to work for everything I attained.

"I have had a great deal of illness and disability and before each siege I have asked, not that I might be cured, but that

of Interior Prayer, English translation, Kegan Paul, Trene, Trubner, London and St. Louis, Mo., B. Herder Book Co., n.d. Our use of the term, as above outlined, is essentially that of Poulain, Part II, Chap. III.

[2] Take, for instance, two married women, one without mystic graces but enjoying continuous recollection (Chapter XII, pp. 225 ff.); and the other with continuous recollection also, but with many other mystic graces (Chapter XVI, pp. 320 ff.).

I might come just a little closer to God. So far, He does not seem to be paying too much attention to me, but so long as I can keep on trying I am willing to make the effort.

"Perhaps I am what you would call a 'conformist.' In so far as I can, I lead a regular Community Life; I am not perfect, but I do make a real effort to do the best I can. At the close of the day when I go to the Chapel, sometimes I accomplish very, very little, but at least I do present myself and maybe some day God will let me know that He is glad to see me.

"With the above as an introduction, you can probably realize how difficult I find the period devoted to *mental prayer*. Most of the time it is all I can do to read from some book. I have used various books for this purpose—*The Life of Christ—Trust—Abandonment*—and a few others. I have made a very great effort to do something about this, but feel that I have not succeeded very well." [3]

Someone might say: "If this nun has not attained recollection in prayer it is her own fault. She has failed in perfect observance of the law of God and the rule of her community. Failure to attain devotion in prayer is always the fault of the one who prays." But how can anyone be certain of the truth of the two statements in this accusation leveled against the good nun?

First of all, who can say with *certainty* that her failures of observance are of such a character that God rightly punishes her by not granting her contact with Himself in prayer? Taking her statement at its face value she has been making a good honest effort for years. Then there are other things in her history that indicate real enthusiasm in doing all she can do to promote the honor and glory of God. She at least feels that she seeks God without ceasing.

Secondly, how can anyone establish the principle that

---

[3] See also the account of a respondent reported in Chapter XII, pp. 217 ff. One might interpret "the peacefully blank state" that this respondent enters into, along with almost continuous wandering of attention, as a shadowy form of the prayer of quiet.

failure in prayer (in the sense of habitual lack of devotion) is always the fault of the one who prays? At all events, let us point out again that St. Teresa of Avila tries to console those who do not experience the mystic graces by telling them that they should not be without hope "for true union can quite well be achieved, with the favor of Our Lord, if we endeavor to attain it by not following our own will but submitting it to whatever is the will of God." [4] She then goes on to point out that the mystic graces make it easier for us to unite our will completely with the will of God. But if we attain to perfect union with the will of God, without the mystic graces, it is far more meritorious.

"But note very carefully, daughters, that the silkworm [self-love] has of necessity to die; and it is this which will cost you most; for death comes more easily when one can see oneself living a new life, whereas our duty now is to continue living this present life, and yet to die of our own free will. I confess to you that we shall find this much harder, but it is of the greatest value and the reward will be greater too if you gain the victory." [5]

Let us try to picture an example of a man who leads a spiritual life with great fidelity but with little devotion. We could imagine him as a layman. He would be, for example, a perfect husband and a perfect father, taking his joy, like St. Thomas More, in his home life surrounded by his wife and children: the consolation and support of all. His home would be a school of the service of God. No one would be able to remember a time when he said an angry or an unkind word. Or we could imagine a member of a religious community. He might be so ordinary that he would not stand out from his fellow religious. But sometime the remark would be passed: "Have you ever seen that fellow break a rule?" He would be a man to whom a superior could go at any time with any charge and find a willing co-operator. But when he himself looked into his interior life, he might feel

---

[4] *Interior Castle*, Vol. V, p. iii, Peers's translation, Vol. II, p. 259.
[5] *Ibid.*, p. 260.

a tendency to be discouraged. He might often sleep, like the Little Flower, during the time of meditation, and like her he might have no devotion in his thanksgivings after Mass. But with heroic prudence and effort he would so arrange the day that he could usually say his office in peace, make his meditation, and devote some time to holy reading. Sporadically and by special effort, during the course of the day, he would pause and be for a moment face to face with God. From time to time he would say to Christ: "Profoundly I adore Thee: ardently would I love Thee: faithfully would I serve Thee." Or he would give wordless expression to the consecration of himself to our Lord with all his power to be, to do, and to suffer.

Such a man would of necessity possess that background peace in his life which derives from freedom from mortal or all fully deliberate venial sin. But he might lack entirely that peace experience, characteristic of the prayer of quiet, which flows from a quasi-perceptual realization of the Divine Presence.

Now the question arises could such a one, having no experience of the sweetness of infused contemplation or any of the mystic graces, attain to the perfection of the love of God and therefore to perfect sanctity? [6]

[6] There have been a number of pronouncements condemning the concept that *mental prayer* is necessary to salvation. These are given by Josephus de Guibert, S.J., in *Documenta Ecclesiastica, etc.*, Rome, Gregorian University, 1931. E.g., mental prayer is so necessary to every man that without it no one can be saved (p. 253, #438). The Holy Office summed up its attitude on various types of mental prayer in 1675 thus: "The Holy Office does not condemn mental prayer which is termed the prayer of the affections and the prayer of quiet, but the assertions of those who in the first place reject vocal prayers and other spiritual exercises used by the Holy Roman Church; and maintain that those making use of the aforesaid types of [mental] prayer are certain of salvation, need no penance, while those omitting it sin mortally" (p. 256, #441). (See the account of the correspondent on pp. 247 ff.)

There is good authority for the concept that the prayer of quiet, or infused contemplation, is not necessary for perfection. From July 1694 to March 1695, the Bishops Bossuet, Noailles, and Fénelon met with Tronson, the Superior of the Sulpician Seminary, at Issy, and laid down certain propositions on pure love and contemplation to which they all subscribed. These *Articles of Issy* have not the authority of a pronouncement of the

What is perfection? St. Thomas tells us that "the ultimate perfection of a thing consists in the attainment of its end. Whence since it pertains to the divine goodness to bring things into being, so also, to direct them to their end." [7] We can be certain that God will direct all men to perfection and surely such a one as corresponds to our fictitious example and the good nun with whose difficulties we opened this chapter. But in what does the perfection of man consist to which God is ever directing the souls of men? Man attains his end, and therefore his perfection, in the love of his Creator. "For it is charity which unites us to God Who is the ultimate end of the human mind, because he that abideth in charity abideth in God, and God in him." [8]

But what then is charity? We have dealt with this above, but let us present the essentials again, so that they may be clearly before the reader's mind in this discussion. In the human mind we can distinguish two types of desires. One seeks things perceived by the senses. The other consecrates us to that which the intellect alone can know. God cannot be perceived by the senses. He can be known only by the intellect. This consecration of ourselves and this choice of a good that can be perceived only by the intellect cannot be a sensory craving. It is an act of the will. Charity, therefore, is an act of the will. [9]

The fact that charity is an act of the will makes it theoretically possible to attain to perfection without any perceptible devotion. One may be perfectly cold and nevertheless truly and irrevocably committed to the service of God.

Church, but merit respect because of the high standing of the signers, two of whom were on other points of divergent opinions. In articles 21 and 22 we read: "The prayer of the simple presence of God or of Quiet and other extraordinary prayers, even passive, approved by St. Francis de Sales and other spiritual writers, received throughout the Church, cannot be rejected, nor regarded as suspicious, without grave temerity." "Without these extraordinary types of prayer one can become a very great saint and attain to Christian perfection" (p. 316, #495).

[7] *Summa Theologica*, 1. Q. CIII, i, corpus.
[8] *Ibid.*, 2. 2. Q. CLXXXIV, i, quoting I John IV:16.
[9] *Ibid.*, 2. 2. Q. XXIV, i.

The mystic graces lead to an increase of charity when God wills to increase charity by their bestowal. The mystic graces normally produce a type of devotion which one may call an intellectual, rather than a sensory, resonance of one's whole being. When our Lord looked on St. Peter, just after he heard the cock crow, we are told by scripture that he went out and wept bitterly. The sorrow he perceived was not caused merely and directly by the sound that he heard. Our Lord's prediction of his fall came before his mind, along with unforgettable memories of the Last Supper and all that Christ had meant for him in the three years of His public life: a host of memories that sense cannot express and intellect alone can understand. A similar host of concepts and an infused knowing of God constitute the intellectual halo of many mystic experiences. At times, especially in the prayer of quiet, the intellectual halo fades into the background of consciousness but the love of God glows with intense warmth and is far more than a cold determined consecration of the soul to God. But the very nature of charity and the omnipotence of Divine Providence make it clear that theoretically God can increase charity and so lead man to perfection without the *warmth* of love. Charity might be defined descriptively as a volitional consecration of the creature to the Creator manifested by an unfailing fidelity in His service. In general a high degree of charity glows with intense fervor. But it may not; and many a severe temptation is conquered by volitional stability, supported, of course, by the grace of God, but unaided by affective warmth. As charity grows toward its perfection it approaches the spiritual marriage of the soul with God.

What St. Thomas calls the essence of perfection, St. John of the Cross terms supernatural union with God which "comes to pass when two wills—namely the will of the soul and that of God—are conformed together in one and there is naught in the one that is repugnant to the other." [10] One

[10] *Ascent of Mount Carmel*, Bk. II, Chap. V, Peers's translation, Vol, I, p. 80.

is guided by faith to this union: "The soul must be like a blind man, leaning upon dark faith, taking it for guide and light, and leaning upon none of the things that he understands, experiences, feels and imagines." [11] This means to St. John of the Cross that the soul cannot trust to the purely natural powers of reason in meditation, nor to sensory or imaginal visions and locutions.

St. John teaches us that it is faith which gives us that dark knowledge of obscure contemplation which is the essence of that quasi-perceptual realization of His presence which glows with divine charity. But he does not teach that one is not guided by faith until one has abandoned meditation and entered on the way of infused contemplation. Nor does he teach that God's illuminating and inspiring graces are given only in truly contemplative prayer.

In the process of developing and perfecting charity, faith and hope are increased along with charity. There is an intimate process of interaction between the three theological virtues. We may distinguish in our spiritual development the following functions:

1. The deepening of our knowledge of the truths of faith. This takes place in many ways: by the action of God's ordinary illuminating graces that accompany the reception of all the sacraments, but particularly the Eucharist, and abundantly in the whole regime of Catholic education, and in various other ways.

There is, however, one type of deepening our knowledge of the truths of faith which belongs exclusively to infused contemplation simply because it *is* one form of infused contemplation. This is a quasi-perceptual knowing and insight into the fullness of meaning of one of the divine attributes.[12] This is something quite different [13] from intellectual penetration into an abstract truth by the aid of God's ordinary il-

---

[11] *Ascent of Mount Carmel*, Bk. II, Chap. IV, Vol. I, p. 74.
[12] See St. John of the Cross, *Ascent of Mount Carmel*, Bk. II, Chap. XXVI, cited below, p. 299.
[13] For an actual example see p. 99.

luminating grace. This quasi-perceptual knowing was termed a "shewing" by Mother Juliana of Norwich in her *Revelations of Divine Love*. And she clearly distinguished between her "shewings" and what she had learned in a natural way by ordinary grace. "I had *two* manners of beholdings: the *one* was endless continuant love; with sureness of keeping, and blissful salvation, for of this was all the shewing. That *other* was the common teaching of Holy Church of which I was before enformed and grounded." [14]

2. Seeing the hand of God in all the trials and sorrows of life. Can it be said that no one sees God's hand in what happens to him and accepts it in loving patience, uniting his will to the will of God, unless he has been granted the *sweetness* of infused contemplation? It would seem that all this might be possible by God's ordinary illuminating and inspiring graces. Very often, however, that insight will be the brighter light of infused contemplation without being recognized as such by the subject.

3. The imparting of a knowledge of God to the soul in mental prayer—in meditation a) by God's ordinary graces, and b) by the special graces of the prayer of quiet or infused contemplation.

Can it be said that it is theoretically impossible for God to lead the creature to perfect conformity of its will with His own without granting it the sweetness of infused contemplation? One must admit this possibility in the light of the infinite power and wisdom of God. St. John of the Cross did not raise the problem of this theoretical possibility, but spoke from his experience with the friars and nuns of the Teresian reform to whom he addressed the *Ascent of Mount Carmel*.

A careful study of the experience of many souls would probably show 1) that most souls whose will is conformed completely to the will of God have attained to the habitual peace and glow of charity of the prayer of quiet; 2) that

[14] *Sixteen Revelations of Divine Love Shewed to Mother Juliana of Norwich (1373), op. cit.*, p. 111.

many who do not attain to the prayer of quiet and to perfection have failed because they did not co-operate fully
with the graces they received; 3) that some souls, through no
fault of their own, never attain to the conscious blessings of
the prayer of quiet or infused contemplation, but nevertheless are led to perfect union of their wills with the will of
God by a kind of dark love of God in patient endurance
of the sorrows and trials of life.

"And one of the ancients answered and said to me: These
that are clothed in white robes, who are they? And whence
came they? And I said to him: My Lord, thou knowest. And
he said to me: These are they who are come out of great
tribulation and have washed their robes and have made them
white in the blood of the Lamb." [15]

Therefore let us cry out with St. Paul: "God forbid that I
should glory, save in the Cross of our Lord Jesus Christ: by
whom the world is crucified to me, and I to the world," [16]
and let God lead us as He will.

We have been speaking of infused contemplation, or, as
it is also termed, the prayer of quiet, as manifested by its
psychological characteristics: a quasi-perceptual realization
of the Divine Presence and a peace experience which glows
with the warmth of the love of God. But underlying these
psychological manifestations is what might be termed the
metaphysical essence of infused contemplation. This is something caused by divine action on the soul through sanctifying grace flowing over into the intellect and activating the
theological virtue of faith, giving rise to this knowing. This
divine action flows also into the will, activating the theological virtue of charity and arousing a certain process within the
soul that is manifested by the peaceful glow of the love of God.
Were faith and charity dead in the soul, there could be no
genuine experience of infused contemplation. Furthermore,
the perfection of the theological virtues is involved in the
very essence of Christian perfection. One cannot be perfected

[15] Apocalypse VII: 13-14.
[16] Galatians VI: 14.

and either of the others left in an imperfect condition if the soul is to attain to Christian perfection.

Ordinarily, faith, hope, and charity are perfected by God's raising the soul to infused contemplation with its quasi-perceptual realization of the Divine Presence and the glow of charity and a resultant yearning to be with Him in eternal life. Our problem may now be more clearly expressed by asking: Can Infinite Wisdom and Almighty Power perfect faith, hope, and charity without granting the soul any quasi-perceptual realization of His presence or the *glow* of charity or a *conscious burning* yearning to be with Him in eternal life? And the answer is that perfect co-operation with the graces which God gives in the trials, sorrows, and sufferings of life will result in an unfailing consecration to His divine will, an unhesitating belief, blind though it may be, in His eternal presence and loving providence, and a patient waiting till He will rend the heavens and come down and take the soul to Himself in eternal life. All this can lift the soul to the heights of perfection without the fair blessings of infused contemplation. But all this is what may be truly termed the metaphysical essence of infused contemplation. All this is what St. John of the Cross terms the "dark spiritual fire of love" [17] by which the soul is purged and cleansed, and so attains to its perfection. And "this dark night is an inflowing of God into the soul, which purges it from its ignorances and imperfections, habitual, natural and spiritual and is called by contemplatives infused contemplation, or mystical theology." [18] Ordinarily infused contemplation is manifested more or less continuously by its psychological characteristics; but it is in the power of Infinite Wisdom and Almighty Power to perfect the soul of man by the metaphysical essence and hold in abeyance the psychological manifestations.

[17] *Dark Night of the Soul*, Bk. II, Chap. XII, Peers's translation, Vol. I, p. 436.
[18] *Ibid.*, Bk. II, Chap. V, Vol. I, p. 405.

II

We must now introduce an important distinction in the meanings of terms used to describe the stages of the spiritual life: particularly the terms spiritual betrothal and spiritual marriage. If true union with God, as St. Teresa of Avila says,[19] can be obtained without any mystic graces other than "dark love" which brings about a perfect union of a human will with the will of God, then a soul might be on a level of sanctity corresponding to that of spiritual betrothal or spiritual matrimony without ever having experienced a betrothal scene or a spiritual marriage. But without the definite scene as a sign (along with its specific effects) no human being might be able to come to any decision on the matter.

It is true that God has destined every soul to perfect union of will with Himself. If the "perfect union of will with Himself" means spiritual marriage then spiritual marriage is the normal end, in this life, of every human being.

St. Bernard says that if the soul loves Christ perfectly it enters into a spiritual marriage with Christ.

"It is our teaching that every soul, even though it is weighed down by sins, ensnared by vices, caught in temptations, a captive in exile, imprisoned in the body . . . though, I say it is doomed without any hope, nevertheless it is our teaching that such a one can pause and consider and not only be able to breathe in hope of pardon and of mercy; but also dare to aspire to nuptials with the Word. Let it not, therefore, tremble at the thought of a marriage compact with God; let it not shrink back from bearing the sweet yoke of love with the King of the Angels. How can it fear any manner of contact with Him, in whom it recognizes the bright image and resplendent likeness of itself?" [20] "Such a conformity weds the soul with the Word. For it is already like unto Him

---

[19] See above, p. 280.
[20] *In cantica*, Sermo LXXXIII, 1, Migne, *P.L.*, Vol. CLXXXIII, p. 1181-C, D.

by nature; and it makes itself like to Him in what it wills, loving even as it is loved. Therefore when it loves perfectly, it marries." [21]

The question now arises: Can the soul love *perfectly* without a very special grace from God? We approach here a problem associated with a pronouncement of the Council of Trent: "If anyone should say that a man, having once been justified, can . . . in the whole course of his life avoid all sins, even venial ones, except by a special privilege of God, such as the Church holds of the Blessed Virgin: Let him be anathema." [22]

Seeing that the canon speaks of *all* sins, it is taken to include not only deliberate venial sins but also semideliberate sins which are committed without due reflection, or out of lack of emotional control over slight aberrations. It is *de fide*, that is "a matter of faith," that one cannot avoid all semideliberate venial sins during a *whole* lifetime without a very special grace from God. It is admitted that if an adult dies shortly after his baptism that he might have avoided all semideliberate venial sins. Hence theologians interpreting the concept of "a whole lifetime" say that it is "theologically certain" [23] that a baptized Christian cannot avoid all semideliberate venial sins *for a long period* without a most special privilege of God which is very rarely granted.

If now to "love perfectly" signifies to attain to a state in which for a long period one never slips even into any semideliberate venial sins, one cannot attain it without a very special grace from God.

Let us look now into some things that St. John of the Cross says about spiritual betrothal and spiritual matrimony. In the following quotation he seems to be speaking of a soul, the

[21] *Ibid.*, p. 1182-C, D. Quoted from the Encyclical Letter of Pius XII on the occasion of the close of the eighth century since the death of St. Bernard, *Acta Apostolica Sedis*, 30 June 1953, Vol. XLV, p. 373.

[22] Session VI, Canon 23, Denzinger-Bannwart, p. 833.

[23] Ludovicus Lercher, *Institutiones Theologiae Dogmaticae*, Vol. IV, Part I. 1., p. 213.

Bride-Soul, who has been betrothed to Christ and, having spent some time in the state of spiritual betrothal, is about to be called to the spiritual marriage.

"The Spouse, the Son of God, sets the Bride-Soul in possession of peace and tranquillity, in the conformity of the lower part of her nature and the higher, cleansing her of all her imperfections and bringing into control the natural reasoning powers and faculties of the soul. . . . First, the Spouse adjures and commands the useless digressions of the fancy and the imagination from henceforth to cease; and furthermore He brings into control the two natural faculties, which formerly to some extent afflicted the soul, and which are those of wrath and concupiscence; and in so far as may be in this life, He brings to the perfection of their objects the three faculties of the soul—memory, understanding and will. Besides this, He adjures and commands the four passions of the soul—namely: joy, hope, grief and fear—which from henceforth are mitigated and brought under control." [24] In other words, the roots of all sins and imperfections are completely destroyed and it would seem that the soul enters upon a long period, possibly lasting even to death, in which it will not offend God by even a semideliberate venial sin. If so, this state demands that very special grace required by the Council of Trent.

Speaking of the life of the soul in the state of spiritual matrimony, St. John of the Cross says that all the mental faculties "tend in their first movements, without the soul's being conscious of it, to work in God and through God. For the understanding, the will and the memory go straightway to God; and the affections, the desires and appetites, hope, enjoyment and the rest of the soul's possessions are inclined to God from the first moment, even though, as I say, the soul may not realize that it is working for God." [25]

[24] *Spiritual Canticle*, Stanzas XX and XXI, Exposition, Peers's translation, Vol. II, p. 296 (second redaction).
[25] *Ibid.*, Stanza XXVIII, Vol. II, p. 343.

III

It is evident that a very special grace is demanded to elevate the soul to the state of spiritual marriage with Christ. Ordinarily, just as no one enters the state of spiritual matrimony with Christ without passing through the state of spiritual betrothal, so no one is betrothed to Christ who is not prepared for it by the prayer of quiet or, as St. John of the Cross terms it, infused contemplation. But is it possible for God to increase the virtue of charity in a soul to a degree *equivalent* to that of spiritual matrimony without granting to the soul the peace of the prayer of quiet? The question is theoretical and as a theoretical question one must answer that this is within the power of Divine Omnipotence. But does He ever do so? Our data suggest, *but do not prove*, that the peace of the prayer of quiet may be dispensed with.

If God does do so, what are the signs of states equivalent to spiritual betrothal and spiritual marriage?

St. John of the Cross mentions a condition essential for spiritual betrothal: being "completely purged from all creature affection (for spiritual betrothal as we say, cannot take place until this happens)." [26] One might say that the nonmystical equivalent of spiritual betrothal must involve at least the complete renunciation of all that does not concern one, persevered in till the soul arrives at a habitual state of freedom from all fully deliberate venial sin and devotes itself as far as it is possible completely to the service of God. *This complete devotion to the service of God cannot entail the neglect of any duty whatsoever.*

I would hesitate to set up any further milestones in this uncharted field, but would like to suggest that the perfect love of God, equivalent to the state of mystical marriage, may have many forms of expression. Ordinarily it should involve the more or less complete elimination of semideliberate venial sins and such a control of desires and emotions that anything

[26] *Living Flame of Love*, Stanza III, 24, Peers's translation, Vol. III, p. 73; also second redaction, *ibid.*, p. 174.

unreasonable in affective mental life can scarcely make its appearance. Continuity of recollection, independent of personal effort, would also be a valuable sign. This would, however, involve the peace of the prayer of quiet. We must count with the rare possibility of going on to perfection by the hard way of many trials and no consolations.

From the fact that St. Thomas teaches that the perfection of man consists *essentially* in keeping the commandments, we should conclude that nothing more than the perfect fulfillment of the will of God can be required as essential to the concept of perfection. St. Thomas conceives of perfection as a condition in which everything is excluded "that hinders the affection of the mind from being wholly directed to God" as well as all that is incompatible with the love of God.[27]

In his answer to the second objection in this article he admits that the perfect in this life still offend God by some venial sins without drawing a distinction between fully deliberate and semideliberate venial sins. The descriptions, given by St. John of the Cross, of perfection in the state of spiritual matrimony indicate that in that state the soul has been given that very special grace spoken of by the Council of Trent. But whether St. John of the Cross means that souls in the state of spiritual matrimony have been freed from all semi-deliberate venial sins, or that they commit them but rarely, one could scarcely maintain that such freedom can be acquired *only* by the mystic grace in which the soul enacts with Christ a scene in which Christ takes it as its spouse and it, in turn, pledges itself to Christ in spiritual matrimony. "By its very nature and essentially (*per se et essentialiter*) the perfection of Christian life consists in charity, principally indeed in the love of God and secondarily in the love of one's neighbor." [28] Secondarily, various other things may be involved, which, however, are not necessarily always present. St. Thomas mentions the vows of the religious life as means, but not necessary elements. One could also mention the

---

[27] *Summa Theologica*, 2. 2. Q. CLXXXIV, ii, corpus.
[28] *Ibid.*, iii, corpus.

sweetness of all the mystic graces including spiritual betrothal and matrimony. But the perfection of charity is essential, and as St. Bernard says: When the soul loves perfectly, it marries.

One never attains to the perfection of charity without the bestowal of extraordinary graces by God. Seeing that God has destined us to perfect charity and spiritual matrimony with Himself, if we are faithful to his ordinary graces the very special graces necessary for perfect charity will certainly be granted.

I V

Does our material give us any indication of what might be the character of such a grace? The following extract from the report of one of our respondents seems to be at least of such a character that it might lead the recipient toward a more perfect inner control of emotional life, and so to the avoidance of many semideliberate venial sins.

"Once in a period in which I was struggling with various forms of interior emotional rebellion, I felt impelled to look up again the meaning of the word Paraclete. I had no idea that doing so had anything to do with interior emotional control. I found the definition: 'Legal counsel in a court of justice.' (It happened that, at that time, I was passing through a rather difficult period and had to watch my behavior.) I had probably noticed the same definition before, but it appealed to me now in a special manner. It recalled a trial at which I was present many years ago, for which an eminent lawyer had been retained. From time to time he would whisper something to the attorney conducting the case, as if saying: 'I would not insist on that: I would bring out such and such a principle.' It seemed to me that this whispering illustrated very well the action of the Holy Spirit on the soul in the difficult situations and storms of emotional life.

"But the matter did not stop there. I entered upon a period in which I seemed to live with the Holy Spirit. From time to time He seemed to whisper to me. (I have a critical tendency to antagonisms.) Once when an antagonistic feeling made me look down on another (for some act I do not now remember) the Holy Spirit seemed to whisper: 'Do you think that I am putting that antagonism into your heart?' And with the whispering the antagonism quickly faded away. On another occasion some one gave me a dig in the ribs, which seemed to me to indicate that he was provoked with me. I expressed nothing but felt sad. My feelings were hurt and I commenced to nurse the idea that I was badly treated. And the Holy Spirit seemed to whisper: 'Never nurse unreasonable notions and feelings.' At the same time I felt an impulse to shake off my sadness, which at the moment was rather deep. And in a little while it was all gone.

"The repeated instructions that I received make me recall the words of the psalmist: 'Thou hast taught me, O Lord, from my youth.' [29] Sometimes the whisperings are accompanied by a peculiar sense of the presence of Him Who whispers; and I experience the truth of our Lord's words: 'But you shall know Him, because He shall abide with you and be in you.' [30] This consciousness struck me as a new experience. For often in the past I had read the passage and I had thought: I have never really experienced the presence of the Holy Spirit within me. Then again, there is a knowing that I should control at once a rising feeling of antagonism, without any semblance of a locution or the consciousness of the presence of One Who is speaking to me.

"I felt that in a few days I had made more progress towards the goal of perfect inner control of emotional life, and particularly towards fraternal charity, than in all my previous life. Before these whisperings commenced I seemed to be, in these things at an absolute standstill." [31]

V

A question that is often asked is: May I desire and ask God to lead me to Him by granting me many mystic graces?

[29] Psalm LXX:17.
[30] John XIV:17.

[31] See continuation below, p. 301.

When the question is asked in this general way, the general answer of approved spiritual writers is an emphatic No. And this is reasonable. The mystic graces cannot be acquired by our own natural industry. They are special gifts of God, Who distributes to all according as they have need. Your life is a warfare and the plan of battle is given to you by the Holy Spirit, the Supreme Master of spiritual strategy. It would be foolish for you to ask and sinful to insist on fighting the battle in your own way.

But spiritual writers in general make a distinction between the prayer of quiet, otherwise termed infused contemplation, and the other mystic graces. And they point out that infused contemplation actually unites the mind and heart of man with God. As long as one enjoys infused contemplation he abides in the love of God and therefore dwells in the depths of the Divine Essence. For the time being, he attains his end: the union of the soul with God. Hence it is generally admitted that if infused contemplation (or the prayer of quiet) be numbered among the mystic graces it is something that may be desired: a thing good in itself that one may pray for.

St. Teresa, after having discussed the nature of the prayer of quiet, writes: "You will desire, then, my daughters, to strive to attain this way of prayer, and you will be right to do so." [32] She goes on to point out that any attempt to produce the prayer of quiet directly, by our own efforts, would be "laboring in vain." The only way, she maintains, is to be humble, recognize our unworthiness, be totally detached from all that stands between us and God and pray for the power to imitate Christ in all things and to be associated with Him in suffering.

St. John of the Cross is very severe on directors who would lay down a fixed rule and limit all souls to the practice of meditation.

"These directors such as we have been describing fail to understand souls that have attained to this solitary and quiet

[32] *Interior Castle*, IV, ii, Peers's translation, Vol. II, p. 238.

contemplation, because they themselves have not arrived so far, nor learned what it means to leave behind the discursive reasoning of meditations . . . and they think that these souls are idle. . . .[33] Such persons have no knowledge of what is meant by spirituality. They offer a great insult and irreverence to God, by laying their coarse hands where God is working." [34]

V I

When, now, we come to mystic graces, such as visions and locutions, we meet with a few priests who take an extreme position in dealing with penitents. They insist that *all* visions and locutions are purely natural phenomena and must not be looked upon as coming from God. I met with one who excepted from this sweeping condemnation visions and locutions recorded in scripture.[35] That such exceptional attitudes should be possible suggests the great importance of all confessors being familiar with the sound principles of mystical theology.[36]

A tendency to reject the miraculous is associated at times with the denial of the supernatural character of all visions and locutions. But one cannot harbor the concept that no miracles are possible and be in harmony with the defined teaching of the Catholic Church.[37]

Nor can one say that all visions and locutions are natural phenomena arising by purely psychological laws of the hu-

---

[33] *Living Flame of Love*, stanza III, 53, Peers's translation, Vol. III, p. 189.
[34] *Ibid.*, 54, p. 190.
[35] See below, p. 309.
[36] There are two rather recent works from which that knowledge may be obtained: John G. Arintero, O.P., *The Mystical Evolution in the Development and Vitality of the Church*, English translation, St. Louis, Mo., B. Herder Book Co., 1949-1951, 2 vols.; and R. Garrigou-Lagrange, *The Three Ages of the Interior Life*, St. Louis, Mo., B. Herder Book Co., 1947-1948.
[37] See *Canons of Vatican Council*, Denzinger-Bannwart, 1813. The demonstration of miracles is required in the process of the beatification and canonization of saints, Codex 2116 ff.

man mind in certain individuals and be in harmony with the general teaching of the Church. Pius XI in two important documents has given such approval to the teaching of St. Teresa of Avila [38] and St. John of the Cross [39] that no Catholic should accuse them of error in any important matters of doctrine. Both St. Teresa and St. John of the Cross repeatedly distinguish supernatural visions and locutions from those coming from Satan and the natural activity of the human mind. The distinction is so common in the writings of saints, theologians and approved writers on mystical theology that it may be said to be part of the general teaching of the Church.

What is the teaching of St. John of the Cross on visions and locutions? We sometimes hear it said that it is very simple: We must reject them and have nothing to do with them and let God accomplish what He may will in us without us. And so it would seem that the task of the confessor is very simple: Tell the penitent to pay no attention to his experiences and go on about his business. But the matter is not so simple. The confessor must be like a conscientious judge. He must know the law and inform himself fully about the case.

St. John of the Cross distinguishes three types of visions: 1) those that are seen as if external objects perceived by the eyes; 2) those that seem to be a sensory imaginal picture and are in the mind rather than in the outside world; 3) those that constitute an intellectual knowing and cannot be expressed in sensory terms.

Concerning the first class, termed sensory visions, he rightly points out that God cannot be perceived by bodily eyes. Therefore "the soul withdraws itself from the means of union with God when it closes not its eyes to all these things of sense." [40] "And it must be known that, although all these things may happen to the bodily senses in the way of God,

---

[38] *Acta Apostolicae Sedis*, Vol. VI, March 7, 1914.

[39] The encyclical of Pius XI on St. John of the Cross mentions explicitly and approves his major works, *ibid.*, Vol. XVIII, August 24, 1926.

[40] *Ascent of Mount Carmel*, Bk. II, Chap. XI, Peers's translation, Vol. I, p. 105.

we must never rely on them or admit them, but must always fly from them, without trying to ascertain whether they be good or evil." [41]

The teaching of St. John of the Cross on supernatural imaginary visions is somewhat more complex. But the following passage seems of special importance: "With regard to all these imaginary visions and apprehensions and to all other forms and species whatsoever, which present themselves beneath some particular kind of knowledge or image or form, whether they be false and come from the devil or are recognized as true and coming from God, the understanding must not be embarrassed by them or feed upon them, neither must the soul desire to receive them or to have them, lest it should no longer be detached free, pure and simple, without any mode or manner as is required for union." [42]

Though St. John is very positive in forbidding the soul to set store by sensory and imaginal visions, he warns the director against all gruffness that would have a tendency to seal his penitent's lips and put an end to mutual confidence.

"But, with respect to what has been said, it must be pointed out that, although we have insisted so much that such things should be set aside, and that confessors should not incite their penitents to discuss them, it is not well that spiritual fathers should show displeasure in regard to them, or should seek to avoid them or despise them, or give their penitents cause to show reserve and not to venture to speak of them, for it would be the means of causing them many inconveniences if the door were closed upon their relating them." [43]

St. John then goes on to point out that the term vision may be applied not only to something that seems to be perceived by the bodily eyes, or manifested by means of the imagination, but also to the intellectual awareness of a presence without any sensory factor in its perception: intellectual visions. Similarly, a truth may be presented to the intellect not only

[41] *Ascent of Mount Carmel*, Bk. II, Chap. XI, Peers's translation, Vol. I, p. 102.
[42] *Ibid.*, Chap. XVI, p. 132.
[43] *Ibid.*, Chap. XXIII, p. 184.

by words that seem to be heard by the ears, or whispered internally, but also by pure intellectual concepts: a knowing without sensory or imaginal words.

These intellectual visions may concern God Himself or creatures. In regard to intellectual visions that concern creatures he says: "These visions, in as much as they are of creatures, with whom God has no proportion or essential conformity, cannot serve the understanding as a proximate means to union with God. And thus the soul must conduct itself in a purely negative way, concerning them, as in other things that we have described." [44]

When, however, the intellectual vision is a knowing of God Himself it is pure contemplation and therefore not to be rejected. "This kind of knowledge is of God Himself and the delight is in God Himself. . . . For this kind of knowledge comes to the soul in direct relation to God, when the soul, after a lofty manner, has a perception of some attribute of God—of His omnipotence, of His might, of His goodness and sweetness, etc.; and whensoever it has such a perception, that which is perceived cleaves to the soul. In as much as this is pure contemplation, the soul clearly sees that there is no way wherein it can say aught concerning it, save to speak in certain general terms." [45]

"And since these manifestations of knowledge came to the soul suddenly, and independently of its own free will, it must neither desire to have them or not to have them; but merely be humble and resigned concerning them, and God will perform His work how and when He wills.

"And I say not that the soul should behave in the same negative manner with regard to these apprehensions as with regard to the rest, for as we have said, they are a part of the union, towards which we are directing the soul." [46]

Turning now to locutions, that is, innerly spoken words that one perceives and which may seem to come from God

---

[44] *Ibid.*, Chap. XXIV, p. 191.
[45] *Ibid.*, Chap. XXVI, pp. 194-195.
[46] *Ibid.*, p. 197.

and not to be formulated by the mind, St. John of the Cross warns of the great likelihood of being deceived. This likelihood arises in part from the ease with which our thoughts naturally clothe themselves in words, by a kind of psychic reflex. Wish fulfillment often directs the trend of our thoughts. One who has strong desires wants to see them accomplished and may easily attribute words that his own mind has formulated to God Whom he thinks will now realize the desire he has so long entertained. The author remembers a good devout soul who came to him many years ago and commenced to talk about the great order we were going to found together. I expressed some doubts. "What," she exclaimed, "has not our Lord told you about it?" "No," I replied. "But," she said, "He told me from the tabernacle that He had."

There is, however, a type of locution which St. John of the Cross says should not be rejected. He terms the words spoken in the soul, in such a locution, *substantial*, because of themselves they work a permanent change for the better in the soul, or take away sadness and flood the soul with peace and joy. Thus one of our respondents was grieving about the death of one who had meant so much in her life. In the depths of her sadness she heard the words: "You have Me." At once the sadness was gone and the soul was flooded with light and peace. We have mentioned several cases of perplexity about a religious vocation being suddenly removed by an interior locution. And in the report above [47] we are told that the Holy Spirit seemed to whisper: "Do you think that I am putting that antagonism into your heart?" The innerly spoken words of the question promptly banished the antagonism. But many a strong emotional drive maintains its attack in full force even though one says to oneself: "Can I possibly think that this urge comes from God?" Concerning substantial words, St. John of the Cross says that the soul "should not reject them, since the effect of these words remains substantially within it and is full of the blessing of God. As the

[47] P. 294.

soul receives this blessing passively, its action is in no way of importance." [48]

Substantial words which produce their effect of themselves may be given for a while as an aid and then fade into illuminations and inspirations that are not to be distinguished from God's ordinary grace. Having been helped by a locution the soul is then left to carry on by God's ordinary grace. This appears from the conclusion of our respondent's report, the first part of which was given above.[49]

"The 'whispering' in the sense of locutions that seemed to come from the Holy Spirit, in a special manner present within me, faded out. It seems as if He came to teach me an important lesson and placed upon me the responsibility of holding fast, with His ordinary graces, to the obligation He pointed out to me. But I was left with a deeper abiding realization of His habitual presence, and a valuable sensitiveness to a duty to control emotions in their first movements; and make excuses for all with whom I came in contact, that I may love others, as Christ loves me. There remained a peculiar consciousness, in the background of my mind, that the Holy Spirit is still watching over me."

Some mystic graces while not giving instruction in the spiritual life flood the soul with divine charity.

A priest writes: "Several times when commencing the Introit at Mass, the Christ Child seemed, in my imagination, to be standing on the altar to my left. His head was crowned with thorns and one or two of the thorns had made wide wounds from which the blood was oozing. He seemed to be very sad about something, but He did not make known to me the cause of His sorrow. It seems to me now that He wanted me to realize how much He suffers from the sins and ingratitude of those whom He loves: all the children of men. Perhaps He was particularly sad about my own lethargy and coldness; and the lukewarmness of all those who by their

[48] *Ascent of Mount Carmel*, Chap. XXXI, Peers's translation, Vol. I, p. 220.
[49] P. 294.

special calling should love Him with a strong and tender devotion. Once, while I was thinking about these things, He stepped over on the altar, all unhindered by the bookstand. As if He were seeking consolation, He rested His head on my shoulder. I felt the prick of the thorns, but alas only the shadow of the pain the Christ Child seemed to be suffering. But my love for Him burned with unbelievable intensity and yet I went on with the Introit and Kyrie in a wonderful, quiet, silent peace of soul."

When the soul burns with divine charity it would be a mistake to make any attempt to quench the flames. And when one feels an impulse to consecrate himself wholly to Christ, and does so with all that is within him, he has good reason to believe that such an impulse is not from nature, but from God. Furthermore, an imaginal vision of the "Christ Child" involves an intellectual element: the awareness of the presence of the Eternal Word.[50]

Rules for Guidance in Regard to the Mystic Graces Based Largely on the Writings of St. John of the Cross

1. God Himself has planned the spiritual life of each individual soul. We must want what He has planned and nothing else.

2. We must not persistently ask Him to give us either many or few or even more of His mystic graces; but ever pray that our lives may unroll as He has planned: uncontaminated by any personal desires.

3. The danger in asking for the mystic graces is that, in doing so, we might be seeking ourselves and not God; our own pleasure, rather than divine service; to be esteemed holy by others, rather than to become holy by sacrifice.

4. We should refrain particularly from asking for sensory and imaginal visions and from praying that God would direct us by locutions. To do so would be to run grave danger of

[50] See below, p. 351, where this intellectual element is more apparent.

being deceived by the mere normal activity of the mind or the machinations of Satan.

5. It is lawful for us to ask for the union of mind and heart with God; and because the prayer of quiet or, as it is sometimes called, infused contemplation, is the union of mind and heart with God, it is lawful for us to desire it. St. Teresa of Avila tells us this explicitly.[51] But even here we must beware of all self-seeking and vanity, and allow God to lead us as He will.

6. We should pay no attention to sensory mystical phenomena that are not concerned directly with God and in which there is no intellectual element that lifts us to a knowledge of the divine attributes and to the love of God, to keeping the moral law, and fidelity to the ideals of the spiritual life.

7. Whenever any mystic grace is associated with such an intellectual element, or is in itself a deeper knowing of God or a quasi-perceptual apprehension of one of His attributes, or leads to the conquest of unworthy emotions and desires, we should allow ourselves to be carried along by the grace and co-operate with the help given us so as to attain to God and conquer sin and imperfection.

Thus St. John of the Cross, after recounting various types of sensory phenomena that the soul experiences in visions and locutions, says that it must pay no attention to the sensory phenomena but "it must set its eyes only upon the spirituality which they produce, striving to preserve it in its good works and to practise that which is for the due service of God. . . . And in this way the soul takes from these things only that which God intends and wills—namely, the spirit of devotion— for He gives them for no other important purpose." [52]

8. Divine manifestations of knowledge which have respect to God "are themselves that union; and to receive them is equivalent to a certain contact with the Divinity which the

---

[51] See above, p. 198.
[52] *Ascent of Mount Carmel*, Bk. II, Chap. XVII, Peers's translation, Vol. I, p. 144.

soul experiences, and thus it is God Himself Who is perceived and tasted therein." [53] . . . "And I say not that the soul should behave in the same negative manner with regard to these apprehensions as with regard to the rest, for, as we have said, they are part of the union, towards which we are directing the soul." [54]

If one will consider various concepts in the theology of St. Thomas Aquinas and the works of St. John of the Cross, one will see how reasonable are the principles that St. John of the Cross lays down for the guidance of the soul in the ways of the mystical life.

St. Thomas teaches that sanctifying grace and the light of glory are one and the same thing, in the beginning and at the consummation of its development. [55] The light of glory in its perfection is the illumination of the soul of man by the Divine Essence Itself acting directly upon the intellect and performing the function of a concept of the mind in the process of perception. In its beginning, sanctifying grace is a change wrought in the essence of the soul and so transforming it that it can be acted upon by the Divine Essence so that it will see God face to face in the beatific vision. [56]

The Council of Trent teaches us that the theological virtues, faith, hope, and charity, are infused into the soul in the process of justification when man receives sanctifying grace. [57] St. John conceives of *infused contemplation as the theological virtue of faith in action.* "For as God is infinite, so faith sets Him before us as infinite; and as He is Three and One, it sets Him before us as Three and One; and as God is darkness to our understanding, even so does faith likewise blind and dazzle our understanding. And thus, by this means alone, God manifests Himself to the soul in Divine light, which

---

[53] *Ascent of Mount Carmel,* Bk. II, Chap. XXVI, Peers's translation, Vol. I, p. 196. For actual examples see above, p. 100, and below, p. 320.
[54] *Ibid.,* p. 197.
[55] See Chapter V, p. 97.
[56] See above, Chapter V, The Theology of Mystic Experience, pp. 90 ff.
[57] Denzinger-Bannwart, p. 800.

passes all understanding. And therefore, the greater is the faith of the soul, the more completely is it united with God." [58] St. John then goes on to say that the soul must walk by faith in its journey to God, "the understanding being blind and in darkness, walking in faith alone; for beneath this darkness, the understanding is united with God, and beneath it God is hidden, even as David said in these words: Darkness was under His feet." He then cites various other references to darkness in Holy Writ and says: "All these mentions of darkness signify the obscurity of the faith wherein the Divinity is concealed, when It communicates Itself to the soul; which will be ended when, as St. Paul says, that which is in part shall be ended, which is this darkness of faith, and that which is perfect shall come, which is the Divine light." [59]

And then several times St. John points out to us that the dark night of the spirit is infused contemplation. For example: "This dark night is an inflowing of God into the soul, which purges it from its ignorances and imperfections, habitual, natural and spiritual, and which is called by contemplatives infused contemplation, or mystical theology." [60]

From this it is perfectly clear that if the soul should set its heart upon experiencing sensory or imaginal visions, it would desert the way of infused contemplation and divine faith for something that is not God. God may choose at times to kindle the fires of charity by some kind of sensible communication, but the soul should never crave the sensory and seek of itself to escape from the darkness of faith. As divine faith goes hand in hand with the infused virtues of hope and charity, as the Council of Trent points out to us, so the life of faith or infused contemplation leads of necessity to the perfection of charity.

And so we have before us now the two ways. Let us name

---

[58] *Ascent of Mount Carmel,* Bk. II, Chap. IX, Peers's translation, Vol. I, p. 98.

[59] *Ibid.,* p. 99.

[60] *Dark Night of the Soul,* Bk. II, Chap. V, Peers's translation, Vol. I, p. 405.

them: the Way of Peace and the Way of Patience. Most devout souls living an interior life walk in the Way of Peace. But from time to time their Way of Peace leads them into the Way of Patience. Few, very few, souls pass their whole life in the Way of Patience; but great will be their reward in eternal life. Peace often illumines the sickroom and the prison cell. But sometimes it does not. Our Lord whispers to the soul: "Be thou faithful unto death and I will give thee the crown of life." And the whisper may give at once patience and fidelity. And so in the slave labor camps of Siberia there seem to be some who are called to live and die in the Way of Patience. And patience hides a hidden peace that makes quiet endurance possible. Those who go far in the Way of Peace have already on earth a foretaste of what it means to live with God in eternity. "I to my beloved and His turning is towards me" expresses the habitual union of the soul with God in the Way of Peace. And those who walk, faltering through physical weakness, on the Way of Patience see God also, but dimly and darkly through the tears of sorrow and trial. Both those on the Way of Patience and those on the Way of Peace yearn for the day and suffer till the hour comes when they shall behold Him Whom the soul loveth in the region of inaccessible light. And the Spouse whispers: "Surely I come quickly," and the soul answers: "Come, Lord Jesus."

CHAPTER **XVI**

The Mystic Graces

PICTURES express more than verbal definitions. Definitions, however, are not to be neglected. Their meaning is grasped better when one can also look at some kind of a picture whenever this is possible. We shall, therefore, commence this discussion of the mystic graces with a picture that is available to us from a rather large mass of material.

"One night I returned home sleepy and tired. There still remained some of the day's office to be said and so I went into the chapel and sat down. I was so sleepy that while saying my office I repeatedly went sound asleep. When I woke in one of these periods I had an imaginal picture of the Blessed Virgin standing on my left. She seemed to be reciting the psalms. As the memory image of the scene comes before me now, she was clothed with beautiful flowing white garments falling in regular folds. There seemed to be a pale blue sash girding her waist. In some way I seemed to penetrate her inner mind. Perhaps I only felt her interior, from the external picture: erect, silent, motionless. She seemed absorbed in what she was doing—reciting the psalms. Her whole being seemed to glow with the love of God. Her whole attitude seemed to say to me: 'This is the way you should say your office, my child.'

"At the time it appeared to me as a pure imagination, and I remember thinking or murmuring: 'I can never do anything

307

like that'; and went off to sleep again. I woke again and there was the erect, motionless figure beside me, absorbed in the recitation of the psalms. Several times I went to sleep and woke again to find the Blessed Mother beside me, showing me how I ought to recite the Divine Office.

"I think it was only the next day that the conviction dawned on me that the whole experience was a precious grace, akin to an imaginal vision, which God had given me to bring about a reform in my manner of reciting the Divine Office."

Those who read the above account will for the most part fall into three classes:

1. Those who, while believing in God, regard with more or less marked distrust any statement that records a vision or a supernatural locution of any kind. To these we may associate some psychiatrists who do not believe in God and who argue fallaciously: The insane have visions and hear locutions; the saints and some who are not saints experience visions and hallucinations; therefore the saints and these others are insane.

Many good Catholics do not go so far as to deny as absolutely false any statement that records a vision or any other mystic graces. Nevertheless they treat such accounts with a degree of suspicion that eliminates them from serious consideration.

One should realize that this attitude may lead to misunderstanding many persons who live a devout life. Taking the term *mystic graces* to indicate all those who answered positively questions 16, 17, 18, 19, 20, and 23, 92 out of 142, or about 65 per cent, had experienced one or more of the mystic graces. The experience, therefore, of phenomena, at least akin to the mystic graces, occurs in about two-thirds of those who lead a devout life.

It is strange to what an extent one may be led by a veritable antagonism to the supernatural. I was once discussing the matter with a Catholic priest. To him, St. Paul was an epileptic because of his fall at the time of his vision of Christ. St. Teresa of Avila was a case of dementia praecox, and the

Little Flower, a constitutional psychopath. Our friend was not a psychiatrist. He denied the possibility of proving with certainty any miracles, or supernatural phenomena such as visions, except those recorded in scripture, maintaining that outside the certainty of faith there is no certainty.[1] This was an extreme that I have seldom encountered.

2. The opposite extreme, which I have met only once, was that of a good priest who said that there must be a basis in fact for the miraculous accounts we find in the acts of the martyrs no matter what evidence of historical criticism may be mustered against any of them.

Between these two untenable extremes there is a wide field in which we must seek an attitude which is at once theologically correct and dictated by sound reason. In doing so we must be mindful of two duties. 1) We must recognize the hand of God when He acts and the voice of God when He speaks. To seriously fail in this duty would be grievously sinful. 2) On the other hand, we must not bring the Church into disrepute by an uncritical acceptance of tales and fables that are without basis in historic fact. These concepts applied to those who seem to experience God's mystic graces will guide the confessor in the direction of souls and the biographer in the task he has undertaken.

Considering these things we may proceed to define the third attitude.

3. Under the term *mystic graces* are to be classified certain normal and fairly common experiences of some of those who lead a devout life, but which seldom enter the consciousness of those who do not lead a devout life. They are special forms of God's illuminating and inspiring graces by which He helps the soul on the road of sanctity to attain union of will, intellect, and heart with Himself. By the metaphorical term union of "heart" I hope to express the subjection of all emotions, impulses, and desires to the domination of reason so that they follow in the wake of the complete subjection to

[1] A similar concept was condemned in the fourteenth century. Denzinger-Bannwart, 558. See also *De fide et ratione contra Bautain*, 1622 ff.

God of intellect and will along with the whole being of man.[2]

One form of the mystic graces is what is termed by St. Teresa of Avila the prayer of quiet. The beginnings of this prayer take place so early in our spiritual life and are found so generally in devout souls, at least in its incipient forms, that we have given it special consideration in treating of the interior life. Outstanding among the various forms of the mystic graces are the prayer of union, ecstasy, interiorly spoken words. Sometimes, but rarely, words are spoken that cannot be distinguished from actual human speech, as when the Lord called the child Samuel in the temple.[3] It is also possible that one may receive the meaning of a statement that could have been expressed in words, but was not. Then there are various types of a consciousness of the presence of Christ or our Lady or one or more of the saints.[4]

To these we must add dreams, though in our questionnaire we did not ask for an account of any dreams that might have been supernatural in origin. The following from the autobiography of the Little Flower is an example of a mystic grace granted in a dream.

When St. Thérèse of Lisieux was suffering in the last stages of tuberculosis she received the favor of being assimilated to the passion of Christ, so that she could experience what it is to feel that one is forsaken by God. She was tormented by temptations against faith, over and above a spiritual darkness that in itself was a very great trial.

"When my heart," she wrote, "weary of the surrounding darkness, tries to find some rest in the thought of a life to come, my anguish increases. It seems to me that out of the darkness I hear the mocking voice of the unbeliever: 'You dream of a land of light and fragrance, you dream that the Creator of these wonders will be yours forever, you think one day to escape from these mists in which you now languish. Nay, rejoice in death which will give you, not

---

[2] See above, pp. 263 ff.
[3] I Kings III.
[4] Discussed more fully in last chapter.

what you hope for, but a night darker still, the night of utter nothingness!' " [5]

Somewhat later in the month of May she tells how the storm had raged ever since Easter. One night she was thinking of how God sometimes has consoled His favored ones by dreams, but felt that that could not be for her for whom "it was night, always night." [6] She fell asleep in the midst of the dark and heavy storm that raged in her soul.

Early in the morning of that night she had a dream in which she saw three Carmelites in mantles and long veils and she knew that these three were visitors from heaven. She felt a very strong desire to look on the face of one of these Carmelites. Great was her joy when the tallest among them walked toward her and lifted her veil and covered her with it. In the darkness that surrounded her by reason of the veil the face of this Carmelite was suffused with a soft light and she recognized the Venerable Mother Anne of Jesus, the foundress of the Carmel in France.

As St. Thérèse goes on to describe the loving smiles of this holy Carmelite and her fond caresses one gets a living picture of the life of charity of the saints in heaven: a charity which in heaven each and all will extend in every meeting and holy conversation, a charity which should find an earthly counterpart in all human relations. The love that we bear to God must flow over and dominate our inner attitudes to all and their outward expression in gentle smiles and holy affability.

The dream of St. Thérèse gives us a picture of the social life of the saints in heaven. It put an end to her dark night of faith. "On waking, I realized that Heaven does indeed exist and that this Heaven is peopled with souls who cherish me as their child." [7]

Anyone familiar with the theory of dreams and their in-

[5] *Soeur Thérèse of Lisieux,* New York, P. J. Kenedy, 1912, p. 141, revised translation, 1927, pp. 156-157.
[6] *Ibid.,* p. 179, rev. trans., pp. 199-200.
[7] *Ibid.,* p. 181, rev. trans., p. 200.

terpretation will recognize that this dream stands apart in a category of its own. There is no sign of the bizarre symbolism of the ordinary dream. It is much more like a vision seen in waking life than the ordinary phantasmagoria of the dream. It put a sudden end to a severe mental strain, and produced an equally sudden bursting of faith into bloom, so that she seemed to know by a quasi-perceptual intuition the substantial reality of "things to be hoped for" and was given by God Himself, far more than was pictured in the dream, the incontrovertible "evidence of things that appear not."

We are now in a position to describe the third attitude of mind toward phenomena reported as mystic graces. The various phenomena classified under the phrase mystic graces may be caused directly or indirectly by God. They may be truly supernatural in character and constitute special aids that God gives to some souls by which they increase in charity and all the virtues and attain to an ever closer and closer union of will, intellect, and heart with Him.

The author confesses that this is his own position. It seems to him that those who deny the existence of God, and by consequence all miracles and supernatural mystic graces as well, feel so unreasonably certain of their own position that they have not carefully examined the available facts with a mind open to conviction. They have assumed the position of Hume. We can have only moral certainty of any miracle; but we know with physical certainty that miracles cannot occur. On this basis the consideration of God and supernatural phenomena are automatically ruled out of court and not considered. But facts are facts and any true certainty, moral, physical, or metaphysical, demands the assent of the human mind. If we have moral certainty of the fact that a miracle took place, we cannot have physical certainty that all miracles are impossible. We must examine the possibility that there is an author of all nature, Whose power transcends the physical forces He brought into being. Our physical certainty is, then, not that miracles cannot occur, but that they cannot occur by the powers of nature. Any candid examination of the problem will show that our physical certainty cannot extend further than this. This physical certainty actually implies the possibility of miracles happening in virtue of the power of the Source and Origin of all that is, Who Himself is the sufficient reason for His own existence and Who by the very concept of His Essence transcends all that we know as nature.

As to those in the second group who regard the mystic graces, especially locutions and visions, as evidence of dementia praecox, I would raise the question as to whether or not this opinion is an example of what Francis Bacon would term *idolum theatri*, that is to say, a concept that is based neither on reason nor experience but which is the traditional doctrine in the group to which one belongs. I think one who has seen, conversed with, and studied typical cases of dementia praecox, and who would then study St. Teresa of Avila in her ordinary daily life would never be able to say that she suffered from dementia praecox. One can study her ordinary life from her letters and the *Book of the Foundations*. There she appears as a normal woman with great executive power, capable of bringing difficult enterprises to a successful conclusion. She has a delightful sense of humor, such as one never finds in a case of dementia praecox. She took a kindly interest in the difficulties of those under her charge. In other words she was a thoroughly normal personality, which no insane person ever is. And yet she heard voices and saw visions. I have in the past argued with psychiatrists who smiled at my naïveté in regarding her as mentally normal. But all consciousness of the presence of Christ or the Blessed Mother or one of the saints cannot be *ipso facto* ascribed to the broad category of the hallucinations of the insane.

Few, however, are so extreme as to regard mystic experiences as pathognomonic of dementia praecox. But many are very suspicious of them and think those who "suffer" from mysticism are in serious spiritual danger. St. John of the Cross lays down the general rule, but with exceptions, that locutions and visions should be allowed to pass without notice, saying that they work their good effect in the soul of themselves.[8] The principle must be applied with some discrimination. Take, for instance, the imaginal vision, cited above, of the Blessed Virgin reciting the psalms. Should the recipient have paid no attention to it and have said: "This is something dangerous. I will have nothing to do with it and recite my office, as I always have, lolling about as I please"?

St. John clarifies what he means by the following words: "The soul must set its eyes only upon the spirituality which they produce, striving to preserve it in its good works and to practise that which is for the due service of God, paying no attention to those representations nor desiring any pleasure of sense." [9] I think the words "paying no attention" in this passage mean that the recipient should not keep mulling over in his mind, "I have had a vision and am getting way up in the spiritual life." As a matter of fact, in the case we have mentioned, the vision, if vision it was, was given to the recipient precisely because he was not getting way up in the spiritual life. And St. John of the Cross in the first part of the passage cited indicates that the recipient must pay a whole lot of attention to what is shown him to be lacking in his spiritual life, and to make use of any means suggested in the vision to improve his spiritual life.

Some visions and other mystic graces are so simple and innocent that it is hard to see how they could do any harm. Let us take another case from our material.

"I consulted a doctor on account of a condition which he diagnosed as severe inflammation of the middle ear. He told me that hearing in that ear would be permanently impaired. He dusted some powder on the ear drum and told me to return the next day. Seeing that I could not hear ordinary conversation with my other ear I looked forward to a permanent

---

[8] See *Ascent of Mount Carmel*, Bk. II, Chaps. XVI and XVII, and above, pp. 297 ff.

[9] *Ibid.*, Peers's translation, Vol. I, p. 144. The word "spirituality" is Peers's translation for *buen espíritu*. The phrase might be translated better by: "the good spirit to which they give rise."

disability which would mean a great change in my life and work. The following morning I was reclining on my bed, somewhat depressed in spirits. Suddenly without seeing anything I became conscious of the presence of Christ, standing behind my head on my left. He seemed to sympathize with me so tenderly that I felt a warm responsive love for Him. I asked Him however for nothing. I just loved Him. He seemed to say to me, 'Would you like to be healed, my child?' I felt: 'I certainly would', and the presence faded.

"When I went to see the doctor he was greatly surprised. The inflammation was gone and my hearing was normal in the ear that had been affected."

One fails to see that a mystic grace of this kind is in any way a danger to the spiritual welfare of the soul. I would not like to deny that some are in danger because of supposed mystic graces. But one should raise the question whether or not the mystic graces that endanger the welfare of the soul are true graces sent by God, or counterfeits due to a heightened imagination set in action by a desire to be numbered among the mystics, or by the father of lies prowling about to find someone whom he may deceive. The love of God, like the "love of our neighbor" worketh no evil.[10]

It is easily seen that many pass judgment on the nature of mystic graces in virtue of their personal attitudes of mind and habitual ways of thinking rather than from a broad and intimate acquaintance with what happens in the interior life of man with God.

The fact that those who do not lead a holy life in any sense of the word seldom or never have any mystic experiences and perhaps even a third of those who do lead a devout life are also devoid of these experiences leads us to recognize that they are entirely unknown to the majority of mankind as conscious events in their own mental life. It thus comes about that many are as suspicious of mystic experiences as a city boy would be of mushrooms he might come across in a field when he was hungry.

[10] Romans XIII:10.

In the first place we must recognize that God, the Supreme Intelligence, directs all intelligent beings to Himself, the Supreme Good and the final end of every created mind. There is a true Light which enlighteneth every man who cometh into the world. This He has ever done by what is termed the natural law which is the dictate of God, the Eternal Law, to every conscience when the mind of man sits in judgment upon conduct. Over and above this, from the beginning, He guided man through a primeval revelation in Paradise, and then through the law and the prophecies made known to the Hebrew people. Finally: "God, Who at sundry times and in divers manners, spoke in times past to the Fathers by the Prophets, last of all in these days, hath spoken to us by His Son." [11] The Eternal Word made flesh, while living with us, established "the Church of the living God, the pillar and ground of truth." [12] And ascending into heaven, almost His parting words were: "Behold I am with you all days even to the consummation of the world." [13] No man can add to nor take away from the deposit of truth entrusted the Church by Jesus Christ.

From the first days of Christianity great saints have been given a special commission in a mystic experience. Thus St. Paul was converted and given his mission to the gentiles in a mystic experience. St. Peter in a mystic experience was taught that he should not impose on gentile converts the food restrictions in force among the Hebrews. [14] St. Augustine in the garden of his house experienced a series of mystic graces in which he heard a voice: "Take up and read! Take up and read." He picked up and read from a book of the Epistles of St. Paul a random passage: "Not in rioting and drunkenness, not in chambering and impurities, not in contention and envy: but put ye on the Lord Jesus Christ, and make not pro-

[11] Hebrews I:1.
[12] I Timothy III:15.
[13] Matthew XXVIII:20.
[14] Acts X:11 ff.

vision for the flesh in its concupiscences." [15] And there shone
a light in his mind and peace filled his heart. A life of sin
was renounced and he lived in celibacy for the rest of his
days.[16] From those early days to the present untold thousands
have experienced mystic graces of many kinds and in some
way they have suddenly or gradually been transformed by
their experiences.

Can we say, in the examples just cited, that these mystic
graces were mere volitional attempts to imagine what was
heard? A study of the context will show that no such concept
can be maintained. It is a general characteristic of the mystic
graces that they break in on the mind independently of any
activity of the one who experiences them. If they appear to
be produced by the experiencer they are fraudulent imita-
tions and not true mystic experiences.

Is the whole course of spiritual development in which there
may be a number of mystic graces, on to and including spiritual marriage with Christ, precontained in the unconscious of
the individual? Or is it a growth which takes place by repeated plantings from without, that is, by the inspirations of
divine grace?

When Freud speaks of the unconscious he finds therein
two types of material: 1) repressed elements that were formerly conscious but which the subject wants to forget, and
2) the whole past experience of the race.[17]

Seeing that there is no evidence that acquired experience is
ever transmitted by heredity, the only way for the experience
of the race to enter the mind of the individual is by what is
handed down in the environment in which the individual develops. *What filters into the unconscious from the experi-*

[15] Romans XIII:13-14.

[16] *Confessions*, Bk. VIII. St. Augustine raises but does not settle the question whether the voice was that of a child or something supernatural. But
he says that he interpreted "it to be no other than a command from God
to open the book."

[17] See Sigmund Freud, *The Ego and the Id*, trans. by Joan Riviere, London, 1927, and *The Unconscious*, in *Collected Papers*, in five vol., London,
Hogarth Press and Institute of Psycho-analysis, 1924, Vol. IV.

*ence of the race must enter the mind through the conscious
experience of the individual.*[18]

What, we may ask, was there in the unconscious of Peter,
the Jewish fisherman of Galilee, that could have erupted and
made him suddenly think that it was lawful to eat the flesh
of swine? Or what was there in the inner consciousness of
Saul, the persecutor of the Christians, on his way to Damas-
cus, to bring them bound to Jerusalem, that could have
erupted and produced a vision of Christ and consciousness of
a duty to renounce Judaism and preach the Gospel of Christ?

These two facts are inexplicable on any theory of the unconscious *with a basis in actual facts;* but they are adequately
explained by the concept of spiritual growth as a series of
plantings from without, that is to say, by the inspirations of
divine grace.

The experience of the individual from birth to death, in
which he commences at some point an interior life and with
or without various mystic experiences goes on toward the
spiritual marriage of the soul with Christ cannot be evolved
from the filtration of racial experience through the environment to the consciousness of the individual. A study of it
would also show that much is not contained in what is read
or heard, but seems to be something new, which arises by a
series of "plantings" due to the inspirations of divine grace.

Furthermore, over and above the psychological content and
character of the mystic grace there is something else that it
bestows. St. Augustine in his *Confessions* describes his long,
vain efforts to free himself from the shackles of impurity. But
with the mystic graces in the garden culminating with reading the passage in St. Paul, there came a sudden change and
he was endowed with power from on high. Facts such as that
must be considered in discussing the origin of the mystic
graces. The Freudian unconscious with its pansexuality would
drive man deeper into the quagmire of impurity, never deliver him from the slavery of lust.

[18] What is here said of Freud's racial unconscious applies also to C. G.
Jung's "Collective unconscious."

St. Teresa says several times that the mystic graces lead to a marked increase in the love of God and a virtuous life. When she was about to write about the prayer of union [19] she went to communion and our Lord said to her: The soul "dies to itself wholly, daughter, in order that it may fix itself more and more upon Me; it is no longer itself that lives but I." [20] In the following chapter she writes of the soul: "Almost without knowing it, and doing nothing consciously to that end, it begins to benefit its neighbors, and they become aware of this benefit. . . . They realize that the soul has virtues, and seeing how desirable the fruit is, would fain help it partake of it." [21]

Not only the prayer of union but all the mystic graces contribute to growth in virtues, and the above passage indicates that this is true not only in the one who is given the prayer of union but also of those among whom the recipient lives.

It should also be perfectly evident to anyone that were the mystic graces due merely to the person's own volitional efforts he would never be able to bring about such changes in himself, let alone in the lives of others. The effects for good which Sister Miriam Teresa Demjanovich had as a novice on the spiritual life of those with whom she lived derived from the mystical graces of which she was the recipient.[22]

Examples of the Mystic Graces

There is a vast difference in the extent to which souls experience the mystic graces among those who have any experience of them at all. In some there has been one and only one isolated mystic grace. One, for instance, mentions having heard words that seemed to come from God which de-

[19] Our question 16 was formulated to see if the soul had experienced anything akin to the prayer of union.

[20] *Life*, Chap. XVIII, Peers's translation, Vol. I, p. 110.

[21] *Ibid.*, p. 112.

[22] See *Sister Miriam Teresa (1901-1927)*, by a Sister of Charity, New York, Benziger, 1936; Theodore Maynard, *The Better Part*, New York, Macmillan, 1952.

cided her vocation. In several, such innerly spoken words have put an end to a period of doubt and led to a decision in regard to their vocation which seems never to have been regretted.

A nun writes: "Once, as a young girl of 17, I had gone to a priest giving a mission to ask some advice concerning a divorced man. I had no intention of speaking about my vocation. At the end of the conversation, I casually remarked that I had thought of the religious life. Father advised me to decide within six months. As I left the rectory and started down the steps to the street, a very definite thought, or was it a voice, said: 'You are going; and as soon as you can get away.' So vivid was it that after many years all the details are as clear to me now as on that day. Another time, about two years ago while waiting my turn for confession, I was much depressed and felt I could not go on. From the tabernacle came an interior *voice* saying: 'Can't you do it for Me?' and at once peace and calm flooded my soul." More than one have mentioned the peace and the lifting of a depression that followed a locution. Such effects can be explained by God's action on the soul; but no man can lift himself by pulling on his own boot straps.

A married woman, though she has not known a clear-cut betrothal scene with Christ, had an equivalent experience. She writes thus: "When I was in the hospital some time ago, after receiving communion, Christ became present to me in a peculiar manner I had never experienced before. From that time He has never departed from me. On leaving the hospital, I would have given a million dollars if I had it, to be able to take along the furniture of the room in which I had spent such blissfully happy days with Christ. I have a constant awareness of the presence of the Blessed Trinity (especially of the Second and Third Persons). This is so vivid that it seems to me that it *is* the beginnings of eternal life. My happiness in being privileged to know and love Christ cannot be affected by the trials and sufferings I have to endure; because I know that they are only ways and means of adding glory to Him. I have been looking forward to and hoping for death for about 25 years (ever since I was in my teens) but for the last dozen years it has almost become an obsession. Once when I was experiencing this yearning, about 2 years ago, Christ said to me: 'I will take you now if you want me to'. I replied, 'I don't want what I want, but what *You* want'. I have experienced no betrothal nor marriage scene such as you describe, but I know Christ and I belong to each other. I have spent whole nights with Him in mental prayer. But my imperfections have not disappeared. I am still struggling with them. You should hear me shout at my youngsters. The goal —Be ye perfect as your heavenly Father is perfect—gets further and further away. I feel that I am the most stupid, useless, good-for-nothing, and miserable of all God's creatures."

A married woman gives the following descriptions of incidents in her spiritual life. She is one of those who is habitually conscious of the Divine Presence the whole day long. Her prayer is habitually that termed the prayer of quiet, and the peace of prayer lasts with her all day long even in the midst of household duties. She writes: "No matter what I read or how I commence my mental prayer, I always wind up in that longing to be just there in the presence of my Eucharistic King by the gift of myself." Usually, she spends in prayer all the time she can possibly spare.

Though she fluctuates between Chautard's sixth and seventh degrees and therefore is not conscious of any fully deliberate venial sins, she writes thus: "Because God is so good and merciful to me, I feel lower and viler than all. In spite of my many weaknesses and sins, He is always loving and tender each time I try again."

At times she suffers because she cannot be united at once with Christ in heaven. From time to time she experiences something akin to the prayer of union and ecstasy, and at various times is conscious of the presence of Christ and our Lady and some of the saints.

"While I cannot say that I am now in the experiences of degree number seven of the questionnaire, it seems to me that in everything I do I am conscious of the presence of God. Devotion to the Holy Eucharist is my greatest joy and concern. It is the whole Kingdom of Christ right here on earth. Many times a day I place myself spiritually in front of the tabernacles all over the world. I am irresistibly drawn to make visits to Our Lord in the Blessed Sacrament whenever possible, at almost any time during the day. I feel a longing to prostrate myself before the Blessed Sacrament. To receive our Lord every morning is my greatest happiness and the only really important thing in this whole world. My greatest sorrow (and I accuse myself of it often) is that I cannot comprehend it deeply enough. Neither am I able to give sufficient adoration to this great mystery. I lament my dullness and weakness in this and often cry out: How can I sufficiently adore and love Thee?"

"Once when I was reading a meditation by Father John Ryan, S.J., in the little 'Fatima Findings,' upon coming to a part that told of the Incarnation (it was just a sentence or two) I was overwhelmed by the sublime mystery of the Incarnation and for a moment I seemed to penetrate into that mystery so far that I seemed to be outside of myself and I felt that I would have died if I hadn't come to myself quickly. I could never describe it, but I know that I grasped it for that moment. There was a terrifying grandeur about it, but it seemed to increase my love and desire to please God.

"Once, in prayer, it seemed almost a physical or bodily experience of Our Blessed Mother preparing me and taking me to my Eucharistic King as a Mother might give her daughter and prepare her for marriage, as if to say: 'You are grown up now and must be a real spouse to the King'. It seemed like a real experience, many things were made more real to me.

"Once when I had been so troubled about the trials and illness of my daughter, I awoke one morning hearing a voice saying: 'I am a little Chicago saint for a little Chicago girl'. I saw a mental image of Mother Cabrini. It was so real and this assurance stayed with me for weeks. I then prayed fervently to Mother Cabrini from then on, and my daughter was helped both spiritually and physically.

"Very often I may be looking at a little flower, or a pool of water or any of the things of nature and for a few moments I am aware of the power and love and grandeur of God, so vividly that I can scarcely contain myself. My faith is increased so much at these times."

A priest gives the following accounts of various mystic graces and other experiences classified according to the numbers in our questionnaire.

"Mental prayer consists for me in a silent resting in the intimate Presence and embrace of my Beloved, Him Who is Infinite Love. Normally, precise *thoughts* and *images*—to say nothing of *words*,—are impossible and repugnant. Rather, my need and attraction in prayer is to surrender all voluntary human activity in a total, trustful, loving yielding-up of my will and my whole being to the Will and Divine activity of the Beloved. This Divine Action is not usually felt—prayer is usually very dry, and far from sweet to nature. Distractions of a very superficial kind tend to allure my imagination and mind, since this prayer gives them nothing to feed on. Thus my *will* often finds itself all alone in its union with the Beloved. But the will is never disturbed, but simply uses these distractions as material for offering my helplessness to God, in utter trust in Him Who is so merciful to me, and Who can in a moment rid me of these distractions if it please Him. Apparently He prefers my state of happy helplessness! So I do not struggle against distractions in a way that would disturb the simplicity of the will's union with God—nor am I discouraged or saddened by them. I simply disown them, refuse to be bothered by them, and leaving them behind, bury my will deeper and deeper in the Will and Heart of my Beloved.

"Obviously there is little in the way of infused grace of prayer—but since I pray simply to please Him, I happily leave all that in His hands. He does teach and guide my soul by His prayer, though it be in a hidden, dark way which I cannot always perceive at the time. It is the science of Love and utter trust, that He teaches, and it is in this spirit of silent love and boundless trust that He enables me to embrace Him in prayer. Having normally no grace for the higher forms of prayer, nor the ability to meditate, I do not offer God a specific prayer; but rather offer Him my nothingness, my whole being, in union with Jesus and Mary, as itself a prayer: the prayer that His beloved Will be done in all souls, at any cost to myself.

"So it is not so much mental prayer (for my mind is so helpless at prayer!) but rather prayer of the will—a will that rejoices in its helplessness and darkness, as a means of expressing its utter loving surrender to its God. It is the prayer of silent praise and gratitude for everything just exactly the way it is.

[Question 13]

"I avoid self-chosen, arbitrary acts of penance, believing that for me, self-denial is most perfect when it consists in the embrace of God's Will and good pleasure moment by moment. I find that this implies a well-nigh constant spirit of self-denial, if I am alert for every tiny sacrifice and contradiction contained therein.

"I do eat as simply as obedience, and the common life, allow; and, with the blessing of obedience, restrict sleep to five hours, in order to spend two more hours in prayer. But this is done, *not* as a penance, but because God thirsts for our prayer, and each waking moment is so precious for Love!

✦

[Question 14]

"Yes, according to the will, but *not* according to human nature. And there is *no* thirst for self-imposed sufferings and humiliations.

[Questions 16, 17, 18]

"There have been a few instances of absorption in God of this sort, but whether they correspond to 16, 17 or 18 I'm not sure.

[Question 19]

"Yes, on a few occasions—but I do not dwell on them. The first and clearest instance was early in my religious life, when I seemed utterly overwhelmed and crushed by my misery and helplessness. I sensed the Presence of Jesus very close in front of me, and heard interiorly the words: 'Have I ever failed you yet? Then why should I begin to do so now?' After a pause: 'I know that you are nothing by yourself, but I will not leave you by yourself'. A little later, but less distinctly: 'I would gladly suffer My entire Passion for just one soul: even yours'. (Also see last example of #20)

[Question 20]

"There has apparently been one vision seen by my bodily eyes, of our Blessed Mother. It is important that it was seen at the age of 16, when I had no knowledge at all of the Catholic faith, or of the Mother of God. So it was quite independent of my imagination or desires.

"I was sleeping alone in a bedroom at home, when for no apparent reason I awoke, to find a woman bending over me, looking down at my face. At my awakening she made no movement nor sound, nor did I. Somehow I was not even startled, but filled with deep Peace. At the first moment I thought it was my mother, though I soon realized in the semi-darkness that it was not, though it was a middle-aged woman who had the air of being my mother—in the way she was bending over me and gazing at me with intense love.

"She was not superficially beautiful, but a wonderful beauty of soul was revealed in a face that bore the marks of great suffering quietly and heroically borne. The gaze of her eyes into mine was the focal point in the experience: a gaze of utter love, a mother's love, containing and absorbing a boundless sorrow—the Mother of Sorrows.

"Some moments seemed to pass thus, in silence and peace. Then gradually she straightened up always with her gaze fixed upon my face, and slowly, soundlessly, moved backwards away from the bed. As she did so, the room began to grow more and more luminous, while she herself, now seen to be clothed in purest white, became more and more radiant though less and less distinct in outline, until finally her form was lost, while her radiance seemed to fill the room. Then this radiance, too, faded, and I was left alone—in utter peace but somehow, inexplicably not startled or excited. Filled with wonder, to be sure, I distinctly remember making very sure I was awake and not dreaming. Then I went back to sleep, and never spoke of the vision to anyone, until it became shelved in my memory, simply as a puzzling mystery. Eight years afterwards, about ½ year after I had received the grace of Faith, while singing the Salve Regina, it suddenly came to me—unexpected and clear—that the Mater Misericordia had indeed 'turned her eyes of mercy upon me'.

"There have been a number of instances, (though none in the last two years), of imaginal visions—always unexpected, and always accompanied by an infused understanding of their meaning. I will mention three of them:

"1. Once, while in private prayer, I suddenly saw interiorly, very distinctly, a beautiful hand holding aloft the Blessed Sacrament. The background was of limitless space. I understood it to represent the constant offering by Our Lady of her Divine Victim-Son to the Eternal Father on our behalf.

"2. Once, while in private prayer, away from the community but at the time of the Community's Communion Mass, I seemed to be in back of Our Lady, who was seated on a chair or throne at the Sanctuary step of the Church facing the Choir, with St. Joseph standing at her side. The Community was coming up in procession to receive Holy Communion from Our Lady's hand. The vision lasted while two or three religious received from her, the Divine Victim.

"3. The last such imaginal vision occurred while I was lying in bed in the Infirmary, and did follow upon a period of several hours in which God seemed to be guiding my prayer and enlightening me upon the Divine Plan of Redemption in a very special way. I was becoming more and more passive to His action, when suddenly I heard interiorly the words: 'And now I will show you a soul entering Heaven'. My mind, completely passive, was shown a soul rising from a place of utter darkness and desolation, and, taking the form of a young child clothed in white, it approached the gates of the Heavenly Jerusalem. And as the child approached, the gates swung open, and all the saints were seen gathered together eagerly and lovingly welcoming their tiny brother. And at the same time I heard interiorly the most exquisite harmonies, sung by the host of Angels. My whole being was filled to overflowing with indescribable joy and a sense of eternal glory, as if I were sharing the experience of that child. Accompanying this brief vision, was the infused understanding that this sudden ascent of the soul from utter darkness to boundless joy signified that the more a soul lovingly endures every possible trial and darkness and suffering on earth, the fuller will be its joy and glory for all eternity. It filled me with a distaste for all consolations—even spiritual ones—and indeed since that moment, for 2½ years, there have been virtually none.

[Question 21]

"Yes, though I see now that there was plenty of self-love mixed in—but the *un*sensible infused understanding that accompanied them was purely good and did indeed urge me to greater generosity and closer conformity to the Divine Will."

Criteria of Genuine and False Mystical Experiences

The technique that we have made use of in this work enables us to get a general picture of the stages of the spiritual life through which man passes in his ascent to God, and also to have a look at some types of mystic experience that some, but by no means all, encounter on the road. It does not enable us to pass a final judgment on these experiences so as in each case to say definitely that this was a supernatural occurrence and had God for its author, that was a counterfeit of the imagination, and something else was due to the Father of Lies. To do this, with some hope of coming to a true decision, one should be able to interview the recipient of mystical favors, and learn from him something about his fidelity to God in the ordinary duties of life.

However, there are certain psychological determining characteristics in the accounts themselves that will help the one who must pass a practical judgment for the direction of a penitent. Let us first consider certain signs of a mystical experience that has God for its author.

If one will consider the various accounts presented in this book he will find examples that will fit into one or more of the following categories:

1. Some mystic experiences seem specifically designed to correct an evident fault in the recipient's spiritual life or mode of behavior, such as the one which we cited in the commencement of this chapter in which our Lady seemed to correct by her personal example a slovenly manner of reciting the office. Similar to this is the following: "Some time ago our Lady seemed responsible for curing me of a rather serious illness. When my vigorous health returned I again started to work very hard and considered myself authorized to cut my sleep way down by sitting up very late at night. After I had been doing this for some time, not without qualms of conscience, it seemed to me one morning, around about the beginning of Mass, that our Lady was speaking to me, being present on my right side. There was no visual image whatso-

ever. She reprimanded me, very firmly but at the same time gently, by a series of concepts rather than by interiorly spoken words. I might express what she said as follows: 'You must keep your rule and get in the full time allowed for sleep. You cannot expect that I will miraculously get you out of all the difficulties that will come to you by your own failure to practise prudence as you should.' "

When any spiritual experience, *by its very nature*, is helpful in our spiritual life we may be fairly sure that it is a grace given by God on the basis of the text: "Every best gift and every perfect gift is from above coming down from God the Father of lights." [23] Was the lesson of our Lady reciting the psalms given by God but the visual image a natural product of the imagination? One might ask: When God wishes to bestow a grace, *does He wait upon the imagination* to first produce an image? If so, would not that make grace dependent on the bizarre and irregular activity of a faculty that seems to know no law? It would seem more consonant with the divine dignity that God should Himself awaken the image in the imagination and illumine the intellect to understand its mystic meaning. The same is to be said of auditory images or intellectual locutions.

But could one be deluded by the devil or his own imagination even though the result of the so-called mystic experience, by its very nature, was helpful in our spiritual life? J. de Tonquédec, S.J., the official exorcist of the Archdiocese of Paris, made this comment: "Illusion in this matter can be without importance, as far as the government of conduct is concerned. From the moment that the results are good, and can be utilized for spiritual profit, it matters little whether they be due to the play of our natural faculties, or to the motion of ordinary grace, wrongly considered as a mystic grace —or even to the action of the demon, who would thus find himself trapped in his own snares." [24]

[23] James I:17.
[24] "De la certitude dans les états mystiques," *Nouvelle Revue Mystique,* 1953, Vol. 75, p. 399.

2. Sometimes when a person is in doubt about what he should do, or is overwhelmed by sorrow or anxiety, a few words that seem to come from Christ or the Blessed Mother or one of the saints will make him suddenly know just what he ought to do, or lift the emotional clouds that hang over him and establish him firmly in peace in the sunshine of divine charity. All this takes no more time than that required to understand what is said. What is given is given; and the recipient receives it without an opportunity to say whether he will take it or not. The only thing left for him to do is to be grateful for a favor that evidently came to him directly or indirectly from God.

3. Some mystic experiences are of such a character that we cannot conceive of them as having been brought about by the subject himself, and at the same time they seem utterly foreign to what Satan could or would do. Of this character is the experience of the married woman cited above, who received communion in the hospital and from that moment entered into a state of continuous and permanent consciousness of the Divine Presence.[25]

The state that she describes is similar to that mentioned by St. Teresa, in the Seventh Mansion of her *Interior Castle*, as what takes place in spiritual matrimony. Few will deny that it is naturally impossible for man to bring about by natural efforts, unaided by divine grace, anything approaching a state of abiding continuous recollection in which one lives always consciously in the presence of the Blessed Trinity. No one should attempt to remain *uninterruptedly* in the Divine Presence. Some who do have become neurotic and suffered a mental breakdown without ever attaining their end. Many have injudiciously made the attempt without suffering anything more serious than complete failure in their efforts to attain this end. It is never attained by personal effort and is rarely given by God. The most we can do is to be faithful to mental prayer, fight against sin in every form, practice reasonable self-denial, from time to time in the course of the

[25] See above, p. 320.

day recall that we ever live face to face with God and bow down before Him in spirit with loving adoration.

When God commences to give shorter or longer periods of a loving awareness of His presence, this recollection is accompanied by a profound peace and inner spiritual joy. It is a state from which anything akin to mental tension is completely banished. Furthermore, it will come and go without one being able to bring it on or to hold on to it when it is present. Anyone who admits that those who describe such states of continuous consciousness of the Divine Presence are giving true accounts of what they actually experience, should also admit that this mystic grace has God for its author.

It will not always be possible to determine whether or not some experiences are due to the grace of God or one's own imagination. When the one who has them, or produces them, is truly humble it will make little difference. The rules of St. John of the Cross, cited above,[26] should be pointed out, and the subject conduct himself as they dictate.

Can there be any such thing as counterfeit mystic experiences produced by Satan in an effort to deceive a soul and wrest it from Christ? All spiritual writers in the Church admit this possibility and even dwell upon it. Is there anything in our data that would enable us to detect such counterfeit mystic experiences? Let us see.

Many of the experiences described in our material may be understood mainly as a picture lesson in the spiritual life of definite value to the recipient. Others, as in those akin to the prayer of union or ecstasy, lift the soul to the heights of divine charity, and the soul, in utter forgetfulness of self and without any focal awareness of the delight it experiences, burns with the love of One it knows to be present, and adores the Creator of all that is.

Whenever the deliciousness of the experience stands out in great prominence, and, therefore, self-enjoyment plays the major role, one should seriously question that it has God for its author. This is particularly true when the experience is

[26] See above, p. 302.

not an isolated event but recurs repeatedly and dominates the whole inner life of the soul. The true love of God is an act by which the will consecrates the soul irrevocably to God. It may be emotionally cold, but in the height of mystic experience all the faculties of man unite in this irrevocable consecration. This consecration, therefore, has the warmth of an intense emotional experience. But in this warmth there is no trace of sexuality. Should sexuality become a prominent element in the experience it should be regarded as a counterfeit of Satan. This suspicion would be confirmed if there is no element of adoration and a love of God that in some manner might be expressed or implied in such words as: *Deus meus et omnia* (*My God and my All*). No harm would ever be done by telling one who has experiences of this kind to pay no attention to them whatsoever. This would demand a great sacrifice, for usually the one who experiences them prizes them highly. But the sacrifice would be of great spiritual value.

In less than one per cent of my cases was there anything that suggested, in the above-described way, a Satanic element. The mystic experiences of those who lead a devout life are, in general, not only innocent and harmless but very helpful in leading them to God.

Let us in conclusion consider the mystic graces, examples of which are now before the reader, in relation to the natural activities of the mind.

We can by voluntary effort imagine Christ or our Blessed Mother or one of the saints as before us. Some can imagine that they see them and also hear them speak. But when they do so, they know perfectly well that all this is a pious exercise that they themselves carry out by the ordinary grace of God. Several have mentioned doing this and have said that they derived great spiritual profit from the exercise, but they in no way confused this exercise with experiencing visions or locutions. Unquestionably many often do this in their daily meditations.

The mystic graces, if ascribed to the natural operation of

the imagination, must be regarded as its involuntary activity which has nothing whatsoever to do with personal effort. Let us consider these involuntary activities of the imagination.

Some years ago that brilliant little German psychologist F. Kiesow, at the University of Turin in Italy, made a study of what he termed *"Freisteigende Vorstellungen."* [27] These are spontaneous memory images that suddenly arise before the mind as a visual picture, with no apparent cause for their presence. In this they have a point of resemblance with various mystic graces. Kiesow's wife for some time kept a record of this spontaneous imagery and did all that she could to trace it back to some perception with which the memory image was associated. An association was found with certainty in only 193 out of 892 cases; sometimes only after painstaking efforts. From the fact that, after long effort only, many associations were found, Kiesow concluded that failure to find associations in a goodly number of cases did not prove that they were absent and jumped to the generalization: no idea arises in mental life except by perception or association.

We are not now interested in the validity of this generalization. But various mental phenomena suggest that it may not give a true picture of the mental life of man. Thus an afterimage from looking at a bright spot does not disappear once and for all, but keeps rhythmically returning, and certainly not in virtue of any association. What are termed hypnagogic hallucinations—the peculiar bizarre visual, sometimes auditory, images that come and go and indicate that sleep is at hand, certainly are not brought into the mind by any law of association. A pathologist having spent hours looking through the microscope may on leaving the laboratory have recurrent visual images of microscopic fields such as he was studying. No law of association accounts for these spontaneously recurring images. Such phenomena might be supposed to indicate a rhythmic reactivation of sensory traces which might, at times,

---

[27] *Über sogenannte "freisteigende" Vorstellungen*, Arch. f. d. ges. Psychol., 1906, Vol. VI. See also Wundt, *Grundzüge der Physiol. Psychol.*, 6th ed., 1911, Vol. III. p. 566.

call before the mind an image recognizable as experienced in the past (sensory memory, according to St. Thomas), or images bereft of all coloring of past experience (activity of imagination, according to St. Thomas).

All these sensory phenomena are quite different from mystic graces. The mystic graces are in general brand-new experiences in which the intellectual content takes precedence over the sensory. Therefore they cannot be the mere activity of imagination and sensory memory. They have often the character of someone giving us important instruction and guidance at a critical moment in our spiritual life, either symbolically or by actual verbal instruction. And not only that, but they may be followed by profound changes in our moral and spiritual life that work a reformation of our personality and whose effects abide *usque ad finem vitae*, even to the end of life. They belong to an entirely different world from the phantasmagoria of sensory mental life which have little if any importance. We have good right to regard them as experiences that derive from that true Light which enlighteneth every man who cometh into this world.

There is also a whole group of phenomena, which we have no more than referred to in this work, that also derive from this Light. I mean the valuable insights that come in any good meditation or in holy reading. It is by these illuminations that God brings us out of darkness into His marvelous light.

Could the mystic graces have any kinship with a dream? One without intimate knowledge of the mystic graces might think the recipient passes into a dreamy state and naturally becomes aware of the activity of the imagination that everyone experiences in dream life.

If one wants to get an insight into the mechanism of the dream one should study what has been termed hypnotic analogies.[28] When one is reading or working at his desk in the daytime, one sometimes falls into a doze and has a short dream. It has been found that such a dream is the mere *con-*

[28] See Psychological Studies from the Catholic University of America, *Psychol. Monographs*, Vol. 27, No. 4, pp. 387-400.

tinuation of the thoughts that were in one's mind just before going to sleep. They are much more easy to analyze than the dreams of the night, separated by some hours from the thought of the day. Thus one went to sleep and saw a shower of faintly luminous rods falling helter-skelter, and heard the words "all things topsy-turvy." This auditory-visual imagery is a *hypnotic analogy* of the train of thought in the subject's mind just before going to sleep. He had failed in something he tried hard to accomplish.

Could a mystic experience in some way involve the mental activity that is characteristic of dream states? When comparing two groups or series of events, it is well to take each series as a whole and compare it with the other as a whole. In this way identity or diversity is much more apparent than if one tries to compare individual items or experiences. Alfred Binet wrote a little book on suggestibility. It has two frontispieces, neither with any legend. They represent two groups of children. I found by actual trial that about 80 per cent of college students were capable of correctly deciding which group represented the suggestible children and which the nonsuggestible. Similarly it is easy to decide with certainty and correctness that one group photograph, or group of photographs, represents children with IQs of sixty to eighty, and another photograph, or set of photographs, represents a group with IQs ranging from one hundred to one hundred ten; though various individual pictures, if compared, would give rise to serious doubts and errors.

If now, one would be given the series of phenomena presented in this book as mystic graces, and an equally numerous series, chosen at random, from dream life, there would be no difficulty in seeing that they constitute two very different groups of experiences. Why, therefore, should anyone, unwilling to recognize supernatural experiences, try to maintain that mystic experiences are mere natural activities of the imagination such as we are all familiar with in dream life?

Then there are, in individual experiences, elements that show that they have nothing to do with going to sleep. For example the imaginal representation of the Blessed Virgin reciting the psalms [29] was not seen when the recipient was asleep, but only when he wakened did he see her standing beside him erect and motionless apparently absorbed in what she was doing.

Some break in on one who is wide awake, chanting the psalms in choir, or reciting the "Our Father" at Mass.[30] They seem no more connected with the immediately previous train of the subject's thought than if someone were to interrupt you and speak to you while you were very busy with the work of the day.

No one can reasonably attribute to the natural workings of the mental powers of man all that transpires in the life of the soul with God. On the other hand, we cannot always be sure whether an event was due to the ordinary help which God ever provides us, or to one of those special graces which He less seldom grants. But whenever anything works within you a definite change for the better, you should always see the hand of God. You should never forget that "it is God Who worketh in you, both to will and to accomplish, according to His good will." [31]

[29] P. 307.
[30] P. 351.
[31] Philippians II:13.

CHAPTER **XVII**

Spiritual Betrothal and
Spiritual Marriage[1]

WE SHALL get a better realization of the mystical state known as the betrothal of the soul with Christ if we pause to give a résumé of the preparatory stages of the spiritual life which lead up to this wonderful mystical grace. This résumé is based mainly on the data of our questionnaire rather than on the literature about spiritual betrothal. Our guiding lines in outlining this process of development will be the extent of freedom from sin and the type and state of mental prayer. The sufferings of life accompany all these stages. They do not come by accident. They are not merely permitted. They are designed by God to purify the soul so that it may become such a being that Christ might be able to choose it as His promised spouse and make the soul conscious of His choice in a scene in which each would promise itself to the other.

The first stage is one which often lasts for years. It is a long and sometimes a bitter struggle with temptation. The deeper a soul may have descended into a life of sin, the longer and the more violent this conflict is likely to be. But God is

[1] These experiences are considered in this chapter as special mystic graces. Equivalent states that are not mystic graces were mentioned above, pp. 291 ff.

not bound by natural laws of time and space. In some souls who have maintained baptismal innocence, this period passes in greater peace. The usual termination of this period is due to, or accompanied by, the entering upon a habitual life of mental prayer, very often, but not always, in the form of some type of meditation. At the same time there commences a more or less vigorous life of self-denial.

This leads by further graces of God to a period of freedom from all fully deliberate sins, whether mortal or venial. One still falls into involuntary venial sin, however, through lack of control of emotional life, also into many imperfections, and slips into conduct which later seems to the soul to have been utterly foolish and unreasonable.

Sometimes in this period or even before, one may experience the first touches of the prayer of quiet. In fact, if we may draw any conclusions from the experience of St. Teresa, the prayer of quiet and that of union may appear very early in the course of the spiritual life. "The Lord began to be so gracious to me on this way of prayer that He granted me the favor of leading me to the prayer of quiet, and occasionally even to union, though I did not understand what either of these was, or how highly they were to be valued." [2] St. Teresa says that at this time she "was not yet twenty years old," but Peers estimates correctly that she could not have been less than twenty-three, because she entered the Convent of the Incarnation late in her twenty-first year.

During this period the soul that is being prepared for spiritual betrothal with Christ is likely to receive some, perhaps many, of the mystic graces described in the preceding chapter. However, in this period occurs the parting of the ways in the history of a soul. Some, as we have seen, will go on to perfect friendship with Christ and the equivalent of spiritual matrimony and will never experience any of the mystic graces, other than the prayer of quiet, and perhaps in rare cases not even that. Others will receive various mystic graces and the inestimable blessing of spiritual betrothal; but only a very

[2] *Life*, Chap. IV, Peers's translation, Vol. I, p. 23.

few of these will in this life attain to spiritual matrimony with Christ. This, as St. John of the Cross remarks, is incomparably higher than spiritual betrothal, but no one enters it without having first passed through the spiritual betrothal.[3]

We must be careful to distinguish between a psychological state in a definite level of mystical development and being made, as it were, officially and canonically the spouse of Christ. This latter takes place on entering the religious life when one makes the vows of poverty, chastity, and obedience. The vows entail an obligation to strive for perfection and so to make oneself such a being as Christ might choose to be espoused to Himself in a mystical experience.

Denis the Carthusian uses the term "Spouse of Christ" in a very general sense. He cites St. Augustine as authority for this use, but gives no reference. "Every rational soul is the spouse of Christ or the adulteress of the devil. For if the soul adheres more to the supreme good than to any created, transitory and vain good, if it gives itself more to virtues than to vices, if it loves heavenly goods more than earthly, then is the soul the Spouse of Christ, but if the contrary is true, it is the adulteress of the devil." [4] Denis then goes on to point out that if the soul is faithful in this first period it will pass to a higher state in which it receives many mystic graces. "In this state you will attain to a life of familiar union with Him. You will be made one spirit with Him, so that very often He will speak to you in the depths of your being and lead you to the contemplation of His hidden secrets, and teach you concerning the mysteries of faith, so that after the divine visitation passes, your mind will glow with the memory of the overflowing sweetness of your heavenly and immortal Spouse." [5]

We must ever bear in mind that all the mystic graces, including betrothal and espousal, are means to help us to attain

---

[3] *Spiritual Canticle*, Stanza XXII, Peers's translation, Vol. II, pp. 308-309.
[4] *De mortificatione vivifica*, Articulus XIV, Opera Omnia XL (Opera minora VIII), pp. 115-116.
[5] *Ibid.*

or to abide in a state of perfect love of God. The heights of perfect charity may be attained without any of the mystic graces at all, or only a very few. So that one who might even be in the state of spiritual matrimony with Christ could not say that by that fact he is superior to any individual who has never received any such favor. For the essence of perfection is not found in the mystic graces as such, but in the perfection of charity, to which they conduce. This may be attained without any of the mystic graces at all, but it seldom is.

A good nun who had received many mystic graces and was evidently leading a holy life answered as follows the question: "Do you feel that you cannot say with certainty that you are spiritually superior to anyone?" "I do feel that I can say with certainty that I am spiritually superior to some, for my contact with others gives me assurance that I have received many spiritual advantages and graces not given to others." This answer may not indicate vanity and in all probability has nothing to do with a Pharisaical sense of personal superiority. It is merely a piece of honesty that shows a lack of instruction. Her answer would be necessarily correct, as well as honest, if perfection could be measured by the number and character of the mystic graces one has experienced. But as we have pointed out, mystic graces do not in themselves constitute perfection, but are means and powerful helps to the increase of our love for God in which perfection essentially consists. One who receives mystic graces should take great care to make full use of the impulse to give up all that does not concern one and live in the love of God. This is particularly true of spiritual betrothal and matrimony. "Unto whomsoever much is given, of him much shall be required." [6] If one has made inadequate use of great mystic graces, he may well be far inferior to one who has closely united his will to the divine will by the ordinary graces which all enjoy.

It may be that the mystic graces are sometimes given to weak souls who without them would never rise toward the perfection of the love of God. But those who for some reason

[6] Luke XII:48.

are chosen for the betrothal or spiritual marriage with Christ are purified for this union not only by great sufferings, the shadows of divine charity, but also by various mystic graces.

The phrase "spiritual betrothal with Christ," in the sense of a mystic grace, should only be applied to a scene in which Christ in some manner manifests His presence to the soul and in which there takes place a little ceremony whereby Christ betroths Himself to the soul and the soul betroths itself to Christ. Needless to say, this scene should arise within the soul, without the soul by imagination or any kind of effort trying to bring it about or continue it once it commences. It must commence and unroll itself entirely spontaneously, as it were, for it cannot be genuine unless it is brought about by Christ Himself.

St. John of the Cross speaks of this scene with Christ as leading to a "lofty estate and union of love wherein after much spiritual exercise God is wont to place the soul, which is called spiritual betrothal with the Word, the Son of God. And at the beginning when this is done for the first time, God communicates to the soul great things concerning Himself, beautifying it with greatness and majesty, decking it with gifts and virtues, and clothing it with knowledge and honor of God, just as if it were a bride on the day of her betrothal. And upon this happy day, not only is there an end of the soul's former vehement yearnings and plaints of love, but, being adorned with the good things which I am describing, she enters into an estate of peace and delight and sweetness of love." [7] A little further on he says: "It is to be noted that in these two stanzas is contained the most that God is wont to communicate to a soul at this time; but it is not to be understood that to all such as arrive at this estate He communicates all that is expounded in these two stanzas, nor that He does so according to one single way and degree of knowledge and feeling. For to some souls He gives more and to others less; to some after one manner and to others after

---

[7] *Spiritual Canticle*, second redaction, Stanzas XIV and XV, Peers's translation, Vol. II, p. 258.

another; though souls belonging to either category can be in this estate of the spiritual betrothal." [8]

It is evident, therefore, from the experience of St. John of the Cross that the spiritual betrothal will present a widely varying group of graces. In some these gifts will be far richer than in others. But if the essence of perfection is the degree to which one loves God, one cannot conclude that the perfection of the betrothed is measured by the richness of mystic experiences. The genuine intensity of charity to which the soul is raised in the spiritual betrothal might be far less apparent than the beauty of the mystic graces.

We must note, however, that an increase of solid virtue accompanies, according to St. John of the Cross, the betrothal of the soul with Christ. God decks it with gifts and virtues as a human lover bestows upon his bride-to-be various costly gifts on the day of their betrothal. It would seem that, in general, the soul would be conscious of a decrease in its moral and spiritual imperfections and an increase in the power of volitional control over emotional expression and sensory desire. This is true of all the mystic graces but especially so of spiritual betrothal. But according to St. John of the Cross some imperfections of sensory nature persist until their complete conquest in the state of spiritual marriage with Christ. "The sensitive part never, until the estate of spiritual marriage, completely loses its imperfections, neither is its strength completely subdued." [9] However, this complete domination of sensory nature is approached toward the end of the period of betrothal as the soul is made ready for its nuptials with Christ.

We must remember that the state of spiritual betrothal is not a static but an intensely dynamic period in which the soul is rapidly and ever more rapidly advancing to the perfection of divine charity. When the word dynamic is here used it does not imply a consciousness of violent personal activity. For the soul is being carried by forces outside itself

[8] *Ibid.*, p. 259.
[9] *Ibid.*, p. 274.

to which it submits in perfect tranquillity. Peace is the dominant characteristic of its daily life.

But that peace is not so profound as to exclude periods in which Christ no longer seems to abide in the soul. St. Teresa and St. John of the Cross speak of these painful absences of the Beloved during the period of the betrothal. Thus St. John of the Cross says: "The absences of her beloved which the soul suffers in this state of spiritual betrothal are very afflicting, and some are of such a kind that there is no grief to be compared with them." [10]

There is another type of suffering that sometimes, but not always, is found in this state. The soul suffers because it realizes that it is still in the flesh and therefore it cannot be perfectly united with the Beloved and behold the Divine Essence face to face. "Oftentimes, therefore, she suffers greatly, especially when her realization of this becomes more vivid." [11] St. Teresa describes transitory states that come on suddenly and last from a quarter of an hour to three or four hours. In these states the soul suffers so intensely because it cannot see God face to face that it seems on the point of death. After one of these attacks she wrote her poem: *"Vivo sin vivir en mi."*

I live yet in myself I have no life,
and my waiting is of such a kind that I die because I do not die.

The phrase "I die because I do not die" was not an example of poetic exaggeration with only a slender basis in reality. She wrote as follows in the *Interior Castle:* "It sometimes happens that, when a person is in the state that you have been considering, and has such yearnings to die, because the pain [of absence] is more than she can bear, that her soul seems to be on the very point of leaving the body, she is really afraid and would like her distress to be alleviated lest she should in fact die." [12]

10 *Ibid.*, Stanza XVI, Vol. II, p. 281.
11 *Ibid.*, p. 287.
12 *Interior Castle*, VI, xi, Peers's translation, Vol. II, p. 327.

These intense sufferings, because the soul does not see God face to face, are not experienced at all stages of the period of spiritual betrothal, and by some in this state they may not be perceived at all.

As the time rolls on the soul grows to a state of perfection that closely resembles that of spiritual matrimony. It may have many severe trials but its peace can no longer be disturbed. Christ dying on the Cross suffered agonies we can never understand, but in the midst of all He beheld the beatific vision and remained in perfect peace. It is to this state that the betrothed of Christ draws near as the time of its spiritual marriage approaches, whether it is to be celebrated in time or in eternity. Already, whenever it desires, it can enter the interior temple of the soul where only a thin veil dims the glory of the presence of God.

II

What is the difference between betrothal to Christ and spiritual marriage? In my data, I have no case which I could be certain of as spiritual marriage, but several that seem to be genuine cases of spiritual betrothal. Let us turn, therefore, to St. Teresa for an account of spiritual marriage.

The soul "is brought into this Mansion by an intellectual vision, in which by a representation of the truth in a particular way, the Most Holy Trinity reveals Itself, in all three Persons. . . . It sees these three Persons individually, and yet, by a wonderful kind of knowledge which is given to it, the soul realizes that most certainly and truly all these three Persons are one Substance and one Power and One Knowledge and one God alone; so that what we hold by faith the soul may be said to grasp by sight, although nothing is seen by the eyes, either of the body or of the soul, for it is no imaginary vision." [13]

It seems that the matrimonial scene is repeated at intervals and that in these scenes there are various symbolic exchanges

[13] *Interior Castle*, VII, i, Peers's translation, Vol. II, pp. 331-332.

of all personal goods, indicative of a true marriage and something more than a betrothal. Thus St. Teresa writes:

"When granting this favor for the first time,[14] His Majesty is pleased to reveal Himself to the soul through an imaginary vision of His most sacred Humanity, so that it may clearly understand what is taking place and not be ignorant of the fact that it is receiving so sovereign a gift. To other people the experience will come in a different way. To the person of whom we have been speaking the Lord revealed Himself one day, when she had just received communion, in great splendor and beauty and majesty, as He did after His resurrection, and told her that it was time she took upon her His affairs as if they were her own and that He would take her affairs upon Himself; and He added other words which are easier to understand than to repeat." [15]

What was possibly St. Teresa's first espousal ceremony with Christ, she thus describes:

"Then He revealed Himself to me, in an imaginary vision, most interiorly, as on other occasions, and He gave me His right hand, saying to me: 'Behold this nail.[16] It is a sign that from today onward, thou shalt be My bride. Until now, thou hadst not merited this; but henceforward thou shalt regard My honor not only as that of thy Creator and King and God but as that of My very bride. My honor is thine and thine is Mine.' " [17]

In this matrimonial exchange of goods, Christ bestows on the soul not only the joys of sanctity and the consolations of the mystical graces, but also the inestimable privilege of participation in His sufferings and trials. The greatest of all Christ's works was the redemption of man by His passion

---

[14] The ceremony of spiritual marriage with Christ is therefore likely to be repeated a number of times.

[15] *Interior Castle*, VII, 11, Peers's translation, Vol. II, p. 334.

[16] The word in the Spanish text is *clavo;* but one fails to see the propriety of a *nail* as a symbol of spiritual marriage. Could it be that St. Teresa intended to write *llave* (key)? Christ gave His bride the key to all His treasures. *Clave* is used for the key of a code.

[17] Relation XXXV. E. Allison Peers. Vol. I, p. 352. Peers dates this event as happening at the Convent of the Incarnation, Avila, 1572.

and death upon the Cross. Besides the gift of Himself, He can grant us no greater gift than to allow us to participate with Him in the salvation and sanctification of men. This we necessarily do as members of His mystical body. The mystical body of Christ carries out the work of the head, the Eternal Word made flesh. This work was accomplished by the passion and death of Christ upon the Cross. Our Lord's passion and death are continued in the Holy Sacrifice of the Mass and in the trials and sufferings of all the members of the mystical body down throughout the centuries. When, therefore, Christ sanctifies a soul and calls it to the mystical marriage with Himself even in this life, the spouse of Christ must expect that the interchange of goods will involve an abundant participation in the passion of the Redeemer of man. And so our Lord said to St. Teresa one day:

"Thou knowest of the betrothal that there is between thee and Me; this means that all I have is thine, and so I give thee all the trials and pains that I endured and thou canst ask of My Father as though they were thine own." [18]

This means that after her mystical marriage St. Teresa could ask of the Eternal Father anything that could be gained by the merits of Christ's passion. But experience seems to show that it also meant that she would have many sufferings and trials by which she would be united with all that the members of Christ's mystical body endure and so she would fully participate in the passion of her Spouse.

Besides the interchange of goods, there is another specific and proper sign of a mystical marriage. It is psychological in nature. In St. Teresa it involved a division of the flow of consciousness into two streams. Speaking really of herself, she wrote thus: "The person already referred to, found herself better in every way; however numerous were her trials and business worries, the essential part of her soul seemed never to move from that dwelling-place. So in a sense she felt that her soul was divided; and when she was going through great trials, shortly after God granted her this favor,

[18] Relation LI, Peers's translation, Vol. I, p. 360.

she complained of her soul, just as Martha complained of Mary. Sometimes she would say that it was doing nothing but enjoy itself in that quietness, while she herself was left with all her trials and occupations so that she could not keep it company. You will think this absurd, daughters, but it is what actually happens." [19]

Apparently this double stream of consciousness is not maintained without interruption. But it does appear and when present allows the espoused to remain in the depth of the Blessed Trinity even while it is carrying on business transactions. This double consciousness of St. Teresa illustrates one thing that may well characterize the society of the blessed in heaven. They will enjoy the beatific vision of the Divine Essence even when in the social life of the angels and saints they commune with one another. According to St. Thomas, our Lord on earth ever enjoyed this beatific vision [20] even in his active life and dying on the Cross.

In the state of spiritual matrimony there will no longer be painful periods during which the Beloved is absent. The Eternal Word will ever be present to His earthly spouse. The soul may still have various duties to perform and will never omit or in any way neglect a single one. But it will feel that its main occupation in life is to commune in love and adoration with the Eternal Word. When work is finished it will hear the call of the Beloved and withdraw to that interior temple of the soul which is ever resplendent with the glory of the triune God.

III

Experiences of Those Who Thought That in Some Way Christ Had Come to Them Without Being Announced and He Had Pledged His Troth to Them and They to Him

Some of those who felt that they had been through a betrothal scene with Christ merely acknowledged the fact but

[19] *Interior Castle*, VII, 1, Peers's translation, Vol. II, p. 333.
[20] A decree of the Holy Office 5 June 1918 makes no other concept tenable. See Denzinger-Bannwart, p. 2183.

gave no description of it at all. One said that it was physically difficult for her to comply with the request. She had been for years in bed as a chronic invalid.

With one it seems to have been an intellectual realization rather than a sensory experience of any kind. "There were no words. I was just certain that I belonged to Him; and I was certain of His great and tender love for Me. This realization that I was betrothed to Christ came before I entered the convent and several times in the novitiate. When I was a young religious and was sent out to teach, I was very much dissatisfied with mission life. I complained to our Lord that I had far less time to spend with Him in the Blessed Sacrament than when I was out in the world. I wanted to leave the community and go to a cloister. So much did I complain to Him, about the lack of time for mental prayer, that one morning during adoration, before I went to school, He said: 'Do not worry about that any more. I shall remain in your heart from communion to communion and, whenever you want to, you can adore Me here present as you would in the tabernacle. Remember always that you must be a living cloister.' That happened over twenty years ago and, ever since, the interior presence of Christ has supplied in large measure for the lack of opportunities to make a visit to Christ in the tabernacle.

"Since the betrothal scenes, there has been a profound and permanent change for the better in my spiritual life. Without disturbance I have been able to pass through many trials; and a wondrous peace and love of God has settled down on my soul. I live with Christ in my interior tabernacle. But in spite of all I am still conscious of imperfections."

One who did not describe the scene said: "It was equal to an engagement, but I knew it was not finished. The spiritual marriage is still hoped for. I believe that all religious are called to spiritual marriage with Christ and that it is the natural, normal and obligatory term of our vocation. The vows, and the taking of them, do not raise us psychologically to the mystical level of spouses of Christ as a mere matter of course. The main factor in such an elevation is a great love which brings about close union with God."

Another answers question 23 affirmatively but does not describe the actual words or the manner of the betrothal. However, she does give its setting. "It took place after Holy Communion. I had a marvellous perception of the divinity of Christ, the eternal God, and of the presence of the 'Three in One' more real than my own presence." She answers questions 24 and 25 in the affirmative and to 26 she says, "Christ seems to be always with me. After my communions, Christ is all Beauty! Light! Love! Once when His Sacred Face came vividly before me His holy eyes seemed to meet mine with a deep and tender Love. If grace has worked such marvels in my soul, what can it not yet do to make me more pleasing to God, if I only cooperate." She feels that she has lost all interest in things not concerned with carrying out the actual communion of love with her heavenly spouse. But she says: "The duty of teaching often absorbs my attention."

She did not give a description of the method of her mental prayer. At times, but not habitually, she experiences something akin to the prayer of quiet with a peace experience that carries over into the day. She devotes to prayer all the time she can possibly spare. Occasionally during Holy Mass at the words *Per Ipsum, et cum Ipso, et in Ipso,* she experiences something akin to the prayer of union. Sometimes also there is something akin to ecstasy. There are imaginal visions of Christ in which she seems drawn close to His thorn-crowned head. And often our Lady seems to be close to her in a kind of intellectual presence. These experiences inflame her love of God and lead her to a closer conformity with His divine will.

✦

One priest wrote that he experienced a betrothal scene with Christ a few years ago, but cannot recall it now. One can scarcely imagine that a genuine supernatural betrothal scene would ever be forgotten.

Another priest writes as follows: "There have been four scenes in my spiritual life which seem to have the character of spiritual betrothal with Christ. The first might be better considered as a preparatory visit rather than as a betrothal. It occurred some twenty to twenty-five years ago. I was standing at my place in choir, during high Mass, with my arms folded. Suddenly Christ seemed to be hovering in the air before me. He stretched out His arm to me. I seemed to have, as it were, a spiritual arm which I stretched out and grasped the hand of Christ. For I remained in reality still standing with my real arms folded. No words were spoken, but the act symbolized that Christ asked me to give myself to Him and I did so with all my heart and soul. And He accepted my allegiance.

"Many years later I was studying St. Louis de Montfort's works on the Blessed Virgin. I concluded to make a private personal retreat and make the act of consecration to the Immaculate Heart of Mary. I did so. Shortly after, during Matins and Lauds, the Blessed Mother, with the Child Jesus in her arms, seemed to hover before me. She came closer and put the Divine Infant in my arms. My heart burned with the love of Christ while I continued to sing the psalms as if nothing at all had happened.

"I think it was only a few days later when the Blessed Mother and the Divine Infant seemed again to hover before me. She held out the Divine Infant towards me and He stretched out His hand to me; and as before, I extended an invisible arm and grasped the hand of the Divine Child in my own. How tiny the little Infant's hand seemed when it was enclosed in my own. We seemed to pledge ourselves, one to another, in spiritual betrothal.

"The scene led to a wonderful increase in my love of Christ and for several years the experience of the Divine Child resting on my left arm, was often renewed during Matins and Lauds.

"Some years later while I was reciting aloud the *Pater Noster* at my morning Mass, I heard very distinctly and quietly the innerly spoken words: '*I take thee for My spouse*'. I found difficulty in continuing to recite the *Pater Noster* aloud and answering in innerly spoken words, '*And I take Thee for my Spouse*'.

"Sometime later, with great devotion, I was chanting Matins and Lauds with the Christ Child. I had not tried to imagine Him present. But He had come to me all of His own accord. The peculiar spiritual warmth caused by His presence seems to me impossible to produce by any personal effort. Consciousness was ever flowing over into acts of love. Sometimes I seemed to be face to face with the Eternal Word in the bosom of the Blessed Trinity. While chanting the *Miserere*, the Christ Child seemed to be a little in front of me and at the words, '*Asperges me hyssopo et mundabor*', He seemed to sprinkle me with holy water, and to laugh a merry laugh that only a child can laugh, and then, to fly in some way through the little space that separated us, and throw His little arms about my neck and to be so glad in a beautiful childish manner that I was now cleansed from all my sins. When I recited the words: '*Averte faciem Tuam a peccatis meis*' He seemed to turn His head quickly away from me, 'in swift child's whim', and as quickly turn back to me. It seemed that His face beamed upon me all radiant with joy. And He said to me, '*Will you be Mine?*'. Intellectually, I swore to be His forever. (All the time I was chanting the *Miserere*.) Again and again during the chanting, He seemed to say in His own inimitable childish manner: '*Will you be Mine?*' '*Will you be Mine?*' And every now and then I was face to face with the Eternal Word in the bosom of the Blessed Trinity.

"No other scene in my spiritual life wrought such a change in me. Ever since I seem to walk with God the whole day long and wake in the morning to live the new day with God, no matter what I may have to do."

Epilogue

IF THE reader has grasped the all-important concept of this book, he will by now have realized the great truth: Each and every human being is destined to be a friend of God. He will then, naturally, say to himself: If the Infinite and Almighty God has invited me to be His friend, the most important thing in life is to live so that I may become such a one that the All Holy might admit to friendship with Himself.

The reader will then ask a practical question: What then precisely must I do to actually enter into the sublime relationship of friendship with the Almighty?

Let us suppose now that I am talking to an earnest soul who has read very little about the things of the spirit, but has been faithful to Sunday Mass since childhood; to one, however, who has seldom thought about God during the week, who perhaps is in too much of a hurry to think about morning prayers, but who usually says a few hurried prayers before getting into bed. To such a one I would say: My child, remember the words of God to Jeremias: "You shall seek me: and you shall find me, when you shall seek me with all your heart." [1]

Think often that God is everywhere and He is ever gazing upon you with eyes of love, asking your love in re-

[1] Jeremias XXIX:13.

turn. "Whither shall I go from Thy spirit? Or whither shall I flee from Thy face? If I ascend into heaven Thou art there: If I descend into hell Thou art present. If I take wings early in the morning, and dwell in the uttermost parts of the sea: even there also shall Thy hand lead me; and Thy right hand shall hold me." [2]

Then, my child, think that you come to God through Christ. "Abide in Me: and I in you. As the branch cannot bear fruit of itself, unless it abide in the vine, so neither can you, unless you abide in Me. . . . If you keep My commandments you shall abide in My love: as I also have kept My Father's commandments and do abide in His love." [3] And then on another occasion He said: "Take My yoke upon you and learn of Me, because I am meek and humble of heart: and you shall find rest for your souls. For My yoke is sweet and My burden light." [4]

You must, therefore, start with a study of Christ: His personality and His teaching. Christ is the Second Person of the Blessed Trinity: "God from the substance of [His] Father, begotten before the ages: man from the substance of [His] Mother, born in time." [5] You are destined to perfect friendship with the Triune God, and your soul will be espoused to the Second Person of the Blessed Trinity Who was born in the stable of Bethlehem.

And how shall this study of Christ be made? By meditative reading. I think you will find that *The Christ the Son of God* by Abbé Constant Fouard [6] will lend itself to this meditative reading. Later you will find that the Gospels themselves will give you ample food for thought. Read and ponder, looking for *ideals of conduct*. But pause to give your heart to your Eternal Lover. St. Teresa of Avila tells us that in our life of prayer it is more important to love much than to think much.

[2] Psalm CXXXVIII:7-10.
[3] John XV:4, 10.
[4] Matthew XI:29-30.
[5] Athanasian Creed.
[6] Longmans, Green & Co., New York.

Then there are many details and problems to be considered in your life with God. You need a little book of instruction. I would suggest the *Introduction to a Devout Life* by St. Francis de Sales. You should arrange your day so as to perform *all your duties* and still have time for Him Who loves you with infinite love. Here is where you will need the guidance of a prudent director.

The necessity of a spiritual director was clearly formulated by St. Benedict in his rule. In speaking of the special personal penances which each should undertake in Lent, he says: "Let each one, however, make known to his Abbot what he offereth, and let it be done with his blessing and permission: because what is done without leave of the spiritual father shall be imputed to presumption and vainglory and merit no reward." [7] St. Benedict's rule expresses the best traditions of the Fathers of the Desert. But the general necessity of counsel in the important affairs of life goes back to the Old Testament as a part of divine revelation bequeathed by God's chosen people to the Church. The sapiential books often speak of it. Thus: "My son, do thou nothing without counsel: and thou shalt not repent what thou hast done." [8] But the sacred writer advises caution: "Be in peace with many: but let one in a thousand be thy counsellor." [9]

St. John of the Cross urges a similar caution: "It is of great importance for the soul that desires to make progress in recollection and perfection to consider in whose hands it is placing itself; for as is the master, so will be the disciple, and, as is the father, so will be the son." [10] Every confessor is not one's spiritual director. One living in the world in a fairly large city would find little trouble in finding a prudent director. By asking a few questions first from one, then from another, one would eventually find a wise confessor, who appreciates the importance of a life of prayer and self-denial, to whom one could go when necessary for spiritual direction.

[7] Rule, Chapter XLIX.
[8] Ecclesiasticus XXXII:24.
[9] *Ibid.* VI:6.
[10] *Living Flame of Love*, Stanza III, 30, Peers's translation, Vol. III, p. 176.

One who has no director may have a period of devotion
and attempt too much and eventually give up all devotional
practices. Thus one respondent, a devout layman, writes:
"At one time I spent at least an hour daily before the Blessed
Sacrament, plus the recitation of the entire divine office and
serving mass and the Rosary. I abstained from all meat, wine,
fish, tobacco and coffee. I would go for months on end
without a penny in my pocket, never seeing a movie or
hearing the radio. I would fast all day Friday—not even bread
besides various other penances. Those were beautiful days.
But little by little I have given up all those habits: every one
of them except daily Mass through which I sit like a dumb
ox. In my heart I want to live only for God. But I feel very
weak and incapable of doing anything for Him."

This report illustrates, I think, how one who trusts solely
to his own judgment may go to injudicious extremes with the
result that he gives up most of his good resolutions. Had he
asked advice and entered on a moderate regime, he could have
added to it for a while in various emergencies, and would
probably have persevered and not have given up.

This leads us to the problem of *your* regime of life. You,
like all who lead a devout life, should be faithful to certain
devout exercises every day. Chief among these devout exercises are Holy Mass and Holy Communion daily, if in
any way possible; and some time to be devoted to mental
prayer and holy reading; a visit to the Blessed Sacrament, the
Rosary; some short morning and evening prayers to be faithfully said on rising and just before retiring. When thinking
about daily spiritual exercises, do not fail to consider Canon
911 of the Codex of Canon Law, which says: "Let everyone
make much of indulgences or the remission before God of
the temporal punishment due to sins." Do you, therefore,
see to it that no day passes without your making a generous
contribution to the relief of the poor souls in purgatory.

And then study and continue to study the lives of the saints.
Choose your heroes from this number. Above all do not fail
to place your spiritual life under the guidance and protection
of the Mother of God.

Be sure that you look upon your various spiritual exercises
as helps toward living in God and regard them as pauses that
will enable you to be conscious of His presence throughout
the day. Remember that God said to Abraham: "Walk before Me and be perfect." Your spiritual life must be conceived of as walking before God, the whole day long. This
you will accomplish if you are faithful to your daily schedule
of spiritual exercises and often pause to think: Christ, my
friend of friends, loves me with infinite love and is ever
waiting for me to turn to Him and in the flash of a moment
give expression—wordless perhaps—to my love for Him.

But what exercises are advised? No one can answer that
question who does not know you and your life. You must
seek a director and talk matters over with him.

When you are just beginning to lead a spiritual life, you
should contrive to make a closed retreat, if in any way possible. Make it the main thing in your next vacation. Ask
someone, or find out in some way, what retreats are going
to be given at the time of your next vacation and write and
make arrangements. When there, tell the retreat master that
the main object of the retreat is to plan your spiritual life;
and before it is over have a talk with him and make out your
daily schedule, however simple it may be, and ask the grace
of God that you may faithfully observe it. Pius XI in an
important encyclical on Spiritual Exercises recommended
that not only the clergy and religious but also the laity should
make a closed annual retreat every year, to be renewed by
a day's retreat every month or perhaps only four times a
year (*Mens nostra*, December 20, 1929). You will do well to
follow the advice of the great pontiff who might well be
termed the patron of the spiritual life. Your monthly day of
recollection might mean doing your everyday work, but
making special efforts to come before Christ in the interior
of your soul many times a day. Remember that no type of
honest life is inconsistent with walking with God and becoming the friend of the Almighty.

Most everything of importance in your spiritual life could
be put under the two categories of prayer and self-denial,

giving to each of these a broad comprehensive definition. You would do well to read again Chapters IX and X above in which prayer and penance are discussed in some detail.[11]

The general rule for renunciation is: Give up everything that does not concern you. "Every one of you that doth not renounce all that he possesseth cannot be my disciple."[12] But that does not mean that a married man should give away all his possessions so that he would no longer be able to care for and educate his children. Renunciation is eminently a personal affair and never means precisely the same thing for any two individuals. As St. Paul says: "Every one has his proper gift from God: one after this manner and another after that."[13] And then to complicate your problem, between that which concerns you and that which does not, there is a wide area of no man's land under dispute. I would suggest that before making any definite resolutions you read the first book of *The Ascent of Mount Carmel* by St. John of the Cross.[14] There you will find the fundamental philosophy of renunciation. Then study the tenth book of the *Confessions* of St. Augustine for the attempt of a great mind to determine for himself his field of renunciation. And then read and reread *The Little Flowers of St. Francis of Assisi*[15] and try to understand his total renunciation and wondrous kindness in providing for the comfort and consolation of those under him. He did not scruple, when in his last illness,

[11] You will need further instruction on prayer than the few words given above in this epilogue. Excellent for a beginner is Joseph McSorley, C.S.P., *A Primer of Prayer*, New York, Longmans, Green & Co. (contains a good list of works on prayer). See also Vital Lehodey, O.C.R., *The Ways of Mental Prayer*, Dublin, Gill and Son; T. V. Moore, O.S.B., *Prayer*, Westminster, Md., The Newman Press. A general conspectus of the forms and stages of mental prayer is given in Godefroid Belorgey, O.C.S.O., *The Practice of Mental Prayer*, Westminster, Md., The Newman Press, 1952. But of most importance to get the spirit of prayer is Saint Teresa of Jesus, *The Way of Perfection*, trans. by Alice Alexander, Westminster, Md., The Newman Press.

[12] Luke XIV:33.

[13] I Corinthians VII:7.

[14] Vol. I of *Complete Works*, trans. by Peers, Newman Press, Westminster, Md., 1949.

[15] Many editions are available.

to ask the Lady Jacopa to cook and bring him certain delicacies he greatly relished and he ate them and enjoyed them.[16] I mention this typical incident in the life of St. Francis of Assisi that you may see that in the matter of self-denial everyone has his own proper gift from God. You must find out what God asks of you. This will require great honesty to exclude rationalizing yourself into the enjoyment of selfish ease. You must also seek the advice of a prudent director lest you go to excess.

You would do well to study the Rule of St. Benedict,[17] particularly the fourth chapter on "The Instruments of Good Works." It contains the detailed suggestions of the great Patriarch of monks for the practice of self-denial. Note that his suggestions commence with the love of God and the Ten Commandments. Then follow the corporal and spiritual works of mercy, and, then, various items which might be grouped under the broad heading "emotional control."

On one of the occasions when our Lord foretold to His apostles His Passion and death, He said: "The Son of man must suffer many things and be rejected by the ancients and chief priests and scribes and be killed and the third day rise again." [18] Then apparently He turned to all those around Him, and in a louder voice said to all: "If any man will come after Me, let him deny himself and take up his cross daily and follow Me." [19] We may look upon the practices, we have just been discussing, as fulfilling our Lord's command to deny ourselves. This practice of self-denial may be regarded as very important, or even necessary, if we are going to obey the second precept and take up our cross daily and follow Christ.

In order to get help to carry in a perfect spirit our daily

16 *The Little Flowers of St. Francis of Assisi*, Catholic Book Publishing Co., New York, 1946, pp. 253 ff.

17 The best translation is that of Dom Oswald Hunter Blair, Fort Augustus, Scotland, Abbey Press, 1934. Latin and English are given on opposite pages.

18 Luke IX:22.

19 *Ibid.*, 23.

cross, we should in our morning Mass [20] come before Christ dying upon the Cross. We might well devote the time from the Sanctus to the Communion to standing in spirit at the foot of the Cross and associating ourselves by love, sympathy, and adoration with our Lord in His agony. Not every morning will dawn upon some great sorrow. But if we learn to live with our Lord in His passion, it will ever be easy to turn from our own sorrow and gaze as it were through our tears at Christ upon the Cross and forget ourselves in a flame of love that ascends to the throne of God.

When after your Holy Communion you leave the Church to go to the duties of your day, you bear Christ within you: not as He was dying upon the Cross or as He was buried in the tomb, but the living Christ with His glorified body. It is Christ Himself, Who now sitteth at the right hand of the majesty on high, Who multiplies His presence in the tabernacles of the Church and in the hearts of the faithful. Even when His sacramental presence fades, the abiding of the Eternal Word remains and you do not do your work alone but He works in you and through you the things He would accomplish in your sphere of life. One Catholic mother had to teach a backward child to walk. It took painful and persevering effort, but the effort was rewarded in the end. She told me, years afterward, that during this period God seemed close to her in a way that could scarcely be described. In some manner He was right before her and she had the consciousness, not that she was training the child and God was looking on, but she felt spontaneously: *We* are training the child. Now whether you ever have any such vivid realization, the real truth is that as long as you are in the state of grace,

[20] The following books may help you to a devotional appreciation of the Holy Mass. F. Desplanques, S.J., *Living the Mass*, Westminster, Md., The Newman Press, 1951; Joseph Kramp, S.J., *The Liturgical Sacrifice of the New Law*, St. Louis, Mo., B. Herder Book Co., 1927; Pius Parsch, *The Holy Sacrifice of the Mass*, St. Louis, Mo., B. Herder Book Co., 1949. For a deep study of its history, Ildefonso Schuster, *The Sacramentary*, New York, Benziger Bros., 1925-1931, 5 vols.

God abides with you and works through you and is with you in all you do.

The concept that the risen Christ is with you should make you look forward to the day when you will rise from the dead and live with the angels and saints in heaven. In that day you will share with Christ the prerogative of absolute control of your emotional life. And that should stimulate you to exercise that control, as far as possible, *now*. "Our conversation is in heaven," [21] said St. Paul. In the original that means: Our manner of life is like that of those who live in heaven: the angels and saints of God. And all that means that you must beg the help of God and do all you can possibly do yourself to live with that perfect emotional control that characterized our Lord on earth and is forever manifested by the angels and saints in heaven.

And so when you leave the Church, after your morning Mass, you leave to live and work with the Eternal Word of God in all you do and say. As the promised bride of Christ you live in the bosom of the Blessed Trinity. The Eternal Father sent Christ into the world and so also He sent you into the world to do His work and be His apostle. As the years roll by, you must approach, more and more closely, to the obedience of Christ. God will not forsake you because of weakness and failure. And as long as you are making a good honest effort you will be able to say truly: "He that sent me is with me; and He hath not left me alone. For I do always the things that please Him." [22]

Living thus it will become a matter of supreme importance to you to co-operate cheerfully with others. You will be approachable to all, offensive to none. You may often feel provoked, but you will never manifest impatience, let alone say an unkind or angry word. You will make many real sacrifices in order to be helpful to others.

There will come a period in your spiritual life when you

[21] Philippians III:20.
[22] John VIII:29.

will never, with full deliberation, say an unkind word or in any way manifest an emotion that would grieve or offend another. But God is calling you to something far more perfect: your conversation, your whole manner of life must become like that of the angels and saints in heaven. You must strive for a Christ-like control of all mental functions so that no unworthy emotion will be able to enter consciousness. Having conquered fully deliberate venial sins, you must go on to the conquest of all semideliberate venial sins and imperfections. This, as we have pointed out, will require, for perfect success, an extraordinary grace from God. You will certainly be granted such help that you will keep on approaching the Christ-like ideal. The final elimination of semivoluntary venial sins is, however, within the realm of possibility.

It would be well for you to pause here and meditate on the following words of Christ. They were spoken by Our Lord at the Last Supper when He asked that all those who would believe in Him through the teaching of the Apostles might be one, as He and His Father are one. "I in them and Thou in Me: that they may be perfect in one: and the world may know that Thou hast sent Me." [23]

The meaning of this prayer is that the sanctity of the faithful may be a silent living apostolate that will turn the world to Christ. Early Christianity was keenly alive to this obligation: the apostolate of the spiritual life which is *living Christ.* St. Peter exhorted the Christian world: "Let wives be subject to their husbands: that, if any believe not the word, they may be won without the word, by the conversation (that is, the manner of life) of the wives." [24] After exhorting Timothy (Bishop of Ephesus) to preach, St. Paul wrote to him: "Be thou an example [25] of the faithful, in word, in conversation, in charity, in faith, in chastity." [26] And to Titus (Bishop of Crete) he wrote: "In all things show thyself an example of

[23] John XVII:23.
[24] I Peter III:1.
[25] That is to say, the type of a true Christian.
[26] I Timothy IV:12.

good works, in doctrine, in integrity, in gravity . . . that he who is on the contrary part may be afraid, having no evil to say of us." [27]

Without the apostolate of the spiritual life, lived by the faithful in those early centuries, Christianity would not have conquered the Roman Empire. Slaves became apostles of Christ in every city of the empire and in regions beyond the sway of the Roman eagles. Not until the period extending from the fifth to the ninth centuries did the great apostles of the nations appear. Strange to say, their preparation was a period spent alone with God in monastic life. St. Benedict of Nursia, who had no conscious intention of initiating a movement for the conversion of Europe to Christianity, laid its foundations when he entered his cave at Subiaco to live as a Solitary. Saints Cyril and Methodius, the Apostles of Moravia, were two brothers. Cyril [28] early in life, to avoid promotion by the emperor, fled to an island in the Sea of Marmora and hid in a monastery. Methodius, also in his early life, resigned a high office in the government to lead a solitary life as an ascetic in a *laura*, that is, a monastery in which hermitages, one for each monk, are grouped around a central church. A study of the great Apostles of the nations will show that the power of their apostolate was derived from their life with God and was in essence the apostolate of the spiritual life. Their work spread because they assimilated their hearers to the apostolate of the spiritual life and then preached by the silence of a life consecrated to God. This apostolate of sanctity continues its work in our day and it is to this apostolate that you are called.

An article by Peter F. Anson, "Missionaries of the Sea," in *Commonweal*, December 7, 1951, calls attention to an interesting attempt to send forth solitaries, living in the world

[27] Titus II:7, 8.
[28] Cyril was baptized Constantine but died early in his ministry. He requested to make his monastic profession on his deathbed and took the name of Cyril. These two brothers invented what is at present the Rusisan alphabet.

alone with God, as apostles to sailors. In 1945 the French
bishops conceived the idea of bringing into existence a body
of missionaries who would do what they could to bring seamen and fishermen to the knowledge and love of God. Now
there are some thirty priests in the *Mission de la Mer*. No
priest goes on the mission of the sea until he has been introduced to the social and economic problems of seamen and has
had adequate experience in their duties by working for some
time with them and becoming an expert seaman himself. On
December 1, 1949, a contemplative community was formed
"of men who planned to spend the greater part of their time
afloat instead of ashore": the Little Brothers of Jesus. "Their
vocation is more in the nature of 'solitaries' (in the spiritual
sense) for each is alone in the midst of a crew made up of
men who are rarely practicing Catholics." Their problem is
to do their hard work in the Divine Presence, and preach by
the silent example of their lives. In the midst of this they arrange in some way to recite the Divine Office alone—for only
one missionary ships on any single boat. They also find time
for an hour of mental prayer, and once a week spend, in the
course of the night, an hour in silent adoration. Only on the
two or three days between voyages, which are two to three
weeks long, is it possible for these contemplatives of the sea
to go to Mass and receive Holy Communion.[29]

There was always room for some difference of opinion as
to whether or not such a life as that of the Missionaries of
the Sea is more proper for priests or for the laity assimilated
to Catholic Action.[30] But it is worthwhile pointing out that
it is not necessary to be a priest in order to exercise it. Nor is
it essential to be assimilated to anything. It would be well for
you to be in contact with the director of Catholic Action in
one of its various fields in your diocese. You would find support as a Benedictine Oblate or a member of one of the third

[29] See also *The Pylon*, Vol. IV, No. 2, April 1952.
[30] Early in 1954 Cardinal Lienart, Bishop of Lille, announced that Pius
XII had ruled that the "priest-worker" movement, as such, must be abandoned. Since then it has been profoundly modified.

orders or of a secular institute such as Opus Dei. But none
of these things is absolutely necessary. The one thing necessary is to love God and show it by living as He wants you to
live. If you do this wherever you are you will preach a
powerful daily sermon by the silent example of a holy life.
Don't wait for somebody to organize you. God Himself will
organize anyone who leads a holy life and will synthesize
all his activities. Seek help, however, in such existing organizations of the Church as seem to supply your personal needs.

But how will all this lead you into the contemplative life
and the mystic graces? If you have understood the lesson of
this book you will understand that you can prepare yourself
to enter contemplative life only indirectly. Pray and ask
God's help to avoid every shadow of sin. "For wisdom will
not enter into a malicious soul, nor dwell in a body subject
to sins." [31] "Blessed are the clean of heart, for they shall see
God." [32] Study the life and teaching of Christ and try to be
like Him. Take up your cross daily and follow Him Who
died for you upon the Cross; and never waver no matter how
deep and long may be the darkness of the years, but believe
without any shadow of doubt the words of Eternal Truth:
"If any one love Me, he will keep My word. And My Father
will love him; and we will come to him and will make our
abode with him." [33]

[31] Wisdom I:4.
[32] Matthew V:8.
[33] John XIV:23.

References to Spiritual Literature

Classic Works on the Spiritual Life

Baker, Augustine, O.S.B. *Holy Wisdom.* New York: Harper and Brothers. 1950. Written in a quaint style and hard to read, but will repay the effort.

Francis de Sales, St. *Introduction to a Devout Life.* Translated by John K. Ryan. New York: Harper and Brothers. 1940.

—— *Treatise on the Love of God.* Translated by Henry Mackey, O.S.B. Westminster, Md.: Newman Press. 1949.

Marmion, Columba, O.S.B.

The following series of books published by B. Herder Book Co., St. Louis, Mo., may, taken as a whole, be conceived of as a general treatise on the spiritual life. They constitute to a large extent a digest of the spiritual teaching of St. Thomas Aquinas.

Christ the Life of the Soul. 1935.

Christ in His Mysteries. 1919, 1923.

Christ the Ideal of the Monk. 1926.

Christ the Ideal of the Priest. 1951.

Rodriguez, Alphonsus, S.J. *Christian and Religious Perfection.* Chicago: Loyola University Press. 1929. 3 vols. A great classic on the spiritual life that will help greatly one who seriously seeks information.

Saudreau, Auguste. *The Degrees of the Spiritual Life.* New York: Benziger Brothers. 1907. 2 vols.

Tanquerey, Adolphe, S.S. *The Spiritual Life.* Translated by Herman Branderis. Westminster, Md.: Newman Press. 1947.

Unequaled for clear, solid, theological information on the spiritual life.

Tissot, Joseph, M.S.F.S., Editor. *The Interior Life*. Translated by W. H. Mitchell. Westminster, Md.: Newman Press. 1949.

History of Teaching on the Spiritual Life

Closely related to the help given by a general treatise on the spiritual life is that which comes from reading a history of the various teachings on the spiritual life.

GENERAL

Pourrat, Pierre, S.S. *Christian Spirituality*. Translated by W. H. Mitchell and S. P. Jacques. New York: P. J. Kenedy and Sons. 1922-1928. 3 vols. Reprinted by Newman Press, 1953, with addition of Vol. 4, translated by Donald Attwater. A most valuable and comprehensive work which will help the reader to avoid reefs on which many have suffered shipwreck.

SPECIAL

Brémond, Henri. *Literary History of Religious Thought in France*. Translated by K. L. Montgomery. New York: Macmillan Co. 1929-1937. 3 vols. Unrivaled for a living detailed picture of religious movements in France in the eighteenth century.

Butler, Edward Cuthbert, O.S.B. *Western Mysticism*. New York: E. P. Dutton and Co. 1922.

After a preliminary grounding in the works of St. Francis de Sales and one of the above general works and when the director feels that the soul is prepared for an introduction to the mystical life, it would be well to study carefully the following works:

1. The first book only of the *Ascent of Mount Carmel*. This will give one the fundamental mystical theology of self-denial. It should, however, be put in practice only under direction.

2. *The Way of Perfection* of St. Teresa of Avila. This will give a good introduction to prayer. Special attention

should be given to what St. Teresa terms the prayer of recollection (Chapters XXVIII-XXIX) and to the wonderful description of the prayer of quiet (Chapter XXXI). The chapters given are those thus numbered in the *Complete Works of
St. Teresa* translated by E. Allison Peers. In the translation
of the text by Alice Alexander the chapters are XXX-XXXI
and XXXIII.

3. One should then read St. Teresa's *Interior Castle*, which
will give an insight into the development of the spiritual life
from its beginnings to the mystical marriage of the soul with
Christ. It is well for all normal minds leading an interior life,
whether in the cloister or in the world, to know the spiritual
life in all its stages.

4. Then one might read *The Spiritual Canticle* of St. John
of the Cross. It tells the same story as *The Interior Castle*.
One will find it much more difficult to understand than St.
Teresa, for St. John uses general abstract terms and St. Teresa
describes actual mental experiences. The *Complete Works of
St. Teresa*, translated by Peers, is published by Sheed and
Ward, New York, and Peers's translation of the *Complete
Works of St. John of the Cross* is published by Newman
Press, Westminster, Md.

5. The soul would now profit by a reading of Pourrat's
Christian Spirituality, referred to above, and some of the following works.

Arintero, John G., O.P. *The Mystical Evolution in the Develop-
ment and Vitality of the Church.* Translated by Jordan
Aumann, O.P. St. Louis: B. Herder Book Co. 1951. 2 vols.
Garrigou-Lagrange, Reginald, O.P. *Christian Perfection and
Contemplation.* Translated by Sr. M. Timothea Doyle, O.P.
St. Louis: B. Herder Book Co. 1942.
——— *The Three Ages of the Interior Life.* Translated by Sr. M.
Timothea Doyle, O.P. St. Louis: B. Herder Book Co. 1947.
2 vols.
Parente, Pascal, S.T.D. *The Mystical Life.* St. Louis: B. Herder
Book Co. 1946.

A List of Readings for the Catholic Mother [1]

Boylan, Eugene, O.C.R. *This Tremendous Lover*. Westminster, Md.: Newman Press. 1951.

Berger, Florence. *Cooking for Christ*. Des Moines: National Catholic Rural Life Conference. 1949.

Breig, Joe. *God in Our House*. New York: America Press. 1949.

—— *My Pants When I Die*. New York: McMullen Books. 1952.

Caussade, J. P. de, S.J. *On Prayer*. Translated by Algar Thorold. New York: Benziger Brothers. 1931.

Coakley, Mary L. *Our Child, God's Child*. Milwaukee: Bruce Publishing Co. 1953.

Day, Dorothy. *On Pilgrimage*. New York: Catholic Worker Press. 1948.

Delany, S. *Married Saints*. Westminster, Md.: Newman Press. 1950.

De Lourdes, Sister, R.S.M. *Baby Grows in Age and Grace*. Norwalk, Conn.: C. R. Gibson. 1951.

Goichon, A. M. *La vie contempletive: est elle possible dans le monde?* Desclée de Brouwer. 1952.

Healy, Kilian, O. Carm. *Walking with God*. New York: McMullen Books. 1948.

Hildebrand, D. von. *Marriage*. New York: Longmans, Green and Co. 1942.

Hope, Wingfield (*pseud.*). *Life Together*. New York: Sheed and Ward. 1943.

Houselander, Caryll. *The Reed of God*. New York: Sheed and Ward. 1944.

Kothen, Robert. *Marriage, the Great Mystery*. Translated by Eva J. Ross. Westminster, Md.: Newman Press. 1947.

Lindworsky, Johannes, S.J. *The Psychology of Asceticism*. Translated by Emil A. Heiring. Baltimore: Carroll Press. 1950.

Magner, James A. *The Art of Happy Marriage*. Milwaukee: Bruce Publishing Co. 1952.

Moore, Thomas Verner. *The Home and Its Inner Spiritual Life*. Westminster, Md.: Newman Press. 1952.

—— *Personal Mental Hygiene*. New York: Grune and Stratton. 1951.

—— *Prayer*. Westminster, Md.: Newman Press. 1951.

[1] Prepared for the author by a friend.

Mouroux, Jean. *The Meaning of Man.* Translated by A. H. C.
　Downes. New York: Sheed and Ward. 1948.
Newland, Mary Reed. *We and Our Children.* New York: P. J.
　Kenedy and Sons. 1954.
Perkins, Mary. *Mind the Baby.* New York: Sheed and Ward.
　1949.
Plus, Raoul, S.J. *Christ in the Home.* New York: Pustet. 1951.
Sheed, F. J. *Saints Are Not Sad.* New York: Sheed and Ward.
　1949.
Sheen, Fulton J. *Three to Get Married.* New York: Appleton-
　Century-Crofts. 1951.
Vann, Gerald, O.P. *Eve and the Gryphon.* Westminster, Md.:
　Newman Press. 1947.
––– *The Heart of Man.* New York: Longmans, Green and Co.
　1945.
Wilson, Alfred, C.P. *Pardon and Peace.* New York: Sheed and
　Ward. 1947.
Zeller, Hubert van, O.S.B. *Praying While You Work.* Spring-
　field, Ill.: Templegate. 1951.

ENCYCLICALS

Pope Pius XI. *Casti Canubii.* New York: Paulist Press. 1931.
Pope Pius XII. *Moral Questions Affecting Married Life.* New
　York: Paulist Press. 1951.

PAMPHLETS

Kalven, Janet. *The Task of Woman in the Modern World.* Des
　Moines: National Catholic Rural Life Conference. 1946.
Mueller, Theresa. *Designs for Christian Living.* Collegeville,
　Minn.: Liturgical Press. 1952.
––– *The Christian Home and Art.* Kansas City, Mo.: Designs
　for Christian Living. 1951.

Readings in Theology

Our spiritual life is an expression within us of the development of the theological virtue of faith. One can help himself
to realize this if he will pause to think that for one who does
not believe in God there can be no true religion nor genuine
religious experience till God calls him to be not faithless, but

believing. One who has no faith in the divinity of Christ cannot understand, much less experience, the spiritual life of the Church. To misunderstand or doubt any of the doctrines of the Church will lead to a serious deficit in our spiritual life. On the other hand a good knowledge of sound theology will help the development of our spiritual life, as well as enable us to carry out the injunction of St. Peter: "Sanctify the Lord Christ in your hearts, being ready always to satisfy one that asketh you a reason of the hope that is in you." [2] There are many souls who would never have lost the faith had they understood its teachings.

A list of "Readings in Theology" is, therefore, not so far out of place as it might seem in a book devoted to the "Life of Man with God." Sound theological thinking is a matter of fundamental importance. It would be well for every Catholic to devote some time to readings in Catholic doctrine. There are two groups to be considered. First there are those with little leisure. They should from time to time look over a pamphlet rack and pick up a booklet or tract that appeals to them. But there is a considerable number who could spend several hours a week in serious reading. If they would devote this to learning about God, Christ, and His Church it would be an important aid to their spiritual life. The following list of books would be helpful in mapping out a course of serious reading and study extending over some years. One should perhaps prepare himself for the study of doctrine by reading a good book on the Holy Scriptures. Robert and Tricot's *Guide to the Bible* would be interesting and helpful. Then one would come to Church history. Mourret's *History of the Catholic Church* would serve as a good foundation, but consult list of works on Church history given below. Mourret introduces many interesting historical details that give a living picture and make for interesting reading. To understand the theology of the Trinity and the Incarnation one must know the Church history of the first centuries. This is given in the first two

---

[2] I Peter III: 15.

volumes of Mourret. Then to understand the theology of grace, faith, and justification, one might pass to Volume V on the Renaissance and the Reformation. With this introduction one would appreciate better *The Teaching of the Catholic Church*, edited by Canon Smith. Some readers would prefer to read a series of small books. Various works in the bibliography that follows will enable them to make such a choice.

I

General Works on Theology in English

Henry, A.-M., O.P., Editor. *Initiation théologique*. Paris: Les Éditions du Cerf. 4 vols. First 2 vols. translated by William Storey. Chicago: Fides Publishers. 1954-1955. An important general work on theology.

Scheeben, M. J. *The Mysteries of Christianity*. Translated by Cyril Vollert, S.J. St. Louis: B. Herder Book Co. 1947. A general outline of Catholic teaching developed from an analysis of its nine great mysteries by a great theologian.

Smith, George D., Editor. *The Teaching of the Catholic Church*. New York: Macmillan Co. 9th printing, 1955. The most valuable general treatise on Catholic theology in English.

Vonier, Anscar, O.S.B. *The Collected Works*. Westminster, Md.: Newman Press, 3 vols. Vol. I, *The Incarnation and Redemption*, 1952. Vol. II, *The Church and the Sacraments*, 1952. Vol. III, *The Soul and the Spiritual Life*, 1953.

PATROLOGY

Bardenhewer, Otto. *Patrology: The Lives and Works of the Fathers of the Church*. Translation edited by J. J. Shahan. St. Louis: B. Herder Book Co. 1909.

Quasten, Johannes. *Patrology*. Westminster, Md.: Newman Press. Two volumes have appeared covering the ante-Nicene period. 1950 and 1953. The introduction gives an account of the history of patrology and an extensive bibliography.

AIDS TO THE STUDY OF THEOLOGY

Bellord, James. *Meditations on Christian Dogma*. Westminster, Md.: Newman Press. 1948. 2 vols.

Journet, Charles. *The Wisdom of Faith: An Introduction to Theology.* Translated by R. F. Smith. Westminster, Md.: Newman Press. 1952. A very valuable general introduction to the study of theology.

Knox, Ronald A. *Enthusiasm: A Chapter in the History of Religion.* New York: Oxford University Press. 1950.

Lubac, Henri de, S.J. *Catholicism: A Study of Dogma in Relation to the Corporate Destiny of Man.* Translated by Lancelot C. Sheppard. New York: Longmans, Green and Co. 1950.

Newman, John Henry Cardinal. *An Essay on the Development of Dogma.* Edited by C. F. Harrold. New York: Longmans, Green and Co. 1949.

Palmer, Paul F., S.J., Editor. *Sources of Christian Theology.* Westminster, Md.: Newman Press. Vol. I, *Sacraments and Worship.* 1955. Most valuable for a picture of the historical teaching of the church in the early centuries.

Parente, Pietro, Antonio Piolanti, and Salvatore Garofalo, Editors. *Dictionary of Dogmatic Theology.* Translated by E. Doronzo, O.M.I. Milwaukee: Bruce Publishing Co. 1951. Contains a valuable bibliography of theology.

II

General Works on the Holy Scriptures and Their Historical Setting

Daniel-Rops, Henry (*pseud.*) *Israel and the Ancient World.* Translated by K. Madge. London: Eyre and Spottiswoode. 1949.

Heinisch, Paul. *History of the Old Testament.* Translated by William G. Heidt, O.S.B. Collegeville, Minn.: Liturgical Press. 1952. Valuable for seeing the Scriptures in their historical background.

Orchard, Bernard, O.S.B., Editor. *A Catholic Commentary on Holy Scripture.* New York: Thomas Nelson and Sons. 1953. This work produced by a body of forty-three contributors is not only a commentary on the text of the Bible, but also a most valuable general and special introduction to Holy Scripture with valuable bibliographies and a set of maps.

Ricciotti, Giuseppe. *The History of Israel*. Translated by Clement della Penta, O.P., and Richard T. A. Murphy, O.P. Milwaukee: Bruce Publishing Co. 1955.

Robert, André, P.S.S., Alphonse Tricot, and various collaborators. *Guide to the Bible*. Translated by E. P. Arbez and R. P. McGuire. Westminster, Md.: Newman Press. 1951. 2 vols. A very valuable general introduction to Holy Scripture.

La Sainte Bible. Translated in French under the direction of L'Ecole Biblique de Jérusalem. Paris: Les Editions du Cerf. 1949—. A series of small volumes devoted to individual books of the Holy Bible. The series constitutes a valuable special introduction to Holy Scripture, with notes on the text of great value.

Steinmueller, John E. *A Companion to Scripture Studies*. New York: Joseph F. Wagner. 1941-1943. 3 vols.

III

General Works on the History of the Church

Fliche, Augustin, and Victor Martin, Editors. *Histoire de l'Eglise*. Paris: Bloud and Gay. 1936-1952. 24 vols. Closes with pontificate of Pius IX, 1846-1878. An extensive history of the Church based on the sources.

Hughes, Philip. *A Popular History of the Catholic Church*. Garden City, N. Y.: Macmillan. 1949. Image Books, Doubleday.

Lebreton, Jules, S.J., and Jacques Zeiller. *The History of the Primitive Church*. New York: Macmillan. 1944-1947. 2 vols. Translation by E. C. Messenger of first volumes of Fliche et al., *Histoire de l'Eglise*.

McSorley, Joseph, C.S.P. *An Outline History of the Church by Centuries*. (*From St. Peter to Pius XII*.) St. Louis: B. Herder Book Co. 1943.

Mourret, Fernand, S.S. *A History of the Catholic Church*. Translated by Newton Thompson. St. Louis: B. Herder Book Co. 1930—. 7 vols. The recent seventh volume carries the work through the French Revolution. Interesting reading with references to sources.

Palanque, J. R., and others. *The Church and the Christian Roman Empire*. New York: Macmillan. 1953. Translation by E. C. Messenger of Vols. 3 and 4 of *Histoire de l'Eglise*.

I V

The Existence of God and the Freedom of Man

Daudin, Henri. *La Liberté de la volunté*. Paris: Presses Universitaires de France. 1950. An interpretation and critique of the concepts of will in philosophers.

Garrigou-Lagrange, Reginald, O.P. *God: His Existence and His Nature*. Translated by Bede Rose, O.S.B. St. Louis: B. Herder Book Co. 1934-1936. 2 vols.

—— *The One God*. Translated by Bede Rose, O.S.B. St. Louis: B. Herder Book Co. 1943.

—— *Providence*. Translated by Bede Rose, O.S.B. St. Louis: B. Herder Book Co. 1937. Treats of Divine Providence and the fundamentals of natural theology.

Grabowski, Stanislaus. *The All-Present God*. St. Louis: B. Herder Book Co. 1954.

Hawkins, D. J. B. *The Essentials of Theism*. New York: Sheed and Ward. 1950.

Marc, André, S.J. *Psychologie réflexive*. Bruxelles: Desclée. Vol. II, *La volonté et l'esprit*, 1949.

Moore, Thomas Verner, O.S.B. *The Driving Forces of Human Nature*. New York: Grune and Stratton. 1948. Human freedom discussed in Chapters XXVII and XXVIII.

Pontifex, Mark, O.S.B. *The Existence of God*. New York: Longmans, Green and Co. 1947. A short treatise on metaphysics. Chapter V deals with free will.

Sheen, Fulton J. *God and Intelligence*. New York: Longmans, Green and Co. 1938.

Smith, Gerard, S.J. *Natural Theology*. New York: Macmillan. 1931. Extensive references and bibliography.

V

Christ, the God-Man

Adam, Karl. *The Son of God*. Translated by Philip Hereford. New York: Sheed and Ward. 1937.

Fouard, Constant. *Christ the Son of God*. Translated by George F. X. Griffith from fifth French edition. New York: Longmans, Green and Co. 1890. 2 vols. Often reprinted.

Goodier, Alban, S.J. *The Passion and Death of Our Lord Jesus Christ.* New York: P. J. Kenedy and Sons. 1933. Often reprinted.

———*The Public Life of Our Lord Jesus Christ.* New York: P. J. Kenedy and Sons. Second edition, seventh impression, 1936. 2 vols. Often reprinted.

Grandmaison, Léonce de, S.J. *Jesus Christ.* Translated by Basil Whelan and Ada Lane. New York: Sheed and Ward. 1930-1932. A careful historical study of the sources.

Guardini, Romano. *The Lord.* Translated by Elinor C. Briefs. Chicago: Henry Regnery Co. 1954. A brilliant portrayal of Christ by a brilliant mind and a deeply spiritual personality.

Hedley, John Cuthbert, O.S.B. *The Light of Life.* New York: Benziger Brothers. No date.

Koesters, Ludwig, S.J. *Believer's Christ.* Translated by J. W. Grundner. St. Louis: B. Herder Book Co. Second edition, 1939. An attempt to present the theology of Christ and the pertinent historical data in language that can be understood by those who are not theologians.

Lebreton, Jules, S.J. *The Life and Teaching of Jesus Christ Our Lord.* Translated by Francis Day. Milwaukee: Bruce Publishing Co. 1935. 2 vols.

Lunn, Arnold. *The Third Day.* Westminster, Md.: Newman Press. 1945.

Prat, Ferdinand, S.J. *Jesus Christ.* Translated by John J. Heenan, S.J. Milwaukee: Bruce Publishing Co. 1950. 2 vols.

Ricciotti, Giuseppe. *The Life of Christ.* Translated by Alba Zizzamia. Milwaukee: Bruce Publishing Co. 1947.

VI

The Holy Spirit

Cunningham, Francis, L.B., O.P. *The Indwelling of the Trinity.* Dubuque: The Priory Press. 1954.

Froget, Bartholomy, O.P. *The Indwelling of the Holy Spirit in the Souls of the Just.* Translated by S. A. Reamers. Westminster, Md.: Newman Press. 1950.

Grandmaison, Léonce de, S.J. *We and the Holy Spirit.* Translated by Angeline Bouchard. Chicago: Fides Publishers. 1954.

John of St. Thomas, O.P. *The Gifts of the Holy Spirit.* Translated by Dominic Hughes, O.P. New York: Sheed and Ward. 1951.

Leen, Edward, C.S.Sp. *The Holy Ghost.* New York: Sheed and Ward. 1937.

VII

Grace and the Sacraments

Joyce, G. H. *The Catholic Doctrine of Grace.* Westminster, Md.: Newman Press. 1950.

Lattey, Cuthbert, S.J., Editor. *Catholic Faith in the Holy Eucharist.* St. Louis: B. Herder Book Co. 1928.

Matthews, John V., S.J. *The Life That Is Grace.* Westminster, Md.: Newman Press. 1953.

Philipon, M. M., O.P. *The Sacraments in the Christian Life.* Translated by John Otto. Westminster, Md.: Newman Press. 1954.

Scheeben, M. J. *Nature and Grace.* Translated by Cyril Vollert, S.J. St. Louis: B. Herder Book Co. 1955.

—— *The Glories of Divine Grace.* Translated by Patrick Shaughnessy, O.S.B. St. Meinrad, Ind.: The Grail. 1946-1950. 5 parts.

VIII

The Church and Its Authority to Teach

Adam, Karl. *The Spirit of Catholicism.* Translated by Justin McCann, O.S.B. New York: Macmillan. 1930. Reprinted by Doubleday and Co., Image Books, New York, 1954.

Brunsman, Johannes, S.V.D. *The Teaching Office of the Church.* Translated by Arthur Preuss. St. Louis: B. Herder Book Co. 1928-1932. 4 vols.

Butler, Basil Christopher, O.S.B. *The Church and Infallibility.* New York: Sheed and Ward. 1954.

Guardini, Romano. *The Faith and Modern Man.* Translated by Charlotte E. Forsyth. New York: Pantheon. 1952. A short but clear and penetrating analysis of various fundamentals of faith.

Huby, Joseph. *The Church and the Gospels.* Translated by Fenton Moran. New York: Sheed and Ward. 1931.

Journet, Charles. *The Primacy of Peter.* Translated by John S. Chapin. Westminster, Md.: Newman Press. 1954.

—— *The Church and the Word Incarnate.* Translated by A. H. C. Downes. New York: Sheed and Ward. 1955. 2 vols.

Koesters, Ludwig, S.J. *The Church: Its Divine Authority.* Translated by Edwin G. Kaiser, C.P.P.S. St. Louis: B. Herder Book Co. 1938.

Lattey, Cuthbert, S.J., Editor. *The Church.* St. Louis: B. Herder Book Co. 1928.

—— *Church and State.* London: Burns, Oates and Washbourne. 1936.

—— *The Papacy. Papers from the Summer School of Catholic Studies Held at Cambridge, 1923.* St. Louis: B. Herder Book Co. 1924. One can get from this book a true picture of the papacy in history from the commission given by Christ to St. Peter to the present, which might otherwise require extensive reading.

—— *The Pre-Nicene Church.* London: Burns, Oates and Washbourne. 1935.

Rivington, Luke. *The Primitive Church and the See of Peter.* London: Longmans, Green and Co. 1894. An important historical work on the infallibility of the Pope and the teaching power of the Church.

IX

The Mystical Body of Christ

Pius XII. *Encyclical Letter on the Mystical Body of Christ.* New York: Paulist Press. 1943.

Anger, Joseph. *The Doctrine of the Mystical Body of Christ.* New York: Benziger Brothers. 1931.

Breton, Valentin M., O.F.M. *The Communion of Saints.* Translated by R. E. Scantlebury. St. Louis: B. Herder Book Co. 1934. A good historical treatise treating of the communion of the faithful on earth with the souls in purgatory and the saints in heaven but accentuating the communion of Christians on earth in the mystical body, the Church, in relation to devotional life.

Goosens, Werner. *L'Eglise corps du Christ d'après Saint Paul.*
Paris: Librairie Lecoffre. 1949. An important little study.
Guardini, Romano. *The Church and the Catholic and the Spirit
of the Liturgy.* Translated by Ada Lane. New York: Sheed
and Ward. 1953. Very important for the understanding of
the spiritual life of the Church in relation to the social order.
Mersch, Émile, S.J. *Morality and the Mystical Body.* Translated
by Daniel F. Ryan. New York: P. J. Kenedy and Sons.
1939. Extensive bibliography.
—— *The Theology of the Mystical Body.* Translated by Cyril
Vollert, S.J. St. Louis: B. Herder Book Co. 1952.
—— *The Whole Christ. The Historical Development of the Doctrine of the Mystical Body in Scripture and Tradition.* Translated by John R. Kelly. Milwaukee: Bruce Publishing Co.
1938.

X

The Blessed Virgin

Brown, Raphael. *The Life of Mary as Seen by the Mystics.* Milwaukee: Bruce Publishing Co. 1951. One will find here an
excellent account of the attitude of the Church on private
revelations, and will learn much of value from the mystic
drama of our Lady's life.
Doheny, William J., C.S.C., and Joseph P. Kelly, S.T.D. *Papal
Documents on Mary.* Milwaukee: Bruce Publishing Co.
1954.
Duhr, Joseph, S.J. *The Glorious Assumption of the Mother of
God.* Translated by John Fraunces, S.J. New York: P. J.
Kenedy and Sons. 1950. A theological weighing of the evidence from tradition. Good bibliography.
Garrigou-Lagrange, Reginald, O.P. *The Mother of Our Saviour
and Our Interior Life.* Translated by Bernard J. Kelly,
C.S.Sp. St. Louis: B. Herder Book Co. 1951.
Montfort, St. Louis Marie Grignion de. *Treatise on the True De-
votion to the Blessed Virgin Mary.* Bay Shore, N. Y.: Fa-
thers of the Company of Mary (Montfort Fathers). 1941.
Most, William G. *Mary in our Life.* New York: P. J. Kenedy
and Sons. Second edition, 1955.
Palmer, Paul F., S.J., Editor. *Mary in the Documents of the
Church.* Westminster, Md.: Newman Press. 1952. Very valu-

able for obtaining the general dogmatic picture of the Mother of God and Catholic devotion to Mary.

Scheeben, M. J. *Mariology*. Translated by T. L. M. J. Geukers. St. Louis: B. Herder Book Co. 1946-1947. 2 vols. A translation of the section on the Blessed Virgin in Scheeben's classic *Handbook of Dogmatic Theology*.

Sheed, F. J., Editor. *The Mary Book*. New York: Sheed and Ward. 1950.

Smith, George D. *Mary's Part in Our Redemption*. New York: P. J. Kenedy and Sons. Second revised edition, 1954.

William, Franz Michel. *Mary the Mother of Jesus*. Translated by Frederic Eckhoff. St. Louis: B. Herder Book Co. 1952. A beautiful historical and devotional life of the Blessed Virgin, based mainly on scripture and theological deductions, and also on nonscriptural sources, references to which are, unfortunately, not given in the English translation.

XI

The Holy Sacrifice of the Mass and the Liturgy

Pius XII. *Encyclical Letter on the Sacred Liturgy*. Washington, D. C.: National Catholic Welfare Conference. 1947.

Desplanques, François, S.J. *Living the Mass*. Translated by Sister Mary Constance, S.C. Westminster, Md.: Newman Press. 1951.

Duchesne, Louis. *Christian Worship: Its Origin and Evolution*. Translated by M. L. McClure. New York: Macmillan. 1931.

Fortescue, Adrian. *The Mass. A Study of the Roman Liturgy*. With a foreword by Herbert Thurston, S.J. London: Longmans, Green and Co. Second edition, 1937.

Garrigou-Lagrange, Reginald, O.P. *The Priest in Union with Christ*. Translated by G. W. Shelton. Westminster, Md.: Newman Press. 1954.

Kramp, Joseph, S.J. *The Liturgical Sacrifice of the New Law*. Translated by Leo F. Miller. St. Louis: B. Herder Book Co. 1926.

Michel, Virgil, O.S.B. *The Liturgy of the Church*. New York: Macmillan. 1942.

Schuster, Ildefonso Cardinal, O.S.B. *The Sacramentary*. Historical and liturgical notes on the Roman Missal translated by

Arthur Levelis-Marke. New York: Benziger Brothers. 1925-1931. 5 vols.

XII

The Last Things

Arendzen, J. P. *What Becomes of the Dead?* New York: Sheed and Ward. 1951.

Garrigou-Lagrange, Reginald, O.P. *Life Everlasting.* Translated by Patrick Cummins, O.S.B. St. Louis: B. Herder Book Co. 1952.

Guardini, Romano. *The Last Things.* Translated by Charlotte E. Forsyth and G. B. Branham. New York: Pantheon. 1954.

Gumpel, Peter, S.J. "Unbaptized Infants: May They Be Saved?" Bath, England: *Downside Review.* 1954. Pp. 342-458. This study does not raise the question whether or not these infants attain perfect natural happiness, but whether or not they see God face to face in heaven. The common view of theologians is that they do not enjoy the beatific vision. Some modern authors seek ways of seeing a justifiable exception to the common view.

Jugie, Martin. *Purgatory and the Means to Avoid It.* Translated by M. G. Carroll. Westminster, Md.: Newman Press. 1949.

Michel, Albert. *The Last Things.* Translated by B. V. Miller. St. Louis: B. Herder Book Co. 1930.

Moreux, Theophile. *What Shall We Become after Death?* Translated by J. F. Scholfield. St. Louis: B. Herder Book Co. 1923.

Pieper, Josef. *The End of Time. A Meditation on the Philosophy of History.* Translated by Michael Bullock. New York: Pantheon. 1954. The reader of this book should bear in mind that before the great tragedy of anti-Christ the world may see a more perfect fulfillment of the prophecy of Isaias.

Sasia, Joseph, S.J. *Future Life.* New York: Benziger Brothers. 1919. New edition.

Schneider, Wilhelm (Bishop of Paderborn). *The Other Life.* Translation revised and edited by Herbert Thurston, S.J. New York: Joseph F. Wagner. 1920.

The Degrees of the Spiritual Life

THE FOLLOWING questionnaire was constructed in the hope of getting a picture of the interior spiritual life from the zero level to its very heights. The first part was made by modifying somewhat the scale to be found in *The Soul of the Apostolate* by Dom J. B. Chautard.[1] It was thought that considerable light would be thrown on an individual's spiritual life by having him place himself on Chautard's modified scale, a) at the present, b) when at the lowest point of his spiritual life, c) when at its highest point. It would have been better to have placed Chautard's various symptoms in vertical sequence, followed by three columns referring to the various periods, a, b, c as just defined, to be marked as present or absent.

In the technique we employed we do not know whether or not the subject grades himself by freedom from sin or by the level of his mental prayer. Stage five becomes ambiguous also because when it is mentioned as the lowest stage we do not know whether in the course of his life a subject *never* committed a mortal sin or did so only rarely. Thus some who mentioned this as the lowest stage of their whole life may never have lost baptismal innocence. However, an attempt to pry too closely might have led some to refuse to answer at all. Out of two hundred answers, eight said that stage six was the

[1] Techny, Ill., Mission Press, pp. 172-174.

lowest in their lives, which implies that they had never committed a cold-blooded, fully deliberate venial sin. We may, therefore, say that 4 per cent of those leading an interior devout life may have worn the robe of baptismal innocence all their lives without staining it by fully deliberate venial sin.[2] Our table shows also that those who have sunk to the bottom have risen to the heights of the spiritual life.

The second part of the questionnaire might be divided into three sections. Questions 1 through 11 were formulated after studying Chapters XIX and XX in the Second Book of the *Dark Night of the Soul*. Here St. John of the Cross is outlining the ten stages of the love of God according to St. Bernard and St. Thomas. Visions, locutions, betrothal and espousal scenes do not figure in these descriptions of the heights of divine charity. It was hoped that they would indicate that a subject had attained to perfect love of God even though he had never experienced any of the mystic graces. The essence of Christian perfection is charity,[3] and perfect charity may be attained without any of the mystic graces. The fact, however, that we asked data on the mystic graces was criticized by some respondents as placing undue emphasis on these extraordinary phenomena. We tried to ward ourselves against this criticism by the paragraph just before question 1 (pp. 387-88). A full study of the spiritual life could not neglect the mystic graces.

The second part consists of questions 12, 13, and 14, in which we try to find out something about the subject's habitual mental prayer, his life of self-denial and his attitude toward sufferings and humiliations.

The third part consists of questions 15 to 30. In question 15

[2] Four per cent is a minimum. We have just called attention to an ambiguity in the determination of stage five. We may say, therefore, that more than four per cent of our respondents have never committed a mortal sin. Taking our group as a fair random sample of those leading a devout life, there must be thousands now living in our country who have preserved their baptismal innocence.

[3] P. 216.

we commence to study various mystic graces. Question 15 is intended to bring out anything akin to the prayer of quiet; question 16, the prayer of union; questions 17 and 18, ecstasy; question 19, locutions; question 20, visions. St. Teresa says that these experiences greatly inflame charity and stimulate the practice of virtues: hence question 21. Question 22 was designed to bring out any influences in one's spiritual life that seemed to be derived from Satan.

Question 23 asks for the descriptions of any betrothal scene with Christ. St. John of the Cross speaks of the soul being decked on this day with "gifts and virtues . . . just as if it were a bride on the day of her betrothal." [4] If this is the case, the soul should be conscious in various ways of a more perfect control of emotional life by reason and of a more intimate union with God. Hence, questions 24, 25, and 26. St. John of the Cross in the same place speaks of the *first* time the betrothal scene occurs. One must expect, therefore, that the betrothal scene will be *repeated:* hence question 27.

St. John of the Cross also says: "The soul does not come to this garden of complete transformation [which is the joy and delight and glory of the Spiritual Marriage] without first passing through the Spiritual Betrothal and through the mutual and loyal union of those who are betrothed." He also says: "I think that this estate [spiritual matrimony] is never attained without the soul being confirmed in grace therein." [5] Hence questions 28 and 29. St. Teresa of Avila dwells particularly on the lack of painful absences in the state of spiritual matrimony.

St. John of the Cross also says: "So long as the soul has not reached this estate of union of love, it must needs practice love, both in the active life and in the contemplative; but when it reaches that estate it befits it not to be occupied in other outward acts and exercises, which might keep it back,

---

[4] *Spiritual Canticle*, second redaction, Stanzas XIV and XV, annotation, Peers's translation, Vol. II, p. 258.

[5] *Ibid.*, Stanzas XXII, Peers's translation, II, pp. 308-309.

however little, from abiding in love with God." [6] Hence question 30. This does not mean that such a soul would neglect or refuse duties imposed by obedience but that as far as it might be allowed it would have no interest in anything except in its inner life of love with God.

In my material I found no one whom I could definitely place in the state of spiritual matrimony.

QUESTIONNAIRE: *The Degrees of the Spiritual Life*

You are requested to study the following questionnaire [7] carefully and fill it in, but not to sign it as it is not necessary to give any indication of who or what you are. It might help to get an insight into the spiritual life, as it is lived, if you would indicate whether you are a member of the laity, the priesthood or a religious community by underlining one of these words. It is to be used in a study of the stages of the spiritual life, the results of which will be made known to others in the hope that the knowledge of the spiritual life thus obtained will stimulate souls to seek perfection.

First study the following seven degrees of the spiritual life [8] and try to estimate honestly, without self-depreciation or exaltation, just where you now are and, if you will, state the lowest degree you were ever in and also the highest.

1. *Hardness of heart—*
    Mortal Sin: Obstinacy in this sin, by ignorance or a maliciously false conscience. Stifling of remorse, or absence of it.
    *Prayer—*Deliberate suppression of all recourse to God.

2. *Christian only outwardly—*
    Mortal Sin: Considered as a slight evil, committed on any occasion or temptation.
    *Prayer—*Mechanical, without attention, always dictated by temporal interest.

[6] *Spiritual Canticle*, second redaction, Stanza XXVIII, 2, Peers's translation, Vol. II, p. 346.

[7] The usual data in a questionnaire, such as date of birth, male or female, et cetera, were not asked for to lessen objections to filling it out.

[8] Adapted from Dom. J. B. Chautard, The Soul of The Apostolate, Mission Press, Techny, Ill. Pgs. 172-174.

3. *Moderate Piety—*
   Mortal Sin: Weak resistance. No flight from occasions, but genuine sorrow and good confession.
   Venial Sin: Looked upon as insignificant.
   *Prayer—*Vocal prayers fairly well said, but seldom.

4. *Intermittent Piety—*
   Mortal Sin: Loyal resistance. Habitual avoidance of occasions. Deep regrets. Penance to atone.
   Venial Sin: Sometimes deliberate, weak resistance, slight regrets.
   *Prayer—*Mental prayer is attempted, but often neglected.

5. *Sustained Piety—*
   Mortal Sin: Never, or very rare, in a violent, sudden temptation.
   Venial Sin: Rarely deliberate. Deeply regretted.
   Imperfections: The soul avoids searching for them so as not to be obliged to overcome them.
   *Prayer—*Constant fidelity in spite of everything to daily mental prayer; meditation likely to pass into aspirations of love.

6. *Fervor—*
   Venial Sin: Never deliberate. Slipped into at times through half advertence. Deeply regretted and fervently atoned for.
   Imperfections: Guarded against and resisted heartily.
   *Prayer—*Mental prayer willingly prolonged. Often a quiet, silent gazing into the face of God.

7. *Relative Perfection—*
   Imperfections: Energetically avoided with great love.
   *Prayer—*Habitual life of prayer even while devoting oneself to exterior work. Thirst for self-denial and humiliations. Hunger for the Holy Eucharist and Heaven. Various infused graces of contemplative prayer.

In which one of these degrees can you place yourself now in your present spiritual life? _____

And, if you will, which was the lowest degree you were ever in? _____. Which was the highest? _____.

When the soul arrives at a state that is a transition from the 6th to the 7th degree, summarized above, there comes a parting of the ways that unite later on the heights of perfection. This parting is not so complete as to exclude all bypaths leading from one road to the other. One of these has few spiritual consolations such as ecstasies and visions. St. Teresa of Avila tells us it is more meritorious. The other has many extraordinary consolations that lead to perfection more rapidly. Perfection in its essence is the degree to which Charity is possessed.

Kindly answer the following questions to indicate on which of these ways you run your spiritual life and also how far you have advanced.

1. Can you say that you have forsaken all that is sinful and all that is not God in order to attain God? _____.

(In answering this question remember that the duties of your state of life pertain to God, and also a certain amount of wholesome recreation. You cannot draw near to God by neglecting your duties.)

(Space is left between questions for a few words of explanation. If more is needed make use of a special sheet giving numbers of the questions.)

2. Can you say that you seek God without ceasing? _____. "Seek ye the Lord and be strengthened. Seek His face forever more." (Ps.civ.A.)

3. Does your love of God give enthusiasm to all you do for Him? _____.

4. Do you feel that you cannot say with certainty that you are spiritually superior to anyone? _____.

5. Do you believe in your inmost heart that you are lower and viler than all? _____.

6. Do you seek yourself in nothing, not even asking God for spiritual consolations; but, forgetting self, are you ever interested in finding something to do that will please God? _____.

7. Do you really suffer and is it painful to you to remain on earth because you want to be united at once with Christ in heaven? _____.

8. Have you a consciousness of running, in your spiritual life, with great rapidity towards God and a perfect life, as the hart to the living waters? _____.

9. Have you a sense of such freedom from sin and all that is not God that you approach God in prayer with great intimacy and boldness and yet God seems to invite and not rebuke you? _____.

[Both items must be "yes" to be termed a positive answer.]
(Instructions set in brackets were not in the original. They are meant for one who might desire to repeat our work.)

10. Can you say, "I have found Him whom my soul loveth. I held Him and I will not let Him go." And does your union with Christ rise at times to such heights that, were moments to broaden into eternity, you would seem to possess the joy of eternal life? _____.

[Both items must be "yes" to be termed a positive answer.]

11. Does your life flow on in a sweet joy and a wonderful love of Christ which is not interrupted even by intense physical pain or great mental trials and sufferings? _____.
[What is meant here is expressed by Msgr. Vernon Johnson writing of St. Thérèse of Lisieux: "Along with that spiritual joy went an equally supernatural peace which suffering, physical or spiritual, was utterly unable to touch." [9]]

Write out on a special sheet descriptions of any actual experiences you may have had belonging under each of these headings (1 to 11) and also under the following (12 to 30). Give each description the number of the question to which it is an answer.

12. (a) Describe on a special sheet of paper, the usual way in which you make your mental prayer.
   (b) Do you often prolong the period set apart for mental prayer? _____
   (c) Do you devote to mental prayer all the time you can possibly spare? _____.

13. What works of self-denial and bodily penance do you usually practice?
[Call negative: all those who mention no positive acts of self-denial; who say: some only of those things prescribed by rule. Call positive: all those who mention at least some practice of self-denial, or those of rule, or those of the priesthood, or the fasts and abstinences of the Church.]

[9] *Spiritual Childhood*, London, Sheed and Ward, 1953, p. 160. This sentence did not appear in the original questionnaire.

14. (a) Can you say that you really thirst for sufferings? _____. For humiliations _____ and desire like Christ to be reputed with the wicked? _____.

(b) Can you say that you would at least suffer such things patiently recognizing in them God's will for you? _____.

15. In mental prayer do you ever enter into a period of profound peace with your whole being infused with the love of God, a peace which remains in spite of the mind wandering at times away from God? _____. Is your prayer habitually of this character? _____. Does the peace continue after your period of prayer is over, and accompany you into the work of the day? _____.

16. Have you ever entered into a state of prayer in which, though you can neither see, hear, nor understand, God seems to have so entered into your soul, that when you return to yourself, you cannot possibly doubt that you have been in God and God has been in the depths of your being? _____.

17. In prayer has your love of God so absorbed you that the body lost sensation of itself for some seconds? _____.

18. Have you ever entered into a state in which you lost all awareness of your surroundings and sensation of all kinds and were completely absorbed in God? _____.

19. Have you ever heard any interiorly spoken words (or experienced them intellectually) that seemed to come in some manner direct from God? _____.

20. Have you experienced any imaginal or other consciousness of the presence of Christ or our Lady or the Saints, or have you seen them as it were right before you as sensory objects? _____.

21. And did such experiences inflame greatly your love of God and urge you to a closer conformity with His will? _____.

22. Have you ever experienced any molestations that seemed to come from Satan, other than ordinary temptations? _____.

23. Have you ever experienced a scene in which Christ seemed to come to you without being announced and in which He pledged His troth to you and you pledged yourself to Him? _____.

Note however that it is one thing by *personal effort* to go through in imagination such a scene, it is quite another when the scene arises without your having anything to do with its coming or with its development. If you have experienced such a spontaneous scene of betrothal, describe it on a special sheet of paper.

24. *After* such a scene did you become aware of a profound and permanent change for the better in your spiritual life manifested for example by the ability to spend an hour or longer in mental prayer without notable distraction, and from time to time by many beautiful visits of Christ to your soul? _____.

25. Did you discover after a bit that you were able to put up with (without being in the least ruffled) trials or indignities which formerly would have made you angry and rebellious?

_____.

26. Did you find that a wondrous peace and love of God had settled down on your soul, and for long periods you were able to live intimately with Christ, although these periods were followed by others in which you suffered greatly from the apparent absence of Christ? _____.

27. Was the betrothal scene ever in any way repeated?

_____.

28. Did there come another such scene of a *special character*, after which you lived habitually with Christ and never afterwards suffered from long painful periods in which He seemed absent? _____. Describe this experience if it was ever yours.

29. Following such a scene did you find that your imperfections had disappeared and no longer gave you any trouble?

_____.

30. Did you then lose all interest in things not concerned with carrying out the will of God, and the actual communion of love with your heavenly spouse? _____.

Check and see if you have answered *all* questions.

Kindly write on blank pages a brief account of how you first commenced to lead a spiritual life and of the influences that made your spiritual life, perhaps, a definitely *interior* life.

[These last two sentences were not in the first copies of this questionnaire.]

Some Objections to Our Procedure

A double objection raised against the attempt made in this book was this: First of all, you will not be able to get people to answer the questionnaire and give an account of anything so sacred as their intimate personal religious experiences. In the next place, if you do get any such accounts you will never be able to tell whether they came from God, the subject's own imagination, or the devil.

As a matter of fact, the returns have been far richer than I had hoped for. As to the evaluation of the returns, I would say that however important that may be, and it actually is very important, it is not the primary object of our study. Before you evaluate the "varieties of religious experience" you must have the data before you. In his book *The Varieties of Religious Experience*, William James attempted to give a picture of religion as it is lived. But he "was not equipped by training and sympathetic contacts to understand religious experience. Unfortunately he was interested in extreme forms of religious experience rather than the usual normal devout life of the believer. He dashes about in the lives of the saints like a bull in a china shop making use of his brilliancy in satire, to hold up to ridicule what he is incapable of appreciating." [10]

Our work is an attempt to find out what is the usual devout life in the Catholic Church. The first part on the daily life of those who live with God present that life in its broad general outlines. Other chapters give an insight into such things as the prayer of a good Catholic and the struggle with temptation. In the second part on the inner life of those who live with God, we try to picture the intimate relation of the soul with God from its beginning to the loftiest height we found in our material: the state of spiritual betrothal with Christ; or, we should say, what seemed to our collaborators to be genuine experiences of the soul in its relationship with God.

It is a contribution of some value to merely present the experiences. But can we be sure that these experiences are not mere natural phenomena of the imagination or deceits of Satan? As Aristotle said of ethics, you cannot expect in this field metaphysical certainty. Though we cannot attain metaphysical cer-

[10] T. V. Moore, *The Driving Forces of Human Nature*, p. 15.

tainty, perhaps we may arrive at a certain degree of high probability or even moral certainty that certain things recounted are examples of God acting on the soul by means of divine grace.

There is a tendency in some to say that any phenomenon is a purely natural event unless there is *conclusive* evidence that no one can reject, that it is of divine origin. There must be indeed a commendable reserve in pronouncing affirmative judgment that an event is miraculous. At the same time we must be conscious of our obligation to recognize the divine when it is present. And in dealing with phenomena not strictly miraculous, but which concern the soul's progress in charity and all the virtues, one should beware lest in refusing to admit the divine, he might slip into Pelagianism.

The evaluation of the real merit and worth of a person's life demands more than the data of a questionnaire. But we can perhaps get a general picture of the usual normal devout life of the Catholic from the data we present. I think that a candid reader will be charmed by the simple spiritual beauty of the Catholic home of which we give a glimpse. One will also see the life of the priest in a parish, of a missionary in a foreign land, of priests and nuns in active work, and of cloistered religious as well, from a perusal of our book. One will also enter into what seems to be the inner life of the soul with God.

In discussing the possibility of all that inner life being a form of deceit, natural or preternatural, one should consider the following:

Anyone can imagine or construct many of the scenes that were reported by our collaborators. But a single scene, the pure product of imagination, quickly passes away. It does not work a transformation for the better in one's whole spiritual life, as sometimes happened with our cases.

"Every best gift, and every perfect gift is from above, coming down from the Father of lights." [11] We have a right to suppose that religious experiences that intensify the love of God, a theological virtue, and reform conduct do not come from Satan, the father of lies.[12]

A priest said to me: "How do you know but what someone will get hold of your questionnaire and play a joke on you and write out a series of extraordinary mystic experiences. I for one

[11] James I:17.
[12] For a more complete study of this problem see Chapter XVI, p. 328.

would take great pleasure in throwing such a monkey wrench into the machinery."

I wonder if anyone with a conscience would, on sober thought, make such an attempt? In the first place it would be a lie and a lie in a serious matter that might do a grave injury. Nor can one conceive of any good that would be accomplished by such an act that would make it worthwhile.

And then to seriously invalidate the study one would have to be intimately acquainted with genuine mystic experiences in order to fabricate a number of accounts good enough to be deceptive. One who had such intimate acquaintance with genuine mystic experience would in general be one who himself led a devout interior life; and such a one would not lie, let alone attempt to do serious injury by a lie.

Further, such an attempt to be of any importance would make itself statistically apparent in what is known as our curve of distribution. There should be a hump at the upper extreme instead of a fading to zero. But as we have said, our curve fades to zero at questions 28, 29, and 30. Instead of there being one or more cases of spiritual matrimony there are none, and only a few cases of spiritual betrothal. One cannot think that my friend's objection is to be seriously considered. It is nothing more than an unlikely possibility. There is no internal evidence from our data that the possibility has been realized in the region where one would expect to find it.

The general tone of the answers indicates attempts to describe truly what has actually been experienced. Sometimes this stands out very clearly. Thus one wrote at question 16: "No point in going any further." Another wrote: "This is where I definitely stop."

I think anyone who reads the quotations from our respondents and the accounts of their lives in the home or in the cloister will realize that our study gives a true picture of the "varieties of religious experience" in the devout life of Catholics of our own day in the United States of America.

One wrote as follows: "About that questionnaire—I am not exactly enthusiastic about that sort of thing, and I can't see just how it is going to benefit a large number by getting an intimate manifestation of conscience from people. There are quite a few questions on the sheets, which are, and should be, asked only rarely. There is also an emphasis on the extraordinary, which leaves me out of the picture and is very harmful to proud souls like myself."

We have already pointed out that, to be complete, our questionnaire had to include queries concerning the mystic graces; but we tried in the questionnaire itself to point out that mystic graces are not essential to charity, which is the essence of spiritual perfection.

I can readily understand that many would not like to write down an account of their spiritual history even without mentioning their own names and with the certainty that there would be no way of associating their account with themselves. Respondents were asked not to mention their names. I hoped in this way to secure greater freedom and reliability. There would be no urge to paint oneself in a more favorable light when no one would ever know who was being painted.

Even saints have written autobiographies that have been helpful to millions down throughout the ages. It will be of assistance to some to know the heights to which ordinary people like themselves have risen by the grace of God. It will be valuable to know that one can rise from the lowest depths to the height of perfection. And because this is so, it seems perfectly lawful to ask people to give a fragmentary account of their spiritual history. No one who had conscientious objections to doing this was compelled to do what he felt he should not in conscience undertake.

On the other hand, some found the study and filling out of the questionnaire a great spiritual help. St. Teresa of Ávila advises us to find out just where we stand in the spiritual life. The questionnaire on the degrees of the spiritual life helps one to do precisely this.

We may conclude with a few comments made by some of our respondents.

"This analysis has been soul searching and has been a great help to self-knowledge. I feel it has done much for my spiritual life and shall eagerly await your contribution."

"Thanks for everything in the questions. They helped me very much."

"I am grateful for the opportunity to answer the questionnaire. If it is of no value to you, it has been of tremendous value to me. I have never been faced up to many of these questions. Do religious women generally have sufficient opportunity?"

"I am a religious. The questionnaire has shown me how far I am from the goal I am seeking."

"The questionnaire has certainly made me realize how little I have accomplished and how much more I could do."

"Studying this questionnaire has been of tremendous value to me and to at least two other people. No matter what the results of the study are, the instrument itself is a powerful spiritual weapon."

"I have reached the age when spiritual things must come first. These pages have helped me to renew my resolutions. Please pray that the love of God will keep growing stronger in me."